Work

Also by Mike Noon

A Dictionary of Human Resource Management *(with E. Heery)*
Equality, Diversity and Disadvantage in Employment *(edited with E. Ogbonna)*

Also by Paul Blyton

The Dynamics of Employee Relations (Second edition) *(with P. Turnbull)*
Reassessing Human Resource Management *(edited with P. Turnbull)*
The Climate of Workplace Relations *(with A. Dastmalchian and R. Adamson)*
Time, Work and Organization *(with J. Hassard, S. Hill and K. Starkey)*
State, Capital and Labour *(with G. Ursell)*
Changes in Working Time

The Realities of Work

Second Edition

MIKE NOON

AND **PAUL BLYTON**

palgrave

First published 2002 by
PALGRAVE
Houndmills, Basingstoke, Hampshire RG21 6XS and
175 Fifth Avenue, New York, N. Y. 10010
Companies and representatives throughout the world

PALGRAVE is the new global academic imprint of
St. Martin's Press LLC Scholarly and Reference Division and
Palgrave Publishers Ltd (formerly Macmillan Press Ltd).

ISBN 0–333–98458–7 hardback
ISBN 0–333–98459–5 paperback

This book is printed on paper suitable for recycling and
made from fully managed and sustained forest sources.

A catalogue record for this book is available
from the British Library.

A catalog record for this book is available
from the Library of Congress

Designed by Claire Brodmann Book Designs,
Lichfield, Staffs

10   9   8   7   6   5   4   3
10   09   08   07   06   05   04   03

Printed in China

Dedication

To Carolyn,
For making my life complete. MN

To Ticky and Barley,
For their love and friendship. PB

Contents

List of figures

List of tables

Preface

The first edition of *The Realities of Work* was written while we were both working at Cardiff Business School. We were jointly teaching a course that was designed to get students thinking about the effects of management practices, policies and initiatives on the lives of ordinary working people. We felt that most of the texts that typical business and management students encountered either ignored the employees, or else treated them as compliant and passive. Of course there were chapters in some books and various academic journal articles that sought to evaluate the employees' perspectives, but no single text brought together the theories and research material in such a way that the employee was seen as central.

Through putting together a course that placed the employee centre stage, we collected material from sociology, social psychology, industrial relations, organisation theory, human resource management, and labour economics, as well as material from our own research. Our objective was to encourage students to consider the employee as the principal actor with a lead role, rather than a support actor with a walk-on part. The result was the first edition of *The Realities of Work*.

In this second edition we have taken on board the feedback, comments and constructive criticisms of our peers and our students. The message was clear: they liked the approach and critical edge to the first edition but the coverage would benefit from slight expansion and the text could be made even more accessible to students. To address the first of these comments we have added two new chapters (on 'knowledge and work' and 'representation at work') as well as expanding the content of some of the original chapters and revising the structure of others. In addition, we have written a new introduction that now explains the rationale and approach of the book. We have been keen to take on board specific comments relating to individual chapters and sections within the chapters, so no chapter has been left unaffected by our revision process. The entire text has also been updated to take into account new research evidence (particularly from outside the UK) and emergent theories.

On the second issue – greater accessibility – we have made some notable changes that affect the overall appearance of the book and others that add opportunities for assessing the understanding of the concepts. In publishers' jargon, these are called 'features' and they are as follows.

Features at the beginning of each chapter:

- A list of 'Key concepts' signposts the important terms that will be encountered. After reading and understanding the chapter, students should be able to define each of these terms.
- The 'Chapter aim' specifies the purpose of the discussion.
- The 'Learning outcomes' signal what ideas and propositions students will gain knowledge and understanding of. Each outcome is repeated at the appropriate place in the margin of the chapter text so that students can easily locate the material relevant to each specific learning point.

Features within each chapter:

- The 'Excerpts' provide examples of research or discuss theories that help to expand upon the points made in the text. They are designed to prompt interest, provide an illustration or act as a discussion point. The text can be read without looking at these excerpts, but it is hoped that they will prove useful in support of the main narrative.
- The 'Exercises' provide the opportunity for students to reflect on the preceding material and assess their understanding. They require students to read the text and apply the theoretical ideas or make use of the concepts. Sometimes this requires them to draw on their own experience; other times they must evaluate the research evidence presented in the text. Most of the exercises can be completed individually or discussed in small groups. They are ideally suited to tutorials/seminars or break-out sessions in lectures.
- The 'To sum up' paragraphs bring together the key points before the text moves on to the next set of issues.

We are pleased with the outcome of these revisions and hope our readership will similarly approve. Yet, while the book looks different and the content has been expanded, our approach remains the same. As we outline in the introduction, we want readers to explore the diversity of theories and approaches to the study of work. We have also sought to maintain an analytical style because we want students to think critically and logically about the issues. We want readers to evaluate the theories and empirical evidence and bring their own perspectives and understanding to the issues. With this in mind, some of the discussion in the introductory chapter is designed to help them develop their skills in critical reasoning.

Finally there are some people we wish to thank. First, our thanks go to the many colleagues who have commented on the text, often informally, and invariably constructively. Their suggestions have been absorbed. Second, we would like to thank the anonymous reviewers of the manuscript. Their comments and attention to detail greatly assisted in the redrafting process. Third, thanks must go to students: those who talked with us about the text and helped confirm where improvements and changes needed to be made; those who were honest enough to tell us that the solid blocks of text in the first edition 'were a bit off putting'; and those who bought the book in sufficient quantities to convince our publisher that a second edition was required. Fourth, we want to express our appreciation for the support and encouragement given to us by our commissioning editor at Palgrave, Sarah Brown.

However, the biggest thank you goes to our families, for whom the realities of *our* work meant sometimes saying no to doing more interesting and enjoyable activities than sitting in front of a computer screen. So, Mike thanks Carolyn for her support and willingness to discuss aspects of the book, even when her own work was pressing, and when we should have been enjoying the walk, the beach or the skiing. Paul thanks Ticky and Barley for making the realities of his life outside work so enjoyable and fulfilling.

Mike Noon
Leicester Business School
De Montfort University
The Gateway
Leicester
LE1 9BH

mnoon@dmu.ac.uk

Paul Blyton
Cardiff Business School
Cardiff University
Colum Drive
Cardiff
CF10 3EU

blyton@cardiff.ac.uk

Exploring the realities of work

KEY CONCEPTS

- Definitions of work
- Classifying work
- Socio-economic classification
- Theories
- Deductive and inductive approaches
- Typologies
- Ideal types

- Methods of data gathering
- Objective and subjective
- Theoretical and empirical
- Qualitative data
- Quantitative data
- Methodological pluralism

CHAPTER AIM

To explain the approach this book adopts to explore, analyse and critically evaluate the experiences of work.

LEARNING OUTCOMES

By reading and thinking about the material in this chapter, you will be able to:

1 Define the term 'work';

2 Outline a system for classifying work;

3 Explain the basic tools a social scientist uses to study work;

4 Summarise the various perspectives from which work can be analysed;

5 Identify the core components around which the rest of the book is structured.

Introduction

Our purpose in writing this book is to convey an impression of work from the perspective of the employee and to examine this through the use of theory and research evidence. There are plenty of books explaining the principles and methods of management, but very few that address what it is like to be *managed*. In other words, the perspective of employees is often overlooked or taken for granted.

Thus, what distinguishes this book is that it is focused on employees. It is about the effects of being managed: the experiences of employees in organisations as they cope with the strategies, tactics, decisions and actions of managers. This means that the main protagonist in our discussion is 'the employee' – although at times other characters make a necessary appearance, such as managers, policy makers, trade unions, the unemployed, and various academic commentators. To explore these experiences, we have drawn widely from the social sciences and have sought to provide empirical evidence and theoretical discussions that are not always to be found in mainstream texts.

Central to our analysis is a conviction that employees actively engage in developing counter-rationalities to management policies and plans. In some circumstances these challenge management, while in others they help to produce conformity among workgroups. As we shall see, these counter-rationalities take several different forms, ranging from gaining additional (unofficial) rest periods to organising work in such ways as to achieve an easing of work pressures, increased income and/or a sense of control. The pervasiveness of such counter-rationalities, and their significance for those involved, indicate the importance of analysing these aspects of work behaviour not as temporary deviations from management orthodoxy, but as persistent and rational responses of groups of workers whose interests only partially coincide with those of management, and who have a vested interest in, for example, preserving their energy, maximising income, having fun and gaining a sense of control over their work situation.

The book sets out to capture the diversity of work experience – the fact that workers experience, in varying degrees, both satisfaction *and* alienation, demonstrate both cooperation *and* resistance, display both common interests *and* opposing ones, and perceive their distinct interests in both individual *and* collective terms. The challenge that faces us it to explore the varied experiences of work – in sum, the realities of work.

Shortly, we will specify the key components of these realities by mapping out the terrain that the book explores. Before doing so, however, it is important to make some key points about how work can be defined and classified, the tools that can be used to explore the concept of work, the perspectives that can be adopted and the particular approach we have taken.

Learning outcome 1

Define the term 'work'.

Defining work

Before reading this section, attempt Exercise 1.1 which is designed to make you think about how we should define work.

What do *you* think?

1 For each of the following statements, decide whether you would classify the task as 'work'. Justify your decision in each case.

a) An electrician installs a power socket in your house.

b) The electrician installs a socket in his own house.

c) Your friend, who 'knows a bit about electrics' installs the power socket in your house.

d) You install the power socket yourself.

e) When the socket has been installed you plug in your games console and play your favourite game.

2 Now, try to write a short definition of 'work'.

If you've completed Exercise 1.1 you have probably arrived at the conclusion that the boundary between work and non-work activity is hazy. Nevertheless you have possibly been able to arrive at a definition of work that you are comfortable with, even though it is not perfect. If you have accomplished this, then you have already developed the line of thinking we want you to adopt throughout this book when exploring the realities of work. In short, this is the view that although the task is complex, contradictory and sometimes frustrating, we can seek to analyse, understand and explain social phenomena.

So how does your definition of work match up to others? The definition of work supplied by the Concise Oxford Dictionary is the 'application of effort or exertion to a purpose'. This is reasonable but not precise enough for our purposes. A more useful definition is provided by Thomas (1999: xiv) who identifies three components essential to work:

1 Work produces or achieves something (it is not an end in itself).

2 Work involves a degree of obligation or necessity (it is a task set either by others or by ourselves).

3 Work involves effort and persistence (it is not wholly pleasurable, although there may be pleasurable elements to it).

We can test the validity of this three-component definition by assessing it against various tasks such as serving a customer in a shop, fixing a broken washing machine, phoning a client, digging a hole, giving a presentation, etc. For example, serving in a shop achieves something (a sale and customer satisfaction), involves obligation (set by the employer) and involves effort (responding to customer needs). The definition also helps to define as work those tasks and chores that are expected of us in our day-to-day lives, such as driving to work, cleaning and ironing clothes, getting the kids ready for school or engaging in small talk with clients/customers.

Generally the definition stands up to scrutiny, but there is one notable problem. Some activities that might be described as leisure pursuits also match the three criteria. For example, sport or gardening (1) achieves something, (2) presents a self-imposed challenge and (3) requires effort and persistence. The same could be said of learning a foreign language or a musical instrument, painting (the house or on canvas), walking the dog, or playing a computer game. In addition, some activities might fit the three criteria but may represent a leisure activity in one context and work in another. Cooking and looking after children are two prime examples of this. Thus, it is not only the activity that defines work, but also the circumstances under which the activity is undertaken.

One way of removing some of this confusion is to focus on work that is remunerated. Indeed, most books on work confine their attention to paid work: employment. Clearly, given the number of people involved, the time devoted to it and its importance as a source of income, this is an important component of work. Further, it is employment in the sphere of visible work that society views as the principal form of work – 'real' work in these terms is seen to be that which is remunerated. But at the same time, such a focus obscures as much as it reveals: the concentration solely on paid work ignores huge areas of work which, if paid for, would equal or exceed the total value of paid work. The main areas of unpaid 'hidden' work are household-based work (cooking, cleaning, child-rearing, home improvement, and so on) and a range of activities falling under the heading of voluntary work. Work may also be 'hidden' if it involves illegal activities, or is undertaken for payment that is not declared to the tax authorities.

What is needed is to strike a balance that gives greater recognition to the different activities that constitute people's work. Further, such a balance is necessary not only because of the scale of the different spheres of work but also because of the key links that exist between the different aspects of paid and unpaid, visible and hidden work. The fact that unpaid work is undertaken disproportionately by one group (women) and that work in the unpaid sphere affects access to paid work, makes the study of the different areas of work more important still. Thus, while some of the issues covered in the book require primary consideration to be given to work in the form of employment, at several specific points, recognition is given to a broader definition of work. The purpose is to underline the significance of the different spheres in their own right and the significance of hidden work for a fuller understanding of the nature and character of employment.

TO SUM UP

Just because it is challenging to arrive at a definition or understand a concept, this does not prevent us from attempting to do so. And just because there are contradictory opinions this does not mean that there is no point engaging with the issues. Our immediate task – or if you like, our work – is to attempt to arrive at useable definitions as a basis for classifying and analysing work.

Classifying work

There are various ways of classifying work, the most common of which are listed in Table 1.1. Such classifications allow distinctions to be made between different groups of employees and therefore provide a basis for developing explanations as to why particular phenomena occur, such as different pay levels, gender differences, different expectations and orientations to work, differences in behaviour at work, and so on. This emphasis on classifying and explaining is the purpose of much social science – which seeks to explore the social world, just as traditional science explores the physical world. (The section below explains some of the basic techniques of social science.)

Table 1.1   Systems of classifying people according to their work

Criteria of classification	Examples
The way jobs are undertaken	Manual/non-manual Skilled/semi-skilled/unskilled
The main purpose of the work	Specific occupational groups
Job status	White-collar/blue-collar
Temporal pattern	Full-time/part-time Permanent/temporary
Work location	Workplace/home Formal economy/informal economy

Source: Based on discussion by Frenkel, Korczynski, Donoghue and Shire (1995)

Throughout the following chapters you will encounter examples of these various methods of classifying work. You will also be introduced to other classification methods which are currently being developed – for example, the distinction between types of 'knowledge workers' (Chapter 8) or between employees expected to deliver different types of 'emotion work' (Chapter 7). There are also classifications within particular categories of work – for instance we identify different types of 'hidden work' within the informal economy (Chapter 12).

In practice, social scientists are constantly finding new ways of classifying work. One of the most recent examples is the new system of socio-economic classification based on a person's type of employment contract, rather than their income. Those at the top have longer-term contracts, receive a rising income, greater opportunities and wider benefits. For a fuller explanation, see Excerpt 1.1, then attempt Exercise 1.2.

New systems of classifying work are being developed for understandable reasons. In particular, changes in the context and nature of work – economic changes, globalisation, new customer demands, technological developments, new management techniques and so forth – mean that existing classifications can become outdated and misleading. For example, Frenkel, Korcynski, Donoghue and Shire (1995: 777) argue that,

> The manual/non-manual distinction is a less meaningful reference point as routine manual work is increasingly automated and the characteristics of skilled production workers become similar to those of technicians. . . . The main purpose of work is also a less reliable criterion as workers undertake a wider range of tasks, for example contributing to improvements in work processes and assuming functions previously undertaken by supervisors and managers.

TO SUM UP

Classification systems are developed to assist our understanding of the dynamic nature of work. They are a means by which people can be grouped together into specific types based usually on the work they do, and through which complexity can be simplified. Such systems are important tools to use when embarking upon the task of studying work – to which we now turn.

EXCERPT 1.1

A new class system

In 2001 the UK introduced a new way of classifying people: National Statistics Socio-economic Classification (NS-SEC). This system is designed to take into account:

- labour market situations: a person's source of income, economic security and prospects of economic advancement;
- work situations: a person's location in the systems of authority and control, and their extent of autonomy at work.

Table 1.2   National Statistics Socio-economic Classification (NS-SEC), with examples

NS-SEC categories	Examples
1 Higher managerial and professional occupations	Company directors, senior managers, police inspectors, doctors, architects, academics, lawyers
2 Lower managerial and professional occupations	Teachers, journalists, social workers, optometrists, operations managers
3 Intermediate occupations	Police officers, secretaries, paramedics, driving instructors
4 Small employers (less than 25 employees) and own-account workers (non-professional)	Shop keepers, farmers, publicans, self-employed electricians, taxi-drivers

▶

▶ **Table 1.2**   National Statistics Socio-economic Classification (NS-SEC), with examples

NS-SEC categories	Examples
5 Lower supervisory and technical occupations	Train drivers, landscape gardeners, railway construction workers, TV engineers
6 Semi-routine occupations	Shop assistants, childcare assistants, receptionists, cooks, hairdressers
7 Routine occupations	Lorry/van drivers, cleaners, waiters, refuse collectors, couriers
8 Never worked and long-term unemployed	

This means that the emphasis is placed on the employment contract and the way that employees are regulated through these contracts in three forms:

1 In a 'service relationship' the employee renders 'service' to the employer in return for 'compensation' in terms of both immediate rewards (such as salary) and long-term or prospective benefits (such as assurances of security and career opportunities). The service relationship typifies Class 1 and is present in a weaker form in Class 2.

2 In a 'labour contract' employees give discrete amounts of labour in return for a wage calculated on amount of work done or by time worked. The labour contract is typical for Class 7 and in weaker forms for Classes 5 and 6.

3 Intermediate forms of employment regulation that combine aspects from both forms (1) and (2) are typical in Class 3.

(Quoted from Office for National Statistics, 2001b: 3–4)

The system also introduces separate classes for those people who have self-employed status or who run small businesses (Class 4) and those who are unemployed or who have never worked (Class 8). Full-time students are excluded from the classification.

EXERCISE 1.2

What do *you* think?

Read Excerpt 1.1 which explains the new way of classifying people according to their employment contract.

1 As a 'student' you are excluded from this classification, but in which class would you put your current part-time job (or a job you have undertaken in the past)?

2 In which class would you put your mother or father's occupation?

3 In which class would you put:

a self-employed plumber?

a plumber employed by someone else?

a plumber who employs 28 other people?

▶

▶

4   What difficulties did you find in trying to classify the plumber in question 3? Reflect on these difficulties and consider the main problems with applying this system of classification.

5   What practical uses does such a system of classification have?

Learning outcome 3

Explain the basic tools a social scientist uses to study work.

Studying work

Conceptual tools of the social scientist

The ideas that you will encounter in the following chapters emanate from people doing a job of work – most of them are social scientists (sociologists, psychologists, economists, political scientists, and so on). Like any other occupational group, social scientists have a set of 'tools' they use. Of course, each person may differ regarding the way they use specific tools for the tasks at hand – and consequently the outcome (output) of their work might differ. The difference between social scientists and other workers, however, is that while many occupations rely on physical tools, social scientists depend on conceptual (abstract) tools. In particular these include theories, models, typologies and different methods of data gathering.

Theories

Definitions of theory

> A formulation regarding the cause and effect relationships between two or more variables, which may or may not have been tested. (Gill & Johnson, 1997: 178)

> A set of systematically interrelated concepts or hypotheses that purports to explain and predict phenomena. (Robbins, 1998, Appendix B: 18)

Theories appear in a variety of forms, but frequently they are formulated as propositions that specify a cause and effect or an association, and present an explanation. To illustrate this, below is a list of theories about work. We have included one theory from each of the chapters in this book – so we will be exploring them later, along with many other theories. You will notice that they are all in the form of a proposition or statement that specifies a relationship between features (concepts). These propositions are testable – in other words, it is possible to attempt to verify them by subjecting them to an investigation.

- Advanced capitalist economies have experienced a decline in manufacturing and a growing dominance of the service sector because of the effects of globalisation.
- Once subsistence needs are met, people work for reasons other than money.
- Employees are working harder than ever as a result of new management practices designed to address the demands of intensified competition.

- Skilled status has often been denied to women through male domination of the political, material and ideological processes of social closure.
- There is an inevitable tendency towards the deskilling of work due to the desire of managers to control and regulate labour.
- Workers are expected to manage the emotions of customers because increasingly, organisations are differentiated by the service encounter.
- Irrespective of their conditions of work, all employees find ways of creating time, space and enjoyment in the working day, which helps them to tolerate the oppressive and exploitative elements of work.
- Ethnic minorities have fewer opportunities in the workplace because they suffer direct and indirect racial discrimination.
- The knowledge of employees is increasingly being expropriated by managers in order to meet the challenges of an information age.
- Employees choose to belong to collective bodies such as trade unions because of a fundamental power imbalance in the employment relationship.
- The formal economy is supported by a vast amount of work that remains hidden from view because it is illegal or unrecognised.

While it is easy to make theoretical statements like this, it is far more difficult to develop methods for testing them. That is the challenge the social scientist is faced with. He or she will devise a way of investigating such theoretical propositions – thereby allowing the theory to be substantiated, rejected or modified. Typically, the process will involve:

1 specifying the concepts involved (defining the problem and reading up on previous similar investigations);
2 formulating a method for investigating the issue (a methodology);
3 undertaking the investigation (doing the research);
4 analysing the findings;
5 publishing the conclusions.

Throughout the book you will find examples of how theorists have developed propositions and then how both they and others have sought to confirm, reject or modify theories as a result of the research.

Of course, at each of these stages different decisions and interpretations could be made by different social scientists, which affects the outcome of the investigation. So, any single theory might result in confirmation from some researchers, rejection by others and modification by yet others. A case in point, as you will see in Chapter 6, is the theory of the deskilling of work: some researchers argue that deskilling has taken place, others suggest a counter-theory of upskilling and a third group suggest that both effects are occurring in different ways. Naturally, this is very frustrating if you are looking for 'the answer', and some people are tempted to ignore certain types of research so as to avoid facing the problem of conflicting evidence. They might even reject the idea of theorising completely and argue that what needs to be applied is simply 'common sense' (see Excerpt 1.2). However, it is preferable to weigh up all the evidence and decide which is more convincing based on the rigour and approach of the research. You will find yourself in that position as you read the following chapters. The important point to remember is that it is fine to be more persuaded by one argument rather than another provided you can explain *why* you are more persuaded.

EXCERPT 1.2

Isn't it just common sense?

You've undoubtedly heard someone comment, 'It's just common sense', when they are trying to justify an idea or give credence to their viewpoint. In practice however, the claim that something is 'common sense' is often used by people who do not wish to, or cannot, explain their reasoning. There are two main dangers of saying 'it's common sense'.

1   It is not always *common*. When we describe an idea, issue, theory or whatever as common sense we often mean that it fits with our own understanding of the world. However, other people from different social backgrounds, ethnic groups, age groups, and so on might not share the same understanding. In other words, the idea, issue or theory is not common to *them*. Just because something is sensible, that does not automatically make it common. For example, taking a siesta during the middle of working days in the summer is common sense in southern Europe – but not in northern Europe.

2   It is not always *sense*. Albert Einstein described common sense as 'the collection of prejudices we have acquired by the age of 18'. In other words, common sense explanations often close our minds to other possibilities. Just because something is common, that does not automatically make it sensible. Some common sense understandings are later proven by rational, logical enquiry and experience to be misguided and ill-informed. Consider, for example the now discredited but once 'common sense' beliefs that the world is flat, that women do not have the right disposition to be successful managers, and that brown corduroy is sexy.

Typically, therefore, social scientists rarely justify something as common sense. They are always seeking to prove their claims and justify their theories and ideas.

Purpose of theories

The point of theorising is to establish a line of inquiry that will raise some specific questions and hopefully lead to an answer (but see Excerpt 1.3). So theorising is an important stage in helping to frame the appropriate questions, rather than blundering about unsure of what you are looking for. However, sometimes there is virtue in approaching an issue without any preconceived theories. Some researchers, for example, prefer to go into an organisation to study a work process or work group with a set of themes, but not developed theories. This alternative approach is often described as 'grounded theory' (a term coined by Glaser and Strauss, 1967) and is designed to uncover concepts, issues and ideas gradually and progressively, from which theory can later be built.

These two approaches can be described as deductive and inductive theorising.

- *Deductive* theories are based on the principles of developing ideas and concepts into a framework or set of hypotheses that can be tested by observation (that is, empirically).
- *Inductive* theories are developed from observation of particular instances and patterns (empirical research) that can then be built into general propositions.

In practice, much social scientific research involves both deductive and inductive theorising.

EXCERPT 1.3

Is there always an answer?

One of the stock responses of a social scientist when asked a question is that 'It depends'. This does not necessarily mean they are failing to give a straight answer but rather that there are many factors that could influence the answer. It might be that the question has not been specified precisely enough, or else there is a range of possible answers to the same question, depending on the frame of reference for the question. It is rather like someone asking 'what one added to one makes'. '2' is an adequate answer, unless they were working in the binary system, or were mixing primary colours, or were referring to different volumes of a liquid, or different products, or opposing magnetic poles ... and so on. In other words, frustrating though it may seem, social scientists must precisely frame and specify questions.

Throughout the chapters you will encounter attempts that social scientists have made to answer questions about working life in organisations. You will see also how different answers emerge to the same questions, and will have to make your own judgement as to which are the most convincing. The more you know and understand, the more you might be inclined to answer, 'Well, it depends' when faced with a question.

Models

Models are simplified versions of the world. They are representations of reality that allow understanding or exploration in an artificial (and safe) environment. For example, airline pilots develop their skills in a flight simulator. This models the real world of flying in two ways: first it provides an exact copy of an airline cockpit controls and the motion of the aircraft, and second it provides a 3D representation of the approaches to different international airports.

In social science, models typically take the form of a visual representation of processes and actions. This means that they are often flowcharts showing the links between different features (concepts, people, departments, materials, and so forth). In this sense, models are often synonymous with theories, and there is a tendency in social science not to differentiate between model and theory. We have adopted this convention in the book, so, for example, Figure 9.1 in Chapter 9 is a flowchart of Marx's theory of the labour process and alienation, but it could just as easily be described as Marx's model of the labour process.

Typologies

Typologies are ways of grouping and classifying different sorts of phenomena. In the previous section we used a typology to distinguish between three different types of theory, and earlier we discussed various classifications of work (which are typologies). The point of developing typologies is to simplify complex social structures and processes and thereby assist in our attempt to understand and explain such phenomena. To illustrate the point, imagine you are with a group of friends deciding where to go and eat. You might ask 'Shall we go Indian, Chinese or Italian?' In effect you have developed a typology of restaurants that simplifies the wide range of possible meals available.

The importance of systematically developing typologies was identified by the influential sociologist Max Weber (1949). He devised the notion of the 'ideal type'. It is a term that is often misunderstood because it is sometimes mistakenly thought to the mean the 'best' type. However, Weber used the term 'ideal type' to refer to the theoretical classification against which any observed types could be matched. For example, returning to our classification of restaurants above, we can say that the three mentioned are all 'ideal types'. One type is not better than another, but each one is distinct from the other two. It also means that if, for example, we found a restaurant that sold mostly Indian food but had a few non-Indian items on the menu we would say that it approximates the Indian ideal type; in other words it does not match it exactly. Again we are not saying that it is better or worse, merely that it is closer to the 'ideal type Indian restaurant' than to any of the other types of restaurant.

Of course our three-type restaurant classification is hopelessly incomplete because we know there are many other types of restaurant (French, Lebanese, Mexican, and so on) that fall outside all three of these categories. But that is also the point of developing typologies. Such systems allow us to identify exceptions, to seek to explain these, and, if appropriate, modify our typologies accordingly.

Typologies are extremely popular – see Excerpt 1.4 for a work-related example. You will encounter plenty more in the following chapters and undoubtedly you will have seen typologies on other courses and in other texts. It should always be remembered that typologies are designed to help simplify the complexity and variety of the social world. This means they are developed to group together similar phenomena. Rarely will you find an exact match between an observed phenomenon and an ideal type.

Using 'ideal types' to classify work

The following quote by Barley (1996: 407) explains how work can usefully be classified into 'ideal types'. However, it also warns how outdated ideal types can become problematic because they provide irrelevant comparisons with which to analyse current jobs.

"The-worker-on-the-assembly-line" is [an] ideal type. It invokes images of an individual, often in an automobile factory, standing beside a swiftly moving conveyor, repeatedly performing the same operation on each assembly that flows by. Boredom, fatigue, routine, lack of autonomy, and little need for thought or education are the hallmarks of such work. Although factory jobs have always been more varied than this, the ideal type nevertheless evokes a constellation of attributes that capture the family resemblance among many factory jobs. The clerk, the professional, the secretary, the farmer, and the manager are other prominent ideal-typical occupations.

Ideal-typical occupations are culturally and theoretically useful. By reducing the diversity of work to a few model images, ideal types assist us both in comprehending how the division of labor is structured and in assigning status to individuals. They help parents shape their children's aspirations. They provide designers of technologies with images of users. They assist sociologists in developing formal models of attainment. It is not clear how we could think in general terms about worlds of work without such anchors. The problem is that ideal-typical occupations are temporally bound.

Like occupational classifications and cultural dichotomies, ideal-typical occupations lose relevance as the division of labor and the nature of work change. For example, the ideal-typical farmer is an independent businessman laboring in the fields from sunrise to sunset with the assistance of a tractor, a few hired hands, family members, and little formal education, but extensive practical knowledge of crops, weather, animals, and soils. Modern farming bears little resemblance. Today, many farmers are subcontractors for agribusiness, have a college education, understand chemical properties of soils and fertilizers, and manage their farms with the help of computers."

Methods of gathering data

When we use the term data (the plural of 'datum') we essentially mean 'information'. Data appear in two basic forms:

- *Quantitative data*: data in numerical form, such as the number of people in a particular workplace, or the percentage of staff on part-time contracts.
- *Qualitative data*: data in non-numerical form, such as employee opinions about their working hours, or a description of a particular work process.

Sometimes the terms 'hard data' and 'soft data' are used respectively to describe the two types of data described above. Our preference, however, is not to use these labels because they have misleading connotations. 'Hard' gives the impression of being strong, fixed and robust, and 'soft' gives the impression of being weak, malleable and feeble, but in practice these descriptions can apply to both quantitative *and* qualitative data. For example, would you trust the supposedly hard data that 90 per cent of hospital workers are satisfied with their salary if you knew the data were based on a questionnaire filled in by only ten hospital administrators? Similarly, would you label as 'soft data' the description by a heart surgeon of the work process in their operating room?

Throughout the subsequent chapters you will encounter both quantitative and qualitative data. In our opinion, social scientists can use both types of data to make sense of the social world. However, not all commentators agree with this view. Some would argue that the social world, by definition, cannot be measured in the same way as the physical world. They might also suggest that it is futile to bring the quantitative methods and techniques used by physical science into the realm of social science, and that the emphasis should be on qualitative data. In contrast, there are others who argue that the social world does lend itself to being measured and explored in the same way as the physical world, and therefore the same quantitative methods and techniques can and should be used, although applied in different ways. These two protagonists (the qualitative and quantitative advocates) would use different methods of gathering data. The qualitative advocate would recommend that research is undertaken using methods such as semi-structured interviews, focus groups, observation and participation. The quantitative advocate would recommend computer simulations, questionnaires, controlled experiments, and statistical analysis.

You will encounter examples of these various research techniques in the following chapters because we believe both viewpoints have something to offer. Indeed, our view is that it is important to study research findings from both qualitative and quantitative researchers because their different approaches:

- can uncover different aspects of the same social phenomenon;
- can account for the same social phenomenon in different ways;
- can encourage us to have open minds on different issues.

By standing in this middle ground between the qualitative and quantitative approaches, we think it is possible to gain a better perspective of the diversity of the social world and the competing explanations of social action and processes. It also allows us to appreciate and comment on the contradictions and paradoxes in work that surface time and again – as you will see.

EXERCISE 1.3

What do *you* think?

Consider the following statement:

'A happy worker is a productive worker'

▶

▶ 1 Is this a theory? Justify your answer.

2 If someone said the statement is 'just common sense', how might you respond as a social scientist?

3 What method of inquiry would you adopt to assess the statement?

Analysing work: ways of looking

Learning outcome 4

Summarise the various perspectives from which work can be analysed.

From the comments in the previous section, it should be apparent that we have purposely adopted an approach that encourages an open-mindedness when analysing work. In particular, we are advocating that you identify how different approaches can be incorporated into an exploration of work to produce a more complete understanding. This is especially the case with regard to three key pairs of perspectives: the theoretical and the empirical; the objective and the subjective; and the past and the present.

Synthesising theoretical and empirical perspectives

Given the central role of paid work to industrial capitalism, and to the individuals therein, it is not surprising that the subject has given rise to extensive theoretical consideration which, at best, offers a stimulating variety of ideas. However, no single theory successfully captures the cross-cutting nature of work experience: the ways in which work encapsulates both conflict and cooperation, satisfaction and alienation, tension and accommodation. We have found that it is useful to draw upon various theories to locate and interpret work experiences and worker behaviour within a broader conceptual framework. In this way, then, the book does not advocate or adopt a single theoretical perspective but is informed by a range of theories, and seeks to tread the difficult – but what is felt to be ultimately the more rewarding – route of incorporating different theoretical insights without on the one hand, becoming shackled to a single orthodoxy, or on the other hand, being guilty of inappropriately cobbling together convenient bits of different theories to form an illogical pastiche.

We have also attempted to achieve a balance between theory and empiricism. There is a rich empirical tradition in Anglo-Saxon academic research that has illuminated our understanding of the experience of work. Moreover, empirical studies display a true plurality of research methods, all of which are legitimate and worthy attempts to explore the realities of work – although, of course, they vary in quality and rigour. Throughout the chapters we have tried to show how different research methods have been used to address a range of questions: methods which range from the ethnographic approach of qualitative researchers to the statistical analyses of quantitative researchers. Similarly, there is diversity in the levels of analysis: from detailed studies of particular workplaces to international comparative surveys. In some instances too, these different methods have been used to address the same research question, producing a plurality of interpretations that compete with one another for theoretical supremacy; nowhere is this better illustrated than over the issue of skill discussed in Chapter 5. As committed, active researchers ourselves, we have a strong conviction that theory and empiricism have a symbiotic relationship: an empirical account devoid of theory is as inadequate as a theory without data.

Synthesising objective and subjective perspectives

The plurality of empirical study also reveals a deeper tension between, on the one hand, researchers whose concern is to explore the objective conditions, processes and causal effects surrounding work, and those who seek to interpret subjective experiences and the meanings that people derive from their work. The former tend to focus on quantitative data while the latter rely more on qualitative data. We have drawn from both perspectives, and have sought to show the increasing importance of recognising a balance between considering the extreme objectivist position of one concrete, measurable truth, and the extreme subjectivist view of a multitude of intangible, impressionistic, equally valid truths. As noted above, we reject the notion that the essence or 'true' experience of work can be distilled into a single thesis or argument. It is one thing to identify common properties, general influences and widespread constraints, but it is another to postulate grand theories supposedly encapsulating the 'reality' of work. For a central problem is that the world of work, and work people's objective and subjective locations within that world, are more complex than that. The activities which constitute work take highly diverse forms, and are conducted in a wide variety of settings, with those taking part displaying the full range of character and biographical variation. In addition, it is clear that people subjectively experience work in a wide variety of ways. Hence, as the book's title indicates, what needs to be sought is an understanding of the *realities*, rather than any all-embracing *reality*, of work. This is not to dismiss the possibility of unearthing various widespread influences or common characteristics of work in contemporary industrial society. But while identifying and assessing these, it is equally important in a book of this nature to give recognition to the diversity of work realities.

Synthesising perspectives of the past and the present

Throughout the discussion we attempt to give a sense of history. All too often management texts fail to acknowledge the historical traditions of work and working, which means that the reasons why particular practices, policies or ideas came into being, are obscured. At worst, such an ahistorical approach has meant that each issue is dealt with as a contemporary problem that can be solved by a quick-fix solution: typically in the form of the latest buzz-word or policy to emanate from self-styled management gurus. It is little wonder that the result is at best a mixed success. Moreover, such an approach shows a contempt for the past that is both ill-advised and anti-academic. In contrast, we have tried to imbue our analysis with a respect for the past in terms of ideas, practices, theories, and research. Our concern is to show that the realties of work are embedded with resonant themes, abiding struggles and unresolved problems. 'New' issues and ideas are often in practice a new expression of the dilemmas and concepts of a previous period.

However, this does not mean that major changes have not occurred in the world of work. Some commentators suggest that the regimes of the past are giving way to a new era where emphasis is shifting from key sectors of work being organised on the basis of large-scale, standardised, mass production operations (with all that entails in terms of the size of organisations, the nature of jobs and patterns of control) to smaller-scale, more flexible forms of organisation, taking full advantage of more flexible technologies to service less standardised, more fragmented and more volatile product markets. It is clear that a combination of factors, including changes in levels of competition, the nature of markets and available technologies, are resulting in significant changes in the character of many work organisations.

In all industrial societies there has been a shift from an emphasis on the manufacturing sector to the service sector. The dominance of the latter as the larger source of employment is well established and in countries such as the UK, there are now four times as many people working in service activities as in manufacturing. Yet, despite their respective sizes, the research attention focused on work in service organisations has remained less than might be expected. Further, besides a general need to reflect more accurately the realities of work in the whole range of work contexts, there is need to represent new aspects of work which the expansion of services has brought about. Two specific examples of this are: the increase in activities involving direct contact with the public and the delivery of 'customer care' where an explicit part of the job is to display a particular set of emotions (Chapter 7); and the greater emphasis on knowledge intensive activities to underpin the information needs of service sector organisations (Chapter 8).

In other, more immediate ways too, the character of work has been changing markedly in recent years. Nowhere is this more apparent than in the growing feminisation of the workforce with many industrial societies approaching a point in their history where a majority of the workforce is female. With the sociology of work criticised for being unreflective of women (see, for example, Tancred, 1995) and with many individual studies criticised (rightly) as being written largely by men about men working in factories, this point in industrial history, when the balance is shifting to a majority of the workforce being female, makes it an appropriate time to consider more closely the contemporary realities of work for both women and men.

TO SUM UP

The above discussion reveals :

- our concern with seeking to explore diversity and variation in the work experience;
- our acceptance of the many interests and tensions within the employment relationship;
- our appreciation of the varied theoretical perspectives on work and methods of research and analysis.

So if you wanted to classify our approach, it would be possible to use the term 'methodological pluralism'. We have explained this in slightly more detail in Excerpt 1.5, but the main point to note is that we consider there are a number of varied, legitimate approaches to both studying and understanding the world of work, revealing different aspects and allowing for alternative interpretations of the work experience for employees.

EXCERPT 1.5

Methodological pluralism

In an analysis of pluralism, McLennan (1995: 57–76) argues that the methodological pluralist has to take a position with regard to ontology (the nature of reality) and epistemology (the way of knowing). This involves deciding whether there can be a pluralist ontology (many realities), a pluralist epistemology (many ways of knowing) or both (many ways of knowing many realities). Consequently, the methodological pluralist can take one of three positions, which McLennan (*ibid*: 73–4) sums up by using three slogans:

1 'Many versions, many (constructed) worlds'
2 'Many (fragmented, temporary) versions, one enduring world'
3 'One (true, valid) version for every single world, but many worlds'

The first slogan reflects the acceptance of both epistemological and ontological pluralism, whilst the second accepts epistemological pluralism, but rejects ontological pluralism. However, it is the third slogan that reflects the position we adopt in *The Realities of Work*: the rejection of epistemological pluralism, but the acceptance of ontological pluralism. To quote McLennan (*ibid*: 74) again:

> [This perspective] maintains that each of the many worlds is perfectly *real*, not just imagined, and for each of these worlds there will (eventually or in principle) be only *one* comprehensive valid theory. Of course, at any given point there are likely to be several plausible versions for each of the various worlds, but it is never legitimate to regard all of these versions as equally valid in principle. (emphasis in original)

Learning outcome 5

Identify the core components around which the rest of the book is structured.

Mapping the realities of work

To reiterate: our objective is to convey an impression of work from the perspective of the employee and to explain this through the use of theory and research evidence. We have drawn widely from the social sciences and have tried to provide empirical evidence and theoretical discussions that are not always to be found in mainstream texts, particularly those concerned with 'how to manage'. In selecting the key issues to include we have focused on how work is experienced and have constructed our narrative around several core questions:

- How do employees understand and make sense of their work?
- How do employees respond to the structures imposed on them through time and space (work organisation)?
- How do employees use their skills, knowledge and emotions?
- How do employees cope with pressure, monotony and a lack of control?
- How and why do employees suffer injustice?
- How do employees represent themselves?

From these central questions we have derived nine segments of the realities of work, each addressing a key theme raised by the questions. These segments constitute the chapters of the book, but to these we have added two further issues: the experience of work hidden from view – where the same questions are pertinent – and the broad context in which the realities of work are experienced. This conceptual map of our terrain is represented in Figure 1.1. The chapters that follow explore each component.

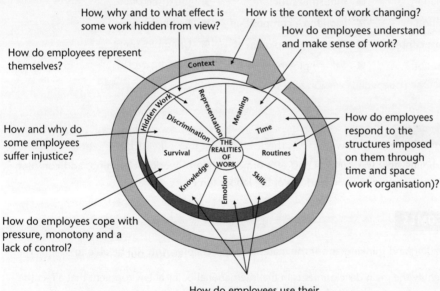

Figure 1.1 Exploring the realities of work

2 The changing context of work

- Political context
- Deregulation
- Privatisation
- Economic context
- Globalisation

- Competitive strategies
- Industrial structure
- Workforce composition
- Part-time employment
- Self-employment

- Location of employment
- Job insecurity
- Redundancy
- Unemployment

CHAPTER AIM

To examine how the political and economic context of work is changing, and consider the main trends in the composition of the labour force.

LEARNING OUTCOMES

By reading and thinking about the material in this chapter, you will be able to:

1 identify the main developments in the international political environment that affect the world of work, particularly trade liberalisation and the growth of supranational alliances;

2 recognise the influence of developments in national political contexts on the nature of work and employment;

3 develop an understanding of the main changes in the overall economic context, particularly the spread of economic globalisation;

4 identify the main changes in the industrial structure, particularly the shift from manufacturing to services;

5 assess the main changes taking place in workforce composition;

6 consider the changing experience of work in terms of changes in levels of unemployment, redundancies, temporary work and job insecurity.

Introduction

The comment is often made that the world of work has undergone dramatic changes over the past 20 to 30 years. Some commentators have gone so far as to characterise these changes as representing a fundamental shift in the nature of capitalism itself: a shift from 'Fordist' to 'post-Fordist' forms of production, from mass production systems to flexible specialisation, from industrial to post-industrial society, or from modern to post-modern forms of organisation (see also the discussion in Chapters 6 and 8). Such broad characterisations usefully signal the breadth and depth of changes taking place and also the ways in which myriad individual changes can be interpreted as part of much broader trajectories. At the same time, it is important to explore the specific changes themselves because such shorthand categorisations constantly run the danger of obscuring as much as (or more than) they reveal. Not only do they encourage (over) generalisations about the direction in which society is heading, they also (and often more implicitly) embody sweeping assumptions about where it has been.

In this chapter it is necessary to cover a lot of ground fairly quickly. Its purpose is to present an overview of how the context of work has been and is changing, and in so doing offer a broad landscape within which to locate the more specific experiences of work that are discussed in later chapters. Even an overview must be selective, however, since contexts can be defined at several levels – an individual worker is located in a particular work setting, but in turn that workplace is situated within a local economy, which itself is embedded in regional, national and international economic contexts. Further, these economic contexts are interrelated with, and influenced by, political contexts that also operate at each of these levels. Thus, in this chapter it is necessary to note some of the main changes that have been taking place in the political context of work over the past two decades, as well as both broad changes occurring within the economic context, and changing patterns of employment. Many of the issues raised in this chapter feed directly into more specific arguments covered in more detail later. For the moment though, the task is to capture a sense of the breadth of change occurring at the different levels. To this end, the chapter is divided into three main sections:

1 The broad changes occurring in the political context of work over approximately the last two decades are reviewed.

2 A similar examination is made of the central (and often closely related) changes occurring within the economic context, together with some of the main responses to those changes.

3 The major developments occurring in the structure and patterns of employment are explored. To illustrate this discussion we draw on OECD data relating to industrialised countries and on data for single countries where this allows us to explore developments in more detail.

Changes in the political context

It is impossible to analyse work without giving some consideration to the political context within which it is located. More accurately, work organisations are embedded within a series of political contexts: the international political environment, the national political context and regional and local politics. These are considered briefly below in an attempt to apply some broad brush strokes on the political backcloth against which the realities of work may be examined. The discussion is confined to the aspects of the political context that have impacted upon the workplace.

Learning outcome 1

Identify the main developments in the international political environment that affect the world of work, particularly trade liberalisation and the growth of supranational alliances.

The international political environment

Of the various international political developments that have been taking place over the recent period that impact upon the world of work, two are particularly notable:

■ the gradual extension of trade liberalisation measures;
■ the creation of supranational alliances in Europe, North America and Asia.

Extension of trade liberalisation

Political intervention over trade is subject to competing pressures as nation states seek to promote trade openness where it enhances economic growth, whilst at the same time seeking to protect more vulnerable domestic industries and markets. The influence of the latter means that many sectors (most notably agriculture but also various manufacturing activities) continue to maintain considerable tariff barriers (duties or charges on particular classes of goods) which have restricted the development of international trade. Nevertheless, since the founding of the General Agreement on Tariffs and Trade (GATT) in 1946, the overall trend both through GATT negotiations and through regional agreements has been towards a gradually more liberalised trading regime. The signing of the Uruguay Round Agreement of GATT in 1994, for example, committed developed economies to further tariff reductions on imports, though many such tariff barriers remain (Milberg, 1998).

The sector in which trading has become most liberalised is that of financial markets through the removal of restrictions on international movements of capital (Milberg, *ibid*: 83). This has acted as a key driver influencing the growth of economic globalisation (see below). Other sectors have also experienced a significant degree of market liberalisation in recent years. Entry into the long-distance telecommunications industry, for example, has been widely liberalised, as has access to local and mobile telecommunications in most industrial countries (OECD, 2000a: 152). Similarly, international air passenger transport has also experienced a degree of market liberalisation in recent years, though market restrictions remain in this, as in many other sectors (see Excerpt 2.1). Where international markets have become noticeably more liberalised is within three major regional groupings of countries in

North America, South East Asia, and particularly Europe. We examine these separately below.

EXCERPT 2.1

Market liberalisation in the international civil aviation industry

Traditionally, the air transport market has been subject to a high degree of State regulation covering market entry, capacity and prices. State ownership was the norm for the majority of the world's major airlines. These carriers enjoyed national 'flag carrier' status and preferential access to international markets through bilateral agreements between national governments.

Pressure for a relaxation in State regulation has come from a variety of sources, most notably growing political support for 'free market' capitalism within a more liberalised and privatised economic regime (many flag carriers have been privatised in recent years).

Following the deregulation of the United States airline industry in the late 1970s, the most significant liberalisation has been in Europe where a single market for aviation came into being in 1997, with any EU-registered carrier gaining the right to operate services within and between any of the EU member states.

This reduction in State control, particularly over the entry of new carriers, operations, pricing and capacity, has had certain immediate effects, most notably the growth of independent low-cost carriers, many operating from second-tier and regional airports. However, relaxation of State regulation over the passenger airline market remains partial. It remains the case that outside regional agreements such as in the EU, the majority of international routes are operated by the two countries involved, and protected by highly restrictive bilateral air service agreements.

Sources: Blyton, Martinez Lucio, McGurk and Turnbull (2001); OECD (2000a).

The growth of supranational alliances

Just as much of the world's trade takes place within and between the three regional areas of North America, Europe and East Asia, so too the main political steps to create regional free markets have also occurred in these regions, through the formation of the North America Free Trade Agreement (NAFTA), the Association of South East Asian Nations (ASEAN), and the European Union (EU). Whilst NAFTA and ASEAN have remained largely economic alliances, the European Union has taken integration considerably further, with member states establishing a widespread political and social agenda, though primarily to support the Union's economic programme.

It is the breadth of this integration in Europe that has made it particularly significant in terms of its impact on work and employment. For example, member states are subject to a growing body of European law which is increasingly impact-ing upon work organisations by obliging employers (and countries as a whole) to comply with European legislation, even where individual national governments are reluctant. For example, the European Court of Justice has in the past forced the British Government to enact additional equal pay provisions to take into account the European legislation covering work of equal value (Rubinstein, 1984). Likewise, in the mid-1990s, the UK Government was required to change the law on employment protection to give part-time workers the same qualifying period as their full-time counterparts in respect of statutory employment rights concerning, for example, redundancy pay and unfair dismissal compensation (Dickens, 1995: 209).

In the process of enshrining European-wide employment rights and better conditions, a key development was the establishment of the European Community Charter of the Fundamental Social Rights of Workers (known as the Social Charter). In 1989 it was accepted by 11 of the then 12 member states (the UK being the exception) as a political proclamation, with no formal legal status. However, it established the direction in which social policy was to develop, and by 1992 the 11 member states acted to begin the process of implementing the Social Charter through the EU institutions by signing a Protocol on Social Policy as part of the Maastricht Treaty (the Social Chapter). Again the then Conservative Government in Britain refused to be a signatory, and it was not until the incoming 1997 Labour Government that this opt-out decision was reversed.

The main vehicle for developing the work and employment aspects of the Social Charter has been through the introduction of European Directives, on such issues as working time, part-time workers, parental leave, sex discrimination and the rights of employees in European multinationals to works councils (Bach and Sisson, 2000). These Directives have been implemented (or are in the process of being so) via legislative changes at the national levels (see below).

A key political logic behind introducing EU-wide legislation has been to harmon-ise conditions and rights of employees across national boundaries. This is seen to be particularly important by the more prosperous states such as Germany which might otherwise fall victim to 'social dumping' – a process whereby companies transfer aspects of production to countries within the EU that maintain lower wages, less employment protection and fewer employment rights, thus decreasing the costs and overheads of labour. Such differentials exert considerable pressure on those member states with favourable employment terms and conditions to lower them in order to provide a competitive environment for the companies located there. The logical consequence of such differentials is a spiralling down or 'race to the bottom' on employment protection, with Europe becoming a domain of decreasing employment rights and increasing insecurity and exploitation – a politically and morally undesirable outcome within most member states.

The national political context

The growing significance of international agreements over trade, and the devel-opment of supranational political alliances notwithstanding, the national political context continues to represent a major source of influence affecting the world of work and developing patterns of employment. As an economic manager, employer and legislator, the State has a major bearing on the experience of work (Blyton and Turnbull, 1998: 140–79). Indeed, as noted above, even key supranational developments such as the implementation of EU Directives are carried out via changes in national legislation (see Bach and Sisson, 2000: 31–3). Similarly, a central aspect of the move towards greater market liberalisation has been the deregulation of individual national economic sectors. This economic deregulation activity has been given a particular impetus by widespread privatisation of former state-owned monopolies. Indeed, in the national political context affecting the nature of work and employment, it is privatisation activity which is among the most prominent national level political developments world-wide in recent years.

Learning outcome 2

Recognise the influence of developments in national political contexts for the nature of work and employment.

Privatisation activity

The 1980s and particularly the 1990s witnessed a substantial growth in privatisation activity throughout the world. Factors encouraging privatisation have included government desires to raise revenues and avoid new investment costs, and the widespread decline in the power of left wing parties that in the past have been more in favour of state ownership (Toninelli, 2000). One estimate is that the overall size of the public enterprise sector in industrial countries halved between the beginning of the 1980s and the end of the 1990s (OECD, 2000a: 154). In 1990, the total proceeds from privatisation were just under $30,000 million, of which the UK accounted for over 43 per cent. By 1997, however, the total global proceeds from privatisation during that year were over $153,000 million – an increase of over five hundred per cent from the 1990 level (OECD, 1999: 130). In the later 1990s, the most active countries pursuing large-scale privatisation programmes were Australia, France, Germany, Italy, Japan and Spain. Around the world, the main sectors that have been subject to privatisation in the recent period are manufacturing, telecommunications, financial services, public utilities and transport (OECD, *ibid*: 135–8).

Unless activities are taken back under public ownership, privatisation is a finite activity and figures indicate that by the end of the 1990s, the proceeds raised from privatisation were showing some fall back from the 1997 peak year (OECD *ibid*: 130). However, as much of the national state-owned sector becomes privatised, it is likely that privatisation at the sub-national level (involving for example, regional airports, local authority leisure facilities, local transportation systems, and so on) will become increasingly important, though the net receipts from such sales are likely to be markedly smaller.

Labour market deregulation

The UK was in the vanguard of the privatisation activity, and for Conservative Governments of the 1980s and 1990s in the UK, privatisation represented a major plank in a broader project of deregulating economic activity. This was particularly marked in relation to the labour market with the objective of allowing employers greater freedom of operation. This policy of labour market deregulation was underpinned by theories of neo-classical economics which hold that economic revival is dependent on allowing market forces to operate free from any 'artificial' constraint or government intervention. It was argued that competitiveness had been hampered in the past by high labour costs caused by the restrictions and rigidities imposed on employers by employment protection legislation, and the power and influence of trade unions. On the basis of this reasoning, successive Conservative Governments from 1979 onwards embarked on a series of incremental changes that sought to deregulate employment and restrict the influence of trade unions. Whilst aspects of these policies were reversed or curtailed by the incoming Labour Government elected in 1997 (by for example, the introduction of a National Minimum Wage and the establishment of rights for trade unions to pursue membership representation cases, as well as the implementation of European Directives, see above) many of the broader labour market policies have remained in place.

Deregulating employment – by such means as extending the period that employees are required to work before qualifying for employment protection rights, by abolishing wage-setting mechanisms for the least organised groups, and by restricting the operations of trade unions (see Blyton and Turnbull, 1998 for details) – had the effect of shifting the balance away from employment protection towards employment flexibility. This greater flexibility carries a number of consequences for those both in and out of work (see discussion of job insecurity below). However, in identifying the full extent and implications of labour market deregulation in the UK, care needs to be taken for it is something of a misnomer to talk of UK Governments 'deregulating' the relations between capital and labour. Relative to many other economies, the labour market and employment relationships in the UK have *never been* highly regulated. In the UK, for example, legislation on such basic employment issues as the maximum hours a worker is permitted to work, or the minimum number of days' holiday a person is entitled to has, until recently, been notable by its absence. The same holds for the type of employment contracts that an employer can offer – for example, unlike various other countries there is no requirement for employers in the UK to justify the offering of temporary rather than permanent contracts. In this respect, the deregulation of labour markets which took place in the UK in the 1980s and 1990s is all the more significant: it removed and reduced regulations in a context already characterised by a low degree of regulation. In a country where labour market regulation is in any event only modest, the further diminution of that basis of regulation has considerable symbolic significance regarding the perceived relations between capital and labour and the lack of any need to protect the latter against the powers of the former.

One of the significant aspects of the UK privatisation activity for patterns of work and employment is that in the past, an important way that the State regulated employment within and around the public sector was via the practice of Fair Wages Resolutions. These were based on the principle that when a private sector firm was awarded a Government contract, its employees should be paid at a level commensurate with equivalent work being undertaken by public sector workers. This was part of a broader State approach to acting as a 'good employer', and disseminating its practices more widely. The good employer approach also extended to its encouragement of trade union representation, leading to very high levels of union organisation throughout most of the public sector. However, the shrinking of the public sector due to privatisation, coupled with the commercialisation of those activities remaining in the public sector, was accompanied by the abandonment of Fair Wages Resolutions. Moreover, the growth in 'competitive tendering' across the public sector in the 1980s and 1990s resulted in most tenders being won on the basis of least cost, with low wage levels being an important means of keeping costs down when tendering. Thus the increase in competitive tendering and the ending of the concept of 'fair wages' acted to remove further 'rigidities' from the labour market concerning wage rates for employees working on Government contracts.

Regional and local political environments

As states such as the UK also move to more devolved political arrangements, political activity at regional and local levels becomes more significant. One of the most vivid examples of how sub-national politics can have an impact on work is the extent to which it encourages (or inhibits) capital investment in an area. In terms of encouraging capital investment, a UK example from the 1980s of local politics playing a key role relates to the location of the Nissan car company in the North East of England. In this instance, various parts of the local State (the local borough authority, the County Council and the local Development Corporation) acted to purchase land in sufficient quantity (over 900 acres) to attract the car-maker with the prospect of being able to expand their operations on the site much above their originally stated plans (Crowther and Garrahan, 1988).

In the UK the local political context has also proved to be a site where an alternative political agenda can by orchestrated from that prevailing at national level. Recently, for example, the elections for a Mayor of London in 2000 created a rallying point for opposition to the national Government's policy of privatising London Underground. Such examples must be treated with caution, however, for whilst they illustrate the potential importance of local politics in the UK, the influence of the latter remains highly circumscribed, both by the increasing power of Whitehall (Hoggett, 1996) and by the general inability of sub-national political mechanisms such as the Scottish and Welsh Assemblies successfully to challenge the decisions of powerful multinationals. For example, when the Anglo-Dutch steelmaker Corus announced in early 2001 its decision to close substantial parts of its steel-making and plating facilities in South Wales with the loss of approximately 3000 jobs in Wales (and 6000 in the UK as a whole), this decision could not be modified by the Welsh Assembly, despite the latter's efforts of persuasion and financial incentives (*Financial Times*, 17 January 2001, p. 6; see also Excerpt 2.2).

The nature of work is influenced by political factors operating at various levels from the international political arena to local political contexts. Many of the political projects being pursued at the different levels are interconnected, including the search for further privatisation, greater labour market deregulation and broader trade liberalisation.

Learning outcome 3

Demonstrate an understanding of the main changes in the overall economic context, particularly the spread of economic globalisation.

Changes in the economic context

Globalisation and competition

One of the most marked economic developments over the recent period has been the progressive globalisation of economic activity. Just as earlier periods of industrial development witnessed a gradual shift in the extent to which enterprises were oriented towards national rather than local markets, the last quarter century has seen a marked increase in the cross-national nature of goods and service production. It needs to be recognised that the term 'globalisation' is problematic. Many different meanings have been applied to it, and some commentators have criticised the term for its implication that what is currently occurring is fundamentally different from previous patterns of development rather than an extension of those patterns (see for example, Hirst and Thompson, 1996; and Kleinknecht and ter Wengel, 1998).

Although the term 'globalisation' has often lacked precision, we concur with the view that there is now compelling evidence that global activity *is* increasing, that national economies are becoming increasingly integrated into global trading relations, and that large companies increasingly make decisions on a global basis, not least as a result of the trade and capital liberalisation measures that political negotiations have brought about (see above). In part too, globalisation reflects the growing number of countries figuring in an increasingly industrialised world, with countries such as Korea, Taiwan, Singapore, Brazil, Mexico and recently Malaysia, Thailand, India and China becoming prominent industrial producers and major international traders.

A workable definition of economic globalisation is 'the integration of spatially separate locations into a single international market' (Blyton, Martinez Lucio, McGurk and Turnbull, 2001: 447). The principal economic dimension to this is simply the reduction in the costs incurred when conducting business on an international basis. This includes, in particular, transport and transaction costs, such as travel time, freight rates and the cost, speed and ease of communication.

Nowhere is the spread of globalisation more clearly illustrated than in the accelerated growth in world trade in recent years. During the 1990s, world trade grew at a considerably faster rate than total output of goods and services. On average, world trade grew by 6.4 per cent per annum during the 1990s (Bank of England,

2000: 234) Throughout that decade, this represented a much higher rate of growth than total output (GDP); indeed in a number of those years (1994/5/7/8) world trade grew at over twice the rate of world GDP. Further, this outpacing and increased prominence of world trade is forecast to continue. Pain, Ashworth, Holland, Hubert and te Velde (2000: 34) for example estimate that world GDP will increase by an average of 4 per cent in the years to 2006, compared to a forecasted annual growth rate of 7.8 per cent in world trade in that period.

EXERCISE 2.1

What do *you* think?

The focus of the discussion here is *economic* globalisation. However, globalisation also has social, cultural and political dimensions which may be said to reinforce the spread of economic globalisation.

Identify an example of social, cultural and cultural globalisation taking place.

(If you wish to develop your knowledge further on these aspects of globalisation, a good starting point is M. Waters, *Globalisation*, London: Routledge, 1995.)

Multinational firms

Within this overall expansion in trade, multinational firms play a very large and increasing role, and as such represent the principal carriers of economic globalisation. Driven by such factors as the differential cost and availability of labour, favourable exchange rates and the importance of being situated within, rather than outside multi-country free trade areas (such as the European Single Market) the scale of multinational activity has continued to grow (Stopford and Turner, 1985). Taking the example of the United States, US multinationals accounted for over four-fifths (83 per cent) of the value of US exports in 1994. A substantial part of this (36 per cent) involved trade between multinational parents and their affiliates, whilst the remainder (47 per cent) involved trade between multinationals and others (Clausing, 2000: 190).

The overall effect of globalisation, the spread of industrialism, and the increased dominance of multinationals has been to intensify competition in many markets. A growing number of local and domestic markets have become exposed to wider competition, either as a result of international trade or through activities of multinationals producing for the 'host' country market. So much so that a worker in the UK Midlands, for example, could work at the (French owned) Peugeot Ryton plant, travel to and from work in their British manufactured Ford or Vauxhall car (both US multinationals in the UK), do their shopping at lunchtime in their local (German owned) Aldi supermarket, and travel into Birmingham at the weekend to purchase household goods at the local (Swedish owned) Ikea superstore, before returning home to watch their UK manufactured (Japanese owned) Hitachi television, picking up a hamburger from the local (American owned) McDonald's on the way.

Intensification of competition

Besides the pervasiveness of multinationals, other factors too can be seen to have fuelled the intensification of competition, not least an accelerated diffusion of new technologies, generally resulting in more restricted technological advantage being enjoyed by individual companies for a more limited time. Related to this, technological advances in telecommunications have accelerated the speed with which companies can effectively operate in geographically dispersed markets, thereby undermining any advantage of proximity and exclusivity which local producers might previously have benefited from.

The effects of intensified competition on work and workers can manifest themselves in a variety of ways depending on how employers respond to the competitive pressure. Decisions such as positioning in markets through acquisition, divestment, or change in location, which markets to operate in, which products to develop or abandon and which technologies to employ, are all likely to be influenced by the nature and intensity of competition. At the same time, however, in the search for competitive advantage and efficiencies, labour and labour costs frequently play a central role. This is often not only true where labour costs represent a high proportion of total costs, but also where labour costs form a much smaller proportion, but are more open to manipulation (at least in the shorter term) than other, more fixed costs. In the international air passenger transport industry, for example, labour costs represent only between 25 and 35 per cent of total operating costs (Doganis, 1994: 18); however, many other costs (for example, the cost of aircraft and fuel prices) are less open to manipulation, thus making labour one of the few 'variable' elements of cost, at least in the short term. As a result, in the face of deregulation and growing competition in the industry, there has been strong pressure on airline managements to improve competitiveness via cuts in their overall labour costs (Blyton, Martinez Lucio, McGurk and Turnbull, 2001).

There are essentially two contrasting strategies that employers may adopt towards labour in its search for competitive advantage: on the one hand, by increasing the output that labour achieves; or on the other, by reducing its cost. In practice, of course, these two strategies do not represent the sole choice available. Rather, they are located at each end of a continuum of responses, with employers likely to seek improvements in their competitive position by a mixture of responses designed to increase performance *and* reduce costs. Variation, therefore, is likely to be not between one extreme and the other but rather between the relative priorities given to performance improvement and cost reduction. Yet, it will nevertheless be helpful to delineate the two ends of the continuum in a little more detail, for they indicate how broad economic (and political) strategies have important ramifications for labour.

- One end of the continuum entails seeking competitiveness through improved performance and presupposes the creation of a highly trained and competent workforce, capable of utilising a high level of skill to yield increased levels of output.
- The other end of the continuum involving a labour strategy based on lowest cost, is likely to entail minimising expenditure on training, resulting in a low skill, low productivity, low cost workforce.

The choice between these strategies (or the relative weight given to each within more complex strategies) is not only an economic choice but also reflects political policies and constraints. An important reason, for example, why employers in Germany have generally pursued a 'high skill, high performance' strategy is partly because State policies on training and vocational education have resulted in an extensive training infrastructure, and a comparatively high level of skill development among the labour force. Added to this, alternative strategies such as minimising labour costs by hiring in workers when demand is strong, then firing them when demand drops, are less readily available to German employers, because of statutory restrictions governing redundancy and dismissal. This contrasts with the UK where there is little regulatory constraint on employers' ability to hire and fire. Given this, and the comparatively low development of national training and vocational education provision in the UK, it is evident how political policies in the two countries have influenced markedly different labour strategies (Boyer, 1988; Brunhes, 1989).

It has been widely argued that the UK has been in the vanguard of those countries pursuing a low cost competitive strategy, with consequences for levels of investment in skills, wage levels (including non-wage labour costs such as sick pay and pension contributions) and the (low value added) nature of much of the productive activity taking place (for a discussion, see Blyton and Turnbull, 1998). The low wage levels and widespread availability of labour (due partly to high levels of unemployment for much of the 1980s and 1990s; see below) have been important factors encouraging a high level of foreign direct investment into the UK compared, for example, to other EU countries. Much of this investment has required only low or modest levels of skill development, with many activities (for example, in the motor components sector and consumer durables manufacture) involving assembly operations of one form or another. The paucity of the education and training structure in the UK compared, for example, to many of its western European counterparts, has been well documented (see, for example, Keep, 1989 and 1994) as has the UK's level of productivity and performance (see Blyton and Turnbull, 1998: 38–46). The broader point for our present discussion, however, is that many of the salient aspects of work – types of jobs available, levels of income, extent of training and skill development, and degree of job security – can only be fully understood within the broader context of overall competitive strategies and the political and economic milieux within which those strategies are formulated and pursued.

EXERCISE 2.2

What do *you* think?

Assume that you are a senior Human Resources manager in an organisation that in the past has competed on the basis of producing high volume goods to cater for the low cost end of a consumer market (selling fixed focus, 'point and shoot' cameras).

▶

▶

Because of a change in consumer behaviour to favour higher specification and better quality equipment, your company has taken the decision to switch its strategy, get out of the low cost end of the market, change its brand name, and compete by producing very high specification, and much more high cost, equipment.

1 In terms of the workforce, what are the main changes that you anticipate will need to be made? List and rank in order of importance.

2 Now rank these again in terms of which change you would begin with (followed by second and third in order of priority for introduction), and explain the reasons for your decisions.

3 In addition to hopefully meeting the objective of successfully switching production to the higher quality output, what other consequences would you foresee arising from the changes you have listed?

Organising production

Aside from the question of overall strategies aimed at higher performance or lower cost, in other ways too, greater competition and the search for more efficient operations have led to significant changes in how organisations approach the tasks of goods and service production. For example, the twin factors of advances in technological capability and the search for greater efficiency have stimulated the development of more advanced forms of production control, with production processes being 're-engineered' or 're-configured' to improve the sequencing and integration of different stages of productive activity within organisations and the efficiency with which production 'flows' through an organisation with the minimum of bottlenecks. Partly this involves the supply of materials and the timing of manufacturing processes being matched more closely to customer orders, so that goods are produced 'just-in-time' to meet delivery requirements, thereby reducing the amount of capital tied up in stocks of raw materials, work-in-progress and finished goods. In terms of the possible impact on people's experience of work (and as discussed further in Chapter 4) one effect of just-in-time operations could be an increase in work intensity, or at least a reduced ability to create greater control over work pace by building up 'banks' of part-finished items, that can be drawn upon to ease work pressures at a later point.

Quality

Closely associated with these changes in production processes has been an increased emphasis on output quality, with Japanese manufacturers such as Toyota leading the way in making the management of quality a key component in overall production and competitive strategy. The increased emphasis on quality has manifested itself in a variety of management initiatives such as quality assurance, quality circles, and Total Quality Management (TQM) (Deming, 1982; Hill, 1991; Juran, 1979; Oakland, 1989), and has given rise to additional phrases in the management lexicon such as 'continuous improvement', 'zero defects', 'internal customers', 'world best practice' and the more commonplace 'right first time'. Much emphasis has come to be given to assuring quality at the point of production rather than at final inspection, in an attempt not only to ensure a better quality product, but in particular to avoid the cost of re-working defective output. Among the effects of these changes for the experience of work has been an increased emphasis on quality assurance and a requirement for workers to take greater responsibility for inspecting their own work and that of their work colleagues.

TO SUM UP

A major development in the economic context of work is increasing economic globalisation, driven primarily by the expansion of multinational firms. Choices between different competitive strategies impact significantly on the nature of work and employment. Other key changes influencing the experience of work include the increased emphasis on more efficient organisation of production and higher quality output.

Changes in industrial structure and employment

Learning outcome 4

Identify the main changes in the industrial structure, particularly the shift from manufacturing to services.

The structure of employment is never static but reflects and delineates patterns of change in particular industries and broader sectors of activity. The pace and some of the contours of change vary from one industrial society to another; nevertheless a number of broad developments are evident, reflected in the changing structure of employment. Measurement of the structure and location of economic activity, the characteristics of the workforce, the nature of employment contracts and patterns of unemployment, redundancy and insecurity indicate the aggregate nature of employment and the ways this is changing over time. A number of measures are inter-connected: the simultaneous growth in service sector, female and part-time employment, for example. Also, some of the trends which can be identified are influenced not only by structural shifts in the economy but also by cyclical factors which act to accelerate or inhibit certain longer term changes at particular periods. At the same time, what is revealing is the robust nature of many of the structural changes. Cyclical effects such as economic recession have in many cases had only a modest influence on several of the aspects of employment change (for example, the growth in part-time working), temporarily slowing some of the trends but rarely causing even a temporary reversal in longer term developments. This is true even of those aspects of the employment experience, such as redundancy, unemployment and job insecurity, which in the past were closely associated with recessionary conditions, but in more recent times have seemingly become rather more loosely tied to overall economic conditions (see discussion of job insecurity, and Excerpt 2.4).

Employment in service and manufacturing industries

Throughout the industrial world, a progressive shift in employment from primary and secondary sectors to the tertiary, service sector has been pronounced (Blyton, 1989: 31–8). In the OECD as a whole more than six out of ten employees work in the service sector, with North America and several European countries registering a level of over seven employees in every ten being located in services. In 1971, the corresponding proportion of employees working in the service sector in OECD countries was five out of ten, and in 1961 just over four out of ten (Blyton, 1989: 37).

Looking at the UK in more detail, in the thirty years between 1971 and 2000, the number employed in manufacturing in Britain fell by almost four million or almost half (Table 2.1). In the same period, the number employed in services rose by more than seven million, an increase of over three-fifths. As a consequence, by 2000 more than four and a half times as many people were employed in the service sector in Britain as worked in manufacturing. When all industries are taken into account (agriculture, forestry and fishing; mining; electricity, gas and water supply; and construction; as well as manufacturing and services) the proportion of total employees engaged in the service sector in Britain stood at over three quarters (76.6 per cent) by September 1995, up from just over half (52.6 per cent) of the total employees in employment who worked in services in 1971. In contrast, manufacturing employment by 2000 had fallen to less than one in six (16.3 per cent) of the total in employment.

Within the service sector, employment in some industries has grown far more rapidly than in others. While employment in the UK finance, real estate and related services, for example, grew by 185 per cent between 1971 and 1996 and the numbers employed in hotels and catering rose by over four-fifths, employment in other sectors showed more modest increases or even decreases over that period, including wholesale and retail distribution (where employment increased by

Table 2.1 Changes in employment in UK manufacturing and services, 1971–2000 (thousands)

Year	Manufacturing	Services
1971	7890	11,388
1981	6107	13,102
1990	4756	16,643
1996	4106	17,213
2000	3958	18,631
Actual change 1971–2000	– 3932	+ 7243
% change 1971–2000	– 49.8%	+ 63.6%

Adapted from: *Employment Gazette* (Historical Supplement 4) October 1994 and *Labour Market Trends*, December 2000

27 per cent), and post and telecommunications, public administration and transport, which each recorded decreases in employment (Blyton and Turnbull, 1998: 51). Similarly, the decline in employment in production industries in the 1970s–1990s period was also very unevenly distributed with the rate of decline in some sectors (for example, coal mining, textiles, and electricity, gas and water supply) more than double that found in others (for example, paper, printing and publishing) (Blyton and Turnbull, *ibid*: 50).

Male and female workers

This increasing predominance of service sector employment has also been reflected in other changes occurring in the nature of the employed workforce, particularly the proportions of male and female, and full and part-time workers in the workforce. The period since the 1970s has witnessed a marked growth in the proportion of the workforce that is female. Several factors are important in accounting for this change, reflecting both changes in the demand for, and supply of labour. Demand side factors, however, are dominated by the shift to service sector employment and the increased opportunities for employment among women in service industries. This has been a key factor behind the increase in women's overall share in the workforce over the past generation. As Table 2.2 indicates, in the late 1950s,

Learning outcome 5

Assess the main changes taking place in workforce composition.

Table 2.2 Change in numbers of males and females in employment in Britain, 1959–1999 (thousands)

	1959	1971	1979	1992	1996	1999
Females	7174	8207	9435	10,395	10,693	11,477
Males	13,817	13,433	13,176	10,911	10,916	10,967
Total	20,991	21,640	22,611	21,307	21,609	23,444
Proportion of females in total	34.2%	37.9%	41.7%	48.8%	49.5%	49.0%

Sources: Employment Gazette and *Labour Market Trends*, various dates

women comprised just over one-third of the total employed in Britain. By the end of the 1990s, this proportion stood at almost one-half: of the 23.4 million employees in employment in Britain in June 1999, 11.48 million (49 per cent) were women. As the participation rate of women continues to rise, the realisation of a feminised workforce, where a majority of the employees in employment are women, is likely in the foreseeable future. Indeed, the 1993 Census of Employment in Britain identified twenty-five counties and Scottish regions (out of a total of 66) where the number of female employees outnumbered their male counterparts (Thomas and Smith, 1995: 369). A workforce where the majority is female is a reality too in various industries in the UK; and in the service sector as a whole, well over 80% of all employees are female.

What do *you* think?

The discussion of the growth in female employment has concentrated on labour demand factors, particularly the expansion of the service sector. In addition, however, there are important labour supply factors which help to explain why a greater proportion of women – particularly those with children – are returning to the labour market to a greater extent than previously.

1 List the main factors that you think account for why a higher proportion of women are now returning to the labour market.

2 Rank these factors in order of importance and give reasons for your choice of the most important.

Part-time employment

Within the overall changes in employment towards a greater proportion of jobs being held by women, the majority of these located in the service sector, there has been a particular growth in the number of people working part-time. As Table 2.3 shows, across the OECD as a whole, around one in six employees work part-time. However, among the members of the OECD, this proportion varies considerably, with eight countries in 1999 showing a part-time proportion greater than one in five of total employees, while seven other countries recorded a level of less than one in ten employees working part-time.

Table 2.3 Incidence and composition of part-time employment[a] in OECD countries, 1990–1999

Country	Part-time employment as a proportion of total employment						Women's share in part-time employment	
	Men		Women		All			
	1990	1999	1990	1999	1990	1999	1990	1999
Australia	11.3	14.3	38.5	41.4	22.6	26.1	70.8	68.9
Austria	..	2.8	..	24.4	..	12.3	..	87.2
Belgium	4.6	7.3	29.8	36.6	14.2	19.9	79.9	79.0
Canada	9.1	10.3	26.8	28.0	17.0	18.5	70.1	69.7
Czech Republic	..	1.7	..	5.6	..	3.4	..	70.9
Denmark	10.2	8.9	29.6	22.7	19.2	15.3	71.5	68.4
Finland	4.7	6.6	10.6	13.5	7.5	9.9	67.2	64.9
France	4.4	5.8	21.7	24.7	12.2	14.7	79.8	79.0
Germany	2.3	4.8	29.8	33.1	13.4	17.1	89.7	84.1

Table 2.3 Incidence and composition of part-time employment[a] in OECD countries, 1990–1999

| | Part-time employment as a proportion of total employment | | | | | | | |
| Country | Men | | Women | | All | | Women's share in part-time employment | |
	1990	1999	1990	1999	1990	1999	1990	1999
Greece	4.0	..	11.5	..	6.7	..	61.1	..
Hungary	..	2.1	..	5.1	..	3.5	..	68.7
Iceland[b]	7.5	9.1	39.7	35.2	22.2	21.2	81.6	77.1
Ireland	4.2	7.9	20.5	31.9	9.8	18.3	71.8	75.7
Italy	3.9	5.3	18.2	23.2	8.8	11.8	70.8	71.5
Japan	9.5	13.4	33.4	39.7	19.2	24.1	70.5	67.0
Korea	3.1	5.9	6.5	10.5	4.5	7.8	58.7	55.2
Luxembourg	1.6	1.6	19.1	28.3	7.6	12.1	86.5	91.8
Mexico	..	7.2	..	26.9	..	13.8	..	65.4
Netherlands	13.4	11.9	52.5	55.4	28.2	30.4	70.4	77.4
New Zealand	7.9	11.3	34.6	37.2	19.6	23.0	77.1	73.3
Norway	6.9	8.2	39.8	35.0	21.8	20.7	82.7	78.8
Poland	..	..	..	..	..	..	..	..
Portugal	3.1	5.0	11.8	14.6	6.8	9.3	74.0	70.8
Spain	1.4	2.9	11.5	16.8	4.6	7.9	79.5	77.0
Sweden	5.3	7.3	24.5	22.3	14.5	14.5	81.1	73.7
Switzerland	6.8	7.7	42.6	46.5	22.1	24.8	82.4	82.6
Turkey	4.9	3.5	18.8	15.1	9.2	7.1	62.5	65.6
United Kingdom	5.3	8.5	39.5	40.6	20.1	23.0	85.1	79.6
United States[c]	8.3	8.1	20.0	19.0	13.8	13.3	68.2	68.4

a Part-time employment refers to persons who usually work less than 30 hour per week in their main job.
b 1990 refers to 1991
c Estimates are for wage and salary workers only.
.. not available
Adapted from: OECD (2000b)

EXERCISE 2.4

What do *you* think?

Look at the data in the last two columns of Table 2.3 dealing with women's share of total part-time employment. In a majority of the countries (16) women's share of part-time employment fell during the 1990s. What factors can you think of that might account for this decline?

In the OECD countries as a whole, over seven out of ten part-time jobs are held by women (in the EU countries the proportion is almost eight out of ten). Overall, around nine out of ten part-time jobs are located in the service sector (see Naylor, 1994 for a detailed historical examination of the growth of part-time working).

Self-employment

In addition to those in the labour force who are employees, there is also a significant minority who are self-employed. Among industrial countries in the OECD, levels of self-employment are highest where agriculture and small family businesses remain major sectors of activity, for example, Greece, Korea, Portugal and Turkey.

In the UK, self-employment increased substantially (by almost half) during the 1980s, due primarily to the twin forces of, on the one hand, high levels of unemployment and limited job vacancies, and on the other hand, State financial support for those moving from being unemployed to self-employment. In addition, as part of their efforts to cut direct labour costs, many companies from the 1980s onwards abandoned employment contracts in favour of commercial contracts by requiring some of their workers to alter their status from being employees to being self-employed. This occurred, for example, among workers operating outside the main workplace, such as service engineers and milk roundsmen, and particularly in the construction sector (see Evans, 1990). Where self-employed individuals are simply selling their skills to an organisation they are sometimes referred to as 'labour only subcontractors' and these comprise a high proportion of the two and a half million enterprises with no employees in existence operating in the UK (Dale and Kerr, 1995: 462).

The growth in self-employment was heralded by UK Governments in the 1980s as a mark of success and testimony to an emerging 'enterprise culture'. In practice, however, much of this newly created self-employment involves low remuneration and long hours. In 1993, for example, full-time self-employed persons worked, on average, around seven hours per week more than employees (Butcher and Hart, 1995: 218). Small businesses are also prone to high rates of business failure and probably attest more to a lack of employment prospects and firms accepting only self-employed status, rather than any significant desire for autonomy within an enterprise culture.

The location of employment

Size of employing organisation

Whilst it is commonplace to think of a 'typical' employing organisation as one that is fairly or very large, in fact of the 992,000 enterprises with employees operating in Britain at the end of 1993, four out of five employed less than ten people while only 17,000 (1.7 per cent of the total) employed more than 100 people. Of these, 14,000 were medium-sized (100–499 employees) and just 3000 were large (500 or

more employees) (Dale and Kerr, 1995: 462). However, these 3000 largest businesses accounted for over one-third (37 per cent) of total non-government
employment. Large-scale enterprises predominate in the energy and water sector,
mining and quarrying, chemicals and parts of the financial sector. Small firms on
the other hand, are particularly numerous in parts of the manufacturing sector
(including printing and publishing, furniture and fabricated metal products) as
well as in agriculture, construction and most service industries (including business
services, entertainment, catering and vehicle maintenance and repair) (Dale and
Kerr, *ibid*: 463).

In terms of trends in firm size, there is some indication that average firm size is
declining and that the proportion of total employees working for smaller firms is
gradually increasing. In part, this reflects the shift from manufacturing to service
activities (smaller firms being more prevalent in service industries), the closure of
many formerly very large establishments (such as steel plants and shipyards) over
the past two decades, and the increase in outsourcing activity by larger firms.
Restricted longitudinal data (covering the period 1988 to 1991) collected by the
OECD suggest a modest trend throughout the main industrialised countries
towards a larger share of employment being concentrated in smaller firms. In the
UK between these dates, for example, the share of total employment located in
firms with less than 100 workers rose from 47 to 49 per cent (OECD, 1995: 124).
Smaller firms also figure prominently in statistics on employment creation. As the
OECD (1995: 128) notes, however, 'volatility in employment levels . . . appears to
be an intrinsic characteristic of small businesses'. In other words, smaller firms
figure prominently in statistics of gross job gains *and* gross job losses (see also Shutt
and Whittington, 1987).

Location of work

As employment in production industries, particularly traditional industries such
as coal, steel and shipbuilding, has declined, so too has the proportion of total
employment located in the main industrial conurbations. There has been a
growing tendency to establish and expand service activities and new manufacturing projects on 'greenfield' sites, often in semi-rural areas (Massey 1988: 61;
see also Sayer and Walker, 1992). Further, for a significant minority of workers,
their work is located in their own home. The 1994 Labour Force Survey (LFS),
for example, gives an estimate of over 640,000 people working at home in
Britain. The earlier 1991 Census put this figure much higher (almost double the
LFS figure) though the definition of homeworking used in the Census also
included those resident in a workplace (such as hotel workers, agricultural
workers, farmers and those 'living over the shop') which increases the total
significantly (Felstead and Jewson, 1995). One of the areas of growth in homeworking in recent years has been the expansion of teleworking – see Excerpt 2.2
below; also, Sullivan and Lewis (2001) for a discussion of gender and telework.
For a thorough analysis of different forms of working from home see Felstead
and Jewson, 2000.

EXCERPT 2.2

Increases in teleworking

According to the Labour Force Survey (LFS), by Spring 2000 there were just over 1.5 million teleworkers in Britain, a rise of just under 20 per cent from a year previously. This total represents over five per cent of the workforce in Britain.

The LFS tracks three different kinds of teleworker: those working exclusively from home, those working mainly from home, and those who are occasional teleworkers – for example working one day a week from home. By Spring 2000, 299,000 teleworkers in Britain were homeworkers, 757,000 teleworkers worked mainly from home, and 447,000 were occasional teleworkers. Of the total, just over two-thirds were men, who were mainly located in professional (for example, journalists), managerial or technical jobs. Women teleworkers on the other hand were more evenly divided between the managerial, professional, technical category and clerical jobs (such as remote-based call centre staff).

Bargaining Report (2001) also quotes a 1999 European study which estimates that around six per cent of the European workforce are teleworkers, with highest proportions in Finland, Sweden and the Netherlands.

The experience of teleworking is mixed. Advantages include time and money saved on commuting, having access to a more flexible work pattern, and potentially providing more employment opportunities for disabled workers. However, the major disadvantage for all types of teleworker (and indeed all homeworkers) is the isolation that homeworking can entail and the lack of a clear distinction between work life and home life.

Unemployment, temporary work and job insecurity

Learning outcome 6

Consider the changing experience of work in terms of levels of unemployment, redundancies, temporary work and job insecurity.

Unemployment

Just as it is difficult to compare unemployment rates between countries because of different definitions of unemployment, so too seeking to draw an accurate comparison of present day rates of unemployment with those of earlier periods is complicated by the many changes made to the basis on which unemployment statistics are calculated. In the UK since the late 1970s, for example, there have been over twenty such changes (see Denman and McDonald, 1996: 18; and Department of Education and Employment, 1995a: 398–400).

Despite these difficulties, however, important long term trends in the rate of unemployment remain evident. The principal one is that levels of unemployment have risen from levels of around two per cent in the 1950s and 60s to a peak of over 11 per cent in the mid 1980s. Even during periods of strong economic growth, unemployment rates have tended to remain higher than the rates prevailing during growth periods a generation ago. Table 2.4 shows a comparative picture among industrial countries for the 1990s, which indicates that whilst unemployment rates fell during the latter years of the decade, unemployment in many countries remained at comparatively high levels.

Table 2.4 Unemployment rates in 25 industrial countries, selected years, 1990–1999

Country	As a percentage of total labour force					
	1990	1992	1994	1996	1998	1999
Australia	7.0	10.8	9.7	8.6	8.0	7.2
Austria	..	..	3.8	4.4	4.5	3.7
Belgium	6.7	7.2	10.0	9.7	9.5	9.0
Canada	8.1	11.2	10.4	9.6	8.3	7.6
Czech Republic	..	..	4.4	3.9	6.5	8.8
Denmark	7.7	9.2	8.2	6.8	5.2	5.2
Finland	3.2	11.6	16.7	14.6	11.4	10.3
France	9.0	10.4	12.3	12.4	11.9	11.3
Germany[a]	4.8	4.5	8.5	8.9	9.4	8.7
Greece	6.4	7.9	8.9	9.6	10.7	..
Hungary	..	9.9	11.0	10.1	8.0	7.1
Ireland	13.4	15.4	14.4	11.7	7.6	5.8
Italy	9.0	8.8	11.2	11.7	11.9	11.4
Japan	2.1	2.2	2.9	3.4	4.1	4.7
Luxembourg	1.7	2.1	3.2	3.0	2.7	2.3
Netherlands	6.2	5.6	7.1	6.3	4.0	3.3
New Zealand	7.8	10.3	8.2	6.1	7.4	6.8
Norway	5.3	6.0	5.5	4.9	3.3	3.3
Poland	..	..	14.4	12.3	10.6	..
Portugal	4.6	4.2	7.0	7.3	5.2	4.5
Spain	16.3	18.4	24.1	22.2	18.8	15.9
Sweden	1.7	5.6	9.4	9.6	8.3	7.2
Switzerland	..	3.1	3.8	3.9	3.5	..
United Kingdom	7.1	10.0	9.6	8.2	6.3	6.1
United States	5.6	7.5	6.1	5.4	4.5	4.2

a 1990, Western Germany, subsequently the whole of Germany
.. Not available
Adapted from: OECD (2000b)

As well as the variation between countries, unemployment rates vary considerably between different groups and different regions. For example, whilst the EU average unemployment rate in 1999 was 9.2 per cent, among 15–24 year olds the average rate was 17.2 per cent (OECD, 2000a: 218). Likewise, whilst the old Länder in Germany (the former West German regions) had an unemployment rate of 8.8 per cent in 1999, the rate in the new Länder (former East Germany) was 17.6 per cent; similarly in Italy, where unemployment in the South was 21.9 per cent in 1999, compared to 5.4 per cent in the North (OECD, *ibid*: 220).

Alongside this trend of gradually rising unemployment over the past four decades, the proportion of the total workforce which has experienced a period of unemployment in recent years is considerable. The prevailing level of unemployment at any particular time comprises the difference between those coming onto the unemployed register and those leaving it. Over a year, these unemployment 'flows' are far greater than changes in the unemployment rate might suggest. During 1994, for example, the overall level of unemployment in the UK fell by just under 400,000 (from 2.89 million to January 1994 to 2.50 million in January 1995). This figure, however, is the product of an inflow of new unemployment registrations of *ten times* that amount (just over 3.85 million) during the year and an outflow of 4.25 million (Department for Education and Employment, 1995b: 354). In a proportion of the cases, the same individuals become unemployed (and re-employed) more than once in any given year, thus figuring several times in the inflow and outflow statistics: studies have shown that between one-third and two-fifths of new registrations are likely to be persons who have previously been unemployed during the same year (DfEE, *ibid*: 355). What the magnitude of the flows also underlines, however, is the breadth of experience of unemployment within the workforce as a whole. It is also a reflection of a growing lack of employment security (see also, below).

The level of unemployment does not reflect the total picture of job shortage, however. In addition to those officially counted as unable to find work, there are millions more who have become prematurely (and involuntarily) retired or have otherwise dropped out of the labour market because of a perceived lack of prospects of finding work. Changes in the participation rates of men in the labour market indicate the scale of this discouragement effect. The proportions of males of working age who are active in the labour market (in work or registered unemployed) has fallen in several industrial countries over the past two decades, to a point where in the UK for example, more than one in four males of working age, and not in full-time education, are not active in the labour market – a degree of inactivity which Hutton (1995: 1) identifies as having 'incalculable consequences' for overall well-being and social cohesion in the country.

Two further points are worth making in regard to unemployment. First, the level of unemployment and the extent to which people have been made unemployed, impacts both materially and psychologically not only on those directly affected. In addition, the impact is extended by a general heightening of awareness of job insecurity and the perceived difficulties that can be experienced in gaining employment once unemployed – difficulties clearly expressed in the scale of long-term unemployment (at the end of 2000, for example, almost one-quarter of those unemployed in the UK had been out of work for at least a year (*Labour Market Trends*, January 2001)), together with the disproportionate presence of some groups (such as younger and older workers and ethnic minorities) among the long-term unemployed. The effects on people's attitudes to work and job insecurity of high levels of unemployment still prevailing in several countries, were vividly summed up in the UK in the 1980s by Ron Todd (then Chief Negotiator at the Ford Motor Company and later General Secretary of the Transport and General Workers' Union) who commented that 'we've got 3 million on the dole and another 23 million scared to death' (quoted by Bratton, 1992: 70). The second point is that the rate of flow of individuals onto unemployed registers has been affected by the amount and circumstances under which redundancies have been declared over the recent period. It is to a more detailed consideration of redundancies that we now turn.

Redundancies

Labour Force Surveys in the UK indicate that between 1990 and mid-2000, over seven million redundancies took place in Britain. Redundancies are nothing new, of course. What *is* new in the recent period, however, are the causes of redundancy. In the past, redundancies were a consequence of economic difficulty, as Cappelli (1995: 577) comments: 'Firms clearly laid off workers because of cyclical downturns or other situations where their business declined, but reductions in other situations were extremely uncommon.' However, increasingly common is the tendency for employers to announce redundancies as a cost-cutting measure even at times when the business and the economic outlook are buoyant. Quoting Cappelli (1995: 577) again, 'workforce reductions are increasingly "strategic or structural in nature" as opposed to a response to short-term economic conditions'. The experience in the UK in recent years bears this out: firms announce redundancies when they are doing badly *and* when they are doing well, with the constant shaving of workforce totals being used as a method of cost control. A key reason for this, Cappelli argues, is that outside the organisation – and particularly among shareholders and investment markets – cutting workforce levels has come to be taken as a sign of restructuring, efficiency-saving and likely improvement in profitability. The upshot is that redundancy announcements can improve share prices. Cappelli (1995: 571) quotes one US study, for example, (by Worrell *et al.*, 1991) which found that stock prices rose on average by about four per cent in the days following layoff announcements that were part of general restructurings (see also Excerpt 2.3).

EXCERPT 2.3

Redundancies at Corus

On Thursday 1 February 2001, the Anglo-Dutch steelmaker Corus announced 6050 redundancies in Britain – more than a fifth of the UK workforce. This followed 4500 job losses made the previous year by the company which was formed in 1999 following the merger of British Steel and the Dutch firm Hoogovens.

▶

> The job cuts announced in 2001 involved the ending of iron and steel-making at its large Llanwern plant in South Wales, the closing of two finishing plants also in South Wales, and reductions in workforce totals at several other plants elsewhere in Britain.
>
> On the day of the job cuts announcement, the company's share price, which had been falling in the previous period, immediately jumped by almost a tenth (9.7 per cent) in its value, rising from 74.75 pence on the close of business on 31 January to 82 pence at close on 1 February.

Temporary work

There are a number of categories of work that are temporary in nature, in that they are limited in duration. These range from jobs that are casual (the work available only on an ad hoc basis) or seasonal, to those which involve fixed-term contracts and temporary work acquired through temporary work agencies. This variety of forms that temporary work can take makes cross-national comparisons of trends in temporary work difficult. The general picture, however, appears to be a mixed one. While some countries (including Australia, France, the Netherlands and Spain) recorded increases in the relative size of their temporary workforces in the 1980s and 1990s, others (for example Belgium, Greece, Luxembourg and Portugal) recorded decreases, and still others (for example, Japan, Denmark and Italy) had levels of temporary work that stayed fairly constant (OECD, 1996).

In the UK, temporary workers represent just over seven per cent of the total employed population – a modest increase from the level prevailing in the early 1990s (Table 2.5).

Table 2.5 Temporary employment in the UK, 1992–2000

	1992	1994	1996	1998	2000
Temporary employees (thousands)	1304	1492	1671	1748	1733
Proportion of total employees (%)	5.9	6.8	7.4	7.4	7.1

Source: *Labour Market Trends*, December 2000

Of the temporary employees in the UK in 2000, slightly more than half were women. The temporary workforce is distributed across a range of industries, though amongst women, a significant proportion of temporary workers are located in teaching, childcare and related occupations, and sales (*Labour Market Trends*, January 2001: 10).

Job insecurity

Higher average levels of unemployment over the past two decades, the high level of redundancies and (in some countries at least) a higher level of temporary working, have made job insecurity a more prominent concern to workers in contemporary workplaces than it was to a majority of their counterparts a generation ago (Burchell, Day, Hudson, Lapido, Mankelow, Nolan, Reed, Wichert and Wilkinson, 1999). The level of insecurity has also been fuelled by a tendency for more jobs to be offered on the basis of fixed term contracts, rather than as indefinite employment contracts. As Allen and Henry (1996: 66) point out, the growth of subcontracting in the private sector and the move towards contracting out of public services has led to a growth in 'precarious employment', where jobs are secure only for the length of the contract. The effect is the creation of 'an atmosphere of pervasive insecurity' (Allen and Henry, 1996: 67; see also Heery and Salmon, 2000). Heightened levels of corporate merger and acquisition activity have also added to this feeling of job precariousness.

At the same time, it should be noted that many employees continue to spend a significant part of their career with a single employer. In 2000, for example, approaching half (46 per cent) of employees in the UK had at least five years' service with their employer, and over one in ten had worked for the same employer for 20 years or more – a figure slightly higher than the proportion (nine per cent) registering at least 20 years' service with their present employer in 1986 and 1991 (Office for National Statistics, 2001a: 88). Thus, a significant proportion of those in employment build up long service with a single employer. For others, however, work is a much more precarious affair with insecurity, redundancy, temporary contracts and unemployment contributing to an overall experience of a fragmented, rather than a unified working life: an experience which Sennett (1998) argues is highly damaging to personal integrity and individual financial solvency, as well as to the degree of societal polarisation between employment rich and employment poor households (see Excerpt 2.4).

EXCERPT 2.4

The end of career?

In the United States in 1999, the *California Management Review* (*CMR*) published a debate over the end of long term jobs. One of the leading proponents on 'the end of career' thesis, Peter Cappelli (1999) argues that factors such as competitive pressures, volatile markets, more demanding shareholders, the need for flexibility, weaker trade unions, changing skill requirements, technological advances, and the like, have combined to bring the 'jobs for life' era to an end. His thesis is that a prolonged period of widespread permanent, full-time employment with predictable advancement, is over and is being progressively replaced by shorter-term employment relationships. Richard Sennett (1998: 22) argues a similar point, commenting that the motto of contemporary capitalism is 'no long term'.

The alternative viewpoint in the *CMR* debate is put by Sanford Jacoby (1999) who argues that this portrayal of contemporary industrial society is not adequately supported by labour market evidence, and is thus an inaccurate one. Jacoby argues that

▶

▶ measures such as average job tenure, and more generally the continuing experience of work in many public and private sector industries, indicates that long-term employment relationships remain widespread, and the notion of long-term careers is far from over. This counter-argument agrees that there are changes occurring, both in the overall labour market and within individual organisations, but that currently these do not amount to support for an 'end of career' thesis.

EXERCISE 2.5

What do *you* think?

1 Which of the arguments described in Excerpt 2.4 do you find the more convincing? What are your reasons for this?

2 If we take Cappelli's argument to be at least partially correct – or if we assume it will become correct – what do you think are the main implications for employees and those managing them?

TO SUM UP

Developments in the structure of work and employment have significantly changed workforce composition in terms of the size and location of workforces and the distribution of employment between service and manufacturing sectors, the proportion of male and female workers, those working part and full-time, as employees or self-employed. Unemployment, redundancy and the growth of non-permanent contracts have created a heightened sense of insecurity for many employees.

Conclusion

This chapter has illustrated some of the ways in which broader influences and developments impact upon the everyday realities of work. Political policies, from local planning decisions to national strategies on deregulation to the harmonisation of employment conditions across countries, have significantly influenced the context within which work is performed. With the growing integration of many national economies into multi-nation associations such as the EU, it may be anticipated that the political influences on work will be increasingly evident at the transnational level in years to come – possibly at the expense of both national and local political mechanisms.

This increasing economic and political association between different blocs of countries has also been one of the influences on levels and patterns of competition within individual sectors and markets. The growth in competition in general may be seen to have affected the experience of work in various ways. In particular, this may have been experienced through a more intensive managerial search for both performance improvement and labour cost reduction – objectives which manifest themselves in a variety of managerial strategies concerning the workforce and which also reflect broader political conditions, such as the degree of statutory regulation of employment and the national provision of education and training. Competitive pressures from rising industrial nations have also been a major factor bringing about fundamental restructuring of most mature industrial societies, with the latter experiencing a decline of many of the sectors on which their industrialism was initially built (such as coal, steel, textiles, and shipbuilding) and the growth of other, primarily service sector, industries. This shift has been reflected not only in a decrease in manual and a rise in non-manual jobs, but also in major changes in workforce composition: the prominence of male production workers has given way to an increasingly feminised workforce, and one in which a significant proportion of employees work part-time.

In addition, an important change in the overall context of work over the past generation has been the degree to which work has, for many, become a more precarious activity. Indefinite employment and long service with a single employer has, for many, given way to a more fragmented job history. Much higher levels of unemployment, coupled with high redundancy rates and job insecurity, have resulted in a growing proportion of the workforce experiencing paid employment as an intermittent, rather than a regular, activity. One of the issues this raises is whether, as work becomes more fragmented and as the experience of non-work becomes more common, the values associated with work show signs of being in decline. It is to an examination of work values that we now turn.

3 The meaning of work

CHAPTER AIM

To assess why people work, with particular emphasis on the economic and moral dimensions of work.

LEARNING OUTCOMES

By reading and thinking about the material in this chapter, you will be able to:

1 evaluate the importance of the economic need to work;

2 assess the economic commitment to employment drawing on survey evidence;

3 explain the meaning of the work ethic;

4 analyse the four key themes of the work ethic:

  (a) work as an obligation

  (b) work as a central life activity

  (c) work as conscientious endeavour

  (d) work as disciplined compliance;

5 outline and evaluate theoretical perspectives that explain the changes in the work ethic;

6 explain how changes in the work ethic might be linked to changes in the psychological contract.

Introduction

Children are frequently asked the question, 'What do you want to be when you grow up?' And full of the idealism of youth, they eagerly reply that they are going be an astronaut, a fashion model, a footballer, or maybe a computer games designer. Years later, when they are adults, the question is rephrased to, 'What do you *do*?' They are more likely now to mutter that they are in insurance, on the check-out at the local supermarket, teach at the local college, or maybe work in a call centre.

These two common questions are significant because both underline the fact that paid employment is generally considered to be a central defining feature of ourselves as individuals. As children we are being judged in terms of our employment aspirations, and as adults we are being assessed in terms of our employment status. In short, paid work is one of the principal means by which we evaluate other people. In this chapter we explore the concept of work and assess why so much emphasis is placed upon what a person does for a living. Our main concern is to analyse the reasons behind why people work (see Excerpt 3.1).

It will be recalled from Chapter 1 that the focus of the book is how employees experience work, so Chapter 3 assesses the meaning of work in terms of two features: the economic necessity to work and the moral necessity to work. In terms of the economic necessity, we explore the material reasons for working and raise the question of whether people would carry on some form of work even if they had no financial need to do so. In terms of the moral necessity we introduce the concept of a 'work ethic' and assess its various elements that are supposedly encouraging people to work irrespective of any economic necessity. In the remaining sections of the chapter, we reflect on how contemporary changes might be affecting the work ethic, in particular the issues of the development of the post-industrial society, greater leisure and changes in the psychological contract.

EXCERPT 3.1

Why work?

A common sense view is that people work simply for money. However, research consistently reveals that the actual reasons why people work are far more complex. Certainly money is important, but employees tend also to give a range of other reasons for working. To illustrate this point, consider the comments below from workers at Swan Hunter Shipbuilders in the UK. The quotes are taken from Bradley, Erickson, Stephenson and Williams (2000: 180–1) and are all responses to the question: 'Why do you work?'

'I want to provide for my family, but I enjoy the trade union side of my work. I like going to meetings, negotiating and helping people.' (Design engineer)

'To keep my family. But I think it's important to do something you enjoy.' (Draughtsman)

▶

'The pay packet. But work is a necessary ethic when you work all your life – it governs your existence.' (Welder)

'For self-respect – I don't want to become a social parasite. And I don't want to be bored. It's good for meeting people and I get a lot of job satisfaction, and for the money too.' (Sheet-metal worker)

'Making a living and getting the self-respect of doing something productive. It gives me peace of mind.' (Driller)

'To exist. I like the job. I come to work to use my skill and to make enough money to have a decent way of life.' (Plater/foreman)

'It's all I know.' (Caulker/burner)

Learning outcome 1

Evaluate the importance of the economic need to work.

The economic necessity to work

Working to live

Intuitively, we know people work in order to earn money to live; it is through paid work that basic needs are satisfied because it provides money for subsistence (food, housing, clothes, and so on). However, there is a major problem with accepting this argument as it stands: can we really talk about the need to work for the purpose of subsistence when most developed societies provide a welfare system that (in theory at least) prevents people from falling below the basic level of subsistence? Social welfare provision in the form of unemployment benefit, housing allowances and free medical care were specifically designed to act as a safety net, preventing people from falling into destitution. It is the prime example of the State intervening to prevent its citizens from being left totally at the mercy of market forces. Both right-wing and left-wing politicians have argued that the benefit system can act as a *deterrent* to work because it provides a supposedly satisfactory standard of living. The issue arises because someone can undertake a week's work in a low paid job and receive the same or lower income than someone claiming welfare benefits. Moreover, when people take a low paid job after being on unemployment benefit, they often lose their entitlement to other allowances, such as housing benefit, and as a consequence find themselves financially worse off at the end of the week: this is the classic poverty trap. In other words, the benefit system can act as a financial disincentive to work, even though the person may be keen to be employed.

In the UK, governments have recognised this problem of financial disincentives, and have introduced a range of 'in work' benefits: means-tested allowances that can be claimed while in employment. Critics of this policy argue that it exacerbates the problem by effectively subsidising employers who pay low wages. Indeed, it actively discourages them from increasing wages as the employee would lose benefit, and the employer would have to take up the supplement currently funded by the taxpayer. There are two alternative policy solutions which both focus on increasing the differentials between paid work and benefit, although they differ dramatically in their approach:

1 *lower benefits*: this approach considers that benefits are the problem, suggesting the need to lower unemployment allowances and other welfare payments to increase the incentive to work for low wages, thus making unemployment seem 'less attractive';

2 *raise low wages*: this approach is aimed at increasing low wages, typically through setting a national minimum wage, which would similarly increase the differential between those who were in work and out of work, but which would be aimed at making low paid work 'more attractive'.

Working to consume

As this discussion suggests, in Western capitalist economies it is not simply the case that people need to work to subsist; rather, people work to earn money to acquire consumer power. Money is the means to the goal of consumption, whether that be commodity consumption (mobile phones, cars, designer clothes, houses, dishwashers, and so forth) or service consumption (for example, drinking, gambling, eating out, using the gym and holidaying). The central distinguishing feature between those people in work and those who are unemployed is that the former have much higher (although varied) levels of consumer power, and consequently more choice about their lifestyles. This rise of consumption was one of the fundamental developments of the twentieth century. Chapter 6 examines the importance of mass production in shaping people's working lives, but worth noting here is the sometimes overlooked fact that mass production developed alongside mass consumption – increasingly the people who produced the goods were those who consumed the goods. Some commentators suggest that the nature of consumption has changed in recent years, from mass to niche markets (Piore and Sabel, 1984), which has helped to sustain consumption as one of the defining features of our identity. Moreover it perpetuates and elevates the importance of getting money to engage in a shopping experience that is increasingly being seen as a leisure activity in its own right (Featherstone, 1990).

Given the importance of the link between work and spending power, it is hardly surprising that when asked, most people will say that earning money is the prime reason they go to work (or want to work in the case of the unemployed). This unremarkable observation was verified in the UK by researchers working on a major project entitled the Social Change and Economic Life Initiative (SCELI) – research to which we make reference on several occasions throughout the book. The researchers questioned people about their reasons for wanting a job, and from analysis of over 5000 responses they found that the majority (68 per cent) said they worked for the money, either to provide for basic essentials, or, in the case of 27 per cent, to buy extra things and enjoy some economic independence from the primary earner in the household. Perhaps the most surprising aspect of this finding is that the figure is not higher than 68 per cent. Indeed, to uphold the (intuitive) assumption that people work simply for extrinsic reward (money for shopping) we

Table 3.1 Summary of the SCELI findings on the reasons for working

	Full-time		Part-time		Self-employed		Unemployed		Housewife returners	Totals
	Men	Women	Men	Women	Men	Women	Men	Women		
Sample size	1786	1026	21	802	248	118	457	272	480	5210
Monetary reasons	75%	69%	70%	66%	69%	60%	69%	65%	65%	68%
Expressive reasons	26%	27%	28%	21%	29%	34%	25%	25%	21%	26%
Other reasons	1%	7%	3%	14%	2%	7%	4%	10%	14%	6%

Source: Adapted from Rose (1994: 294); percentages have been rounded.

might have predicted the figure to be 95 per cent or more. However, an astonishing 26 per cent said that they did not work for money reasons, but for 'expressive' reasons, in other words for the intrinsic rewards work can bring, such as enjoyment, satisfaction and a sense of achievement. Moreover the percentage of people indicating these expressive reasons remained very similar irrespective of the gender or employment status of the respondent. (See Table 3.1 for a summary, and Rose, 1994, for a comprehensive analysis of the SCELI data.)

Post-materialism

The fact that a significant minority of people say that they work for the intrinsic reward leads some commentators to argue that materialist values in advanced capitalist societies are waning. For example, Inglehart (1997) suggests that many people increasingly are opting for interesting and meaningful work, rather than high salaries. This reflects a 'post-materialist' orientation to work, emphasising quality of life. The term 'downshifting' is sometimes used to describe people who have given up high-flying careers and large salaries for a less work-focused, less materialist way of living. While this post-materialist lifestyle is undoubtedly adopted by some people, the key question is, how widespread has it become? Is it the start of a new trend, or merely the response of a small minority of people to the increasingly stressful nature of work?

An analysis of this hypothesised increase in post-materialism was undertaken by Russell (1998) using data from the International Social Survey Programme. Her analysis focused on a comparison between three European countries (Britain, West Germany and Italy) in two periods of time: 1989 and 1997. The survey measured a range of attitudes to work from which could be generated an overall score for extrinsic and intrinsic work attitudes for each country. The post-materialist thesis predicts that compared with 1989, the score in 1997 for the extrinsic value of work will have decreased while the score for the intrinsic value will have increased. The results (see Table 3.2) reveal a mixed picture that leads Russell to conclude that while there is some evidence of post-materialist values, the overall thesis is not borne out by the data. To explore how this conclusion might have been reached, attempt Exercise 3.1.

Table 3.2 Comparison of extrinsic and intrinsic work values

	Britain		Western Germany		Italy	
	1989	*1997*	*1989*	*1997*	*1989*	*1997*
Overall extrinsic value score	3.2	3.1	3.2	3.1	3.2	3.2
Overall intrinsic value score	3.3	3.2	3.4	3.4	3.3	3.2
Numbers	750	604	703	722	611	530

Notes: Respondents were asked 'How important do you personally think the following items are in a job?': high income; job security; good opportunities for advancement; an interesting job; a job that allows someone to work independently. Their responses were scored on a scale of 0 to 4 – the higher the score the higher adherence to the particular item being considered. An extrinsic value score for each respondent was calculated by averaging the first three items. An intrinsic value score was based on the last two items. The overall score for extrinsic and intrinsic values is the average across all respondents.
Source: Adapted from Russell (1998: 92)

EXERCISE 3.1

What do *you* think?

Examine the data on extrinsic and intrinsic work values shown in Table 3.2.

1 Describe the main similarities and differences between the countries.

2 Assess which of the countries most closely fits the post-materialism predictions. Explain your reasoning.

TO SUM UP

The analysis so far suggests that the majority of people say they work mainly for economic reasons and extrinsic values predominate. Logically it follows that if, by some stroke of luck, someone acquires a fortune, they would leave work to live a life of leisure. In other words, people are not committed to employment for anything other than the extrinsic financial reward it brings. But is such an apparent 'common sense' notion supported by the empirical evidence? We can address this question by first examining a recent study in Britain, and then assessing a larger international study.

The commitment to employment

British evidence

A survey of employment in Britain (Gallie and White, 1993) assessed the attitudes of 3855 people in 1992 regarding a wide range of issues concerned with work. One

Learning outcome 2

Assess the economic commitment to employment drawing on survey evidence.

of the questions was directly concerned with employment commitment and asked respondents:

> If you were to get enough money to live as comfortably as you would like for the rest of your life, would you continue to work (not necessarily in your present job) or would you stop working?

In response, 67 per cent of people indicated that they would continue to work, and there was very little difference in the replies of men and women (68 per cent compared with 67 per cent). Assuming this sample to be representative of the wider working population, it suggests that the majority of people derive more from work than their wage packet.

However, it might be argued that such intrinsic satisfaction from work depends on the nature of the job being done, and that professional workers might be more inclined to stay at work irrespective of financial security, than semi-skilled manual workers. Gallie and White (1993) took this into consideration in their analysis and found that the majority of people in *all* job categories would continue to work even if there was no financial need, although the proportions increased the higher the job level of the respondents. In addition, the survey revealed that employment commitment was highest among people in their early 20s and declined with age.

The general impression is that the majority of survey respondents were committed to the principle of being employed, but it is important to note several points:

- They were not necessarily committed to their particular jobs.
- They were not committed to working full-time, but rather stated a preference for a working week of between 16 and 30 hours.
- They did not necessarily want to maintain their existing conditions of employment, such as work environment and location.

A further point to think about is that the respondents may have been reflecting the socially desirable norm of being 'in work' rather than demonstrating an individual commitment to employment. This is an issue we return to later in the chapter when we consider the moral necessity to work, but, for now, let us assume that the respondents *are* committed to employment. This prompts an additional question: 'What is causing this individual commitment to work?'

From their analysis of further questions asked in the survey, Gallie and White (1993: 67–9) isolate seven influences on employment commitment. To summarise their argument, we can say that employment commitment will be stronger:

1 the more qualifications the person has;
2 the greater their feeling of having been successful in their career;
3 the higher they value 'hard work';
4 the more they feel they have personal control over their destiny;
5 the higher their preference for their current job;
6 the lower their preference for 'an easy life';
7 the higher their attachment to their current organisation.

Of course this does not mean that all these influences have to be present before a person feels committed to employment, but it indicates the possible range of influential factors. Overall, the survey suggests that people in Britain demonstrate a commitment to employment; so how does this compare with other countries?

International evidence

One of the most comprehensive international comparative studies is the 'Meaning of Working' survey (MOW, 1987) which analyses evidence from eight countries. Respondents from these countries were asked what they would do about work if they won a lottery or inherited a large sum of money and could live comfortably for the rest of their lives without working. This is known as the 'lottery question' and is frequently used by social researchers in order to get a general view about a person's commitment to employment. The responses to the lottery question are presented in Table 3.3, ranked according to country. It can be observed that although the majority of people in each country would continue to work, it is in Britain and Germany where the greatest proportion of people indicated that they would stop working – proportions noticeably higher than the next ranked country, Belgium (around 30 per cent for Britain and Germany, compared with 16 per cent for Belgium). When examining the proportions of people who would continue in the same job or who would want to work under different conditions, the ranking is virtually inverted, with respondents from Japan and Yugoslavia (and to a lesser degree, Israel) demonstrating the highest commitment to their existing employment. In contrast, respondents from Britain are the least inclined to want to remain in their existing job. Similarly, for the USA, Belgium, Germany and the

Table 3.3 Responses to the 'lottery question' from the Meaning of Working survey

Ranking	Percentage of respondents who, if they were financially secure, said they would....					
	stop working		continue working in the same job		continue working but under different conditions	
1	Britain	31	Japan	66	Britain	53
2	Germany	30	Yugoslavia	62	USA	49
3	Belgium	16	Israel	50	Belgium	47
4	Netherlands	14	Netherlands	42	Netherlands	44
5	USA	12	USA	39	Germany	39
6	Israel	12	Belgium	37	Israel	37
7	Japan	7	Germany	31	Yugoslavia	34
8	Yugoslavia	4	Britain	16	Japan	27

Source: Adapted from MOW International Research Team (1987)

Netherlands a greater proportion of people would want to continue to work under different conditions rather than remain in the same job, although the differences between the proportions are much smaller than those in Britain. Taken overall, the MOW data show that people generally have a commitment to employment (although not necessarily to their current job) and that this is affected by national setting as well as age, occupation, individual differences and life experiences.

TO SUM UP

The evidence therefore suggests that it is not enough simply to argue that people work for extrinsic rewards. Clearly, income beyond the subsistence level is an important reason for working, but surveys reveal that a large minority of people work for reasons other than money (the expressive needs, noted above) and that a majority of people say they would continue to work even if there was no financial need compelling them to do so. It seems that other factors influence attitudes to work; factors which, some have argued, constitute a moral necessity to work.

EXERCISE 3.2

What do *you* think?

This is an exercise you can undertake if you have a part-time job. Next time you are at work:

- ask your co-workers the 'lottery question';
- encourage them to explain their answers.

Write down a few notes to remind yourself of their opinions, then later on answer the following questions:

1 How similar or different are their responses from each other?

2 How might you explain any differences of response?

3 How do their responses compare with those from the research reported in this chapter?

Learning outcome 3

Explain the meaning of the work ethic.

The moral necessity to work

Implicit in much of the discussion in the previous section is the notion that work is 'good': a virtuous, dignified and worthy activity for people to engage in. In other words, there is a moral dimension to work, commonly accepted by society, which values endeavour and enterprise through employment, above leisure. Being 'in work' becomes morally desirable irrespective of any financial or social benefit that may accrue to the individual. This moral dimension to work is usually called 'the work ethic', and has traditionally been associated with characteristics such as diligence, punctuality, obedience, honesty and sobriety. So where does this moral dimension to work come from? And what relevance does it have for our understanding of contemporary orientations to employment?

One of the best accounts of the development of the work ethic in the UK is provided by Anthony (1977). Drawing on Weber (1930) he traces the work ethic from the roots of Protestantism in the seventeenth century, which defined work as a religious calling, either through the Lutheran belief that a state of grace could be achieved through endeavour, or the Calvinist doctrine of predestination whereby work became part of a lifestyle demonstrating one's salvation. The Protestant work ethic became the foundation upon which the ideology of work associated with industrialisation and capitalism was built. As Anthony (1977: 44) argues,

> Work had every advantage. It was good in itself. It satisfied the selfish economic interest of the growing number of small employers or self-employed. It was a social duty, it contributed to social order in society and to moral worth in the individual. It contributed to a good reputation among one's fellows and to an assured position in the eyes of God.

Similarly, in his consideration of the work ethic in the United States, Rodgers (1978: 14) argues,

> The central premise of the work ethic was that work was the core of moral life. Work made men useful in a world of economic scarcity. It staved off the doubts and temptations that preyed on idleness, it opened the way to deserved wealth and status, it allowed one to put the impress of mind and skill on the material world.

Other commentators have noted how the work ethic seems to be a feature of a wide range of societies, and have suggested that it seems to be a universal human value – see Excerpt 3.2.

EXCERPT 3.2

The work ethic: a universal concept

The work ethic is often referred to as the Protestant work ethic in the UK and Australia, and in the US as the Judeo-Christian ethic. These religious labels have sometimes been used to imply that there are distinct features to the work ethic that makes it prevalent only in Protestant-dominated countries. As we note in the main text, these usually emphasise the value and importance of duty, commitment, effort and obedience. However, commentators have suggested that these features of the work ethic can be found in many cultures and among many nationalities, so it is not uniquely Protestant. To illustrate this point, consider the following quotes.

▶

The Islamic Work Ethic

'The concept of the Islamic work ethic (IWE) has its origin in the Quran, the sayings and practice of Prophet Mohammed, who preached that hard work caused sins to be absolved and that "no one eats better food than that which he eats out of his work". For instance, the Quran often speaks about honesty and justice in trade, and it calls for an equitable and fair distribution of wealth in the society. The Quran encourages humans to acquire skills and technology, and highly praises those who strive in order to earn a living. The Quran is against laziness and waste of time by either remaining idle or engaging oneself in unproductive activity... The Islamic work ethic views dedication to work as a virtue. Sufficient effort should go into one's work, which is seen as obligatory for a capable individual.

... In addition, work is considered to be a source of independence and a means of fostering personal growth, self-respect, satisfaction and self-fulfilment. The IWE stresses creative work as a source of happiness and accomplishment.

... Hard work is seen as a virtue, and those who work hard are more likely to get ahead in life. Conversely, not working hard is seen to cause failure in life (Ali, 1988).

... In brief, the Islamic work ethic argues that life without work has no meaning and engagement in economic activities is an obligation.' (Yousef, 2001: 153.)

The Buddhist Work Ethic

'Reading from interpretations of Buddha's teaching on the ethics of material progress (Nanayakkara, 1992).... Buddha encouraged the proper utilization of human resources to develop the economy. Therefore he presented a very effective work ethic to motivate the workforce. But this work ethic encouraged teamwork and in its widest connotation meant an appropriate attitude toward work. Religion seems to play a major role in this and it is argued that contrary to popular belief that Buddhism is pessimistic in outlook, there is abundant textual evidence that Buddha formulated a work ethic that encouraged workers to put forth their best effort. Buddha singled out laziness as a cause of the downfall of men and nations and urged that everyone should put forth effort. He stressed that one should be one's own master. He encouraged qualities such as initiative, striving, persistence, etc.' (Niles, 1999: 858.)

The Catholic Work Ethic

'Roman Catholic bishops will instruct their flocks that manual work can be a remedy for self-indulgence, dishonesty and individualism. A new paper, 'The Spirituality of Work', by a committee set up by the bishops of England and Wales, states that going out to work does not guarantee salvation, but it helps. However, the paper also issues a warning of one danger of work: "It is a prime way of creating wealth, and so presents the risk of serving only to fill the human horizon with a lust for wealth and possessions." The committee of Catholic laity and workers sets out a list of

▶ prayers, hymns and meditation for use in the workplace. They should be used while giving "proper attention to safety at work", the paper advises. The concept of the "work ethic" as promoted by St Paul, traditionally thought of as a Protestant ideal, is embraced. "Mother Teresa of Calcutta understood that all people were called to holiness – even journalists" the paper states. The committee cites the suggestion in St Paul's letter to the Ephesians "that manual work, or labour, is a suitable remedy for individualist, self-indulgent and dishonest styles of life".' (*The Times*, 2001, January 16)

Although the notion of the work ethic is seductive, it presents us with an analytical problem: how do we disentangle the notion of a moral commitment to work from that of an economic need to work? Can we really argue that there was a general acceptance of a work ethic in industrialising nations prior to the advent of social welfare systems? And even after the emergence of decent wages, is the moral dimension to work any easier to pin down? To put it another way, 'Are workers on the assembly line related to their work by a "bond based on the need for cash from which all moral commitment is absent and which can be easily broken?"' (Anthony, 1977: 286, quoting Beynon, 1973).

To answer these questions, four key themes associated with the work ethic need to be examined:

1 work as an obligation (emphasising duty);
2 work as the central life activity (emphasising commitment);
3 work as conscientious endeavour (emphasising effort);
4 work as disciplined compliance (emphasising obedience).

Each of these will be considered in turn, although as the discussion reveals, in practice there is a considerable overlap and merging of the themes.

Work as an obligation

This theme reflects the importance of doing one's utmost to seek paid employment rather than remaining 'idle'. In the UK such an obligation to work is enshrined within the social welfare system because a person must prove they are 'actively seeking work' before they are entitled to any welfare benefits. But studies of the attitudes of the unemployed reveal that there is a widespread desire not to be perceived as 'lazy', even if remuneration levels from work are only marginally higher than unemployment benefit (see for example, Turner, Bostyn and Wight, 1985). To a large extent this may be the result of the desire to be a 'good provider' for one's family. A study of basic life values conducted in the mid-1960s (Yankelovich, 1973) for example, revealed that 80 per cent of American adults linked the importance of being the breadwinner to masculinity. So, being 'in work' not only conferred economic power on the individual, it helped to forge a masculine identity – a man who was unemployed, was not only unable to provide for his family, he was also less of a man. More recently, this has been illustrated in a study

Learning outcome 4a

Analyse the first key theme of the work ethic: work as an obligation.

of the gender-specific consequences of unemployment in a town in Britain (McKee and Bell, 1986: 141):

> The loss of the male economic provider struck deep chords among both wives and husbands and a passionate defence of men's right to provide was invariably raised . . . Fundamental emotions concerning self-esteem, self-image, pride, views of masculinity, respectability and authority resounded in the expressions of both men and women.

Alternatively, it might be argued that the perception of work as the means of becoming a self-reliant provider for one's family is being eroded in Western capitalist societies because of the growth of unemployment. It is a forceful argument, particularly when there has been an abandonment of the political commitment to achieving full employment, meaning that some of the blame can be displaced onto the Government for failing to provide enough jobs. In other words, as Offe (1985: 142–3) put it:

> [As] the experience (or the anticipation) of unemployment, or involuntary retirement from working life increases, the more the effect of moral stigmatization and self-stigmatization generated by unemployment probably wears off because, beyond a certain threshold (and especially if unemployment is concentrated in certain regions or in certain industries), it can no longer be accounted for plausibly in terms of individual failure or guilt.

Of course, the opposite view can also be argued: as work becomes more scarce the value placed on it (its scarcity value) rises. This can help to explain why most of the unemployed continue to search for work even when conditions offer little hope of secure, long term, full-time employment. In a further twist to the argument, it may be suggested that when a person is faced with unemployment, they are likely to cope much better (in terms of their mental health) if they do not see work as a duty (Warr, 1987). In other words, a strong work ethic might help motivate a person to hunt for work, but it might have a detrimental effect on their ability to cope if they are unable to find a suitable job. Conversely, a weak work ethic may help a person to accept being unemployed, but in so doing may inhibit their motivation to gain employment.

An attempt to assess the pervasiveness of 'work as a duty' was undertaken in the international survey on the Meaning of Working (MOW, 1987). The researchers examined two issues:

1 *obligation* to work: the view that everyone must work to the best of their ability and thereby contribute to society.

2 *entitlement* to work: the view that everyone should have the right to a meaningful and interesting job with proper training.

These are two separate dimensions, and so an individual's orientation to both can be measured. The MOW researchers were able to plot the responses from each

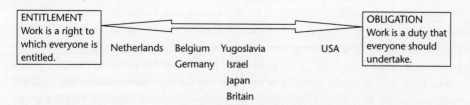

Source: Based on findings from MOW International Research Team (1987)

Figure 3.1 National comparisons in attitudes to work entitlement and obligation

country to demonstrate how the orientation to (1) obligation to work (duties) and (2) entitlement to work (rights) can vary in different national settings. The important aspect to consider from these findings is the overall balance exhibited by respondents from each country – these differences are illustrated in Figure 3.1.

Work as a central life activity

This theme stresses that paid work is the most important part of life, being superordinate to all non-work activities. Some of the most revealing empirical evidence can again be found in the Meaning of Working survey (MOW, 1987: 79–93). The researchers defined work centrality as 'the degree of general importance that working has in the life of an individual at any given point in time' (1987: 81). They developed a method of measuring work centrality that involved asking people to assess working against four other important aspects of their lives: family, community, religion and leisure. Overall, the analysis revealed that in terms of importance and significance, respondents judged work to be second only to family. In the combined national samples, 40 per cent placed family as most important while 27 per cent placed working as most important among the five key life roles (MOW, 1987: 252). Of additional interest are the effects of three variables: age, nationality and gender. The first two we shall deal with briefly, but the third warrants more detailed comment.

Effect of age

A person's work centrality tends to increase with age. The finding is perhaps not surprising given that people may be promoted or take on more responsibility within an organisation the older they get, coupled with the tendency for a person's social life to 'slow down' with age, although family is likely to take a more central role.

Effect of nationality

Work centrality varies according to national differences. The data revealed that respondents from Japan were considerably more work-centred than those from other countries, in particular Britain whose respondents displayed the lowest degree of work centrality.

Effect of gender

Men typically have higher work centrality than women. Caution should be exercised in interpreting this finding, however, because it does not necessarily mean that

Learning outcome 4b

Analyse the second key theme of the work ethic: work as a central life activity.

women are innately less interested in work; rather it might reflect the different roles widely expected of men and women. It is still the case that domestic obligations (particularly cleaning, cooking and childcare) are disproportionately undertaken by women (see Chapter 12) which not only requires them to be less work-centred (more time and thought must be devoted to the family), but can provide an alternative focus to their lives from which they might derive a sense of fulfilment. As Hakim (1991) points out, there has been a failure to recognise how the female labour force is composed of at least two distinct groups that differ dramatically in work orientations: those who choose full-time work, and those who choose the homemaker role. She states:

> [The first] group has work commitment similar to that of men, leading to long-term workplans and almost continuous full-time work, often in jobs with higher status and earnings than are typical for women. The second group has little or no commitment to paid work and a clear preference for the homemaker role; paid employment is a secondary activity, usually undertaken to earn a supplementary wage rather than as primary breadwinner, and is in low-skilled, low-paid, part-time, casual and temporary jobs more often than in skilled, permanent full-time jobs. (Hakim, 1991: 113)

Of course, it is debatable whether or not women are really as free to choose their roles as Hakim suggests; indeed, as we shall argue in other chapters, the research on the impact of patriarchy in constraining these 'choices' is convincing (for analysis of the key debates see Walby, 1986, 1990 and 1997). Nevertheless, for men, the choice of being homemaker is still not widely accepted by society so, in this sense, the moral obligation to be work-centred is imposed more upon men than women, and the general expectation by employers is that a man will want a full-time job, whereas a woman will settle for part-time work.

In addition to domestic obligations, there may be structural reasons for the lower work centrality reported by women. As we note throughout the book, women are disproportionately represented in jobs which tend to have lower pay and benefits, lower status, less autonomy, less responsibility and less job security. Moreover, these poor quality terms and conditions are frequently a feature of part-time jobs, the majority of which are undertaken by women (see Chapter 2). This is perpetuated because the widely-held assumption that women (in general) have low work centrality means a woman in a full-time job is frequently faced with male managers and coworkers who assume that she is less committed to a career in the organisation because she may leave to start a family (supposedly deferring to her family-centred values): an assumption largely reinforced through the biological fact that only women can have children.

> Managers' perceptions of job requirements and procedures for assessing merit have been shown to be saturated with gendered assumptions...Feminists can argue (as they have for years) that not all women get pregnant, but it seems

unlikely that this will stop managers thinking 'yes, but no men will'. (Liff and Wajcman, 1996: 89.)

Finally, it is worth noting how these possible reasons for lower work centrality can link together. The imbalance of domestic responsibilities means that many women find part-time work more convenient, and consequently find themselves in jobs which are both intrinsically and extrinsically poorly rewarded. In this instance, employment becomes de-centred, yet is endured to provide either an adequate income for the family, or an independent income for the women. So among women working part-time or women not in paid employment, it would not be surprising to find lower work centrality. The proper way to assess whether gender affects work orientation would be to compare like with like: men and women in full-time jobs with similar status and terms and conditions. In practice, of course, this is an extremely difficult comparison to make given the deeply gendered horizontal and vertical segregation of labour.

Irrespective of gender, Moorhouse (1984) challenges the view that, for the majority of people, work is a central life activity in any sense other than occupying the majority of their waking hours. He argues that there is a need to distinguish between what people find important (qualitatively central) from that which occupies large amounts of their waking time (quantitatively central). It is only the former, he argues, that offers any sociological insight into working lives. However, the MOW (1987) research revealed a high work centrality on *both* measures: people found work important and it occupied large amounts of their time. But, like all the surveys of this type, it still leaves us with the conundrum of whether people find work important *because* it occupies large amounts of their time – in other words, to use Moorhouse's terms, whether its quantitative centrality determines its qualitative centrality. In addition, such an approach fails to broach an arguably more interesting question: whether people think work *ought* to be so central (both qualitatively and quantitatively). In part we can address this issue by examining the third theme of the work ethic: conscientious endeavour.

Work as conscientious endeavour

Irrespective of the work being undertaken, this theme of the work ethic emphasises the importance of doing a job *diligently*. No matter how menial the task, the individual is encouraged to put effort and care into it in order to produce the best outcome. It is summed up in the maxim: 'If a job's worth doing, it's worth doing well'.

A contemporary expression of this can be seen in the management rhetoric of 'customer care'. Typically, these are initiatives requiring all employees not only to show great respect, but to make the customer feel as though they are being individually looked after. This increasingly requires the employee to manage their own emotions so as to elicit a good feeling in the minds of the customers. This 'emotion work' is being recognised as so important for the competitiveness of contemporary

Learning outcome 4c

Analyse the third key theme of the work ethic: work as conscientious endeavour.

organisations that even those people in low paid, low status, jobs such as shopwork are required to be increasingly diligent in this aspect of their work. It is an issue that is explored in detail in Chapter 7.

The theme of conscientious endeavour also implies *activity*, whether this is physical or mental. The extent of activity of course varies from job to job and task to task. People may place different value on different forms of activity – in particular the difference between manual and non-manual work. Those who value the former tend to invoke the idea of dignity in physical labour, and sometimes suggest that a person has not really done 'a fair day's work' unless they have 'got their hands dirty'. The stress on the virtue of practical rather than cerebral or emotion-based activity has been frequently used to differentiate work supposedly suited to men from that supposedly best undertaken by women. In effect this has perpetuated the gender division of labour by constructing an artificial gendered notion of what constitutes skilled work (see Chapter 5) and increasingly defining customer contact jobs as emotion based, and therefore more suited to women (see Chapter 7). The importance of the physicality of work for men is neatly summed up in the following quotes from male print workers in Cockburn's (1983) study of technological change in the printing industry:

> I like to do a man's job. And this means physical labour and getting dirty, you understand . . . working brings dignity to people I think, they are doing something useful, they are working with these [he demonstrated his hands] that have been provided for that. That's what it is all about. Craftsmanship. (Quoted in Cockburn, 1983: 52)

> People have to work and get their hands dirty, you get more satisfaction out of it than those people that sit there, you know, like a tailor's dummy at an office desk. (Quoted in Cockburn, 1983: 108)

The roots of this notion of work are deeply embedded, and are particularly evident in working class culture, especially among men (see for example, Collinson, 1992). This is vividly illustrated by Willis's (1977) classic study of a group of working class 'lads' which reveals how a counter-school culture constructs and reinforces the value of physical labour over mental work:

> Manual labour is outside the domain of school and carries with it . . . the aura of the real adult world. Mental work demands too much, and encroaches – just as the school does – too far upon those areas which are increasingly adopted as their own, as private and independent . . . Thus physical labouring comes to stand for and express, most importantly, a kind of masculinity and also an opposition to authority . . . It expresses aggressiveness; a degree of sharpness and wit; an irreverence that cannot be found in words; an obvious kind of solidarity. It provides the wherewithal for adult tastes, and demonstrates a potential mastery over, as well as an immediate attractiveness to women: a kind of machismo. (Willis, 1977: 103–4)

Coupled with the importance of *diligence* and *activity* is a further element of conscientious endeavour: the notion that work has some purpose; it constitutes an activity that is valued by others; it is *productive*. This is important because considerable effort may go into activities for which people do not get paid. Indeed, Moorhouse (1987) has argued that people are as productively active (if not more so) in their leisure pursuits as they are in their work. Witnessing the effort that goes into activities as varied as gardening, DIY, creating your own website, sport, embroidery and amateur dramatics confirms this point. Similarly, a huge proportion of highly productive activity is unpaid – notably domestic and voluntary work – while the informal, underground economy (from car boot sales to drug dealing) is a vibrant arena of productive (and paid) activity which is rarely acknowledged by wider society (discussed in Chapter 12).

However, while diligent productive activity is possible in a variety of spheres, it becomes entwined with work centrality – the previous theme of the work ethic – and as a consequence is identified with employment. As Jahoda (1979: 313) argues,

> Work roles are not the only roles which offer the individual the opportunity of being useful and contributing to the community but, without doubt, for the majority they are the most central roles and consequently people deprived of the opportunity to work often feel useless and report that they lack a sense of purpose.

The unemployed are therefore not only deprived of the economic rewards derived through work, they are also denied the moral approval of their conscientious endeavour if they use their initiative to find paid work unofficially (for example, cash-in-hand jobs) or fill their spare time with non-paid productive (and self-rewarding) activities like voluntary work, gardening, writing poetry and so on.

Work as disciplined compliance

This fourth theme of the work ethic is particularly important since it underscores two components essential to capitalist production: the acceptance of the management prerogative and obedience to time structures.

Learning outcome 4d

Analyse the fourth key theme of the work ethic: disciplined compliance.

The management prerogative

The 'management prerogative' refers to the right of managers to direct the workforce as they deem fit, based on their 'expertise'. It can be associated with a style of management that stresses the unitary nature of the employment relationship, that is, the absence of any major conflict of interest and the position of management as the sole legitimate authority. This concept of unitarism, originally defined by Fox (1966) received particular attention during the 1980s with the emergence of a new rhetoric of human resource management (HRM) which similarly emphasises the common goals of employees and managers in organisations. HRM ignores any plurality of interests and imbalance of power in organisations and invokes the idea of organisational commitment and co-operation to secure efficient and effective performance directed towards strategically-designed corporate goals, invariably embodied in a nebulous mission statement. The employees' disciplined compliance with the values and goals of the organisation is perpetuated by management through the development of employment policies and a corporate culture that stress individualism and either marginalise, or completely remove, any collective representation through trade unions (for a full discussion of the multi-faceted nature of HRM, see Legge, 1995).

Obedience to time structures

The second element is disciplined compliance with the time structures imposed by management. The working day provides a time structure which clearly differentiates periods of work and leisure. Traditionally, the Monday to Friday '9 to 5' pattern of working hours provided structure not only to the working day, but to the whole of working (and waking) lives. As discussed in Chapter 4, however, these time patterns are undergoing substantial change in contemporary society. Nevertheless, the majority of people still have a structure imposed by the time routines of their paid work. The importance of this structure is often not evident until people are faced with its removal, particularly through the loss of their jobs. One of the fore-most researchers on the effects of unemployment sums it up succinctly:

> Not only manual workers but everybody living in an industrialised society is used to firm time structures – and to complaining about them. But when this structure is removed, as it is in unemployment, its absence presents a major psy-chological burden. Days stretch long when there is nothing that has to be done; boredom and waste of time become the rule. (Jahoda, 1982: 22)

For people out of work, the problem becomes how to fill the unstructured days, and how to create new structures to take the place of the one they have lost. It is well illustrated by the following quotes from two different studies of unemployment – one in Scotland, the other in England. The first quote is by an unemployed woman in her mid-thirties, and the second by an unemployed male steelworker of the same age.

> I used to think it'd be great not to work . . . when I was working . . . I'd 'imagine having a day off' – it was a treat. Now, I've got every day, and every week, and every month . . . and maybe every year . . . to do *nothing*. There never used to be enough hours in the day for me when I was working . . . now, I know what an hour is . . . it just drags 'round. (Quoted in Turner, Bostyn and Wight, 1985: 485, emphasis in original)

> When you're employed you make use of all your time. You come home from work, have a quick bite to eat, a cup of tea, and get stuck into some job you've got to do. You know you've only got a set time. But when you're unemployed you've got all the time in the world and you think, ah, I won't do that today, I'll do that tomorrow. You take a slap-dash attitude, which is wrong. (Quoted in Wallace and Pahl, 1986: 121)

If all four themes are put together, the work ethic can described as the belief that it is the duty of everyone to treat productive work as their central life activity and to perform it with diligence and punctuality under the direction and control of managers. Rarely would such a complete submission to the work ethic be expressed by an individual, but elements of the four themes *are* reflected in attitudes to work, as has been illustrated by the research findings quoted above (attempt Exercise 3.3 to assess your own position). The general point emerging from the discussion so far is that work is seen by many people as a worthy activity in its own right, over and above the economic rewards it brings. This leads the analysis into the issue of whether the moral dimension to work is changing; more specifically, whether as a result of changes in the structure and nature of paid employment the work ethic is in terminal decline and is ceasing to have any contemporary relevance.

EXERCISE 3.3

What do *you* think?

1 Consider the following statements. For each, note down whether you agree or disagree with the sentiment being expressed, and explain your reasoning.

(a) It is the duty and responsibility of everyone to work.

(b) Work should be the most important part of your life.

(c) You should work hard and conscientiously, no matter what the task.

(d) You should respect the authority of others in the workplace and comply with the rules and regulations.

2 In your role as a student, would you describe yourself as having a strong or a weak work ethic? Justify your answer with examples of when you have exhibited behaviour that reflects a strong or weak work ethic.

The demise of the work ethic?

As already noted, recent survey evidence about why people work is inconclusive. It reveals that the majority of people on the one hand state that economic need urges them to work, yet on the other hand say they would continue to work even if there was no economic necessity for them to do so. Despite this ambiguous evidence, some politicians and academics argue that people are increasingly instrumental in their attitudes to work and suggest that there has been a steady deterioration in the work ethic. Within this perspective it is possible to identify two explanations that account for the demise of the work ethic. They each suggest

Learning outcome 5

Outline and evaluate theoretical perspectives that explain the change in the work ethic.

a fundamental shift has occurred in the economic context: (1) to a post-industrial society, or (2) to a leisure society.

A shift towards a post-industrial society?

This explanation stresses the impact of economic developments and argues that the work ethic is in decline due to structural changes in society which has meant that we have moved from an era of industrialisation to a 'post-industrial' age. The argument contends that while the work ethic was an appropriate basis upon which to build industry, it no longer has a relevance in a post-industrial society. This approach is most closely associated with Bell (1973 and 1976) who argues that advanced industrial economies are undergoing a shift to become post-industrial societies. This is occurring through changes in the social structure including a transformation in the economic base from manufacturing to services, which leads not only to increasing numbers of people being involved in the delivery of services but also increasing demand for, and consumption of services: from tourism to participative sports; from psychotherapy to massage parlours. Concomitant with this structural change is an increasing importance of information-handling activities which means more white-collar jobs requiring higher levels of education and training, and the emergence of professionals as the dominant group, deriving influence through specialist theoretical knowledge. We examine these ideas in more detail later in Chapters 6 and 8.

If we apply Bell's thesis, it challenges the notion of the work ethic in two principal ways:

- First, it means that a work ethic developed for an age of industrial production is no longer relevant for a structurally different society: one based on the increasing consumption of services.
- Second, it suggests that the work ethic will cease to have any moral influence. There will no longer be a moral necessity to work because the post-industrial society is shaped by technological advances, increased efficiency and greater theoretical knowledge, so the cultural realm will have diminishing influence compared with the economic realm.

Critics of Bell (for example, Webster, 1995: 30–51) would argue that his whole notion of a post-industrial society is misfounded because it creates a false dichotomy between manufacturing and services, when in practice the two are interdependent (Gershuny and Miles, 1983). The service sector is helping to sustain the manufacturing sector through 'producer services' (Browning and Singelmann, 1978) such as banking, insurance, marketing and distribution. What is more, there is an increasing expansion not only of service work, but also of service products, so the move may be towards a 'self-service' economy (Gershuny, 1978). For example, people drive cars rather than use public transport, and buy washing machines and vacuum cleaners rather than using laundry and cleaning services. This more complex picture of social and sectoral change suggests there is a continuity of economic development rather than a dramatic structural shift; so it follows that the work ethic might similarly adapt to reflect these changes in patterns of production and consumption. It also brings into question Bell's assumption that the social structure can be separated from the realm of culture – if there is no structural shift, then similarly there is a question mark over the supposed disjuncture with culture (even if one accepts such a separation as feasible in the first place).

A shift towards a leisure society?

Gorz (1982 and 1985) argues that the work ethic has ceased to have relevance because of the emergence of increased leisure time which is 'liberating' people from work. He argues that technological change has led to labour-saving work processes and the creation of a post-industrial age in which leisure and productive activity outside work are increasingly important. Work ceases to be central in people's lives in terms of hours spent working: Gorz (1985: 40–1) projects a future scenario where people will be engaged in work-sharing with the equivalent of no more than ten years of full-time work during their life. Similarly, it is envisaged that income would not be based on having a job or the amount of work performed; instead everyone would be guaranteed a minimum income in exchange for a right to work (and an obligation to perform socially necessary work). Demand for goods and services would be stimulated by the guaranteed minimum income for all, but consumption would only be one side of the equation because the liberating factor for Gorz is the contraction of economic and market activity and the 'expansion of activities performed for their own sake – for love, pleasure or satisfaction, following personal passions, preferences and vocations' (1985: 53). This 'autonomous activity' could take any form, providing it stemmed from individual choice, and so, for some, this *would* involve competitive, free enterprise for financial gain. In other words, the purpose of life is self-fulfilment which will differ from person to person, so with less work time and more free time people can be allowed to pursue fulfilment in whatever manner they choose.

To summarise two volumes of work into a single paragraph does Gorz an injustice, not least because his vision of the future is so counter-intuitive to the capitalist understanding of the exchange relations of the market and the social relations of work that it may seem a utopian mirage. Certainly there are many aspects of Gorz's thesis that can be criticised, but the discussion here will be confined to three main problems with the notion of leisure replacing work, and hence representing evidence of the demise of the work ethic.

■ First, there is the difficulty of what 'leisure' means. There is a range of activities, from housework to amateur dramatics, for which a person does not get paid yet which fills up their time, but it is questionable whether they all could be described as leisure, since most involve (unpaid) effort and many are obliga-tions (especially to the family) rather than free choice (see Chapter 12 for a full discussion). Indeed, perhaps these activities equally demonstrate a work ethic, since they display many of its alleged features. So, if a type of work ethic is evident in leisure activities, the move to a leisure society will not enervate the work ethic so much as refocus it.

■ Second, there is a problem with the location of the work ethic. Even if it is assumed that more leisure time *will* encourage the majority of people to relinquish any commitment to the moral necessity of work, this does not automatically lead to the demise of the work ethic. As Veal (1989) argues, and as expressed in the criticism of Bell's thesis, the work ethic is a cultural phenomenon and, as such, will not be dislocated easily. On the contrary, the resilience of the work ethic might inhibit the moral acceptability of the type of leisure society that Gorz envisages.

> The possibility remains . . . that the work ethic exists within the culture – not necessarily in the hearts and minds of the workers, but among the media, educationalists, the ruling classes, and so on. Thus it has an official existence, rather like an established religion, without being embraced by the population as a whole. In that case, it could be hindering progress towards a more 'leisured' society. (Veal, 1989: 268)

■ Third, theories of a leisure society simply fail to stand up to scrutiny. Many people in work are working longer and more intensely (as we explore in Chapters 2 and 4). This means it is false to suggest that the work ethic is under threat because of people having more leisure time and shifting the balance of their lives away from work towards leisure activities.

TO SUM UP

The conclusion to be drawn from Bell and Gorz is that the traditional work ethic must be abandoned because it is dysfunctional in contemporary society: it is not suited to the changing patterns of employment which emphasise the service sector and force a redefinition of the roles of work and leisure. However, while there is evidence to support each writer's analysis of the structural change (much of which was assessed in Chapter 2) it does not necessarily signal the demise of the work ethic. Instead, what may be occurring is a realignment of the components of the work ethic to match contemporary economic circumstances. Before reading the next section, read Excerpt 3.3 and then attempt Exercise 3.4.

EXCERPT 3.3

New work expectations

'Young people today are at the cutting edge of the revolution in our workplaces. They expect to change jobs and learn new skills repeatedly. Their approach to work is transactional. They trust less and rely on themselves more.

In place of old-style corporate loyalty, economic reality has taught them that they must keep their options open. Pension plans and steady career advancement have less

▶

▶attraction than what an employer can teach here and now. Fixed jobs have less appeal than project-based work which provides variety, builds expertise and increases marketable and transferable skills.

Young people have a different vision of how their security can be achieved. The key is employability, and security is increasingly seen to come from having the skills and confidence to move between jobs.

The Protestant work ethic, encouraging hard work, loyalty and commitment in return for economic security, is no longer in keeping with the spirit of the times. Balance is the buzzword.'

Source: Quote from *The Guardian*, 'Balancing work life and personal life: new workers', 6 January 1999

EXERCISE 3.4

What do *you* think?

Read Excerpt 3.3 and then answer the following questions:

1 Does this quote sum up your view of work? If not, which elements do you disagree with?

2 It is suggested that you will not be guaranteed economic security.

   (a) How do you feel about this?

   (b) What problems might this present in ensuring you get a satisfactory life-style?

3 The quote suggests these are the expectations of *all* young people. Which groups of young people are most and least likely to share these expectations?

The work ethic and the psychological contract

Learning outcome 6

Explain how changes in the work ethic might be linked to changes in the psychological contract.

It can be argued that the work ethic is being challenged because of changes in workplace employment practices that put different demands and obligations on employees – changes that have occurred because of greater intensity and dynamism of the competitive environment. Much of this change has been described in Chapter 2, where in particular we noted the impact of globalisation. One of the concepts used by some commentators to assess the impact of these broad structural and economic changes is the 'psychological contract' between employees and employers (for example, Grant, 1999; Herriot, Manning and Kidd, 1997; Rousseau, 1995; and Sparrow, 1996). It is necessary to define this concept before looking at how it is supposedly changing workplace values and thereby affecting the work ethic.

There are various definitions of the psychological contract from different authors, but it can be described as:

> The beliefs of each of the parties involved in the employment relationship about what the individual offers and what the organization offers. For example, an individual employee might be willing to offer loyalty to the organization and in return expects to get security of employment. Unlike the employment contract, the psychological contract is not written down and changes over time as new expectations emerge about what the employee should offer and what they can expect to get back in return. (Heery and Noon, 2001: 288)

In reviewing the research that has been undertaken into changes in the psychological contract, Martin, Staines and Pate (1998) suggest that two contrasting views exist about the effect on employees: the pessimistic view and the optimistic view:

1 The pessimist view concludes that competitive market pressures have led to changes in the structure and processes of organisations (such as delayering, JIT production, flexibility and teamworking) and an obsessive focus on the customer. This results in:

   ■ work intensification;
   ■ reduced job security;
   ■ neglect of employee welfare and satisfaction;
   ■ fewer career opportunities;
   ■ less training and development.

   The consequence is that employees feel let down by employers as their expectations of 'the deal on offer' are no longer being met. The psychological contract has been broken.

2 The optimistic view concludes that despite these competitive pressures, 'the traditional psychological contract built around job security and a career is still alive and surprisingly well' (Guest, Conway, Briner and Dickman, 1996: 1). There is:

   ■ greater employability;
   ■ more demand by employees for training and development;
   ■ greater functional flexibility among employees;
   ■ more mobility between organisations.

   Consequently the psychological contract is intact in some organisations and being 'redrafted' in others to accommodate the new competitive conditions.

Excerpt 3.4 is an imagined dialogue between a pessimist and an optimist. They bring forward different arguments to represent their views. You will see the tendency is for the pessimist to believe that the work ethic has disappeared, while the optimist is suggesting it persists, although in a modified form. Read the Excerpt and then attempt Exercise 3.5.

Dialogue between a pessimist and an optimist

We noted in the discussion that there are two contrasting viewpoints about the way the psychological contract is changing, and it is clear that they lead to different conclusions about the effect on the traditional work ethic. To explore how the arguments might differ, let us imagine a dialogue about the main components of the work ethic (commitment, obedience, effort and duty) between a pessimist and an optimist. Their discussion might go along these lines.

Regarding commitment

Pessimist: Commitment is undermined by job insecurity. Increasingly, employees are expected to be committed to the organisation, but fixed term or temporary contracts undermine this. Can such employees really be committed if the organisation shows no commitment back to them by refusing to provide a permanent contract? The same is true for employees working part-time but who would prefer to work full-time – why should they be committed to the organisation? They are more likely to search for a full-time job in another organisation.

Optimist: Employees are more likely to get their fixed-term and temporary contracts renewed if they show commitment to the organisation. In this sense job insecurity might encourage commitment.

Pessimist: But is this really commitment? Can commitment really be created through an environment of fear of job loss? Surely commitment is also about loyalty – and that works two ways: the employee demonstrates loyalty to the organisation and in return expects loyalty back. The organisation's need for a numerically flexible workforce undermines its goal of a committed workforce.

Regarding obedience

Optimist: Increasingly, employees are expected to demonstrate their loyalty to the organisation through sharing the beliefs and values of the organisation – the organisation's culture.

Pessimist: But this is often simply compliance. An employee knows what is expected of them and simply complies with management rules. There is no real need to believe in the organisational culture – rather it is sufficient to work as if you believe it.

Optimist: Some employees will believe in and live the values – they share the culture and this is the ideal situation both for them and the organisation. Others will pretend to share the values, but maybe this is sufficient. After all, as long as they behave as though they believe in the culture, what's the problem?

▶

Pessimist: The problem is that managers have constantly to monitor employees to ensure they are complying. It produces an environment of low trust.

Regarding effort

Pessimist: Effort is no longer enough. Increasingly employees are judged according to their output through performance management systems, rather than their input.

Optimist: Employees have always been judged according to output. Most employees will accept this as fair providing they are told in advance the criteria on which they are being judged. Besides, it is increasingly important for employees to demonstrate the correct behaviour at work, such as caring for the customer, so any good performance management system should take these aspects into account.

Pessimist: But work is also becoming intensified. Employees are expected to put in more effort at work. People are required to work harder than ever.

Optimist: People are working smarter. The slack and the waste are being removed from work processes and employees are concentrating more on those aspects that add value. It is not necessarily requiring more effort, but rather a refocusing of effort.

Regarding duty

Pessimist: People are learning to accept that unemployment is normal. The flexibility that organisations require means that everyone will experience periods of being unemployed. They may not like it, but they have no choice. As a result, unemployment is less likely to be seen as a stigma, and work is less likely to be considered a duty – it is simply an economic necessity.

Optimist: The idea of work being a duty has long since disappeared. The practical reality is that people work to consume, and the more and more goods and services on offer, the greater the consumption. Not only does this encourage people to seek work, it also encourages them to seek to develop new skills so that they will always be employed. It is the notion of 'employability' which replaces the old-fashioned idea of a job-for-life in the same type of work. This also puts pressure on employers to provide training opportunities.

Pessimist: But this means that the employee will not be encouraged to be loyal to the organisation.

Optimist: Loyalty is important but it can be over-rated. Organisations in rapidly-changing environments need flexible employees, so labour turnover can be healthy.

Pessimist: So why should an employer offer training if he or she knows the employee will leave to go to another organisation?

▶
Optimist: That's the trade-off. The price of flexibility for the employer is investment in training and skills development.

What do *you* think?

Read the dialogue between the pessimist and the optimist in Excerpt 3.4.

1 Analyse the arguments of the pessimist and the optimist. Which parts do you find most and least convincing?

2 For the sections on (a) obedience and (b) effort, imagine how the argument might continue. Think of a suitable reply and counter-reply from the two protagonists. *Alternatively*, you could role play this with another student: one of you can take the role of the pessimist and the other the role of the optimist, and then try to continue the dialogue from one of the sections. See how far you can get using logical arguments to make your points.

Of course, the views of both the pessimist and the optimist might be valid. For some employees the psychological contract has been breached and they resent this, while for others a change in the psychological contract might be welcomed. Indeed, Herriot (1998: 107) questions the notion of *the* psychological contract and argues that 'different individuals will have different perceptions of their psychological contract; there will be no universal notion of what "the deal" is in any one organisation.' This is an important point for two reasons. First, it reminds us there is diversity among any workforce regarding their values and orientations to work (thereby emphasising the importance of a pluralist perspective). Second, it alerts us to the possibility that 'the psychological contract' is a misconception – so, perhaps the same can be said about 'the work ethic'.

The misconception of the work ethic?

It is possible to argue that a supposed 'demise the work ethic' is without foundation because it is based on the false assumption that a work ethic was generally held by people in the first place. There can be no overall demise, if there was never any *general* acceptance of a work ethic. As Rose (1985: 16) states, 'A possibility is that some sections of the working population did in the past hold work values approximating to a work ethic...while many others were affected in lesser degree by public doctrines about work deriving from it'. Essentially this is an argument for diversity; it suggests that there are, and always have been, numerous orientations to work and that the notion of a monolithic work ethic misrepresents this diversity.

This does not preclude the possibility of changes in work values, but it rejects the view that a general shift has occurred. This emphasis on diversity is argued by Moorhouse (1987) who stresses the importance of gender, class and ethnicity upon work values:

> The meanings of work are not likely to be neat and simple, or form some uncomplicated 'ethic', but are rather likely to be jumbled and variegated, so that any individual has a whole range of types and levels of meanings on which to draw, and with which to understand or appreciate the labour they are doing at any particular moment. (Moorhouse, 1987: 241)

We have considerable sympathy with this view, especially since one of our starting points (as outlined in Chapter 1) is to demonstrate the plurality and subjectivity of work experiences. Often, people invoke the work ethic as simply a synonym for a positive attitude to work, even though, as has been shown in the foregoing discussion, it reflects a selection of values, not all of which will be adhered to by those claiming to have a strong work ethic. Our analysis suggests it is probably a gross oversimplification to write and talk about a single work ethic because the term has a variety of meanings which can easily lead to confusion or ambiguity in interpretation – a type of problem we will also encounter in dealing with other concepts in the study of work, the best example being skill (Chapter 5). However, when any of the themes associated with the 'traditional work ethic' are in evidence in contemporary society, we may justifiably use the plural term *work ethics* to signify the persistence of a moral dimension to employment beyond the economic need.

Conclusion

Throughout, this chapter has been addressing a fundamental question: why work? The evidence indicates that economic need remains an important feature of work, but this does not explain the entire picture. The majority of people say that they would continue to work even if there was no economic compulsion to do so, which suggests that work may also be fulfilling other needs. Aside from earning money (extrinsic need) people are likely to cite a variety of intrinsic needs that work helps to satisfy, many of which reflect the moral dimension to work, for example, the search for achievement, creativity and fulfilment, or a sense of worth, purpose or duty. In other words, work is perceived as the right sort of activity to be engaged in; a message that is powerfully reinforced through a shared culture in capitalist societies, and most typically expressed as a work ethic. As has been noted, the work ethic concept has a variety of meanings, but in so far as it charac- terises a moral dimension to work, it remains an important feature of work orien- tations, and talk of its demise is premature.

Clearly, work provides an opportunity to socialise with people outside of the family and virtually all work involves interaction with other people – co-workers, managers, subordinates, customers, clients, and/or the public. We can speculate, therefore that work fulfils an important social need in people. As Jahoda (1982: 24) argues:

> Outside the nuclear family it is employment that provides for most people this social context and demonstrates in daily experience that 'no man is an island, entire of itself', that the purposes of a collectivity transcend the purposes of an individual. Deprived of this daily demonstration, the unemployed suffer from lack of purpose, exclusion from the larger society and relative isolation.

The research evidence reveals that rarely do people express social factors as a reason for working, yet throughout the subsequent chapters numerous examples are evident of the importance of the social dimension of work:

- how time (Chapter 4) and skills (Chapter 5) can be socially constructed;
- how social interaction helps people to get through the working day (Chapter 9);
- the social phenomenon of discrimination (Chapter 10);
- the social dependency that drives some employees to seek collective representation (Chapter 11);
- the social isolation which characterises some aspects of hidden work (Chapter 12).

For most people work is a place to socialise, and complex social systems develop within the workplace which often spill over into leisure time. Moreover, whole communities may be socially linked through the workplace where there is a single major employer within a locality – for example, a car plant, a hospital, a large retail store or a call centre. Similarly, organisations are often seeking to establish and reinforce their own corporate culture which encourages identity with the organisation through social interaction. In short, work is an important source of social interaction, but for the majority of people the meaning of work lies more in its economic and moral contribution to the human condition.

4 Time and work

- Time and capitalist development
- Time consciousness
- Time discipline
- Controlling working time
- Work absence

- Duration of working time
- Part-time work
- Presenteeism
- Overtime
- Arrangement of working time

- Shiftworking
- Annual hours
- Zero hours
- Flexitime
- Utilisation of working time
- Intensity of work

CHAPTER AIM

To identify the importance of time in the overall experience of work and assess the approaches of management and workforce to working time issues.

LEARNING OUTCOMES

After reading and thinking about this chapter, you will be able to:

1 understand the importance of time consciousness in the development of industrial capitalism;

2 recognise how attendance and absence behaviour illuminates the degree of employees' time consciousness;

3 distinguish different employee coping strategies towards aspects of working time;

4 assess current issues in the duration of working time, including the practice of long hours working or 'presenteeism';

5 identify patterns of change in the arrangement of working time;

6 assess developments in the utilisation of working time and the debate over work intensity.

Introduction

Time is a key component in work as it is in all aspects of human activity. The way time is experienced is fundamental to an individual's overall experience of work. Having too much time to complete a task can slip easily into feelings of boredom. The sense of having too little time can be a major contributor to work-related stress. Even where tasks can be finished comfortably within a given time, dissatisfaction can still arise if the tempo of work remains unchanging. Indeed, introducing variety into the pace of work is an important means of reducing the monotony inherent in many jobs. Where such variation in the tempo of work does not occur naturally, many employees will seek to create it, at times by speeding up their work pace and at other times by working more slowly. This breaking up of the working period into distinctive segments, each with their own temporal characteristics, is one strategy that many work people employ to 'get through' a monotonous working day (see Chapter 8).

All workplaces function on the basis of an array of overlapping time schedules. These vary enormously, ranging from a few seconds for specific and repetitive tasks (such as on many assembly lines or in making up orders in a fast food outlet; see Chapter 6) to many years for the planning, construction and commissioning of major plant, such as a new steel works, or the siting of a new office headquarters. The clock is critical in every contemporary work organisation, allowing the coordination of multiple, simultaneous, and complex activities in ways which could not be achieved without the close synchronisation made possible by accurate time measurement. This ability to synchronise individual activities within an over-all production process has been a key feature of industrial development. The ability to measure time in finely divided units has allowed greatly improved levels of coordination, and thereby a growth in the scale and complexity of operations. This has brought with it an unleashing of productive capacity through a much increased division of labour. Indeed, for writers such as Mumford (1934: 14), 'the clock, not the steam engine [was] the key machine of the industrial age', the critical innovation which set the industrial revolution firmly in motion. So too for Hassard, who comments that,

> As the machine became the focal point of work, so time schedules became the central feature of planning. During industrialism the clock was *the* instrument of co-ordination and control. The time period replaced the task as the focal unit of production. (1989: 18, emphasis in original)

Just as organisations as a whole function by utilising many different time-scales, individual workers operate on the basis of a diverse set of time schedules. These may range from the short cycle times of a machine-paced task, to the length of their working day, working week, working year, and ultimately working life. Further, working time is experienced in both an objective and a subjective way. For example, for many workers, particularly those working in factories, the working day is punctuated by bells or buzzers, objectively signalling the start and finish of defined working periods, meal times and rest breaks. In addition, however, the clock subjectively dominates many workers' thoughts about work; its hands or digits often advancing all too slowly for those locked in laborious tasks and wishing to be elsewhere.

As we discuss later in the chapter, three aspects of working time impact particularly upon the overall experience of work:

1 *the duration of the working period*: how long people work importantly shapes their overall experience of time at work. Since the early nineteenth century, the issue of the length of the working period has been a major focus for employment relations, with campaigns by workers and social reform groups to reduce working time regularly confronting employers opposed to any reduction in the length of productive activity.

2 *the arrangement of working time*: to many workers, equally important to the amount of time they spend at work is *when* those hours are worked – that is, how the agreed working time is scheduled or arranged across the 24 hours of the day and the seven days of the week. Longer opening times and economic pressures to operate plant and equipment more intensively are two of the factors acting to increase employers' demands for extending the working period.

3 *the utilisation of working time*: besides questions of duration and arrangement, the relationship between work time and overall work experience is influenced by the extent to which working time is actually spent in productive activity – that is, the degree to which working time is utilised. The utilisation of working time may be changed either by altering the pace of work or by changes in the length and frequency of non-productive periods. Integral to this issue of work time utilisation is the question of whether or not work is becoming a more intensified activity over time. Evidence on this is reviewed later in the chapter.

These three interrelated elements – the duration, arrangement and utilisation of working time, or what Adam (1990) calls the *time, timing and tempo* of work – combine to shape workers' overall experience of their working time. In turn, these temporal aspects form a key element in the broader experience of work. Yet, issues of time have in fact been the focus of comparatively little research enquiry. The ubiquitous nature of time in human existence has probably acted against it being addressed directly as a research topic. The subjective nature of working time has been particularly under-recognised, with too common a tendency to view work time in terms of 'clock time' – regular, unerring and one-dimensional – rather than an aspect of social existence which is experienced in a variety of ways.

Further, despite the overall character of working time being the outcome of the interplay of elements of duration, arrangement and utilisation, there has been a tendency for those campaigning for change to address themselves to only one of these aspects, such as the length of the working day, the hazards of night work, or the need in certain activities for greater rest periods. At times, the result of this over-focused attention has been that changes introduced to one aspect of working time have been accompanied by unforeseen (and from the worker's point of view, potentially disadvantageous) changes in another: for example, reductions in the working period being secured only by conceding an increased tempo of work, or a greater spread of working time across the week.

While the complexity of working time has generally suffered from insufficient attention, leading writers on the world of work such as Karl Marx and F. W. Taylor did recognise the centrality of work time to capitalism and to efficient work organisation. While Marx (1976) analysed the particular relationship between the working period and the creation of surplus value, Taylor (1911) was concerned with the most efficient ways in which an individual's work time could be utilised: a concern which subsequently gave rise to generations of 'time and motion' study.

The remaining sections of this chapter are concerned with the two views of time in the workplace:

- the main developments in (and the implications of) management's approach to working time;
- the ways in which workers subjectively experience working time and attempt to alleviate perceived negative aspects of managerially-defined time patterns, through the development of alternative time-reckoning systems.

The chapter begins, however, with a discussion of workers' internalised attitudes towards working time. It can be argued that, if the development of more closely controlled and coordinated time schedules marks out capitalist industrial organisation from its predecessors, then employer efforts to assert control over workers' time have been much assisted by employees bringing to their job:

- a growing sense of *time consciousness* – that is, an increased awareness of time;
- a sense of *time discipline* – a growing self-control over the organisation of one's time

It is argued that the upshot has been a developing sense among the labour force of the importance of punctuality, regularity and what constitutes a 'fair day's work'.

TO SUM UP

Time is a critical component of work and organisation; employees' experience of work is heavily influenced by their experience of working time. The arrangement and utilisation of time, as well as its overall duration, combine to shape employee experiences of time at work.

The (partial) growth of time discipline

The making of a capitalist time consciousness

It has been persuasively argued, particularly by E. P. Thompson (1967), that the creation of a greater time consciousness and time discipline among the workforce

Learning outcome 1

Understand the importance of time consciousness in the development of industrial capitalism.

represented a key feature in the development of an urbanised, industrialised economy. For Thompson, developments such as the spread of the school system, with its emphasis on punctuality and its daily diet of bells and whistles, helped to embed a stronger time consciousness and time discipline into the labouring classes (see also Lazonick, 1978). The importance of time-keeping taught in schools was reinforced by the moral edicts emanating from church and chapel about the degradation associated with idleness, the duty to view time as a scarce resource, and the importance of exercising time thrift by employing all time, including working time, to its greatest effect (see also discussion of the work ethic in Chapter 3).

Other significant factors for Thompson include the spread of clocks and other time-pieces which heightened general awareness of the time, and probably more importantly, the emergence of an acquisitiveness among the labouring classes. This last factor reflects the argument that, prior to the development of capitalism, the lack of available goods for purchase and the general absence of opportunities for workers to progress beyond their existing material position, resulted in most people holding a view of work as something necessary for subsistence, but that once a subsistence level had been reached, any desire to continue working, rather than spend time in other activities, diminished. Hence weavers, for example, might 'play frequently all day on Monday, and the greater part of Tuesday, and work very late on Thursday night and frequently all night on Friday' in order to make a sufficient wage (quoted in Pollard, 1965: 214). In this way, while the weavers could not avoid the necessity of earning an income, they retained a measure of control over the timing of their work.

An aspect of this control over working time which extended beyond the textile districts was the honouring of 'Saint' Monday: while Sunday was the rest day from work each week, large numbers of workers also habitually took many Mondays as unofficial holidays (or 'holy-day' – hence 'Saint' Monday) to extend their weekend (Reid, 1976). With the growth of capitalism and larger scale production, however, Thompson (1967) argues that there was more for workers to spend their wages on. As a result, bourgeois values relating to ambition, hard work and thrift became increasingly reflected among a working class desirous of improving their lot. Aspirations towards greater material comfort no longer remained the preserve of the middle and landed classes, but also (and in however small a way) the ambition of much poorer workers. According to Thompson, the overall effect of these various influences was to create a different attitude among workers towards time, leisure and income, increasing their propensity for regular time-keeping, in order to maximise their wages and thus their purchasing power.

Pollard (1963 and 1965) similarly emphasises the importance of time discipline and regular attendance for the development of the nineteenth century factory system. However, unlike Thompson, who focuses particularly on the development of an internalised self-discipline towards time-keeping, Pollard places greater emphasis on the role of external factors, particularly the actions taken by employers to impose greater time discipline. For Pollard (1965: 213) the developing factory system required 'regularity and steady intensity in place of irregular spurts of work'. This did not come easily to the new factory operatives and had to be reinforced by systems of rules, backed by punishments. For example, many nine-teenth century employers sought to control lateness by imposing fines or by locking the factory gates after the start of the work period, thereby forcing anyone arriving late to lose a whole day's pay (Pollard, 1965: 215).

These attempts to establish regular attendance and punctuality were part of a broader employer effort to enforce a strict factory discipline towards work habits, standards of cleanliness and drinking. Enforcement took the forms of elaborate rules, close supervision, fines, corporal punishment and summary dismissals for even minor transgressions. Despite their distinct emphases on internal and external influences on the development of time discipline, however, Thompson and Pollard reach the same conclusion that gradually the industrial workforce came to exhibit a greater time discipline.

Yet, while a reading of Thompson and Pollard might suggest that the question of workers' time discipline was settled during the nineteenth century, with workers abandoning their previous lackadaisical approach to time-keeping in the face of overwhelming opposition from school, church, and employer, on closer inspection it is clear that the employers' victory was never complete, and that in several important respects workers' time discipline has remained partial and problematic (Whipp, 1987).

TO SUM UP

Industrialisation has been accompanied by important developments in time con-sciousness and time discipline. Nevertheless, working time remains a contested 'frontier of control' between management and labour, with each seeking ways to exert greater influence over different aspects of the working period.

Insights into workers' attitudes towards time discipline can be gained through examining issues relating to the extent to which people turn up for work (their attendance and absence patterns) and what time-related practices they engage in while at work. It is to these that we now turn.

EXERCISE 4.1

What do *you* think?

Thompson (1967) identifies time discipline as critical to the development of industrial capitalism.

1 Do you think it is correct to give time discipline such an important place in the development of industrial capitalism? What reasons do you have for saying this?

2 Think about your own sense of time discipline. Would you say that you have a strong or a weak time discipline? What aspects of your behaviour best reveal your level of internalised time discipline?

▶

3 What have been the most important influences on the development of your time discipline – your family; school; peer group; or other influences? Rank the influences in order of importance.

Learning outcome 2

Recognise how attendance and absence behaviour illuminates the degree of employees' time consciousness.

Attendance at work

'Most workers', as Edwards and Scullion (1982: 107) point out, 'attend work for most of the time'. Nicholson (1977: 242) has made a similar point: 'Most people, most of the time, are on 'automatic pilot' to attend [work] regularly.' Whether the driving force is internalised values, habit, economic necessity or fear of employer sanctions, employees' attendance at work is characterised far more by regularity than by absence. Yet, while workers' time discipline towards attendance is high, it is rarely complete: many workers occasionally absent themselves even when they are able to go to work. In a study of attendance and absence in Britain, for example, Edwards and Whitston (1993) found that, on average, workers had been absent from work on over 16 days during the previous year. Studies undertaken in parts of Western Europe indicate that countries such as Germany and the Netherlands may have absence levels up to twice this rate (Prins and de Graaf, 1986, cited in Edwards and Whitston, 1993: 220).

Voluntary absence

Of course, absence from work (and its related time-keeping aspects of lateness and leaving work early) may be due to illness and thus be involuntary and unavoidable. However, it is also clear that a proportion of total absence is voluntary and avoidable. Voluntary absence goes by different names at different times and in different regions – 'skiving', 'having one off', 'taking a sicky', 'swinging the lead', 'on the hop', and 'wagging' are a few such expressions. For obvious reasons, precise data on voluntary absence are difficult to obtain (admitting to being voluntarily absent could cost workers their jobs). However, evidence from different periods indicates a persistent tendency for some workers to 'skive off' from work occasionally. McClelland (1987) for example, identifies the continued practice of Saint Monday throughout the latter half of the nineteenth century in the North East of England engineering industry, even though it was under attack from employers. A graphic description also exists of the tendency for boilermakers before the First World War to extend their holidays. As Pollitt (1940: 59) recounts,

It was at Tinker's boiler-shop in Hyde that I first learnt the custom of the brick in the air. The first day after a holiday we would all ... make a ring in the yard, and the oldest boilermaker ... would pick up a brick, advance to the centre of the ring, and announce 'Now lads. If t' brick stops i' th' air, we start; if t' brick cooms down, we go whoam'. I do not remember any occasion on which we did not 'go whoam'.

Likewise, in the 1920s, an estimate for the dock-working industry indicates that on average over nine million man hours a year were lost through bad time-keeping (Wilson, 1972: 77). Some industries, such as coal-mining, have long been characterised by comparatively high levels of absence, with unauthorised absence frequently higher before or after annual or statutory holidays, particularly among younger age work groups (McCormick, 1979: 146–7). More generally, absence levels in different industries and organisations have shown a considerable resistance to decline (indeed many have risen) despite increased managerial attention. There is no indication either that attendance patterns of white-collar workers are any less subject to the taking of voluntary absence than the manual worker examples cited above.

Many organisations seek to control lateness and absenteeism by different means of time-recording and by a variety of punishments and incentives, including disciplinary action (ultimately ending in dismissal) for those persistently absent and, less frequently, bonuses for those attending punctually every day in a given period. Nevertheless, for some employees, going absent from work clearly represents a way of fulfilling family or other responsibilities, or gaining a respite from excessive work pressures. For others, taking occasional days off acts as a way of coping with 'the routine frustrations of going to work' (Edwards and Scullion, 1982: 110), an escape from the continuous daily repetition of work, eat, and sleep. As one woman in Edwards and Scullion's study put it, 'It's not really boredom with the job. It's just that things get too much for you and you need a rest; you feel generally fed up' (*ibid*: 110).

In this way, workers occasionally relax the moral pressure of time discipline. Of course, temporary absence will rarely resolve the source of work pressure for individuals but it might help cope better with those pressures. In their study of nurses in two North American hospitals, for example, Hacket and Bycio (1996) found that occasionally going absent did not generally mean that things got better for employees, such as in relation to their stress levels or their physical health. Nevertheless, these authors suggest that the occasional absences taken by the nurses may have acted to keep these work pressures at manageable levels, and prevent the stress levels and other effects from getting any worse.

The gap between a 'complete' and the 'actual' time discipline of workers is also reflected in attitudes toward the legitimacy of voluntary absence. In their study of attendance in four organisations, Edwards and Whitston (1993) sought opinions on three hypothetical situations: a worker taking an extra day off having recovered from an illness; a working parent taking time off to look after a child who is ill; and a worker staying at home to get away from work pressures. Over four-fifths (84 per cent) of the male and female workers interviewed accepted the legitimacy of going absent in at least one of these hypothetical cases – a pattern of response which the authors concluded reflected 'a widespread acceptance of the need for workers to go absent in situations which management might see as voluntary or illegitimate absence' (*ibid*: 45; see also Exercise 4.2).

What do *you* think?

You work in an organisation where some employees are regularly absent and their behaviour seems to receive little attention from management. The absences make the jobs harder of those attending work because of the extra work that needs to be covered. The resulting extra fatigue, and the annoyance at those regularly absenting themselves builds up and you begin to take occasional days off yourself, but far fewer than some of your colleagues.

1　Do you think that your behaviour is justified? Why or why not?

2　What does your behaviour signal with regard to your time discipline?

3　If you were a manager in the organisation, what steps would you take to manage the absence problem differently?

4　What do you think would be the different consequences of your way of managing absence?

Organised absence

While much voluntary absence is unorganised, in the sense that it is an action taken by an individual without the involvement of others in a work group, by no means all absence is unorganised. Heyes (1997: 70) for example, describes the organisation of 'knocking' in a chemicals plant, whereby pairs of employees collaborated such that the voluntary absence of one of the pair would result in overtime working by the other (paid at a premium rate), these roles being reversed at a later date in order to share the financial gains from the joint 'knocking' activity.

In other situations, work groups have been able to arrange their work in such a way as to enable individuals to take turns in having some time off. Historically, in the dock-working industry, for example, dockers employed a system known as 'welting' (also known in some areas as 'spelling') whereby half a gang absented itself from work for an hour or more, with the other half of the gang leaving off the work when the first half returned. The development of this informal arrangement appears to have been widespread; Wilson (1972: 215), for example, identifies a similar arrangement operating in dock work in many different parts of the world. Such a practice not only provides an easier work regime for those involved, but may also extend jobs over a longer period of time and could even result in increased earnings if, as a result of the 'welt', work was carried over into (premium-paid) overtime.

Just as dockers engaged in welting would be highly unlikely to be recorded by management as absent, Edwards and Scullion (1982: 102) identified a similar pattern operating in a metals factory, where workers with a relatively high degree of control over their work organisation had developed a working pattern which enabled individuals to take it in turns to leave the factory for up to half a day, without being recorded as absent. It is important to note that such time-keeping arrangements stem not only from the way that workers have organised their work, but also from managerial tolerance of the behaviour – or to put it differently, management's unwillingness (or inability) to enforce their control over the work organisation to ensure that all the workforce are engaged in productive activity for the whole of the work period. As discussed later, this issue of work time utilisation is one which, in recent years, has been subject to increased managerial scrutiny.

It is also important to note that, just as work group norms may encourage absence as an informal element in the effort-reward bargain, work group norms and peer pressure can also act in the opposite direction. For example, where there exist high work loads and tight staffing levels, voluntary absence may be viewed very negatively by the group, since one person's absence is likely to put significantly greater pressure on those attending (Nicholson and Johns, 1985). Similarly, in some work settings, there is a norm of very high levels of attendance, possibly reflecting a high degree of job commitment among the group (Savery, Travaglione and Firns, 1998). Someone taking more absence than the rest of the group in such a setting may incur peer pressure to conform with the group attendance norm.

As well as acting to encourage or suppress voluntary absence, attitudes held by the work group may also influence perceptions of what constitute 'legitimate' reasons for voluntary absence. For instance, a work group of female employees may acknowledge the 'legitimacy' of voluntary absence to care for a sick child, irrespective of the work pressure implications for the remainder of the group attending work.

Controlling absence

Accounts of work organisation in general, and studies of absence behaviour in particular, suggest that there exists a widespread tendency for managers to tolerate a degree of voluntary absence without making concerted efforts to suppress it. In part, this probably reflects the difficulties management typically face in trying to establish whether individual, short-term absences are voluntary or involuntary. Absences are likely to attract greater management attention, however, where they exceed a level judged to be 'acceptable', or where production systems are so highly interdependent and/or where staffing levels have been created which contain so little spare capacity, that ensuring cover for absent individuals is far more difficult. As noted earlier, managerial efforts to control absence can range from giving bonus payments for unblemished attendance records to holding interviews with those whose absence or lateness exceeds a certain level, and ultimately invoking disciplinary procedures ending in dismissal for those persistently absent or late. Clearly, the existence of such sanctions and the ultimate threat of dismissal will affect many people's decisions over whether or not to go absent voluntarily, and how frequently. Besides this threat of sanctions, an additional discouragement to frequent absence for many (particularly those engaged in manual work) is that being absent from work can incur a significant loss of income where sick pay benefits are lower than earning levels.

These instrumental reasons (fear of job loss and desire to maintain income) are important factors in controlling levels of voluntary absence. Yet, at the same time, the persistence of voluntary absence underlines the fact that employers have so far failed in their endeavour to instil into their work force a complete time discipline, with many workers continuing to exhibit some measure of discretion over their level of attendance. In other words, management's continued need to monitor attendance, and their lack of success in totally suppressing voluntary absence, indicates a continuing tension between two temporal rationalities:

- on the one hand, a managerial rationality based on the twin notions of the definition of the working period and the requirement for workers to utilise the whole of that period in productive activity;
- on the other hand, an employees' counter-rationality which emphasises such needs as breaking up the monotony of work or reducing work pressures by occasional absence or lateness.

TO SUM UP

The tension between these two working time rationalities represents a continuing source of conflict and accommodation in the overall employment relationship. While management seek to maximise utilisation of the working period, employees seek to mitigate the physical and/or psychological effects of a demanding or unchanging work period. The resulting tension is, as we shall see, one that is relevant not only for assessing recent efforts by management to impose greater control over employees' opportunities for operating alternative time schedules, but also for considering in what ways (and how effectively) workers are able to resist these efforts and maintain a counter-rationality in relation to their working time.

Learning outcome 3

Distinguish different employee coping strategies towards aspects of working time.

Employees' temporal coping strategies

Exercising control over working time

One of the ways that employees can mitigate the effects of the temporal routine of their work is by being able to modify that routine, at least to some degree. The ability of employees to control their time has been found to have a considerable impact on their overall experience of work. Macan (1994) in a study of US public sector employees, for example, found that those employees who perceived themselves to have control over their work time were significantly more satisfied, and reported themselves as having lower work stress levels, than their counterparts who did not perceive themselves as having much control over their work time.

Modifying work time routines can occur by various means. One of these is where flexible working hours, or 'flexitime' arrangements exist. With flexitime, employees are able to vary their start and finish times, provided that they are present during a core period (for example, between 10am and 3.30pm) and provided that the contractual hours total is worked over an agreed period. As well as formally organised flexitime systems, less formal arrangements are also fairly widespread. Studies of flexitime show that they are generally very positively regarded by employees, and can also yield various benefits for the employing organisation. Indeed, a meta-analysis of twenty-seven studies of flexitime concluded that 'flexible work schedules favourably influenced productivity, job satisfaction, absenteeism and satisfaction with work schedule' (Baltes, Briggs, Huff, Wright and Neuman, 1999: 505; see also further discussion of flexible working hours below).

This importance of being able to exercise a degree of control over working time is also well illustrated in a study conducted by Berg (1999) involving steel workers in thirteen steel plants in the United States. Berg found a significant positive relationship between the extent to which a company was perceived as helping its workers balance work and family responsibilities and workers' overall job satisfaction. This balance was achieved by informal procedures such as supervisors allowing workers to come in late or leave early to take care of family responsibilities, or more formal procedures involving time away from work to deal with family issues (Berg, 1999: 130).

Excerpt 4.1 can usefully be compared to Berg's findings, as it also involves a study of steel workers (in this case, in the UK). The case highlights the effects of removing employee discretion over working time, and the effects this had on employee attitudes.

EXCERPT 4.1

Employee response to work time restrictions

As part of a study of employee attitudes to the introduction of teamworking, employees from two steel finishing plants were surveyed, with responses from over 800 workers. In these plants the introduction of teamworking had been accompanied by two other changes in working time. These entailed, first, the introduction of a new shift system which fixed the rotas for both rest days and holidays for individual employees for the following five years. Second, management at the plants had introduced a much tighter control over the previous practice of employees informally changing shifts with co-workers to accommodate non-work activities (such as sporting events and children's activities). Management's espoused aim in banning these informal swap arrangements was to build up team coherence by keeping the teams working together more closely than had been the case with previous work crews.

However, the restrictions imposed both on the timing of holidays and the informal shift swaps were poorly received by many employees, not only because of the way they constrained employees' flexibility over working time, but also because these constraints were seen to be unfairly distributed, with only those on shifts being subject to the restrictions, whilst those working only the day shift – including the majority

▶

▶ of managers – retained the freedom to take holidays when they wished. The following comments are typical of many:

The most contentious issue with teamworking is the five shift working rotas which no shift worker in the works wanted. It is a totally inflexible system with no provision for social events, family needs or sickness. It is the most demoralising aspect of the new regime e.g. it will now be three years until I can take my child on holiday during the school's summer break.

Whoever thought of the five shift system obviously did not have any family to think of.

Holidays: we are told when to take them. This is very annoying when it appears that management can take a day off when it suits them.

I find it impossible to book any time off for a social event or family occasions as all holidays and rest days are pre-arranged for us by management.

The main reason for the apathy and rock bottom morale among shift workers in my plant is the new work rota . . . whereby [the company] tells us when to have all our holidays as well as our normal days off. There is no flexibility. We feel we are automatons owned by [the company]. All the hardship is put on shift workers . . . while day workers and managers are unaffected and probably don't know the resentment that we shift workers feel . . . We don't like having our leisure time dictated to us.

These negatively perceived working time changes contributed to a lowering of morale at the plants. Overall, over four in five (83 per cent at one plant and 84 per cent at the other) thought that morale had declined since the introduction of team-working, despite perceived positive effects of teamworking such as greater job variety, more opportunities to use their abilities and greater freedom to choose their method of working.

Such was the negative reaction to the working time changes that when the researchers returned to the plants one and a half years later, they found that whilst the new working time rota remained in operation, the ban on informal shift changes had been relaxed as a result of the employee reaction.

Source: Bacon and Blyton (2001)

'Making' time and 'fiddling' time

If one frontier of control over working time is whether or not workers attend work, rather than voluntarily absenting themselves, another involves control over the working period itself: the extent to which the work period, as defined by management, is actually spent working. Production problems, such as shortage of materials and production bottlenecks, are among several possible causes of non-productive periods (White, 1987). In addition, however, non-productive time can be fashioned by workers themselves to achieve an easier work regime (and as a result, a more favourable effort-reward bargain). As Ditton (1979) and others have pointed out, workers can achieve such time manipulation in a number of ways.

Two of those ways, however, are particularly worthy of comment – what Ditton calls 'making' time and 'fiddling' time.

Making time

Making time involves arranging work in such a way as to produce breaks which would not occur otherwise. Traditionally, a common means of achieving this is by what Blauner (1964: 100) terms 'working up the line' – a pattern of accelerated working which results in workers building up a 'bank' or 'kitty' of finished output, which can then be drawn upon to create a break or an easier work period (see also Burawoy, 1979; and Ditton, 1979 on this practice). As Blauner's reference to a 'line' suggests, this practice has been particularly associated with assembly-line operations, but in many other situations too, in both manual and non-manual settings, scope has existed for workers to alter their tempo of work by building up banks of finished output in this way. In Edwards and Whitston's (1993: 301) study, this practice was known in one plant as 'using the back of the book', referring to workers completing tasks, but not immediately recording them (see also Webb and Palmer, 1998).

Fiddling time

In addition to making time, managerially-defined work time structures can also be 'fiddled' in various ways. At their simplest, such fiddles can take the form of employees delaying the start of work, covertly extending the length of meal breaks or leaving off work before the official end of the working period. In situations where work time is recorded by clocking equipment, time fiddles may also involve manipulating the clocking procedures, such that time officially recorded as having been spent working is greater than the time actually spent at work (a fiddle which may involve, for example, workers being clocked-out by others, the former having already left; see Ditton, 1979; also Scott, 1994). In addition, other ways that time might be fiddled include sabotaging equipment or otherwise causing a machine breakdown, resulting in a pause in work while repairs are carried out (see also the discussion of sabotage in Chapter 8).

Mars (1982) argues that in jobs which are dominated by repetitive, *short-cycle* activities, workers' ability to control time is likely to be exercised particularly through their ability to slow a job down. An example of how this can be effected is by employees seeking to manipulate the way that jobs are timed by work study engineers. If employees can convince those timing the jobs that they actually take longer to perform than is really the case, then any resulting 'standard' times established will allow employees to complete the required work with a reduced tempo of work, than would have been the case if the tasks had been allotted a shorter standard time.

Where jobs have more of a *linear* than a short-cycle character, however, such as the tasks of refuse collecting or bus driving, which involve travelling along a route, Mars (1982) argues that the source of workers' time control is more likely to lie in speeding up the work process. By so doing, this will potentially create unofficial free time mid-way or at the end of the task. As an example of this working time strategy, Mars quotes Blackpool tram crews who, if they succeeded in making the journey along the designated route in a faster time than was timetabled, secured an additional unofficial break period.

> The main aim of being a tram conductor is to control the job and to stop it controlling you. This is why tram crews will go to all sorts of extremes to get a tram from A to B ten minutes earlier than it should get there so that they can get a ten-minute break the other end. The times are so worked out that if you follow the route properly you'll never get any tea-break at all and you'll be working your guts out for the whole shift. So the main aim of the job as I see it is to fiddle time. (Blackpool tram conductor quoted by Mars, 1982: 82.)

Notable in this conductor's comment is the importance given to wresting some control of time away from the managerially-defined timetable, without which the latter's time-reckoning system would be overly burdensome. We return to this issue again later.

EXCERPT 4.2

Fiddling time on the factory floor

The following are extracts from an account of participant observation within a British-based subsidiary of a Japanese manufacturing company, given the pseudonym of Telco. The company is a supplier of products to motor vehicle manufacturers, with a workforce of 400. The authors identify various ways that employees made some additional time for themselves during the working day.

'Making time represented action to gain pockets of space away from the drudgery and physical demands that were a consequence of the routine, continuous and fast-paced nature of work at Telco.'

'[One] task was to perform a series of checks on the finished units as they came to the end of the line. First, they would be put on a machine for a specified time which simulated hot conditions, to ensure that they responded appropriately. Then they went to the 'lumo' (illumination) booth, where a complete electronic functional test was performed. Finally, they went to inspection and packing. The women had worked together on this section for several years, and familiarity with the operations also meant that they had found a number of shortcuts which they exploited. For example, with the heating process, rather than leave the units on the machines for the specified length of time demanded by the work standard, when the unit had indicated that it responded appropriately to the temperature, it was removed and replaced with another, irrespective of whether the full time cycle had been completed'.

'The ability of this work-group to manipulate standard operating procedures allowed them to collude to gain some control over the pace of work. The use of the

▶

▶ 'lumo' booth provides an example of this collusion. The 'lumo' booth is completely enclosed with a full-length black curtain, thus preventing anyone from seeing in. Only one operator was supposed to work in the 'lumo' booth, but it provided an ideal meeting place for the workers in this group to chat, knowing that even if the work became backed up they could clear the backlog quickly by shortcutting official operating procedures.'

Source: Webb and Palmer (1998)

EXERCISE 4.3

What do *you* think?

Think about a job you have worked at in the past.

1 What ways of gaining some time for yourself can you recall? If there were several, rank them in order of importance.

2 (a) Using Mars' distinction, did your job involve mainly short-cycle or linear activity?

(b) To what extent were the ways that you adopted to gain some control over time consistent with Mars' argument about the different opportunities that jobs provide for controlling time?

3 If there were few or no ways for you to gain any control over your work time, why was this? If there were several reasons, what were the most important?

Coping with monotony

In accounts of workers seeking to manipulate working time, a commonly referred to objective is to counter the effects of monotony and boredom. Altering the otherwise unceasing tempo of repetitive tasks represents an attempt to introduce greater variety and thereby assist workers to 'get through' their working day (see Chapter 8). One means of achieving this is by breaking up the day into different temporal segments. A particularly vivid account of workers breaking up a monotonous working day by punctuating it with differently characterised time periods, remains that by Roy (1960) and his description of 'banana time'. While observing a work group in a US garment factory engaged in the repetition of very simple operations over a long (12 hour) work day, Roy was particularly interested in how workers dealt with the 'beast of monotony' without 'going nuts' (1960: 156).

Central to the workers' coping strategies was the division of the day into different elements (over and above the formally recognised meal times and coffee breaks). These additional interruptions occurred almost hourly and were very short in duration. The breaks were designated as different 'times' and normally featured not only the consumption of some food or drink, but importantly were also a focus for a period of interactive banter between the members of the work group. 'Peach time', for example, occurred when one member of the work group produced some peaches to share, invariably accompanied by verbal banter from the others about the (poor) quality of the fruit. An hour later came 'banana time', which routinely involved one member of the group stealing (and eating) a banana from another's lunch box, again to the accompaniment of much verbal banter. 'Window time' came next, followed by 'pick up time' and later 'fish time' and 'Coke time'. These different times punctuated the day, acting as a focus of jokes and other social inter-action, and capturing the attention of members of the group, giving them some-thing to think about as they resumed work. The combined effect was to make an otherwise monotonous work day pass more easily.

> The major significance of the interactional interruptions lay in . . . a carryover of interest. The physical interplay which momentarily halted work activity would initiate verbal exchanges and thought processes to occupy group members until the next interruption. The group interactions thus not only marked off the time; they gave it content and hurried it along. (Roy, 1960: 161)

TO SUM UP

Just as some workers may seek to modify an unchanging work period by temporarily absenting themselves, modifying their work time pattern and by fiddling or making time, so too Roy's portrayal of the 'banana time' group highlights another means by which a work group has introduced greater temporal variation into an otherwise uniform work period. In all cases the effect has been to introduce not only temporal variety, but also a degree of counter-rationality into the formal (managerially-defined) working time rationality.

This interplay of managers' and workers' rationalities over working time is far from static. Indeed, significant developments in the arrangement and utilisation of working time have been evident in recent years, many of which have important implications for workers' overall experience of working time, and the extent to which they are able to influence and modify management's formal work time ration-ality. As the next section examines, changes (and notable areas where there has been an absence of change) are also evident in relation to the duration of work time.

Recent developments in the duration of working time

The total time people spend at work is determined by many variables including:

- their age of entry into, and exit from the labour market;
- whether work is full or part-time;

- whether work involves overtime and/or short-time working;
- the amount of absence from work;
- length of paid holidays;
- experience of unemployment;
- the extent to which maternity, paternity or unpaid leave is taken;
- whether individuals are involved in single, dual or multiple job-holding.

Learning outcome 4

Assess current issues in the duration of working time, including the practice of long hours working or 'presenteeism'.

While the factors influencing overall work time are thus many and diverse, historically two aspects of working time duration – the length of the working day and working week – have periodically acted as a prime focus of contest and dispute between employers and employees. Just as workers have sought improvements in remuneration for their work, so too they have also periodically campaigned for reductions in working hours. These calls for shorter hours have often met with opposition from employers, who have claimed that cuts in working time would damage their competitiveness. Yet, as a result of several factors – not least, continued increases in labour productivity and employers' periodic preference for reductions in hours rather than conceding higher wage settlements – the length of the basic working week in Britain has fallen considerably over the past century and a half, typically from over 60 hours to less than 40 hours per week (Blyton, 1985 and 1994).

Yet, despite this reduction in basic weekly hours, many workers in practice continue to work far longer than this as a result of high levels of overtime working (and in some cases, multiple job-holding). A recent estimate for the UK, for example, indicates that over one-third (36.4 per cent) of men and almost one-tenth (9.9 per cent) of women in employment usually work more than 45 hours per week (Labour Force Survey, May 2000). Indeed, so significant is the amount of hours worked in excess of basic hours that the average working time of many full-time employees has actually increased over the past two decades. As well as the UK, this has also been the subject of much discussion in the United States, notably Schor's (1991) account of 'the overworked American' and more recently Jacobs and Gerson (2001) who identify that the increase in work time is particularly evident if family rather than individual work patterns are considered.

The long hours worked among some groups and in some organisations have given rise to a debate over 'presenteeism'; we consider this below, before examining paid overtime working in more detail.

EXCERPT 4.3

Rewarding overtime

A complete picture of overtime working has been difficult to establish as most available data have generally related only to paid overtime, whereas in reality a substantial amount of overtime worked (and disproportionately that undertaken by higher levels of non-manual employees) is not paid for specifically.

▶

▶ Questions in the 1998 Workplace Employee Relations Survey (WERS), however, shed additional light on this aspect of working time. The WERS results are presented in the chart below and indicate that among those working overtime, almost four out of five normally received payment or time off for overtime worked, whilst over a fifth were not normally paid or received time off for overtime (Cully, Woodland, O'Reilly and Dix, 1999: 157–8). Whilst the vast majority of operative, assembly and craft workers were paid for their overtime working, around two-thirds of managers and professionals did not receive payment or time off for their overtime hours.

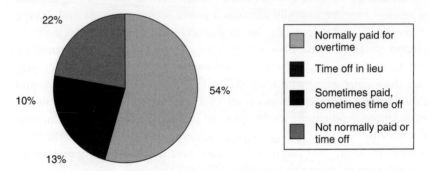

It is evident from other WERS responses that reasons given for working unpaid and paid overtime are distinct. Among those who received payment, the financial incentive was the main reason for working overtime, whilst among those not getting paid, job commitment was a more important factor.

Presenteeism

The Workplace Employee Relations Survey (WERS) 1998 findings show that almost a third (32 per cent) of managers and a fifth (21 per cent) of professional workers in Britain reported usually working over 48 hours per week, most of it without additional payment (Cully, Woodland, O'Reilly and Dix, 1999: 155). The tendency for many managerial and professional groups to work long hours of unpaid overtime is now attracting greater research interest. Some of this is focused on the pressures that employees feel under to demonstrate their commitment to the job by being at their desk for long hours each day. The term that has been coined for this is 'presenteeism' (the opposite to 'absenteeism' or absence from work) (Cooper, 1996; Simpson, 2000). There are many reasons why presenteeism may exist, among them workload pressures, fears over job insecurity, and a desire for promotion. It is also clear that some organisations operate a 'long hours' culture in which there are pressures to conform to the work time norm in order to succeed. Perlow (1999: 68–9), for example, comments on this in her study of software engineers in the United States:

Simply being physically present was thought to be critical to one's success. ...Engineers perceived that the longer they worked, the more they were given credit for contributing and, therefore, the more highly they were regarded by their managers.

One of the key variables influencing long hours working is the work time pattern of those in senior positions in a workplace. Such individuals may not only expect similar time commitment from their subordinates, but may also acts as role models for how to achieve a senior level job within the organisation (see Excerpt 4.4 below).

EXCERPT 4.4

Having a workaholic for a boss

Tim Delaney's typical working day begins at 8.15 in the morning and ends at 9pm. As head of the London advertising agency Leagas Delaney, he frequently expects to put in extra hours on Sunday morning if there is work to be done.

Delaney is, by most people's definition, a 'workaholic' [...]. He says that his long hours are driven by a desire 'to get the work done, to do the right thing, and not to let people down', as well as perfectionism. 'When you are writing an ad,' he points out, 'you can always make it better.'

He also expects the people who work for him to put in long hours. 'If someone left the office at 5.30 each day and the results were fabulous, then I'd say OK,' he says. 'But in this business there are so many opportunities to be seized that it's unlikely that anybody would be justified in doing that.'

He feels no compunction about asking his staff to work weekends, and says that although they might feel occasional resentment, they respect him. 'Everyone wants their general to be leading them by example. What they don't want is somebody who tells them: you do this, I'm going out to dinner.'

Delaney may be an exceptional taskmaster, and advertising a demanding business, but the evidence in recent years indicates that people in the UK are working increasingly long hours. Ten per cent of the population or more could be regarded as 'workaholics' by virtue of the hours they put in.

But what is it like to work for someone like that? Is it inspiring, or is it just stressful?

The Chartered Institute of Personnel and Development (CIPD) has just carried out some research into the subject which appears to show that, for most people, having a workaholic boss is regarded far more positively than might be expected, although there is a clear danger that you will feel under pressure to work longer hours yourself. [...]

The CIPD's new report, *Married to the Job?* looked at how other workers perceived workaholics. Some 38 per cent surveyed said their bosses worked more than 48 hours a week; 28 per cent described that person as a 'workaholic'. But 70 per cent of this

▶

▶

latter group regarded the boss in question as a 'good example' and only three per cent said they resented the long hours he or she worked.

Melissa Compton-Edwards, the report's author, says the research showed that many people are inspired by a boss who works long hours, but it also demonstrated a downside: nearly a third said their workaholic boss would sometimes pressurise or bully them when he or she couldn't cope, and a quarter of those who had a workaholic colleague said they ended up working longer hours themselves in order to avoid looking lazy.

Source: Alexander Garrett, 'Business: Work: My name is Tim . . . I'm a workaholic: Is the 'lunch is for wimps' culture healthy?' *The Observer,* 4 Feb, 2001

A long hours culture may not only be an organisational characteristic – whole societies, such as Japan, have also been characterised as operating a long hours culture, with employees demonstrating their commitment to the group through their long work hours and their tendency to work at least a part of their holiday entitlement (Shimonitsu and Levi, 1992). Recently, technological developments such as mobile phones, pagers, laptop computers and e-mail mean that an increasing proportion of individuals remain in touch with, and contactable by, their employing organisation even when they are away from work (Fuchs Epstein and Kalleberg, 2001: 13).

Presenteeism has a number of potentially detrimental aspects. Simpson (2000: 164) for example, highlights how it can act unfairly against women in organisations, due to men often being in a better position than women with children to stay much later than the official end of the working day. Secondly, long work hours are frequently linked to the inefficient organisation of work time. Perlow's (1999) study referred to above, for example, highlights the way in which improved scheduling of work allowed shorter work days to be achieved among the software engineers she studied.

EXCERPT 4.5

Cross-national variation in work patterns

In a cross-cultural study, Perlow demonstrates that there is nothing inherent in software engineering that called for a particular long hours requirement. After spending time with engineers performing similar software activities in organisations in China, India and Hungary (each part of a larger joint venture with a US-based multinational corporation), the author found quite distinct attitudes in the three countries to the working day and working at weekends.

▶

▶ For example, engineers in China worked a relatively short, intensive eight hour day from 8am to 5pm with a one hour lunch break. These engineers rarely worked weekends. The engineers in India in contrast worked a longer day (most working 9am to 7pm, but often stayed later) with regular weekend working, especially on Saturdays.

The engineers in Hungary fell somewhere in between these two extremes, working longer hours when work pressure required, but also enjoying the greatest flexibility of the three in determining their work hours. Perlow comments that in Hungary, the engineers typically worked from 9am until 6pm, sometimes 7pm, but it was not unusual for someone to come in later, leave early or work from home. These engineers however, put in longer hours (including weekends) when work required it such as the final day before installing a new system.

Source: Perlow (2001)

EXERCISE 4.4

What do *you* think?

Perlow's research shows that the same activity being carried out in three different countries is associated with three distinct work patterns.

What do you think are likely to be the main factors giving rise to this variation? Identify the possible factors operating at (a) workgroup (b) company and (c) societal levels.

Further, many studies over several decades have demonstrated a link between long hours, fatigue, declining productivity and increased accidents and injuries (see for example, Rosa, 1995). In terms of the effects of long hours on individual health, an extensive meta-analysis of twenty one studies undertaken by Sparks and colleagues (1997) concluded that there is a small but significant relationship between poorer physical and psychological health and longer work hours. On the latter, Ferrie and Smith (1996: 47) in their study of several thousand adults found that those working very long hours (60 hours a week or more) were twice as likely to report a depressed mood, compared to those working fewer hours.

The studies in this area have largely concentrated on the people working the long hours, but account needs also to be taken of the physical and psychological impact of those long work hours on other family members, and on the distribution of child rearing and other domestic responsibilities (See Ferrie and Smith, 1996; Jacobs and Gerson, 2001; also Chapter 12).

Paid overtime

It is clear even from the information available on weekly work hours that among some groups, paid overtime working is the norm. In Britain in 1999, for example,

50 per cent of male full-time manual workers and almost 30 per cent of female full-time workers received overtime pay in the period surveyed by the *New Earnings Survey* (NES) (in addition, 19 per cent of full-time male non-manual workers and 16 per cent of female full-time non manual workers received overtime pay). Overall, male manual workers in Britain worked an average of 4.9 overtime hours per week in 1999, adding over 12 per cent to the average basic work week (*New Earnings Survey*, 1999, Part F). Later, there is a discussion of whether or not work has become more intensive over time; these high levels of overtime working however, indicate that for many, work is also characterised by its *extensiveness*, the long work days of a significant proportion of the work force resulting in work occupying a large part of individuals' total waking hours.

Within Europe, average weekly hours of full-time employees in the UK are particularly high. Full-time employees in the UK work the longest hours per week of the EU countries. As Table 4.1 highlights, this is true for both male and female full-time workers, though is particularly marked among men.

Table 4.1 Average hours usually worked[1] per week by full-time employees in the EU, 1998 (in rank order)

Country	Hours	
	Males	Females
United Kingdom	45.7	40.7
Portugal	42.1	39.6
Greece	41.7	39.3
Spain	41.2	39.6
Germany	40.4	39.3
Luxembourg	40.3	37.4
France	40.3	38.7
Austria	40.2	39.8
Sweden	40.2	40.0
Finland	40.1	38.2
Italy	39.7	36.3
Denmark	39.3	37.7
Netherlands	39.2	38.5
Belgium	39.1	37.5
EU average	41.3	39.0

[1]Includes regularly worked paid and unpaid overtime
Source: Labour Force Surveys, Eurostat

Among EU member states, the UK also has the highest proportion of workers working in excess of 48 hours – the maximum length of the working week specified in the EU Directive on Working Time (for a discussion of the Directive, see Incomes Data Services, 1996; and Trades Union Congress 1998). In 1994, the European Commission reported that almost half of the male workers in the EU who worked over 48 hours were employed in the UK (cited in Sparks, Cooper, Fried and Shirom, 1997: 392). The extent of long hours working in the UK has also increased considerably since the early 1980s – up by over 48 per cent between 1984 and 1998 according to one estimate (Trades Union Congress, 1998: 5). Among the industries where long hours working involving paid overtime was especially common for men in 1999 were parts of manufacturing, construction, the retail sector, bar work, security services and mining and quarrying. For female employees, bar work was the activity most associated with long hours working in 1999 (*New Earnings Survey*, 1999, Part F).

These long work hours in the UK reflect a disproportionately high level of overtime working. Several factors may account for this high level of overtime working in the UK, including the past absence of statutory controls (prior to the introduction of the Working Time Directive) on the maximum number of work hours an individual is permitted to work. Also significant for many workers is the importance of overtime earnings for supplementing (low) basic wage levels. Groups such as security guards, for example, are often reliant on high levels of overtime earnings to boost a relatively low basic wage. Overall, while for the average male manual worker in Britain in 1999 overtime earnings represented over one-eighth of their total earnings, this proportion was significantly higher within particular sectors and occupations.

Further, although overtime is often paid at a premium rate (such as time-and-a-half, or double time) it represents a preferable option for many employers, compared with introducing shiftworking and hiring additional staff. Overtime potentially offers not only a more flexible means of extending the working period, but may also reduce any pressure on employers to raise basic wage levels, since the availability of overtime work is offered as an incentive to attract and retain staff in otherwise low paying jobs. For the employees involved, however, it means that the overall experience of work is strongly coloured by the long hours spent at work and the resulting diminished opportunity for pursuing other, non-work activities. In a number of (mainly manual) occupations, the requirement to undertake overtime is a contractual obligation. As noted above, in others (among many white-collar, managerial and professional occupations) there is a widespread expectation that additional hours (paid or unpaid) should be worked to complete tasks that are outstanding, and more generally that working long hours is a sign of commitment (and an unwillingness to work extra hours viewed as an indication of a lack of commitment).

The pattern of working time is characterised not only by some experiencing very long hours of work, but also by a growing diversity of working time schedules, including a significant proportion of the work force employed for only a very few hours each week. In practice, the pattern of hours in paid work is both gendered and polarised, with a large number of men working long weekly hours and large numbers of women (as discussed further below) working comparatively few hours in paid work each week.

Hours of part-time workers

The overall growth of part-time working, and the fact that most part-time jobs are held by women, has already been noted (see Chapter 2). An important aspect of part-time working is that the hours of many part-time jobs are very small indeed. Like the tendency for many full-time jobs to involve long weekly hours, this tendency for many part-time jobs to comprise very few hours is particularly evident in Britain compared with other EU countries (Rubery, Fagan and Smith, 1995), and is also evident in the United States (Jacobs and Gerson, 2001: 41).

As Table 4.2 indicates, in Britain approaching half of part-time male workers and around two-fifths of female part-time workers work 16 hours per week or less, while one in five of the men and approximately one in eight of the women normally work fewer than eight hours per week. The trend is also towards an increase in these shorter part-time schedules. A survey of average hours change in Britain between 1983 and 1993, for example, found that average hours of part-time workers had fallen by almost five per cent over this period, while among their full-time counterparts, there was little discernible change (Butcher and Hart, 1995: 215). For employers, part-time working in general, and the use of short schedules in particular, allows the concentration of workers at times when work pressures are at their highest. For many employees, however, jobs comprising only a few hours per week yield only very limited income, often leading to the necessity for multiple job-holding.

Table 4.2   Distribution of work hours of those working less than 30 hours per week, Great Britain, 1999

Percentage with normal basic hours in the range	Males %	Females %
8 or less	19.6	12.9
8–16	27.0	26.2
16–21	19.0	26.5
21–30	34.3	34.4

Source: *New Earnings Survey*, 1999, Part F, Tables F43, F44

Zero hours contracts

If some jobs are characterised by their short duration, others operate on the basis of no guaranteed duration at all. 'Zero hours' contracts (also known as 'reservism' and 'on call' arrangements) involve employers guaranteeing no definite hours to employees, but simply calling on workers as and when required. In some sectors, such as education, similar arrangements have long existed in the form of teachers being 'on supply' with work being offered, usually at very short notice, to cover absence or other reasons for regular teachers being away from the classroom.

More recently zero hours contracts have developed, initially in the retail sector, again primarily as a means for employers to cover absence.

Such contracts provide employers with both a very high degree of temporal flexibility, and at the same time, extend only minimal contractual commitment to those employed under such arrangements. The workers hired on such contracts are typically afforded no job security, and no guarantee of earnings or hours; yet, these contracts are restrictive in that employees need to keep themselves available ('on call'), which acts to reduce their opportunities for pursuing other activities. However, despite their limitations, it is not the case that zero hours contracts are accepted by employees only because nothing more secure or predictable is on offer. Indeed, there are groups, such as students and those recently retired, for whom the occasional work entailed in zero hours contracts may fit very well with their other commitments and lifestyle.

There has been little aggregate information on the development of zero hours working. The WERS found zero hours contracts to be operating in five per cent of workplaces in 1998, more commonly in the private sector (reported in six per cent of workplaces) than in the public sector (two per cent of workplaces) (Cully, Woodland, O'Reilly and Dix, 1999: 34–5). However, other estimates of the actual numbers of employees with zero hours contracts put the current total at less than one per cent of the total workforce (see for example Equal Opportunities Commission, 1998: 34; Arrowsmith and Sisson, 2000: 302), indicating that at present many organisations reporting the use of zero hours contracts operate these for only small numbers of staff.

TO SUM UP

Working time patterns are increasingly characterised by diversity, with very long weeks worked by some co-existing alongside very short weeks worked by others. Despite a downward trend in basic weekly hours of full-time employees, many continue to work far longer than the basic week, by undertaking a large amount of paid or unpaid overtime.

Changes in the arrangement of working time

Growing diversity in working time patterns

There have been several factors in recent years encouraging employers to increase their total operating hours. In the service sector, this reflects partly the general increase in opening hours which has taken place: as a result, for example, of the liberalisation of Sunday trading, changes in licensing hours for outlets selling alcohic drinks, extension of banking hours, and evening opening of retail and other service activities. In manufacturing, increased investment in technology, coupled with a faster rate of technological obsolescence, has forced employers to

Learning outcome 5

Identify patterns of change in the arrangement of working time, including annual hours and zero hours contracts.

consider more ways to increase capital utilisation in order to maximise returns on investment.

The result of a gradually declining basic work week and the pressures to maintain or increase operating times, has been greater de-coupling of individual work hours from operating hours. This means that instead of an organisation's operating time being the same as the employees' work period (for example, 9am to 5.30pm) the operating time is lengthened (for example, to 10pm) with the additional time being covered for example, by a part-time shift. Such de-coupling is, of course, not new. Those industries where shiftworking has been common practice, such as hospitals, hotels, continuous process operations, transport services, postal services and parts of the engineering sector, have long been used to a distinction between the length of the operating period and individual work hours. What *is* new in more recent years is the spread of this arrangement into areas where traditionally shiftworking has been comparatively rare, such as in retailing and financial services. Further, this pressure to extend hours impacts not only on weekdays but also on weekends.

Nowhere is this more evident than in the banking sector, where in Britain Saturday opening has become a norm, and in retailing, with the increase in Sunday trading. Thus, when viewed in combination with the greater use of a wide range of part-time schedules, an effect of this extension of operating/opening hours has been to create an overall working time pattern which is diverse, not only in terms of the number of hours which people work, but also in terms of when they work those hours. A popular belief, for example, is that a majority of people still work Monday to Friday, from 9am to 5pm or thereabouts. In practice, however, this is far from the actual experience of the majority of employees. In Britain, for example, only around a third of employed men and women operate such a working time pattern (Table 4.3; see also Hill, 2000).

Table 4.3 The timing of work weeks for men and women in Britain

Timing of work	Percentage of employees
Full time, Monday to Friday, starting between 8–10am, finishing between 4–6pm	34%
Full-time, Monday to Friday, other hours	7%
Part-time, Monday to Friday	11%
6 or 7 day week	23%
1 to 5 days, some weekend work	11%
1 to 4 days, no weekend work	14%

Source: Hewitt (1993: 23)

Similarly, a large-scale study of working fathers and mothers in their thirties by Ferrie and Smith (1996) found that the majority of fathers worked outside normal working hours, with two-thirds working in the evenings and six out of ten at weekends (Figure 4.1). Over a third also worked at some part of the night. It was more likely for those men in professional, managerial and other non-manual jobs to work in the evening, while manual workers were the ones more likely to work at night or weekends. Among women, four out of ten worked in the evening or weekend, and between one in six and one in eight at night.

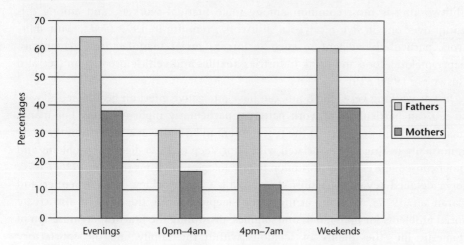

Figure 4.1
Proportions of fathers and mothers[1] working unsocial hours

Adapted from Ferrie and Smith (1996: 19).

[1] The National Child Development Study from which these figures are taken is a longitudinal cohort study which has followed the lives of all those in Great Britain born in a specific week in 1958. The sample size for working fathers and mothers reported in this table was over 3600.

EXERCISE 4.5

What do *you* think?

What are the main implications of the results shown in Table 4.4 for parental roles and family life?

In thinking about your answer you may want to bear in mind the comments made about the effect of night working in the following section on shiftworking.

Shiftworking

There are various ways that an employer may schedule working hours to create a longer working period. The use of overtime for this purpose has already been noted. In addition, a long-established means of lengthening the working period is by shiftworking; a simple definition of shiftwork is 'a situation in which one worker replaces another on the same job within a 24-hour period' (Ingram and Sloane, 1984: 168). Various shiftwork patterns exist:

■ some extend across the whole day and week – for example, continuous three-shift working, with shifts starting for example, at 6am, 2pm and 10 pm;

■ others extend the productive period but not across the entire day or week – such as 'double day' shifts, for example 6am–2pm and 2pm–10 pm.

Many, though not all employees, receive an extra payment (a shift premium) for working shifts. In 1999 an average of one in eight men and one in twelve women employees in Britain received a shift premium (*New Earnings Survey*, 1999, Part F). Shiftworking is most common among male manual workers, and among this group over one in five received a shiftwork premium in 1999 (*ibid.*), with shiftwork particularly evident in such sectors as metal manufacturing, chemicals, paper-making, food and drink industries, textiles and vehicle production (see also Bosworth, 1994: 619).

Just as working very long hours can have a negative effect on health (see above), so too can particular shiftwork patterns, particularly night-working. For many, night shifts (and in particular the requirement to be active at a time when the body is normally resting) are associated with poor sleep quality, digestive problems and other consequences of the disruption to physiological rhythms (Blyton, 1985: 67–70; for a detailed review of issues surrounding night working, see Carpentier and Cazamian, 1977). Working at night and sleeping during the day can also create social problems for individuals and families, disrupting the practical organisation of domestic life, the quality of relations within the family and the satisfactory performance of parental roles (Mott, Mann, McLoughlin and Warwick, 1965).

Compressed work weeks

One reason why the proportion of employees working shifts has not gone even higher is the replacement of formal shiftwork systems with alternative working time arrangements which extend the productive period, but do not incur the wage premia usually paid to workers on shifts. One example of these arrangements is that of 'compressed' work weeks, whereby employees work their total weekly hours in longer work periods but for fewer than the normal number of days (for example, working for twelve hours a day for three days rather than seven and a half hours for five days). Across a work force as a whole, the effect of this can be to create longer work periods without the use of a formal shiftwork system (Poor, 1972; Baltes, Briggs, Huff, Wright and Neuman, 1999).

Seasonal and annual hours

Attempts by employers to extend the length of the productive work period have also been accompanied, in a growing number of instances, by attempts to re-define what constitutes normal work hours, in order to reduce the amount of time attracting (premium paid) overtime rates. Examples of negotiations over the re-definition of normal and overtime periods have become widespread, occurring, for example, in Australia (see discussion in Deery and Mahony, 1994: 333–5) and Germany, where extensive negotiations over working time during the 1990s have included discussions on payments for Saturday working, and temporary increases in weekly hours without incurring overtime payments (Blyton and Trinczek,

1995). In the UK and elsewhere, an example of managerial efforts to reduce reliance on overtime during busy periods has been the introduction of 'seasonal hours' working, whereby the normal work week is lengthened during busy periods and reduced during slacker times. A number of consumer electronic firms in the UK, for example, operate this pattern, with longer work weeks (up to 44 hours) in the months prior to the busy Christmas period, with shorter hours in the following months to bring the average work week back to 39 hours. For the employer this arrangement both reduces overtime payments during the busy months, and also reduces excess labour capacity in the quieter periods (Blyton, 1994: 517–8). For employees, however, this seasonality of the working period can be more problematic, since it is likely to entail both a loss of overtime earnings, and eliminate any discretion they may have enjoyed over whether or not to work overtime.

An extension of seasonal hours arrangements are 'annual hours' contracts, under which employees work an agreed number of hours per year, with working time schedules (including holidays) determined at the beginning of twelve month cycles. Such arrangements usually build in flexibility for employers either by establishing a schedule where more hours are worked during busy periods, or by leaving some of the agreed total hours as non-rostered work time, for which employees are effectively 'on-call' and can be brought into work to cover unforeseen circumstances (Arrowsmith and Sisson, 2000: 299–302; Blyton, 1995; Pickard, 1991).

Seasonal and annual hours arrangements create not only the potential for reducing overtime costs, but coupled with this, enable a closer matching of available labour with levels of output demand. Together with arranging hours to cover longer operating periods, this desire for a closer matching of work schedules with output demand has become a second major focus for employers. In some sectors, demand fluctuates considerably over the working day and week. In parts of the retailing industry, for example, demand rises significantly during lunchtime periods and towards the end of the week. One of the ways working time schedules have been arranged to reflect this is via the introduction of various part-time schedules which increase the volume of available labour during busy periods. Hence, it has become common practice in retailing to schedule part-time workers to work during lunch periods and/or at weekends.

Flexible working hours

In addition to employers' activity in the area of the arrangement of working time, two ways in which employees also exert some influence over how work hours are arranged are through flexible working hours systems and via informal working time arrangements. According to recent British Government statistics, just over one in ten full-time employees in Britain (8 per cent of men and 13 per cent of women) and approaching one in twelve part-time employees, work flexible working hours or 'flexitime' (Office for National Statistics, 2000: 74). However, when the Workplace Employee Relations Survey asked employees if they had access to flexitime if they needed to because of domestic circumstances, almost a third (32 per cent) of employees said they could work flexitime if needs be (Cully, Woodland, O'Reilly and Dix, 1999: 144).

Other arrangements which provide some flexibility to employees include school term-time working and job sharing. In 1999, one in ten female part-time employees (and half that proportion of full-time female employees) worked on a term-time only basis, with a much smaller proportion (2.7 per cent of female part-time employees) working on job sharing contracts (Office for National Statistics, 2000: 74).

Flexitime working remains far more common among non-manual workers, particularly in larger public (and recently privatised) service sector organisations, than among their manual counterparts and others located in manufacturing and smaller establishments in the private sector (Wareing, 1992). Beyond formal flexitime systems, however, it is evident that a proportion of employees operate less formalised systems which provide an element of choice over start and finish times. Those in higher level jobs typically enjoy greater access to this informal flexibility: for example, in Wareing's (1992) study, half the employees in professional occupations had a measure of flexibility over their start and finish times, compared to less than one in ten of those in semi-skilled occupations. It is also evident that many employees secure a degree of flexibility over working hours by reaching informal 'understandings' with other workers and with management in relation, for example, to start and finish times. Such informal agreements are also reflected in much of the overtime that is worked. As noted above, for a proportion of workers, overtime working is a contractual obligation. However, in a large scale study in Britain, Marsh (1991) found that in the period immediately prior to her survey, more than three male full-time workers in every ten and over a quarter of full-time female workers had agreed to work extra time at short notice – a far higher proportion than the six per cent who indicated that they were required by their contract to work overtime (see also Horrell and Rubery, 1991).

TO SUM UP

Much paid work takes place outside what has traditionally been thought of as the normal working period. Employers are increasingly concerned to use different contractual arrangements and shiftwork patterns to arrange working time in such a way as to maximise labour coverage and flexibility, and minimise labour cost. Formal and informal flexitime arrangements are one means by which employees can exercise a degree of choice over the scheduling of their work hours.

Learning outcome 6

Assess developments in the utilisation of working time and the debate over work intensity.

The utilisation of working time

Just as increased attention has been given to arranging working time to cover longer opening/operating periods, and to concentrating labour time at periods of highest work pressure, greater attention has also been paid in recent years to increasing the extent to which labour time is effectively utilised. In the 1980s,

White (1987: 51) estimated that in engineering in Britain between 20 and 40 per cent of paid time was non-productive. As noted earlier, part of the explanation for this will lie in scheduling and production problems such as shortages of materials, equipment breakdown, and a lack of orders, together with possible poor managerial organisation and instruction concerning the tasks to be completed.

As we have seen, however, non-productive time can also be fashioned by workers themselves to create an easier or more varied work tempo. Against this background, three recent developments relating to work time utilisation are particularly noteworthy:

1 *The re-definition of the working period*: the introduction of practices designed to define the working period exclusive of, rather than inclusive of, preparatory activities such as changing into and out of work clothes and walking to and from the actual work area. Efforts to tighten the definition of the working period have centred on practices such as 'bell to bell' working, which refers to the bells or buzzers announcing the start and finish of working periods, with employees required to be in position to commence working when the bell for the start of the shift sounds, and only terminate work after the bell which signals the end of the shift (Blyton, 1994: 520).

    Such managerial attempts to impose a time-reckoning system which minimises non-productive time, together with responses by workers to operate a counter system which creates or extends additional rest periods, have been a feature of capitalist industrial development throughout its history. Karl Marx (1976) for example, remarked on employers' continual efforts to maximise 'surplus labour time' – that is, that part of working hours creating surplus value – by seeking to extend the working period and by efforts to minimise the 'porosity' of the working day: the number of holes or 'pores' in the working day when workers are not actually working. Marx (1976: 352) characterises employers as continually 'nibbling and cribbling' at workers' meal-times and other breaks in an attempt to maximise the quantity of labour effort. As current managerial interest in bell-to-bell working and similar practices illustrates, this issue of non-productive work time continues to be a significant one for twenty-first century management as was the case for their nineteenth century counterparts.

2 *'Lean' systems*: the introduction of just-in-time (JIT) and similar process systems whose development has been facilitated by advances in information technology, and which form a major element in the development of 'lean' manufacturing systems, also have potentially important implications for work time utilisation. Under a JIT regime, for example, emphasis is placed on work 'flowing' continuously through the different stages of production, with components arriving 'just-in-time' to be incorporated into the manufacturing process, with only minimum stocks held of materials, work-in-progress and finished articles (Turnbull, 1988). Among other implications, this method of organising production potentially undermines any ability workers may have to build up 'banks' of finished work which, as discussed earlier, may then be used to create an additional break or an easier work pace later in the working period.

3   *Flexible working*: the growth of task flexibility during the past two decades represents a third area of workplace change with potentially important implications for time utilisation. The issue of labour flexibility has been much debated and it is clear that actual developments in flexibility have not necessarily been in the ways, or to the extent, that many of the early predictions and prescriptions suggested (see, for example, Atkinson, 1984; see also Blyton, 1992; Cross, 1988; Pollert, 1988). Nevertheless, it is also evident that, cumulatively over the period since the early 1980s, developments in work organisation based on broader job definitions, reduced skill demarcations and enlarged jobs, have led to significant changes in the way that individual tasks and work groups are organised. Some blurring of skill boundaries and widespread development of greater flexibility among less skilled workers have increased the mobility of labour between tasks within workplaces and been part of a shift towards more tasks being covered by fewer workers, as organisations seek cost cutting through staff reductions.

EXCERPT 4.6

Unions reporting work reorganisation

In a study of trade unionists in more than four thousand workplaces, Waddington and Whitston (1996: 158–9) identified developments in flexibility as the most prominent in a series of work reorganisation measures, with much of the development in flexibility occurring in the recent period. Over a fifth (23 per cent) of respondents indicated that management had introduced significant levels of task flexibility, most of this over the previous three years. Levels of multi-skilling were lower, with 16 per cent indicating significant development. While developments in multi-skilling were most pronounced in the private sector, task flexibility was more marked in public services, such as in the health service where, for example, general assistant grades had replaced former, more specialist, grades (*ibid*: 164).

Related to the growth of flexibility in many work contexts has been the introduction of teamworking (Procter and Mueller, 2000). Waddington and Whitston (1996: 158) in their study found a lower incidence and growth of teamworking compared to more general flexibility developments. Nevertheless, as management attempts not only to locate more responsibility for performance within work groups themselves, but also increase flexibility through greater worker interchangeability and reduce costs by cutting the number of supervisory posts, it may be anticipated that interest in teamworking will continue to expand in coming years. In some contexts, working in teams has proved only marginally different from prior systems of work organisation based around less formal (but nonetheless important) work group arrangements. However, the circumstances under which teamworking has been adopted (often in contexts of job reductions, lower staffing levels, and increased emphasis on quality assurance, for example) mean that, for many, teamworking is part of a significant change from what has gone before, not least in the additional responsibilities held by the team over such areas as task allocation and quality.

Harder work?

The above aspects of workplace change, coupled with evidence of rises in productivity in the 1980s, have prompted writers such as Elger (1990 and 1991) to consider the extent to which this productive gain was the result of work becoming more intensive (see also Guest, 1990; Metcalf, 1989; and Nolan, 1989). More recently Green (2001) has undertaken a detailed analysis of evidence on changing work pressures and work effort.

The question of whether or not workers are working harder is, in practice, difficult to answer with any degree of accuracy, for it is complicated by various factors, not least the lack of any systematic study of effort. Other factors, too, complicate comparisons of effort: for example, the experience of working harder can be the result of a faster work pace, a longer work period and/or reductions in the extent of non-work time (Elger, 1990). Further, effort may comprise the expenditure of either (or both) manual and mental energy; hence, identifying a decline (or increase) in one may not give an accurate picture of what has happened to levels of effort overall. Thus, it is frequently argued that automation and the other technological changes have reduced the degree of physical effort required to perform many jobs. The decline in employment in manufacturing in general, and in heavy industry such as iron and steel-making, shipbuilding and coal mining in particular, has also been adduced to argue that the number of jobs in the labour force as a whole requiring high expenditure of (physical) effort, is likely to have declined.

Yet, various attitude studies show that despite the decline of heavy industry, many workers report having experienced an *increase* in effort over recent years, both in terms of physical and mental effort. Clearly there are potential bias problems if relying on asking workers whether or not they are working harder than they used to. However, the strength and consistency of worker opinions on questions of effort suggest support for the argument that effort levels have indeed risen. Green (2001) cites a large number of studies to show that during the past twenty years, employees have consistently reported that they are working harder and under greater pressure. For Green (2001: 68) the evidence creates 'a picture of continually rising work effort over the last two decades'. Green also points out that surveys undertaken at different time periods point to the growing importance of 'fellow workers or colleagues' as a key source of work pressure by the late 1990s. As Green (2001: 70) remarks, 'It seems that peer pressure has come into its own as a source of labour intensification.'

Elger (1991) argues that the drive for greater flexibility has contributed to labour intensification because reductions in work force numbers in many organisations, with the fewer remaining workers covering more tasks, has resulted in more intensified work regimes. This is echoed in the study by Edwards and Whitston (1991:

where, for example, one of the factors affecting the perceived increase in effort levels among British Rail platform staff was that the standard labour allocation had been cut from three workers per railway platform to two. Similarly, in the study cited in Excerpt 4.6, a prominent characteristic of the plant under investigation was continued cuts in workforce numbers, with those remaining required to cover a broader range of tasks. Further, just as competitive pressures in the private sector have fuelled a search for lower labour costs (and thus potentially stimulated labour intensification), so too political demands for more efficient public services have led to a corresponding search for reductions in labour costs, as in-house groups have been forced to compete with external providers of similar services. This was one of the factors affecting the hospital ancillary workers in Edwards and Whitston's (1991: 597) study, where competitive tendering had led to work remaining in-house, but only through cuts in labour costs and the need to work harder to complete the tasks.

TO SUM UP

Greater attention has been paid in recent years by management to increasing the productive use of working time. One of the outcomes of this has been employees consistently reporting that they are working harder. Developments such as flexibility and teamworking are among the factors contributing to this experience of labour intensification.

Conclusion

Time is a central factor shaping the experience of work. What this chapter has underlined is the diversity of time schedules: a diversity reflected in the different amounts of working hours, the ways those hours are variously arranged across the day and week, and the degrees to which working hours are actually utilised in productive activity. What has also been stressed is the different ways that management and workers perceive working time. On the one hand, a managerial rationality emphasises the linear quality of time, the importance of regularity for the coordination of different time schedules, and the importance of maximising the productive use of working time. On the other hand, there is a workers' counter-rationality seeking, in part, to mitigate the negative aspects of an unchanging work tempo. These two rationalities exist in a state of mutual influence, with the result that the formal time regime defined by management typically bears only partial resemblance to actual working time patterns performed by their employees.

These two rationalities also reflect a tension between the objective and subjective nature of time. The managerial rationality is essentially based on a linear view of time as 'clock time': time as a scarce resource, and a commodity capable of being 'spent', 'wasted', or 'lost' – its objective character summed up in the classic temporal cliché of capitalism, 'time is money'. On the other hand, however, workers experience time at work subjectively: it can pass quickly or slowly, can be varied or monotonous, and for many will be experienced as a cyclical (rather than a linear) phenomenon, with one day more or less repeating the cycle of the previous day; or even one hour repeating the pattern of the previous. As has been noted, the creation of circumstances to improve the way time is experienced can take various forms, ranging from occasional absence to escape the routines of work, to the creation of different 'times' within the working day, when the tempo of work is altered and the regularity of time suppressed.

The relationship between the objective and subjective character of time, and between a managerial rationality and a workers' counter-rationality towards time, represents an on-going tension in the employment relationship. On the one hand, for example, continuing levels of voluntary absence indicate workers' ability to ward off managerial attempts to impose a comprehensive time discipline on its workforce. On the other hand, management's introduction of tighter staffing levels and practices such as bell-to-bell working signal their pursuit of higher levels of working time utilisation. The tension between the two rationalities may be expected to continue for the foreseeable future, and manifest itself within particular aspects of working time. For example, management's efforts to cut labour costs by restricting the periods defined as overtime (via arrangements such as seasonal and annual hours contracts, and varied part-time schedules) are likely to be countered, to a degree at least, by workers seeking to establish an easier pace of work which allows, among other things, unfinished work to be carried over into (premium paid) overtime hours. Such a carry over of work into overtime remains particularly important in those low paying jobs where workers rely heavily on overtime earnings. Of course, an obvious cost to those working long hours is the reduced time available for non-work activities and responsibilities. In broader societal terms, the cost is also that while many are working very long hours to earn an acceptable wage, others remain unemployed for want of available work. Overall, it is a situation satisfactory to neither group. However, despite an on-going debate over work-sharing and the reorganisation of working time, to date this has remained an issue on which there has been a lack of political will to bring about any significant change.

5 Work skills

KEY CONCEPTS

- Skill in the person
- Skill in the job
- Skill in the setting
- Complexity and discretion

- Tacit skill
- Social closure
- Ideological, political and material processes of social closure

- Social regulation
- Social construction of skill
- Gender and skill

CHAPTER AIM

To explore the concept of skill and critically evaluate three different approaches to its definition and measurement.

LEARNING OUTCOMES

After reading and thinking about this chapter, you will be able to:

1 identify three approaches to evaluating skill;

2 explain how to assess skill in the person and recognise three main problems with this approach;

3 explain how to assess skill in the job:

   (a) using the concept of complexity

   (b) using the concept of discretion;

4 explain how to assess skill in the setting using the concept of social closure;

5 appreciate how skill can be seen as a socially constructed phenomenon that has disadvantaged women through:

   (a) ideological processes

   (b political processes

   (c) material processes.

Introduction

Of all the concepts we come across when studying work and employment, 'skill' stands out as the most difficult to pin down. Yet, strangely enough it is perhaps one of the few topics that most people might claim to have an understanding about. If you ask someone about a job, they would more than likely be able to tell you whether it is skilled or not, and they would probably be able to give a reasonable explanation as to why they considered it skilled. The problem, however, is that we all stress different aspects of a job in evaluating whether it is skilled or not.

In a survey (Francis and Penn, 1994) respondents reported over 16 different definitions when asked the question 'What do you think is meant by the term *skilled job*?'. However, there was some convergence around five main characteristics: training, qualifications, apprenticeship, experience and high abilities. Interestingly (although not surprisingly) the researchers found that different types of employees emphasised different features of skill (see Table 5.1). Francis and Penn conclude that different occupational groups will categorise skill in different ways, which suggests that a person's conception of skill is largely based on his or her own experiences of employment.

Table 5.1 Various meanings of the term 'skilled job'

Feature of skilled work identified as important	Most likely to be identified as important by:
Apprenticeship	Older, male, manual workers (particularly those possessing apprenticeship qualifications)
Training	Younger, female, public-sector service employees (particularly those possessing higher level qualifications)
Qualifications	Women (particularly in retail distribution) Younger respondents People with lower-level qualifications
High abilities	Men People with higher-level qualifications
Experience	No specific group

Based on Francis and Penn (1994). The survey comprised 987 adults aged between 20 and 60, and was undertaken in Rochdale, UK in 1986.

In extreme cases, the lack of consensus over what constitutes a skilled job is less important because the job attributes are diverse enough for people to reach general, if not specific agreement – for example, most people would probably agree that the surgeon's job is more skilled than the hospital porter's job, or that the teacher is more skilled than the school caretaker. But some comparisons are far more problematic – to illustrate this, complete Exercise 5.1.

What do *you* think?

For each of the pairs of jobs listed below, decide which is the more skilled and justify your decision. In other words explain the criteria you are using to decide how skill should be evaluated.

- The hotel receptionist compared with the security guard
- The computer games software programmer and the paramedic
- The cleaner and the car-park attendant
- The insurance broker and the travel agent
- The police officer and the social worker

To reach an agreement on comparisons such as those in Exercise 5.1 it is necessary to achieve consensus on what is meant by the term 'skill'. This is not an easy task because skill is a definitional minefield. However, in the rest of the chapter we will enter this dangerous territory and explore the theoretical concept and its empirical expression.

But first, we must ask, why worry about defining skill at all? This is a reasonable question, and the answer, as explained below, is that the concept of skill is fundamental to the status that people attach to different occupations, and is frequently linked to pay. Moreover, skill is a key factor in determining the structure of employment, most notably in the way it acts to reinforce the gender division of labour in society.

Learning outcome 1

Identify three approaches to evaluating skill.

Locating skill

The first puzzle that needs to be solved is the problem of where skill resides. Is it part of:

- the person?
- the job?
- the setting?

Cockburn (1983: 113) suggests all three aspects need to be taken into account. In her study of (male) printworkers she argues that :

> There is the skill that resides in the man himself, accumulated over time, each new experience adding something to a total ability. There is the skill demanded by the job – which may or may not match the skill in the worker. And there is the political definition of skill: that which a group of workers or a trade union can successfully defend against the challenge of employers and other groups of workers.

A closer consideration of Cockburn's research will be undertaken later in the chapter, but it is worth pausing to give some thought to her three categories because each suggests a different approach to examining skill.

1 *Skill in the person*: Any analysis that concentrates on the *person* is likely to attempt to identify individual attributes and qualities, and seek to measure these through, for example, an aptitude test under experimental conditions; typically this approach has been taken by psychologists. Similarly, a questionnaire might be administered to assess the individual's education, training and experience, which could then be used as a proxy for skill – a method frequently adopted by economists.

2 *Skill in the job*: If the analytical focus is the *job* then the concern is less with the person performing the task than with the requirements embedded in the task itself. In this case, attention would be turned towards the complexity of the tasks required to perform the job competently – an approach typically taken by management theorists. It would also include the extent of discretion over the work – an issue of particular interest to industrial/employment relations theorists.

3 *Skill in the setting*: If the focus is on the political and historical *setting*, an analysis would be assessing the way skill has developed over time and has been 'constructed' by different interest groups, rather than being a feature of the person or the job – an approach pursued by some sociologists, but more usually by historians.

These differences in approach to analysing skill are summarised in Table 5.2. It illustrates how the focus tends to be associated with different methods of analysis and shows how academic disciplines have tended to address different aspects of skill.

Table 5.2 Approaches to the analysis of skill

Focus	Principal area of concern	Typical method of analysis	Typically adopted by:
Person	Individual attributes acquired through: * education * qualifications * training * experience	Questionnaire surveys Aptitude tests/ experiments	Economists Psychologists
Job	Task requirements * complexity * discretion	Job analysis Job evaluation	Occupational psychologists Management theorists Industrial/employment relations theorists
Setting	Social relations	Case studies of industries and occupations Ethnographic studies of workplaces	Social historians Sociologists

TO SUM UP

It is possible for several theorists to arrive at contrasting conclusions about skilled work because they are focusing on different features and are using different methods of analysis.

Having charted the terrain, it is necessary to explore each of these areas in closer detail. To do this the rest of this chapter has been divided into three sections, each analysing a different aspect of skill: the person, the job and the setting. Each section draws out the strengths and weaknesses of the particular approaches, thereby demonstrating that there is no simple way of assessing skill. Following this, a final section illustrates the contemporary importance of the concept of skill by examining how it perpetuates the gender division of labour.

Learning outcome 2

Explain how to assess skill in the person and recognise three main problems with this approach.

Skill in the person

In this first approach, skill is generally considered to be a possession of the individual. It can take numerous forms – for example, knowledge, dexterity, judgement, linguistic ability – but the assumption is that it is accrued by the individual as a product of accumulated education, training and experience. At first sight, this is an attractive conception of skill because it is relatively easy to measure and produces quantifiable data that can be incorporated into statistical analyses. For example, a person can be asked to complete a questionnaire listing their years in formal education, number of qualifications, amount of training undertaken, and on-the-job experience. It is not surprising, therefore, that many labour economists are satisfied with these measures as a proxy for skill. This is typified by the approach of human capital theorists (for example, Becker, 1964) who argue that in a market economy, a person's human capital will determine their value as an employee. From this perspective it is argued that people can choose, as individuals, to increase their human capital through taking advantage of educational opportunities and training. Or conversely, they can choose to ignore these opportunities, with the consequence of lowering their relative value in the labour market. For human capital theorists, responsibility for success in work clearly lies with the individual; they invoke the notion of a meritocratic society, where individual endeavour is rewarded.

Problems with the human capital approach

Three problems are immediately apparent with this approach;

1 *Inequality of opportunity*
   The approach assumes that everyone has the same opportunity of access to the activities that improve human capital. Yet this is clearly not the case. For

example, private education generally provides children with better facilities, smaller class sizes and a more intense learning environment, but such education is only available to the minority of children whose parents can afford it, together with a small number who are awarded scholarships. Similarly, take the example of experience: in order to gain work experience, a person has to be offered a job, but when there are high rates of unemployment allowing employers to pick and choose, a person with no work experience is less likely to be offered a job, so they are consequently unable to gain work experience. It is a classic Catch-22. Both examples illustrate the fundamental problem that people do not compete on equal terms, because, to use a well-worn metaphor, there is not a level playing field to begin with.

2 *Validity of the skill measures*

A more general problem is whether the variables of education, training and experience are valid measures of skill. The number of years a person spends in formal education is linked to qualifications attained, but even then it does not necessarily mean that the skills learned will be appropriate or transferable to the work setting. Similarly, while the measurement of training may be a better indicator of industry-specific knowledge and aptitude, it does not take into account the applicability of the training to the current context. For example, the training a photographer's assistant receives in traditional darkroom printing techniques has not permanently added to their human capital because this skill is becoming redundant due to the new technology of digital cameras and computer manipulation of digital images. The skill may remain in the person, but it is the economic and technical context that determines the value of the skill. The same is true of experience. Forty years' experience of mending mechanical typewriters represents a huge amount of diagnostic skill and understanding of the machines, but the word-processor has made much of this accumulated experience valueless in a very short time.

3 *Use value of the skill*

Should measurement include only those attributes that have a current value – in other words the measurement of 'skills in use' rather than skills possessed? For example, if a person learns to speak Welsh and gains a qualification proving their competence, does this constitute a skill? If it has some market value, human capital theorists would say yes, but if few employers require Welsh speakers, its value is severely reduced. In other words, skill is not a fixed concept, but is relative to its market value. In this sense, all knowledge and abilities can be seen as potential skills, but it is the demand for them and their supply that give them value. Therefore, measuring the skills possessed by the person can be misleading without exploring the labour market context.

To address some of these problems of measurement, researchers sometimes associate education, training and experience with the individual's job (for example, see Excerpt 5.1). Using this method, the amount of relevant education, training and experience needed to perform the job competently is set as a skill benchmark. In an analysis of the US and Canada, Livingstone (1998) found considerable discrepancies between the skills people possess compared with the skills they are expected to use at work. He describes this as the education-jobs gap and argues that the rise in educational qualifications and work-related knowledge has outpaced the development of jobs where people can put this knowledge to use. In effect, there is 'underemployment' of the skills available in the labour market. It seems that Livingstone has shown that there is considerable truth in the long standing joke that that many workers use more skill driving to work than they are required to use when they get there.

EXCERPT 5.1

Measuring skill in the person

The Social Change and Economic Life Initiative (SCELI) was a large-scale research programme conducted in the UK during the late 1980s. The researchers used five different indicators of skill by asking people the following questions:

1 What qualifications would be needed to get your type of job if someone was applying for it now?

2 What length of training did you receive for your kind of work after completing full-time education?

3 What amount of time did it take you to learn to do your job well?

4 Do you have direct responsibility for supervising the work of others?

5 Do you consider your work to be skilled?

The first three of these indicators reflect qualifications, training and experience (common quantitative measures of skills), whilst the fourth indicator seeks to measure one aspect of job content (responsibility for others). In contrast, the fifth indicator is an attitudinal measure, revealing the respondent's perception of their job. (Further findings from this study will be examined in Chapter 6.) The SCELI approach is still ostensibly focused on the individual, but it begins to acknowledge the importance of the job setting.

Source: Based on Gallie (1991)

Similarly, occupational psychologists have tended to focus their attention on the individual and sought to measure 'skills' by using aptitude tests, often administered under experimental conditions. Typically, this approach tries to match the person to the job, thus skills assessments can be used as part of the job selection process – for example, through psychometric tests (designed to reveal cognitive abilities such as IQ), simulation exercises (to reveal qualities such as leadership) and work sampling (to reveal practical abilities, such as asking a candidate for a secretarial job to input data into a spreadsheet). While a full discussion of the pros and cons of the occupational psychologist's approach to skill measurement is beyond our immediate concern, it is worth noting that psychologists themselves disagree about how skills should be measured. For some, it is only under controlled experimental conditions that skill can be assessed (for example, Seymour, 1966) while others argue that skills can only be assessed in the specific context in which they are used (for example, Rogoff and Lave, 1984). In this latter case, the occupational psychologists are bridging a gap by arguing that it is possible and desirable to have two foci: the individual *and* the job setting.

TO SUM UP

The approach of assessing skill in the person tends to view skill as an attribute possessed by an individual, and sometimes described as a person's human capital. While this appears to be a relatively simple way of assessing skill, the problems lie in the methods of measurement and then putting these into practice (see Exercise 5.2).

EXERCISE 5.2

What do *you* think?

Imagine you are devising a new skill-based pay system for an organisation which is supposed to encourage job flexibility and retraining.

1 Should each employee be paid according to the skills they possess or just the particular skills they use?

2 What might be the consequences of paying them according to all the skills they possess?

3 What might be the consequences of paying only for the skills they use?

Skill in the job

In this section the analysis focuses on assessing the skill required by the job, rather than the skills possessed by the person doing the job. Two different aspects of skill are considered: *complexity* and *discretion*.

Assessing the complexity of jobs

Learning outcome 3a

Explain how to assess skill in the job using the concept of complexity.

It seems reasonable to suppose that the more complex the tasks required by the job, then the more skilled the job is. This suggests that all one has to do is measure the extent of complexity and thereby arrive at a skill level. The assumption is that by this means it is possible to derive an *objective* measure of complexity. This is a seductive idea because it would mean that different jobs could be compared and ranked according to their complexity, and that this in turn could be reflected in systems of status and remuneration. Indeed, this has been attempted through job evaluation schemes (Thomason, 1980). On paper this seems a feasible and logical exercise. However, in practice such an exercise is notoriously difficult because evaluating job content is essentially a *subjective* experience. Two main difficulties are encountered:

1 *The difficulty of observing*

Imagine being in the position of observing a job and assessing its complexity. The job might appear complex if it is unfamiliar. For example, to the observer who cannot drive, driving is likely to seem a very complex activity involving physical coordination, spatial awareness, concentration and quick decision-making. Yet for the seasoned driver it might not be viewed as a complex skill at all, not least because it is a widely-shared ability. This presents a paradox: a fair evaluation would necessitate the observer having a familiarity with the task, but this familiarity may lead the observer to under-value the task. In other words, there are problems with relying on observation because of the subjectivity of the observer.

2 *The difficulty of asking*

A possible alternative approach is to ask the person doing the job to identify its complexity. But this also poses problems for similar reasons: familiarity and adeptness may lead a person to under-value a task. As Attewell (1990: 430) argues:

> [Mundane activities] become socially invisible to both the actors performing them and to observers familiar with them . . . They become buried within their practitioners – either psychologically in the form of habits and non-conscious information-processing or somatically in muscles and neurons (knack, deftness and cunning).

This suggests that both observation and self-assessment would lead to a general conclusion that much of human activity in work (as well as outside) is not complex, and by implication, requires little skill. But, as Attewell points out, this is particularly ironic because when a person achieves a high level of competence, they have internalised procedures and routines such that they can accomplish the task 'without thinking'. For the novice, each situation and each problem is unique and uncertain and so he or she must apply conscious thought, but 'the maestro has been there before and has more (non-conscious) routines to apply' (Attewell, 1990: 433). To put this another way, beginners rely on abstract rules which have been derived by others, and they use these to guide their progress and accumulate experience; experts rely on context-bound knowledge that they have developed through experience, and are therefore less conscious of the decision-rules they are using.

In a similar vein, Manwaring and Wood (1985) identify the importance of considering 'tacit skills' (based upon the analysis of Polanyi and Prosch, 1975; Koestler, 1976; and Kusterer, 1978) to suggest that work necessarily involves the internalisation of learning so that tasks can be performed successfully by drawing on unconscious thought, and that different degrees of awareness are required both within and between jobs. The greater the frequency of unfamiliar situations, the less likely the adequacy of the existing routine, and so the greater the awareness required. From this perspective, it might be argued that skill is embedded in *all* jobs but tacit skills are taken for granted rather than being formally recognised.

A further illustration of this is the extent to which social skills generally remain unrecognised unless the job specifically requires direct social interaction with clients and customers (see Chapter 7 on emotion work). This is well illustrated by Burchell, Elliott, Rubery and Wilkinson (1994) who used a questionnaire survey to compare the perceptions of employees and managers regarding the skill content of a range of job categories. They found that the greatest divergence occurred over the perceptions of social and organisational skills needed for production and service jobs; managers rated the importance of these skills considerably lower than the employees who were actually doing the jobs.

In contrast, research into the work of customer service representatives (CSRs) in the financial services sector in Australia and Japan has revealed the increasing importance and recognition of social skills. Korczynski, Shire, Frenkel and Tam (1996) explored the everyday work of front line staff dealing with telephone queries from customers. They found that the social skills played a vital role in:

- establishing a rapport with the customer;
- assessing the attitude of the customer;
- persuading the customer to purchase a product.

In fact management at two of the three organisations studied recognised that social skills were so vital that they changed their recruitment policy – no longer selecting graduates but instead employing a range of people with social skills.

Findings such as these have an important contemporary relevance because although communication and cooperation have always been demanded by most work processes, social and organisational skills are increasing in importance through new employee relations policies such as teamworking, quality and empowerment, and the increase in customer-facing work through the expansion of the service sector (see Chapters 2 and 7). Employees may therefore be required increasingly to use tacit skills that have traditionally lain outside the wage-effort bargain.

Assessing the extent of discretion in jobs

An alternative way of assessing skill (although not necessarily mutually exclusive with complexity) is to examine it in relation to the *discretion* that employees can exercise when undertaking their jobs and hence the amount of control they have over their work. As shall be explored Chapter 6, this approach to the analysis of skill has been most closely associated with a perspective that argues that there is a general tendency under capitalism towards the deskilling of jobs (Braverman, 1974); but this debate can be postponed for the time being, because there are still a number of definitional problems to address.

Learning outcome 3b

Explain how to assess skill in the job using the concept of discretion.

The amount of discretion

Discretion is about choosing between alternative courses of action. The greater the amount of decisions required by an activity, then the greater the skill level. So the more an employee is able to exercise his or her judgement, then the more skilled a task may be said to be. In this way skill levels might be assessed by examining the amount of rules employees are obliged to follow: the more rules, the less scope for discretion and the lower their skill will be judged to be. This distinction between prescribed (rule-dominated) and discretionary (choice-dominated) work was first conceptualised by Jaques (1956 and 1967). While it is a useful schema, it must be treated with caution, as Fox (1974: 19–20) points out:

> It is easy to accept . . . that no work role can be totally discretionary. The occupant of the most elevated post has to operate within prescribed limits, usually a great many. It may be more difficult, however, to accept that all jobs contain discretionary as well as prescriptive elements. Surely many jobs in our kind of industrial society are *totally* prescribed; totally without discretion? Such a view cannot be sustained. However elaborate the external controlling structure of mechanical, administrative, technical or policy prescriptions, some residual element of discretion always remains. (emphasis in original)

This resonates with our earlier discussion about tacit skills, which argued that all jobs require discretion to be exercised, even though such discretion may not be identified by the job description or acknowledged in the reward system. The problem of using discretion as an indicator of skill is that we are focusing on the visible when many of the choices and judgements exercised in the work process remain invisible.

The time-span of discretion

A second concept identified by Jaques (1967) is the 'time-span of discretion'. This is the length of time that a person is allowed to exercise their discretion free from surveillance by superiors: the longer a person's period of autonomy, the higher their skill level. Again, however, this is somewhat limited in its usefulness as far as defining skill is concerned. A major problem with the time-span of discretion is that it fails to take into account the significance of the task and the consequences of making a mistake. For example, a gardener may be allocated a patch of land to tend and be left completely alone for long periods. He has few rules to follow and could work incompetently for weeks before it came to anyone's notice. Conversely, the anaesthetist exercises her judgement within a strict framework of rules and even a slight error will come to the attention of her work colleagues within minutes.

Discretion is also a misleading indicator because it fails to take fully into account the interdependence of many jobs in contemporary workplaces. The notion of discretion tends to evoke an image of a romanticised past reminiscent of the craft worker, which is really an inappropriate benchmark for current jobs. As Attewell

(1990: 443) argues, 'the ideal of the artisan conceiving an object, choosing tools and procedures unconstrained by external rules or routines, and fabricating the object from first to last step is so at odds with the reality of modern work that everyone today, from managers down, appears deskilled'.

TO SUM UP

The common theme that links the two notions of skill as *complexity* or *discretion* is that both approaches emphasise skill as being principally about the requirements of the job. From this perspective, skill is seen as an objective feature of work and therefore can be measured through an analysis of job content both in terms of technical complexity and discretionary requirements. Consequently, researchers tend to view skill as consisting of sub-components, each of which can be measured. A good example of this approach can be seen in Excerpt 5.2 – read it and then attempt Exercise 5.3 to test your understanding of this section.

EXCERPT 5.2

A model of skill in the job

Rolfe (1986 and 1990) has devised a model of skill consisting of six 'substructural' measures (see below). These are used to explore skill changes brought about by new technology affecting different occupational groups. Rolfe's approach is qualitative, so she does not develop quantitative measures of skill for the components. Her model is used to help direct her analysis and interpretation.

Technical complexity | 1 | complexity of tasks
| 2 | knowledge
| 3 | range and variety of tasks

Discretion | 4 | decision-making and judgement over product/process
| 5 | control over the organisation of work
| 6 | supervision

EXERCISE 5.3

What do *you* think?

Use Rolfe's model of skill (Excerpt 5.2) to analyse the jobs that you were asked to compare in exercise 5.1 at the beginning of the chapter. They are listed again below for your convenience.

▶

▶

It is important to be systematic in your analysis. Take each of the six components in turn and assess each pair of jobs.

- The hotel receptionist compared with the security guard
- The computer games software writer and the paramedic
- The cleaner and the car-park attendant
- The insurance broker and the travel agent
- The police officer and the social worker

Now consider these questions:

1 Have you arrived at different conclusions than your previous assessment of these jobs?

2 Was Rolfe's framework helpful? Explain why or why not.

3 Were there any problems in applying it?

4 Has it produced a more systematic and defensible set of conclusions about the comparative skill levels of the jobs than your first attempt? Explain why or why not.

Learning outcome 4

Explain how to assess skill in the setting using the concept of social closure.

Skill in the setting

An assumption underpinning both the 'skill in the job' and the 'skill in the person' approaches is that the concept of skill can be objectively defined. But both approaches can be criticised for being overly rational because they often ignore the historical development of skill. Conceptions of skill are not dispassionately developed on blank pieces of paper; they are socially and politically negotiated over time, and reflect the power and influence of diverse interest groups. This has been the case because skill is considered a measure of worth (both social and economic). As Sadler (1970: 23) has observed, skill is

> to a considerable extent determined by social factors present in the work situation and in the occupational culture at large ... [and therefore includes] the evaluations placed on particular kinds of activity and on particular classes of individual and the actions of organised pressure groups directed at safeguarding the earnings and job security of particular trades and professions.

Consequently, to understand skill it is important to examine the setting in which the valuation of skill is negotiated.

As a starting point of the analysis, it is important to consider one of the fundamental concepts of sociology as defined by Weber (1947) and elaborated by Parkin (1979) and Kreckel (1980). This is the notion of 'social closure' whereby people with a shared interest protect themselves by acting collectively to form a group that is in some way demarcated. Entry to the group is regulated by the existing members, thus they may chose to exclude or include outsiders depending on whether it serves their interests.

> Whether a relationship is open or closed may be determined traditionally, affectually, or rationally in terms of values or of expediency. It is especially likely to be closed, for rational reasons, in the following type of situation: a social relationship may provide the parties to it with opportunities for the satisfaction of various interests, whether the satisfactions be spiritual or material, whether the interest be in the end of the relationship as such or in some ulterior consequence of participation, or whether it is achieved through co-operative action or by a compromise of interests. If the participants expect that the admission of others will lead to an improvement of their situation, and improvement in degree, in kind, in the security or the value of the satisfaction, their interest will be in keeping the relationship open. If, on the other hand, their expectations are of improving their position by monopolistic tactics, their interest is in a closed relationship. (Weber, 1947: 127–8)

In the case of an occupational group, social closure provides the means of establishing a position at least partially autonomous of labour market competition. Instead of being exposed to the vagaries of the free market, the group is united by a 'consciousness of difference' (Weber, 1947: 127) and a willingness to act to regulate itself and influence market forces. This process of achieving occupational social closure is vital in establishing skilled status, and the next section explores it in more detail.

Social closure and skilled status

The overall process of occupational social closure is composed of three interacting sub-processes:

1 an *ideological* process, whereby individuals recognise a shared set of values and beliefs, and reinforce these symbolically;
2 a *political* process, whereby group members act collectively, combining their resources in pursuit of common goals. There will remain a plurality of interests within the group, but they have a mutual interest in combining together and institutionalising their relationship (for example, in the membership of a trade union);
3 a *material* process, whereby members of the group seek to appropriate the tools and technology of the work process and to control or (at least) to influence the work organisation.

These processes are represented by a diagram (see Figure 5.1) and are described in more detail.

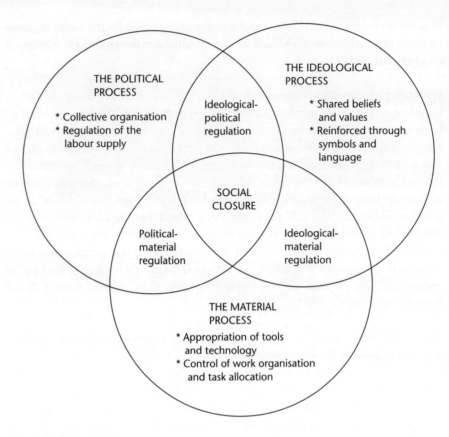

THE POLITICAL
PROCESS

* Collective organisation
* Regulation of the
labour supply

Ideological-
political
regulation

THE IDEOLOGICAL
PROCESS

* Shared beliefs
and values
* Reinforced through
symbols and
language

SOCIAL
CLOSURE

Political-
material
regulation

Ideological-
material
regulation

THE MATERIAL
PROCESS

* Appropriation of tools
and technology
* Control of work organisation
and task allocation

Figure 5.1 The processes of social closure

The ideological process

A key component of social closure is the shared beliefs and values of the occupational group. In this respect the group can be characterised as a sub-culture seeking to establish and ring-fence its separate identity (Turner, 1971). One of the most important ways that the group maintains this distinct identity is through the manipulation of occupational language and symbols. For a group wishing to lay claim to skilled status, it allows opportunity to mystify the work, obscuring the mundane activities and portraying an image of complexity. Language acts as a particularly important regulatory device because it can be used both to exclude and include. In this sense it demarcates the in-group from the out-group – it draws a line between 'us' and 'them'. Thus, being able to talk in occupational argot and jargon symbolises membership of the group by identifying those who have accrued enough experience and familiarity with the occupation to speak and understand the exclusive language. For example, many people have encountered the techno-speak of computer technicians – an impenetrable jargon that is meaningful to them but simply bemuses others.

New entrants to an occupation are quickly reminded by language that they are on the periphery. For example, newcomers in an engineering plant might be sent for the 'long stand', the 'long weight' (wait) or the left-handed screwdriver – thereby exposing their naivety and lack of familiarity with the setting. Symbolic regulation is similarly enacted through rituals, rites of passage, initiation ceremonies, humour and other forms of social control – examples of these are explored in Chapter 9 (see also Excerpt 5.3).

The political process

As well as the shared values and beliefs leading to a collective identity, a group must support this through its own representative body that allows members of the occupation to organise and act collectively. Typically it has been trade unions and professional associations that have performed this role (see Chapter 11 on representation at work for a full discussion). Such organisations reveal that the occupational group has a collective interest that is different from, and separate to that of the organisation where members of the occupation are employed. In other words, it suggests that in some instances employees have a dual commitment: to the employing organisation and to the body that represents their occupation (the trade union or professional association). In some instances this poses particular dilemmas. For example, a hospital doctor may wish to prescribe a particular drug or treatment because it is in the best interests of the patient, but might also be conscious of the high financial cost to the hospital of doing so, with the resultant loss of treatment for other patients. The doctor's professional commitment (to provide the best care for the particular patient) conflicts with his or her organisational commitment (to use hospital resources effectively to care for patients in general).

The occupation's representative body also plays a key role in regulating the supply of labour. This is important if the members of an occupational group wish to create a premium price for their work. In normal circumstances the scarcity of appropriately 'skilled' employees will push up the wage that an employer is willing to pay to secure their labour power. Restricting the availability of labour is therefore in the interest of an occupational group. The control of supply has traditionally occurred through the regulation of entry into the occupation. To regulate entry, for example, a trade union typically sought in the past to establish a 'closed shop' (also known as a 'union shop' in the US), which obliged employers to offer work only to workers who held union cards and were therefore deemed appropriately skilled to be able to accomplish the work safely and with competence. By limiting membership to those who were appropriately qualified, the union could control the labour supply. It could also impose sanctions on members who broke union rules or acted against the interest of co-workers, by suspending their membership and consequently preventing their continued employment. Similarly, professional groups, such as lawyers, doctors and accountants also operate a type of 'closed shop' (although they do not use this term) because to practise one has to have passed the exams set by the profession and be a member of the relevant professional association.

Overall, the control of supply helps to build skilled status by restricting the size of the occupation, thereby conferring on it the notion that only those with special ability can do the job. Coupled with this is the increased price of labour which suggests work of special value, thus further reinforcing the status of the job.

The material process

In addition to controlling entry, occupational groups also need to control or exert influence over the way the work is accomplished. This can be achieved through two routes. First, the organisation of the work and the allocation of tasks. This means regulating which person is allowed to undertake particular jobs. Traditionally this has encouraged demarcation whereby specific employees are limited to certain tasks according to their level of training and seniority. The second route is by appropriating the tools and technology associated with the work. This means that the workgroup seeks to control how the technology is put to use, and to prevent access to it by other groups. Penn (1985: 121) expresses it as follows:

> Skilled manual workers in mechanised factory milieux are defined by their high degree of social control over the operation and utilisation of machinery. These exclusive controls involve a double exclusion, both of the management from the direct or complete control over the labour process and of other workers who offer a potential threat to such controls.

In other instances appropriation involves redefining the tools or technology (see Excerpt 5.3 for a good example). However, the recent emphasis on functional flexibility and teamworking, whereby employees are expected to be able to undertake a wider variety of tasks, potentially undermines the material process of social closure because it widens access to particular tasks among the existing workforce. Nevertheless, as we shall see in Chapter 9, employees find creative ways to reassert their influence over work processes, so control of the material process continues to be a relevant tactic for contemporary employees.

EXCERPT 5.3

The symbols of skill in everyday occupations

There is symbolism embedded in the 'tools of the trade' which help to differentiate an occupational group and allow claims to skilled status. This is particularly well illustrated by the case of construction workers discussed by Steiger (1993). Combining his findings with the work of Riemer (1977) and Applebaum (1981) he argues that owning and being able to use the 'tools of the trade' properly is an important feature of defining skill, not least because the tools – and by definition the skills one possesses – are in full view. Common tools, such as the shovel used by the labourer, are looked down upon whereas more specialised tools carry skill status. 'Rarity is important because . . . only "rare" specialised tools are emblematic of skill. That rarity is important should be of no surprise in a capitalist economy' (Steiger, 1993: 555).

Interestingly, Steiger also cites the example of plumbers for whom technological advances (such as the advent of plastic piping) have reduced the need for specialist tools. The plumbers' response has been to shift the emphasis away from the tools on to their ingenuity and ability to improvise. In this sense, their occupational closure has

▶

▶become symbolised not through the visibility of tools (which are readily available to anyone) but through the invisible 'know-how' which only the 'skilled' plumber has acquired. This is particularly noteworthy because it takes us back to our earlier discussion of tacit skills. The plumbers are elevating the importance of their embedded knowledge that cannot be appropriated by others, or replaced by new technologies.

TO SUM UP

In order for an occupational group to lay claim to skilled status it must establish its separateness and distinctiveness. It can achieve this through engaging in the three processes of social closure outlined above – ideological, political and material. These three processes operate concurrently and are mutually reinforcing, but social closure is achieved only when *all three* processes are enacted.

Social closure or social regulation?

An important point to note is that social closure is an ongoing process that changes over time. Just as groups can build upon the ideological, political and material processes to construct closure, they can also lose closure through the neglect or undermining of one or more of the processes. In other words, groups may display forms of *social regulation* which fall short of social closure. This is illustrated by the intersections in Figure 5.1, and they constitute three different types:

■ *political-material regulation*, where a group has a representative body that influences the labour supply, the organisation of work and the use of technology in the workplace, but does not share a collective identity through a common set of values;

■ *ideological-material regulation*, where a group shares an identity through a common set of values, influences the organisation of work and the use of technology in the workplace, but has no representative body and cannot control the supply of labour;

■ *ideological-political regulation*, where a group shares an identity, and has a representative body that influences the labour supply, but cannot influence the organisation of work and the use of technology within the workplace.

The introduction of new technology is typically seen as a development that can affect all three of the processes. It can challenge the ideological process by breaking down traditional lines of demarcation between tasks, and thereby blurring the boundaries between occupational groups and their separate identities. It can influence the political process by forcing a reappraisal of the qualifications and training needed to undertake the work (thereby affecting the labour supply). And it can reconfigure the material process by redesigning the jobs and requiring the use of different equipment and tools.

It is upon full social closure that a group bases its claim to skilled status, although social regulation provides opportunities for constructing difference on which claims to a skilled identity can then be built. Now attempt Exercise 5.4.

EXERCISE 5.4

What do *you* think?

Choose an occupation from the list below and assess the extent to which it has achieved social closure. Use Figure 5.1 to guide your analysis.

If the occupation has not achieved full social closure, which type of social regulation has it achieved?

- Accountant
- School teacher
- Journalist
- Fire fighter
- Hotel receptionist
- Website designer
- Personnel/human resource manager
- Refuse collector
- Minister of religion
- Nanny
- Taxi driver
- Actor

You might want to repeat this exercise several times to see the differences between occupational groups. You could also try it out on any other occupation or job with which you are familiar.

Strong and weak social construction of skill

There is a further question that needs to be considered: is skilled status *solely* a product of social construction, or do objective (technical) factors also have an effect? In addressing this question, Littler (1982) argues that the social construction theory of skill can occur in either a strong or weak form.

- In the *strong* form, skilled status can be achieved through social closure without necessarily any inherent task complexity or knowledge (a position originally put forward by Turner, 1962). In such a scenario, the power of the workgroup and the ability to act collectively is more important than their technical knowledge.

The 'talking up' of the skilled nature of the work is therefore crucial to its construction as a skilled job.

■ In the *weak* form (exemplified by More, 1980 and 1982) technical skill (complexity and knowledge) is a necessary basis for socially constructing skilled status. However, this does not guarantee the attainment of skilled status, so the occupational group must enact social closure and develop a collective power base. In other words, technical skill is simply the starting point.

In addition, Attewell (1990) identifies a third form which acknowledges that skilled status can be achieved with or without technical skills being present (in this sense it combines the strong and weak forms). However, there is an important caveat which points to the dynamics of the process: if skilled status is achieved in the absence of technical skill, the status itself provides the opportunity over a period of time for the occupational group to appropriate technical skill and thereby strengthen its claim to skilled status.

So far, the discussion has focused upon how skill definitions are constructed by occupational groups. However, there is a far more pervasive impact of social construction which raises some serious issues concerning fairness and equality.

Gender and skill: the social construction of disadvantage

It is possible to argue that a form of social closure exists which centres not on occupational group, but on gender. The evidence suggests that just as an occupational group may seek to construct a notion of skill in its own interest, so too have men acted as a social group; they have constructed skill in such a way as to benefit their own gender and to disadvantage women. To substantiate such a statement, we need to examine the evidence built up by academics who argue that all analysis of work must explore gender as a central and integral factor (see in particular, Bradley, 1989; Walby, 1986). As a framework to locate our arguments, we will use the three interlinking processes discussed above: the ideological, political and material processes of social closure.

Gender and the ideological process

Underpinning the concept of skill is an ideology of gender which labels certain attitudes and forms of behaviour as masculine and others as feminine. These identities are perpetuated not just in the workplace, but throughout the whole of society (although they may vary slightly from culture to culture) and result in the stereotypes we hold about what constitutes being a man or being a woman. It is not surprising, therefore, that work is a domain which similarly reinforces these images. It has already been suggested in Chapter 3 that work provides people with a social identity; thus it can be a domain for the expression of gender. As Matthaei (1982: 194) found, 'a basic force behind sex-typing of jobs was the workers' desires to assert and reaffirm their manhood or womanhood and hence their difference from the opposite sex'.

Learning outcome 5a

Appreciate how skill can be seen as a socially constructed phenomenon that has disadvantaged women through ideological processes.

Jobs therefore tend to be associated with attributes of gender stereotypes which reflect (and reinforce) dominant cultural beliefs about male and female. For example, jobs requiring physical strength, stamina, or logical thought have traditionally been considered men's jobs, because those are attributes supposedly possessed by men, while women, allegedly being innately sensitive, patient and dextrous, have been cast as suitable for caring, boring, repetitive and intricate work.

The source of this belief is the view that a work role is a reflection of a 'natural' ability, in other words, determined by and constrained by biology. For example, in Cockburn's study of printworkers (1983: 171–90) the men argued that their job was not suitable for a woman and offered a number of commonly-held views as to why women could not and should not do *their* work:

- women lacked the strength;
- there was too much standing involved;
- they lacked the mental ability;
- they did not have the right temperament (aversion to technical work);
- they were too temperamental (emotional, bursting into tears);
- they were unreliable (because of menstruation);
- they would be exposed to bad moral influences (swearing, horseplay, vulgarity);
- they would force men to behave differently.

For the printworkers, women represented a threat because their entry into the occupation challenged the ideology of what constituted male work:

> It's man's work. If you hear of a man secretary, a lot of people raise a few eyebrows. Well, it's the same with a woman working alongside a man doing *his* job ... if I said to my mates I was working with a woman, they would feel, say, oh, he's doing a woman's job – because they can see that a woman *can* do it. (A compositor quoted by Cockburn, 1983: 180, emphasis in original)

Similarly, a Transport and General Workers Union shop steward at an electrical components factory in Britain is quoted by Charles (1986: 163):

> There's been a great increase in humdrum jobs like the jobs here, that you wouldn't get a man doing ... But the women can sit at a bench eight hours and pick up little fiddly screws and put them in. I think it's fantastic, and they can go for week in week out, you know – but you'll never get a man doing it, so that's why you need ... women working.

But such opinions are not exclusive to men. Consider, for example, the views of these women quoted by Pollert (1981: 99) in her study of a tobacco factory:

> Kate (stripping room): I can't imagine a man doing my work. It's too boring for a man. Women have much more patience.

Gale: Men'd go mad. It'd kill them with boredom! Girls are expected to do that kind of thing. Girls are thought to be the weaker sex.

In white-collar work, there is similar evidence of sex stereotyping of skill. A vivid example of this is provided by Collinson and Knights (1986) whose case study of an insurance company reveals how the male managers manipulated the setting (the work organisation), the recruitment process, selection criteria, and rationale for promotion to segregate the office according to gender, and to justify this in terms of business rationale. The effect was to produce a subordinate situation for women, which is then used against them and rationalised as being a product of their gender. To illustrate this, consider the quotes below (taken from Collinson and Knights, 1986: 155, 158, 162, 165).

Branch manager: Women aren't taken seriously in the insurance world. It can be a soul-destroying job. Inspectors have to advise our professional clients who recommend insurance and pensions to their clients and we want them to recommend us. Yes, it can be a soul-destroying job, and women are either not hard-bitten enough to ride off insults or those that can are pretty unpleasant people.

Office manager: My job is to keep them [the female clerical staff] as busy as possible . . . You can't keep all six happy at the same time. With some you can tell their monthly changes, even the other girls say so. Sometimes when they're having a good chunner [moan] about the inspectors I have to impress on the girls that if it was not for the men, there'd be no jobs for them, if the blokes don't go out and sell insurance.

Personnel officer, Head Office: The door is always open to move into the career structure, but we've found by and large, they're girls who are not particularly ambitious, looking forward to getting married, leaving and having a family and that's about the measure of it.

Senior pensions clerk: I'm very temperamental, you see. This is another thing Mr Brown [the branch manager] drew to my attention. I can get annoyed very easily and I also get strong moods. He said 'There's no way you could go out to a broker with some of the moods you have'.

The assumption frequently made is that work is not a central life interest for women. Research evidence reported in Chapter 3 suggests this is a false assumption when comparing the work orientations of men and women in *full-time* work. However, the view persists that the central life interest for all women is the family (either their existing one or the prospect of one) and hence they are considered more willing to tolerate boring, repetitive jobs with low career prospects and little responsibility. But we should not overlook the circularity of this argument: are women allocated tedious work because they are perceived to have a lower work orientation than men, or might it be that they have a lower work orientation *because* they only have access to boring, repetitive, low paid, undervalued jobs? Further, not only does stereotyping of men's work and women's work preordain the type and range of jobs that either gender are supposedly able to do competently, it also disadvantages women in terms of the valuation of 'women's work'. The argument is summed up by Jenson (1989) who identifies the way work performed by women tends to be seen as involving some natural female 'talent', whereas work done by men is viewed as involving a learned skill.

EXCERPT 5.4

Gender and skill

The critical importance of gender in defining skill was first explored in a keynote article by Phillips and Taylor (1986). They conclude, 'it is the sex of those who do the work, rather than its content, which leads to its identification as skilled or unskilled' (1986: 63). In arriving at this position they bring out two important issues which help to identify the importance of the ideological process of social closure:

1 Where men and women work in similar processes, doing jobs of similar content, men are more likely to achieve skilled status. The research of Rubery and Wilkinson (1979) into box and carton manufacture is used to illustrate this point. The production of cartons and paper boxes involves a similar process except that whilst box production involves exclusively female labour, carton manufacture is undertaken by men and women. The latter is recognised as semi-skilled; the former as unskilled. Similarly, Spradley and Mann (1975) reveal that the work of waitresses is equally as demanding of a range of abilities as the work of bartenders, yet, unlike the (male) bartenders, the waitresses do not enjoy skilled status.

2 Where new work processes were introduced allowing employers to deem some jobs 'female' from the outset, the work tended to be classified as low-skilled, 'not simply by virtue of the skills required for it but by virtue of the "inferior" status of the women who came to perform it' (Phillips and Taylor, 1986: 61).

In an excellent analysis of women's work in a range of industries, Bradley (1989) argues that the hosiery industry provides the best example of the feminisation of an occupation, whereby women are brought in not directly to take over the work of men, but to work on newly reorganised and degraded work processes. Thus, women are at a disadvantage from the outset: 'The work of women is often deemed inferior simply because it is women who do it. Women workers carry into the workplace their status as subordinate individuals, and this status comes to define the value of the work they do.' (Phillips and Taylor, 1986: 55)

The contemporary pattern in the occupational structure is a general under-valuation of jobs where women predominate, with this disadvantage frequently institutionalised and consolidated by job evaluation schemes that either fail to recognise all the attributes of jobs mainly performed by women, or else value such attributes lower than comparable work mainly performed by men (Horrell, Rubery and Burchell, 1994; Neathey, 1992; Steinberg, 1990). The overall effect is a relatively lower pay rate for jobs where women predominate. For example, job evaluation schemes typically rate fiscal responsibility (for example, devising budgets or counting cash) higher than social responsibility (for example, caring for the sick or minding young children). Indeed, we will explore later (Chapter 7) how social skills are often taken for granted and frequently undervalued by employers. Another example: physical strength (a supposed male natural ability) is often rated higher than dexterity (a supposed female natural ability). The danger is that the evaluation process is widely considered to be fair because it is seen as an *objective* measure of skill – but, as noted earlier in this chapter, such an assumption is naive.

So, in Steinberg's words, 'job evaluation systems...have been constructed to embed cultural assumptions about what constitutes skilled and responsible work in a way that significantly benefits men through the work they have historically performed' (1990: 454). They institutionalise and perpetuate the ideology of masculine and feminine work, and in this way assist in the ideological process of social closure.

Gender and the political process

Learning outcome 5b

Appreciate how skill can be seen as a socially constructed phenomenon that has disadvantaged women through political processes.

In many settings men have been proactive in seeking to protect and differentiate their skills from those of women. The situation is summed up well by Steinberg (1990: 476):

Skill determinations are socially constructed in highly political contexts, in which males – whether employers or employees – exert considerably more power to maintain their definitions of skill...Struggles over the meaning of skill between employers and (primarily male) employees have been frequent, bitter, and hard fought. When employees have won, males have maintained their skill designations and wage rates, even in the face of the deterioration of job content. When employees have lost...skill designations are lowered, wage rates deteriorate, and male employees exit to be replaced by women.

As work processes have changed, men have sought to hold on to their skilled status. Often this has been to the detriment of women (as we elaborate below) such that 'skill has been increasingly defined against women – skilled work is work that women don't do' (Phillips and Taylor, 1986: 63).

Trade unions have played an important role in this political process in providing the means by which male workers can organise and exclude women from their trades (Hartmann, 1979). At no time was this more evident than during and after the First World War. In the period leading up to the war, British Government officials secured an agreement with union leaders to allow a temporary dilution of skilled labour in munitions and other industries related to the war effort ('dilution of skill' referring to workers who had not served apprenticeships undertaking tasks previously performed by skilled workers). With so many men having volunteered, and later been conscripted into the army, this skill dilution opened up opportunities for women to undertake work formerly the preserve of male skilled workers, and at pay rates comparable to the skilled rates. However, as part of this agreement between Government and unions, it was also agreed that customary practices over the hiring of skilled workers would be restored after the war – thus, the skill dilution and the opportunities this provided for many women was, for the vast majority, short-lived (Ursell and Blyton, 1988: 109).

The historical analysis of gender relations in employment by Walby leads her to conclude that 'from the last quarter of the nineteenth century an increasing proportion of trade unions used grading and segregation as their response to women's employment, rather than the exclusionary strategy . . . It is almost never the case that a union which included men did not follow one of these two patriarchal strategies' (1986: 244). Thus the political process of organising through trade unions has acted to the detriment of women in terms of both access to 'skilled' work, and the attainment of skilled status for jobs where women predominate. Furthermore, research shows that the domination of the male agenda persists within trade unions, and that 'a wide gap exists between what the unions claim for women and what they deliver, but more to the point, between what they claim and what they *attempt* to deliver' (Cunnison and Stageman, 1995: 237–8, emphasis in original).

Gender and the material process

Learning outcome 5c

Appreciate how skill can be seen as a socially constructed phenomenon that has disadvantaged women through material processes.

Cockburn (1983, 1985 and 1986) explores the importance of material aspects of male domination. Through this she is able to identify the way that men appropriate the tools and technology which gives them an advantage in constructing notions of what constitutes skilled work. Her argument is based on the importance of two related concepts: physical effectivity and technical effectivity.

Physical effectivity

The first part of Cockburn's argument is that the physical differences between men and women are often exaggerated to the benefit of men. Obviously there are biological differences between men and women but these limit either gender in only a very small range of tasks – most of which are not work based. Similarly, there are physical differences in average height and body weight, but again these are not necessarily impediments to most jobs. Gender differences are encouraged through childhood and socialisation – men being expected to participate in physical activities, women in sedentary endeavours. As a consequence, men, on average, attain physical effectivity to a greater extent than women.

Technical effectivity

The second part of Cockburn's argument concerns the appropriation of technical effectivity: familiarity with and control over machinery and tools. As noted above, such control is important in constructing a skill identity. Cockburn argues that men have historically acquired control over the design of technology and work processes, and as a consequence this perpetuates existing patterns of dominance. As Wajcman (1991: 41) puts it, 'men selectively design tools and machinery to match their technical skills. Machinery is designed by men with men in mind. Industrial technology thus reflects male power as well as capitalist domination.' This does not necessarily imply an organised conspiracy against women by men, but it certainly reflects a gender-centricity resulting in some machinery and tools being too bulky or heavy for the 'average' woman. There are exceptions to this which prove that alternative approaches are available. Clarke (1989), for example, shows how the increased availability of female labour in Sweden prompted Volvo to invest in the design of tools ergonomically suited for the 'average' woman, and to develop hydraulic lifting devices to lessen the physical requirements of vehicle assembly. But such examples remain rare.

Generally, technical effectivity is sustained through an ideology that perpetuates the notion that men are technically more competent than women. Nowhere is this more evident than the division of labour in the home (see for example, Oakley, 1974 and 1982; Pahl, 1984). Cockburn vividly portrays this in a chapter entitled 'The kitchen, the tool shed' (1985: 198–224) – essential reading to appreciate fully the subtlety of her argument. She illustrates how men not only acquire technical effectivity through work but can use this to improve their social standing in the community, through, for example, being the person who can fix cars or do some rewiring. Women, on the other hand, are discouraged from transporting any technical skills into the home. A woman may use pliers, screwdrivers, Allen keys and a soldering iron at work, but at home these are almost invariably kept for the exclusive use of men, and are locked in the tool shed. Acutely aware of the benefits of technical effectivity in constructing advantage, men jealously guard their knowledge:

> Men's know-how is seldom passed by men to women as a cost-free gift, taught in a serious, generous and genuine way. Often it is hoarded behind a cachet of professional knowledge or craft skill and handed out sparingly, reluctantly. Sometimes it is dispensed from a great height and purposefully used to put women down. (Cockburn, 1985: 202–3.)

The two components of physical and technical effectivity constitute the material of male power. As Cockburn (1986: 97–8) argues, 'the process...involves several converging practices: accumulation of bodily capabilities, the definition of tasks to match them and the selective design of tools and machines'. It is an important argument because it demonstrates how the material power base, constructed historically, is perpetuated to the benefit of men.

TO SUM UP

Through exploring the ideological, political and material processes, it is possible to see how skill has been constructed in a way that advantages men. In particular, the work of Cockburn demonstrates the way men have (in some occupations) appropriated

▶

▶ technology through ideological, political and material means and use it to define their own work as skilled and women's work as unskilled. In this sense, there is an on-going process of gendered social closure. This is embedded in the power of occupational groups and their institutions and the patriarchal structures of management. Finally, try to apply these concepts by attempting Exercise 5.5.

EXERCISE 5.5

What do *you* think?

Return to the occupations listed in Exercise 5.4. Select one of the occupations and then use the framework of the three processes (ideological, political and material) to evaluate whether there is evidence of gendered closure. Repeat the exercise several times because evidence will vary according to which occupation you select.

You should then compare your analysis with that of other students.

Conclusion

The controversy surrounding skill is likely to continue as long as there remain different theoretical perspectives from which to look at the problem of what skill is and how (or if) it can be measured. Once again, it demonstrates the importance of acknowledging the plurality of approaches to a particular problem. By exploring the diversity of meanings, this chapter has been able to explain the principal competing interpretations of skill. Instead of suggesting there is one way of looking, the analysis has explored different angles and produced a more complex picture with greater depth. As the different viewpoints have been brought into focus, so new aspects of the notion of skill come into sharp relief.

As has been shown, the social construction of skill can be used to integrate the different approaches because it provides a framework for understanding the way both technical (objective) measures and social (subjective) meanings of skill can be negotiated. In other words, skill is constructed by drawing on meanings that incorporate all three foci explored above: the person, the job and the setting. These provide the resources that allow the claim to skilled status to be made. Attainment of this claim, however, depends on the successful enactment of the political, ideological and material processes of social closure.

The concept of skill is important because it has wide ramifications. It has been shown how it has been used by different interest groups to lay claim to status, special treatment and higher rewards. In particular, it was noted how this has impacted on the gender division of labour with a dramatic under-valuing of the work of women.

There is a further issue that remains unanswered: to what extent might there be a general historical shift in the nature of skill? Might skill be hard to define because work is continually changing and demanding different abilities? And if such a change can be detected, in which direction is it heading? Are people becoming less skilled or more skilled? These are the questions that lie at the heart of the next chapter.

6 Work routines and skill change

CHAPTER AIM

To explain the dominant forms of work organisation and explore competing theories of skill change.

LEARNING OUTCOMES

After reading and understanding this chapter you will be able to:

1 describe the main features of Taylorism and assess their relevance to contemporary work;

2 describe the methods and application of Fordism;

3 explain the theory behind the deskilling thesis;

4 outline and evaluate the main criticisms of the deskilling thesis;

5 explain the theory behind the upskilling thesis;

6 outline and evaluate the main criticisms of the upskilling thesis;

7 describe alternative approaches to examining skill change;

8 use the work categorisation framework to analyse jobs;

9 explain the relationship between skill change and work organisation paradigms.

Introduction

This chapter addresses a puzzle that has occupied the minds of researchers and theorists for decades: whether the fundamental shifts that have been occurring in the overall nature of work are causing people to experience either deskilling and degrading, or upskilling and enrichment, of their working lives. We have previously noted (in Chapter 2) some of the structural changes occurring in patterns of employment, but here we assess the impact of these broader employment dynamics by focusing on the nature of work tasks. To explore these issues, the chapter is divided into five sections. The first examines two dominant traditions in work organisation – Taylorism and Fordism – using contemporary examples to illustrate the central principles of each. This provides the basis for the next three sections, each of which examines a different perspective on how work is changing: the deskilling thesis, the upskilling antithesis, and the attempts to synthesise these contrasting approaches. The fifth section of the chapter develops a conceptual framework to integrate the analysis.

Dominant traditions of work organisation: Taylorism and Fordism

Routine work in the service sector – burgers and Taylor

Imagine the scene: you are visiting a city for the first time; it is lunchtime and you are feeling hungry; you do not have much money to spend on food; and you only have 30 minutes before your train leaves. As you look along the busy, unfamiliar street you recognise a sign in the distance: a large yellow letter 'M'. A sense of relief overwhelms you as you head for that emporium of American pulp cuisine: McDonald's. Any uncertainty and anxiety has been replaced by the predictability of the McDonald's experience: no matter where you are, you will get the standard tasting burger, covered with the same relish, lodged in the same bun, served in the same packaging for consumption in the familiar decor of the restaurant. Consistency is McDonald's strong selling point – you know exactly what you are going to get when you order your Big Mac and large fries, in any one of McDonald's 28,700 outlets in 120 countries. Of course, to guarantee such a standardised product, the work processes as well as the food have all been standardised. So leaving aside the issue of the product itself, how can we characterise and understand work at organisations like McDonald's?

If we use a metaphor, we can describe McDonald's as a well-maintained machine in almost every aspect of its operations, from the customer interface to the centralised planning and financial control (Morgan, 1986). Employees at McDonald's (or 'crew members' as they are called) are treated as components of this machine. Each receives simple training to perform a number of tasks which require little judgement and leave little room for discretion. Crew members are given precise instructions on what to say, what to do, and how to do it. They are the necessary

Learning outcome 1

Describe the main features of Taylorism and assess their relevance to contemporary work.

'living' labour, joining the precisely-timed, computer-controlled equipment, that cook the burgers, fry the potatoes, dispense the drinks, heat the pies, record the order and calculate the customer's change.

> Much of the food prepared at McDonald's arrives at the restaurant pre-formed, pre-cut, pre-sliced and pre-prepared, often by non-human technologies. This serves to drastically limit what employees need to do...McDonald's has developed a variety of machines to control its employees. When a worker must decide when a glass is full and the soft-drink dispenser needs to be shut off, there is always the risk that the worker may be distracted and allow the glass to overflow. Thus a sensor has been developed that automatically shuts off the soft-drink dispenser when the glass is full. (Ritzer, 1993: 105–6)

This logic of automation is extended to all the processes, with the consequence that the employees push buttons, respond to bleeps and buzzers and repeat stock phrases to customers like subjects in a bizarre Pavlovian experiment. The dehumanising effects can often be seen in the glazed expressions of the young people who serve. But the most poignant, if not ironic, aspects of all this is that one of the world's most successful multi-national corporations at the beginning of the 21st century relies on labour management techniques that were developed at the beginning of the 20th century. Indeed, the pioneer of 'scientific management', F.W. Taylor, would have certainly recognised and endorsed the principles of rationality upon which McDonald's is organised.

EXERCISE 6.1

What do *you* think?

Managers at the global fast food chain, McDonald's, have begun to recognise that they may have gone too far in adopting the sort of standardisation associated with Taylorism. The crew members (the employees) in all McDonald's restaurants have been obliged to greet and say goodbye to all customers in the same manner, according to a set script. However, McDonald's research revealed that customers disliked this, and as a result crew can now speak to customers however they want – within accepted boundaries of politeness, of course. The managers of McDonald's describe this as empowerment.

1 Are McDonald's right to move away from this aspect of standardisation? Why, or why not?

2 Is the abandonment of standardised scripts really 'empowerment' for the crew members?

3 Should other aspects of McDonald's be less standardised?

4 What are the advantages and disadvantages of standardisation?

F. W. Taylor's guiding principles

The ideas of Taylor have been well documented elsewhere (see for example, Kelly, 1982; Littler, 1982; Rose, 1988) so it is necessary here only to reiterate the central principles, to see how closely aligned the contemporary work processes at McDonald's are to concepts that were originally published in 1911. Efficiency was Taylor's guiding obsession. His own work experience as an engineer led him to believe there was an optimum way of performing any job: the 'one best way'. It was the task of management to discover this through the application of rigorous scientific testing which involved breaking all activities down into their smallest components, and systematically analysing each step. No activity was too complex or too mundane to be subjected to this scientific analysis, argued Taylor (see Excerpt 6.1).

Having discovered the 'one best way' of performing a task, management's responsibility was to allocate tasks to employees, attempting to fit the right person to each job. The employee should have the requisite skills, acquired through systematic training, to complete the task at hand, and no more than those required by the job.

EXCERPT 6.1

Applying scientific management

Taylor illustrates his theory with the example of managing pig-iron handling and shovelling.

'Probably the most important element in the science of shoveling is this: There must be some shovel load at which a first-class shoveler will do his biggest day's work. What is that load?...Under scientific management the answer to this question is not a matter of anyone's opinion; it is a question for accurate, careful, scientific investigation. Under the old system you would call in a first-rate shoveler and say, "See here, Pat, how much ought you to take on at one shovel load?" And if a couple of fellows agreed, you would say that's about the right load and let it go at that. But under scientific management absolutely every element in the work of every man in your establishment, sooner or later, becomes the subject of exact, precise, scientific investigation and knowledge to replace the old, "I believe so," and "I guess so." Every motion, every small fact becomes the subject of careful, scientific investigation.' (Taylor, 1911: 51–2)

'Now one of the very first requirements for a man who is fit to handle pig iron as a regular occupation is that he shall be so stupid and so phlegmatic that he more nearly resembles in his mental make-up the ox than any other type. The man who is mentally alert and intelligent is for this reason entirely unsuited to what would, for him, be the grinding monotony of work of this character. Therefore the workman who is best suited to handling pig iron is unable to understand the real science of doing this class of work. He is so stupid that the word 'percentage' has no meaning to him, and he must consequently be trained by a man more intelligent than himself into the habit of working in accordance with the laws of this science before he can be successful.' (Taylor, 1911: 59)

Emerging from Taylor's principles of organising the work process is a distinctive managerial ideology in which four themes dominate:

1 *Division of labour*: this involves the separation of manual work (the doing) from mental work (the thinking). By removing from the employee any discretion over the organisation and execution of work, managers are able to secure control over the method and pace of working. As we shall see, this can have important consequences for determining the skill definition of a work activity.

2 *Planning*: managers play an important role in planning each activity to ensure that it is in line with business objectives. In pursuit of these objectives, employees are to be used dispassionately, along with capital equipment and raw materials, in the search for greater efficiency, productivity and profitability. As a consequence, rigorous selection and training of people (to inculcate required behaviours) become critical management functions.

3 *Surveillance*: based on the assumption that people cannot be trusted to perform their jobs diligently, there needs to be control through close supervision and monitoring of all work activities. Hierarchies of authority are constructed giving legitimacy to surveillance, and simultaneously constructing a 'division of management' (Littler, 1982: 53).

4 *Performance-related pay*: Taylor's deeply-entrenched belief was that people were essentially instrumental, and so money could be used as a powerful motivator providing it was linked directly to the productivity of the individual: a linkage achieved by piece-rate payment systems.

While the logic of Taylorism is impeccable, the conditions of work it produces are often dehumanising and bleak: a set of highly segmented work activities, with no opportunity for employees to use their discretion, and a system of close supervision to monitor their work performance. However, the practice of Taylorism has not necessarily followed the theory as closely as its original protagonist would have wished, leading some commentators (notably, Edwards, 1979; and Palmer, 1975) to argue that Taylor's influence has been overstated because the practical impact of his ideas was limited – not least due to the collective resistance exerted by employees through trade unions.

It is certainly the case that in Taylor's own lifetime the diffusion of the principles of scientific management was modest. Many managers remained unconvinced about the possibility of planning and measuring activities sufficiently accurately to enable the 'science' to work. There were also competing ideas about the nature of job design from the human relations movement (starting with the famous Hawthorne experiments in the 1920s) which brought out the importance of the social factors at work, thus challenging the rational-economic assumptions underlying Taylor's theory of work design (for a full analysis see Schein, 1965).

Notwithstanding these reservations, Taylor's ideas *have made* (and continue to make) a crucial impact on the thinking about job design and the division of labour. Indeed, as Littler (1982) argues, we must be cautious of assuming a linear progression of management theory where each set of ideas neatly supersedes the previous ones.

The persistence of Taylorist principles in organisations like McDonald's is testimony to the resilience of Taylorism. Moreover, it demonstrates how service organisations can use features of 'classic' Taylorism in a similar way to manufacturing industry. Indeed, we might ponder whether shovelling chips into a paper cone is the twenty-first century equivalent of shovelling pig iron into a furnace which Taylor studied a century earlier.

The pervasiveness of a Tayloristic division of labour in the expanding service sector was noted by Ritzer (1993). He contends that McDonald's represents the archetypal rational organisation in search of four goals: efficiency, calculability, predictability and control. McDonald's is a contemporary symbol of a relentless process of rationalisation, where the employee is simply treated as a factor of production. Ritzer's thesis (rather pessimistically) is that both theoretically and empirically this constitutes a general process of 'McDonaldisation' which extends beyond work into the culture of society (Ritzer, 1998). His conclusion suggests that there is an inevitable tendency towards a dehumanisation of work – a theme that echoes the work of the deskilling theorists, whose ideas are explored after considering a second key actor in the design of jobs in the twentieth century.

EXERCISE 6.2

What do *you* think?

Taylor was obsessed with finding the ultimate solution to the problem of organising work. He believed that by analysing and measuring work activities it was possible to find the optimum method of performing every task. In effect, he was suggesting that by careful, scientific, logical analysis, using his guiding principles, managers can find the best way of managing.

1 What is your opinion about Taylor's theory? What are your reasons for agreeing or disagreeing with him?

2 Why do some organisations follow his methods, whilst others reject them?

3 Why is such an old theory still in use today?

4 What types of activities lend themselves most to Tayloristic forms of organisation?

5 Are some work activities impossible to Taylorise?

Routine work on the assembly-line – chickens and Ford

Learning outcome 2

Describe the methods and application of Fordism .

If asked to visualise an assembly-line, many people would probably have an image of a car plant, with a steady procession of partly-finished vehicles passing groups of workers (or robots) who are rapidly attaching windscreens, wheels, trim and so on. This has been the pervasive image of assembly-line work, not least because its innovative form was originally developed and exploited by the Ford Motor Company – an issue that we return to.

First, though, imagine a different contemporary work setting. You are in a massive room dominated by the sound of humming and churning machinery, while intermittently the voices of the all-women workforce can be heard. The room is cool and the air laden with the smell of blood. Overhead, weaving around the factory is a conveyor from which hooks are suspended; hanging from each hook is the carcass of a dead bird. It is a chicken factory, comprising a variety of 'assembly-lines' that convert live birds into the cellophane-wrapped ready-for-roasting meat displayed in supermarket freezers.

The work is Tayloristic in the sense it is segmented into simple, repetitive operations. For example, 'packing' involves four distinct tasks each performed by different employees: inserting the giblets and tucking the legs in; bagging the chicken; weighing it; and securing the top of the bag. But not only are these and similar tasks around the factory simple and repetitive, the pace of the work is also relentless. This is vividly portrayed by an employee performing 'inspection' in such a chicken factory, interviewed for a television programme, 'Dangerous Lives':

EMPLOYEE: The line was coming 'round with about four and a half thousand birds an hour and you used to have to check the chickens for livers, hearts or anything, by putting your hand in the backside of a chicken, feeling around and then bringing anything out, dropping it in the bin, and then going on to the next. Used to be, sort of, every other chicken.

INTERVIEWER: You were doing two chickens at a time?

EMPLOYEE: Yes, both hands in chickens together. You hadn't got time to wipe your nose or do anything really.

INTERVIEWER: Did that line ever stop?

EMPLOYEE: Only if they had a breakdown, you know, a pin went in the line, or there was a breakdown or anything.

INTERVIEWER: So you were doing over 2000 chickens an hour?

EMPLOYEE: Yes.

INTERVIEWER: 14,000 chickens a day?

EMPLOYEE: Yes.

INTERVIEWER: What did you think about that?

EMPLOYEE: Hard work. Real hard work!

Similar experiences of unremitting 'hard work' have been found by researchers studying the harsh realities of factory life in different industries, for example, Pollert (1981) in the tobacco industry, Westwood (1984) in hosiery, Cavendish (1982) in motor components, Beynon (1973) and Linhart (1981) in cars, and Delbridge (1998) in auto components and consumer electronics. In Chapter 9 the experiences of employees are explored in closer detail, but for now, the emphasis is on the work organisation principles which give rise to the assembly-line.

Henry Ford's methods

The name most commonly associated with the development of the assembly-line is that of Henry Ford, whose unique contribution was in adapting Taylorist principles to a factory setting geared to the mass production of standardised products. Ford established a production method benchmark against which assembly-line work has since been assessed, and the term 'Fordist' has come to be used to describe the combination of linear work sequencing, the interdependence of tasks, a moving assembly-line, the use and refinement of dedicated machinery and specialised machine tools (for a detailed discussion, see Meyer, 1981). It has been argued that Fordism is therefore distinguishable from Taylorism in that it constitutes a form of work organisation designed for efficient mass production (Wood, 1989).

The success of Ford, however, can only be fully understood if seen as part of a system of industrial organisation that also sought to create, perpetuate and satisfy, mass consumption. The development of mass markets provided the demand for large numbers of rapidly-produced standardised products, epitomised by the output at the Highland Park factory which rose from 13,941 Model-T Fords in 1909 to 585,400 by 1916 (Williams, Haslam and Williams, 1992: 550). This volume of mass production was only possible because of the development of capital equipment capable of producing on a large scale and the creation of an efficient electricity supply to drive the machinery. In other words, mass production, mass consumption, technological innovation and segmented work organisation were ingredients in Ford's recipe for success. Consequently, as Littler (1985) has argued, Fordism came to predominate as the preferred form of organising work for mass production. It was adopted by Ford's main competitor in the US, General Motors, and then by Ford's European rivals – Austin, Morris and Citröen. Fordism also transferred to other, newer, industries such as electrical engineering and chemicals.

A widely-accepted view is that Fordism is synonymous with mass production, rigidity and standardisation, and that the impact of the ideas pioneered by Ford has been widespread. However, there are some voices of dissent. Notable among these are Williams and colleagues (1987 and 1992) who contend that Fordism has become a stereotype, distorted over time by British and US academics who are keen to attribute failing industrial performance to the persistence of an outdated form of production. In a detailed analysis of Ford's production operations at Highland Park (1909–19), Williams, Haslam and Williams (1992) reveal a picture of greater flexibility and less standardisation of the product than most texts on the subject would suggest. Overall, however, such findings do little to dispel the picture of an authoritarian work regime with closely monitored, machine-paced, short-cycle and unremitting tasks.

As the chicken factory example illustrates, Fordist principles persist in contemporary work settings and these are not restricted to factory work. It can be argued that the assembly-line has been transposed into the service sector. For example, McDonald's might be interpreted as displaying Fordist elements in terms of its mass production of standardised products for mass consumption. Similarly, the supermarket in general, and check-out operations in particular, epitomise a Fordist approach to retailing: the customer's items pass along the conveyor and are swept across the bar-code reader by an operator who performs a monotonous series of repetitive actions. The flow-line, the dedicated machinery and the segmented work tasks are evidence of Fordist principles of work organisation. Thus the chicken, as an object for consumption, is typically reared through (Ford-like) battery farming, is slaughtered and processed in a Fordist factory, and is sold through a Fordist retail outlet (the supermarket) or even consumed as chicken pieces in a Fordist restaurant.

EXCERPT 6.2

The white-collar assembly-line

In an analysis of call centres in Scotland, Taylor and Bain (1999) argue that although not all call centres are identical, many of them can justifiably be labelled 'white-collar factories' because employees are subjected to Tayloristic management techniques and the type of work organisation normally associated with the assembly-line. Their research reveals the following:

'The typical call centre operator is young, female and works in a large, open plan office or fabricated building ... Although probably full-time, she is increasingly likely to be a part-time permanent employee, working complex shift patterns which correspond to the peaks of customer demand. Promotion prospects and career advancement are limited so that the attraction of better pay and conditions in another call centre may prove irresistible. In all probability, work consists of an uninterrupted and endless sequence of similar conversations with customers she never meets. She has to concentrate hard on what is being said, jump from page to page on a screen, making sure that the details entered are accurate and that she has said the right things in a pleasant manner. The conversation ends and as she tidies up the loose ends there is another voice in her headset. The pressure is intense because she knows her work is being measured, her speech monitored, and it often leaves her mentally, physically and emotionally exhausted.

'There is no question that the integration of telephone and computer technologies, which defines the call centre, has produced new developments in the Taylorisation of white-collar work.' (*ibid*: 115)

TO SUM UP

The significance of Taylor, Ford and mass production for the way work has been organised is profound. These principles and methods changed the work process by introducing greater amounts of rigidity and regulation, which, in turn, had important consequences for the skill content of jobs. In particular, this raises the question of whether work, in general, is becoming less or more skilled. The evaluation of the different attempts to answer this question begins with the deskilling thesis.

Thesis: the deskilling of work

Learning outcome 3

Explain the theory behind the deskilling thesis.

1974 saw the publication of one of the most influential books concerned with the study of work: Harry Braverman's *Labor and Monopoly Capital*. Braverman's thesis is that an inevitable tendency towards the degradation and deskilling of work takes place as capitalists search for profits in increasingly competitive economic environments. His contribution to the study of work must not be underestimated. Although his thesis has since been subjected to a great deal of criticism, it played a fundamental role in injecting adrenaline into the lethargic 1970s body of industrial sociology. This revitalisation of labour process analysis is expertly examined by Thompson (1989) and the subtleties of the debate are assessed in Knights and Willmott (1990). The discussion below draws from this rich vein of theory, but does not attempt to do full justice to the various complexities of the debate.

Harry Braverman's argument

At the risk of over-simplifying, Braverman's argument runs as follows. Managers perpetually seek to control the process by which a workforce's labour power (its ability to work) is directed towards the production of commodities (goods and services) that can be sold for a profit. The control of this labour process is essential because profit is accumulated through two stages: first, through the extraction of the surplus value of labour (the price of a commodity greater than the costs incurred in its production); and second, through the realisation of that value when the commodities are actually sold. These two stages are frequently referred to as 'valorisation'. In other words, managers are seeking to control the way work is organised, the pace of work and the duration of work, because these affect profitability. Thus, control of labour is the link between the purchase of labour power and valorisation. In Braverman's analysis the managerial obsession with labour control is key to understanding capitalism and leads managers to seek ways of reducing the discretion exercised by the workforce in performing their jobs. In order to exert their own control over the workforce and limit the control and influence of employees, managers are seen to pursue a general strategy of deskilling which, according to Braverman, can be identified in two forms: organisational and technological.

Organisational deskilling

Organisational deskilling is embedded in the Tayloristic principle of the separation of the conception and execution of work. The conceptual tasks (the more challenging and interesting parts of the job, such as planning, diagnosing problems and developing new working methods) are transferred to technical and managerial staff, while the execution of the work (often the mundane, less challenging part of the job) remains in the hands of shopfloor workers. Theoretically, this process allows managers both to limit the discretion of the shopfloor workers and to secure a monopoly over technical knowledge about the work, which can then be used to exercise greater direct control over the activities of the workforce.

A necessary consequence of the separation of conception and execution is that the labor process is now divided between separate sites and separate bodies of workers. In one location, the physical processes of production are executed. In another are concentrated the design, planning, calculation and record-keeping...The physical processes of production are now carried out more or less blindly, not only by the workers who perform them, but often by lower ranks of supervisory employees as well. The production units operate like a hand, watched, corrected, and controlled by a distant brain. (Braverman, 1974: 124–5)

Technological deskilling

Technological deskilling occurs when automation is used to transfer discretion and autonomy from the shopfloor to the office (from blue-collar to white-collar workers) and to eliminate the need for some direct labour. Braverman focuses on the example of the operation of machines by numerical control (NC) – a process whereby the planning and programming of the machines was undertaken away from the shopfloor by technical staff, who prepared punched paper tapes that contained the information for the machine to run automatically. Prior to NC, the machinists would use their own judgement and discretion to set and operate the machines, but they have subsequently been left with only the relatively simple tasks of loading and switching the machines. In other words, a technological development (NC) allowed the separation of task conception from task execution. Numerical control has more recently been superseded by computer numerical control (CNC) which works on the same principle of separation of programming and operation, but is controlled through a microprocessor. This sort of new technology does not *inevitably* lead to a deskilling of work, but Braverman argues that managers selectively use automation to this end, in order to secure their central objective of exerting control over labour.

In reality, machinery embraces a host of possibilities, many of which are systematically thwarted, rather than developed, by capital. An automatic system of machinery opens up the possibility of the true control over a highly productive factory by a relatively small corps of workers, providing these workers attain the level of mastery over the machinery offered by engineering knowledge, and providing they then share out among themselves the routines of the operation, from the most technically advanced to the most routine... [But such a possibility] is frustrated by the capitalist effort to reconstitute and even deepen the division of labor in all its worst aspects, despite the fact that this division of labor becomes more archaic with every passing day...The 'progress' of capitalism seems only to deepen the gulf between workers and machine and to subordinate the worker ever more decisively to the yoke of the machine...The chief advantage of the industrial assembly-line is the control it affords over the pace of labor, and as such it is supremely useful to owners and managers whose interests are at loggerheads with those of their workers. (Braverman, 1974: 230–2)

There have been plenty of writers willing to comment on Braverman's work. McLoughlin and Clark (1994) divide these into 'sympathisers' and 'agnostics' (see Table 6.1). The main criticisms and revisions to Braverman's thesis are summarised in the next section, but before reading this, attempt Exercise 6.3.

Table 6.1 The key critics of Braverman's thesis

Sympathisers	Agnostics
Accept the general approach but offer some refinement.	Acknowledge some value in the approach, but consider it inadequate.
Friedman (1977a, b, 1990)	Littler (1982)
Burawoy (1979)	Wood (1982)
Edwards (1979)	Littler and Salaman (1982)
Zimbalist (1979)	Knights, Willmott and Collinson (1985)
Armstrong (1988)	Knights and Willmott (1986, 1990)
Rose (1988)	Watson (1986)
Thompson (1989)	

Based on McLoughlin and Clark (1994)

EXERCISE 6.3

What do *you* think?

The UK Government established a 24 hour health helpline (called NHS Direct) that people can ring to check their symptoms rather than going straight to their local doctor (GP). They can receive advice about non-prescription drugs and possible courses of treatment from qualified nurses, using computer databases.

Analyse this using your knowledge of Braverman's thesis.

Six common criticisms of the deskilling thesis

Learning outcome 4

Outline and evaluate the main criticisms of the deskilling thesis.

Criticism 1: The deskilling thesis ignores alternative management strategies

Friedman (1977a, 1977b and 1990) argues that it is false to assume a single trend towards deskilling, since this fails to acknowledge the occasions when it is in the interest of managers to pursue other strategies which leave some discretion in the hands of employees: a strategy of 'responsible autonomy' rather than the 'direct control' which Braverman described. Friedman had in mind job enrichment and quality circles, but a contemporary expression of responsible autonomy is the notion of 'empowerment', whereby individual employees are expected to take responsibility for their own actions and initiate improvements in the way they work for the benefit of the organisation as a whole. Under responsible autonomy, employees are not deskilled but management continue to control the labour process. Thus, the argument here is that there is a wider choice in the mechanisms employed by management for the accumulation of capital than Braverman suggests.

Criticism 2: The deskilling thesis overstates management's objective of controlling labour

The control of the labour process is not an end in itself, but a means to achieving profit. To concentrate solely on labour control objectives ignores the importance of valorisation.

> It is not simply the *extraction* of surplus value in the labour process which is problematic for capital, but the *realisation* of that surplus through the sale of commodities in markets . . . In other words we need to consider the *full circuit* of industrial capital as the starting point for analyses of changes in the division of labour: purchase of labour power; extraction of surplus value within the labour process; realisation of surplus value within product markets. There is no sound theoretical reason for privileging one moment in this circuit – the labour-capital relation within the labour process – if our objective is to account for changes (or variations) in the division of labour. (Kelly, 1985: 32, emphasis in original)

Moreover, the assumption that labour issues (rather than, for example, product development, marketing, or investment) are the central concern of management during strategy formation, is highly questionable (Purcell, 1989 and 1995). Thus, as Littler and Salaman (1982: 257) contend, the process of capital accumulation acts beyond the labour process:

> The firm is primarily a capital fund with a legal corporate personality, linked to a production process . . . While the production process results in a flow of income to the firm, this does not preclude alternative sources playing a major role or even a predominant one e.g. currency speculation, cumulative acquisition and asset stripping, commodity speculation, and credit manipulation of various kinds.

Child (1972, 1984 and 1985) has highlighted the importance of political manoeuvring by managers in an organisation who, as key decision-makers, are making 'strategic choices' that reflect their own values and vested interests. Thus, the argument here is that the internal politics of the organisation have a greater impact on deciding how the work is organised and on the skill requirements than Braverman implies. The logic of capitalist accumulation may remain the over-arching tendency, but this can be mitigated by managers at all levels who are defending their vested interests.

As a consequence, the criticism is that Braverman's thesis underestimates the diversity and complexity of management objectives. The assumption that there is a single shared objective by management – that of labour control – ignores the plurality of interests within management, and the diverse and sometimes competing objectives (Batstone, Gourley, Levie and Moore, 1987; Buchanan and Boddy, 1983; Buchanan, 1986; Child, 1985). For example, in research into technological change in the UK provincial newspaper industry undertaken by one of the authors (Noon, 1994) it was found that when managers were questioned about the objectives of introducing new technology, they stressed different reasons which seemed to reflect their own functional responsibilities. In other words, the objective of increased control over labour was not the primary focus for most managers. Instead, they said technological change provided new opportunities in terms of product quality, product development, production control, efficiency, and flexibility, together with a reduction in labour cost. This suggests that while labour control objectives may be relevant, they must be placed within the context of broader business objectives. As Armstrong (1989 and 1995) argues, the pervasive influence of management accountants at board level in UK companies tends to lead to more strategic thinking based on financial concerns rather than human resource matters.

Criticism 3: The deskilling thesis treats labour as passive

Employees have not been totally compliant, and have resisted change towards deskilling through both trade union collective action and individual action. Indeed, Edwards (1979) argues that management has sought more sophisticated forms of control as a direct response to (and as a way to suppress) worker resistance. He argues there has been a shifting reliance from the 'simple control' typified by the methods of direct supervision that Taylor advocated, to the 'technical control' of the mechanised assembly-line (and more recent developments in computer technology) and the 'bureaucratic control' of workplace rules, procedures and a regulated internal labour market.

Criticism 4: The deskilling thesis understates the degree of consent and accommodation by employees

The work of Burawoy (1979) stands as an important counterpoint to Braverman in that it explores the extent to which the workforce *consents* to its own subordination. In part, this contrasts also with the previous criticism because it suggests that, rather than challenging management control of the labour process, the workforce may develop an informal culture that offers alternative definitions of the work situation and provides the opportunity for meaningful activity. The labour process is thereby redefined as a type of game through which the employees can derive satisfaction (for example, by beating the clock, outwitting the supervisor, or manipulating the machinery). These games act as powerful means of social regulation (self-control) among the work groups, and obscure the exploitative nature of the labour process. In so doing, they unwittingly provide alternative additional sources of control for management. Such a brief summary hardly does justice to the subtleties of Burawoy's work, but these issues will be analysed in more detail in Chapter 9.

Criticism 5: The deskilling thesis ignores gender

Beechey (1982) has argued that several problems emerge from the gender-blind nature of Braverman's argument. First, he fails to appreciate the importance of women's distinct role as domestic labourers because of his 'conceptual isolation of the family from the labour process and of both the family and the labour process from an analysis of the capitalist mode of production as a whole' (Beechey, 1982: 71). Second, his discussion of the pre-industrial family can be criticised for romanticising the past and ignoring the existence of patriarchal structures. Third, his concept of skill fails to explore gender dimensions; an issue already analysed in detail in Chapter 5, where it was noted that the social construction of skill is particularly important in creating 'gendered jobs', resulting in the under-valuation of women's labour power and skills.

Criticism 6: The deskilling thesis overlooks skill transfer possibilities

The failure of Braverman to recognise that deskilling in one area of work may be compensated by upskilling in another, is most forcefully argued by Penn (1983 and 1990) whose ideas are examined in some detail later. However, it might be argued that this constitutes one of the most unfair criticisms of Braverman. As Armstrong (1988) points out, Braverman explicitly recognised that change would occur unevenly across industries, and that in some instances new skills and technical specialities might be temporarily created within the workforce.

A defence of Braverman's thesis

The most persuasive defence of Braverman comes from Armstrong (1988) who argues that:

> any sensitive reading of his work should reveal that Braverman actually regarded the deskilling tendencies of technical change as a system-wide dynamic or 'law of motion' in capitalist economies which could, temporarily and locally, be interrupted or reversed by a variety of factors, many of which have been rediscovered by his critics as supposed refutations. (Armstrong, 1988: 157)

This is an important point because, like all meta-theory, Braverman's thesis will never be able to explain all contingencies, yet this does not necessarily mean its analytical thrust is worthless. Indeed, as Armstrong suggests, many of the 'critics' are in practice offering revisions and amendments to the theory, rather than rejecting it.

Another defender of Braverman, Spencer (2000) suggests that the constant revisions and modifications to Braverman's original ideas by subsequent labour process theorists (academic commentators and researchers) show they have lost sight of the subversive intent of Braverman's original text, and have become obsessed with the social relations of the workplace, rather than the broader critique of capitalism. In short, Spencer laments the way that Braverman's ideas have been brought into the mainstream, and now run the risk of aiding rather than tormenting capitalism.

While some commentators (for example, Lewis, 1995) remain unconvinced by defenders of Braverman, a re-reading of the original text reveals that Braverman had a less deterministic approach than is frequently attributed to him. Therefore, the deskilling thesis needs to be seen as an overall tendency, rather than a universal law applying in all cases.

> Braverman does *not* propound a universal law of deskilling. What he *does* claim is that there exists a general tendency for deskilling to occur in capitalist economies which will become actual where products and processes make this possible and where its effects are not masked by initiatives aimed at changing technology for other reasons. (Armstrong, 1988: 147, emphasis in original)

If Braverman's thesis is to be countered, it should be (and can be) challenged on comparable terms: rather than a tendency towards deskilling, there is an opposite trend towards upskilling occurring within capitalist economies. It is to this antithesis that the discussion now turns.

Antithesis: the upskilling of work

Learning outcome 5

Explain the theory behind the upskilling thesis.

Whereas the deskilling thesis drew from Marxist economic theory and the crisis of capitalism in industrial societies, the upskilling thesis is based on the economics of human capital theory within a new era of capitalism: the post-industrial society. Human capital theorists (Becker, 1964; Fuchs, 1968) suggest that increasingly, firms are investing in their workforce through greater training provision, thus the emphasis is shifted to 'human capital' as a central means of accumulating profit. It is held that rapid advances in technology require a more educated, better trained workforce in order to cope with the increasing complexity of work tasks (Kerr, Dunlop, Harbison and Myers, 1960; Blauner 1964). In turn, this is linked to an ever-reducing demand for manual/physical labour as Western capitalist economies undergo a structural shift away from manufacturing towards service sector activities (Fuchs, 1968).

This shift in the economic base of advanced industrial societies is considered by commentators such as Daniel Bell (whose ideas are summarised in Chapter 3) to signal a fundamental transformation to the post-industrial society, in which theoretical knowledge becomes 'the axis around which new technology, economic growth and the stratification of society will be organized' (Bell, 1973: 112). In other words, the upskilling thesis suggests that the general tendency is towards more complex work requiring higher levels of skill. As a consequence, the shift in the pattern of work organisation will not be towards degradation (as Braverman suggested) but to an enrichment of work.

The upskilling thesis has more recently found expression in the concept of 'flexible specialisation' propounded by Piore and Sabel (1984). They argue that the crisis of accumulation under capitalism is leading to an important shift away from Fordism towards more craft-based, flexible, innovation-led, and customer-focused work organisation. Thus, just as the move from traditional craft production to mass production constituted 'the first industrial divide', the move from mass production to flexible specialisation is described by Piore and Sabel as 'the second industrial divide'. The new emphasis lies on flexible production systems which can meet the demands for customised products in increasingly diversified markets. In particular, developments in microelectronic technology allow for more flexibility in the use of capital equipment: machinery no longer needs to be dedicated to specific tasks but can be re-programmed to perform a variety of tasks. More traditional production methods typically involve long set-up times for the machinery which mean large production runs are necessary to recover the cost; short production runs for small batches are an inefficient use of the equipment. In contrast, computerised machinery requiring shorter set-up times enables greater diversity of (small batch) production without incurring the inefficiencies. In other words, economies of *scale* are now complemented by economies of *scope*. This is important because customers are supposedly becoming increasingly discerning and want a greater variety of goods which allow them to express their individual identity (Sabel, 1982). There-fore, economies of scope become a necessity in a dynamic, competitive market. Computerised production and information processing capabilities provide the technological infrastructure, and allegedly bring with them a demand for upskilled rather than deskilled labour.

Five criticisms of the upskilling thesis

Learning outcome 6

Outline and evaluate the main criticisms of the upskilling thesis.

Generally, the upskilling thesis has failed to stimulate as vigorous a debate as the deskilling thesis – indeed it might be argued that it has been greatly neglected as a theoretical proposition of general skill change, and consequently remains under-developed. However, the related flexible specialisation thesis has provoked consid-erable academic discussion (see for example, Hyman, 1991; Smith, 1989; Williams, Cutler, Williams and Haslam, 1987; Wood, 1989). Consequently, it is possible to identify five major criticisms of the general upskilling thesis.

Criticism 1: The upskilling thesis oversimplifies the link with technical change

Lee (1982) argues that the drawing of a causal relationship between technical change and rising skill must be seen as a simple technicist generalisation. Like the deskilling thesis, it fails 'to consider the institutional "filters" which complicate the relation-ship between production methods, skill levels and class' (Lee, 1982: 147).

Criticism 2: The upskilling thesis overstates the extent to which advanced technology requires higher skill levels on the shopfloor

Indeed, the upskilling thesis is as vulnerable as its deskilling counterpart to the criticism that there are numerous managerial objectives which reflect vested inter-ests and political manoeuvring, so the design of work will be based on these just as much as on 'technical' decisions about skill requirements. For example, in their study of United Biscuits, Buchanan and Boddy (1983) show that even within one company there can be a mixture of skill changes associated with the introduction of advanced technology which makes any generalisation of upskilling or deskilling difficult to substantiate. Similarly, Sorge, Hartman, Warner and Nicholas (1983) reveal how computer numerical control (CNC) technology was used by British managers to deskill the shopfloor workers and turn them into mere machine minders, while in Germany the same technology was implemented in such a way as to integrate the (skilled) programming into the work of the operators, thereby enhancing their skill.

Criticism 3: The upskilling thesis assumes that the growth of the service sector will create skilled jobs

Empirical evidence, however, reveals this to be a gross over-simplification; companies like McDonald's, for instance, epitomise the success of service sector expansion while embodying some of the worst elements of monotonous, routinised, low-discretion work. For example, there has been extensive growth in the number of call centres where jobs are frequently highly-prescribed, monotonous and boring. Based on their survey of Scottish call centres Taylor and Bain (1999: 109) sum it up as follows:

> Call centre operators have joined, with flight attendants, shop assistants, fast food and waiting staff, the swelling ranks of service workers whose performance at work is shaped by the objective of customer satisfaction. All these employees, in various ways, are required to conform to pre-determined phrases, scripts, and modes of behaviour and delivery. If anything distinguishes the call centre worker it is both the extent to which they are subject to monitoring and the unrelenting pressure to conform to acceptable forms of speech, whether scripted or not. It is difficult to conceive of another occupation where the entire working shift requires the articulation of the same vocal patterns in such a repetitive and uninterrupted sequence.

In comparison, Korczynski, Shire, Frenkel and Tam's (1996) detailed analysis of three call centres (two in Australia and one in Japan) lead them to argue that while the customer service representatives have routine aspects to their work, it is misleading to equate their jobs with the sort of routine work typically found in factories. This is because service work relies on the extensive use of social skills when dealing with customers, which can provide a source of creativity for the employee. In short, they are cautious not to equate service work with routinisation or deskilling, yet also suggest that there is little evidence of substantial upskilling taking place, even though there were some opportunities for it to occur in their case study companies.

Criticism 4: The upskilling thesis overstates the extent of change

Generally, theorists who support the upskilling thesis, and those who support flexible specialisation in particular, assume that a radical break with Fordism is taking place. However, this understates the resilience of mass production for mass markets.

For example, the almost insatiable demand for consumer electronics over the past two decades typically has been met by the supply of goods manufactured using production systems that are labour intensive and low skilled (see for example, Delbridge, Turnbull and Wilkinson, 1992; Sewell and Wilkinson, 1992). Similarly, the flexible specialisation thesis over-states the extent to which small batch production will create upskilled and multi-skilled workers. As Pollert (1991) and Smith (1989) point out, small batch production can and has adopted low skilled, short cycle assembly-line techniques. Hence, the criticism here is that the upskilling thesis relies on a false dichotomy between mass and craft production.

Criticism 5: The upskilling thesis needs to be put into a global perspective

With the rise of the multinational organisation it is no longer sufficient to consider change simply in a national context. For example, a shift in the manufacture of consumer electronics from Western Europe to South East Asia removes the demand for low-skilled work in one country, only to increase its demand in another. As a result, it becomes problematic to try to interpret a fall in the demand for low-skilled labour in one national context as a sign of general upskilling. Equally it may indicate a global redistribution of demand for skills, reflecting the mobility of capital in the search for lower labour costs and the pursuit of greater profitability.

EXERCISE 6.4

What do *you* think?

Both the theories claim that there is a 'general tendency' towards either deskilling or upskilling. Based on the comments and criticisms above, you might have been persuaded more by one set of arguments than the other. But suppose you wanted to test which of these theories is correct.

1 What research techniques could you use?

2 What particular issues would you need to think about? Remember you are assessing a *general tendency* in skill *change*.

TO SUM UP

The upskilling thesis is as ambitious as the deskilling thesis in attempting to arrive at a theoretical framework that reflects a general tendency of skill change in one direction. However, in both cases the unidirectional argument needs to be qualified – as the various criticisms have shown. Indeed, the question of whether the dynamics of skill change can be simplified in such a way is highly problematic. A more robust theoretical approach might be to hypothesise multi-directional change within different sectors, industries, occupations and tasks. Three approaches which address such a synthesis are examined in the next section.

Syntheses: polarisation, compensation and the dual impact of automating and informating

Learning outcome 7

Describe alternative approaches to examining skill change.

The polarisation of skills

One of the most thorough of recent attempts to assess the changing experience of work has been that embodied in the research project known as the Social Change and Economic Life Initiative (SCELI). Part of this research focused on the changing nature of skill (Penn, Rose and Rubery, 1994); some of the findings from the study have already been explored in Chapter 5. Importantly for our present discussion, the researchers specifically addressed the question of whether there had been a general trend towards upskilling or deskilling during the 1980s. The conclusion from this survey is that a complex picture of skill change emerges and neither the upskilling nor deskilling thesis adequately explains skill change in the UK. Excerpt 6.3 provides a summary of the main findings.

EXCERPT 6.3

Patterns of skill change in the UK – summary of the main findings from SCELI

Skill change within occupational classes

- A higher proportion of employees reported an increase than a decrease in the skill level of their jobs over the last five years.
- This trend was less marked for non-skilled manual employees, where a greater proportion reported that their skill levels remained static.
- Those experiencing upward occupational mobility were more likely to report skill increases, the greatest increase being those who moved from manual to service occupations.
- Those who remained in the same job experienced less upskilling.

Skill change within sectors

- The general pattern was upskilling rather than deskilling.
- Non-skilled workers in manufacturing experienced upskilling in greater proportions than their counterparts in the service sector.
- In the service sector, there was a marked difference between public and private organisations; the latter having a much greater proportion of low skilled jobs.

Automation and skill

- The use of advanced technology varies between occupations – only 39 per cent of the respondents were using automated or computerised equipment.

▶

▶   ■ In every occupational class, work with advanced technology was associated with higher skill demands.

Gender and skill

■ The skill requirements of the women's jobs (measured by qualifications needed and training) appeared substantially lower than those of the men. Women and men are doing very different types of work.
■ Both men and women were more likely to have increased than decreased their skills, although a greater proportion of men had done so (56 per cent compared with 45 per cent).
■ A greater proportion of men than women were working with advanced technology, so consequently benefited more from its positive impact on skill.
■ Women in male-dominated occupations were twice as likely as women in feminised occupations to have experienced an increase in their skills.
■ Women in part-time employment were in jobs with lower skill requirements than men doing part-time work.
■ Much of the difference in the experience of skill change between men and women can be explained by the negative impact of part-time work. When full-time jobs of men and women are compared, the gender differences in terms of skill change virtually disappear.

Overall

■ Deskilling was rare.
■ The most common experience was upskilling.
■ The argument best supported by the evidence is the polarisation of skill.

Source: Summarised from Gallie (1991).

The SCELI research suggests there has been a *polarisation* of skill associated with three distinct factors: existing skill differentials, advanced technology and gender. To quote the conclusion of Gallie (1991: 349–50):

Those that already had relatively higher levels of skill witnessed an increase in their skill levels, while those with low levels of skill saw their skills stagnate . . . Those that have been in a position to use advanced technology in their work have seen their skills increase; those that have not had this possibility, have been much more likely to see their skills remain unchanged. Finally, the evidence points to a deep gender divide in skill experiences. It is men above all that have benefited from the progress of skills in the 1980s, while women are much less likely to have seen their skills increase. The central factor connected with this would appear to be the existence of a major sector of part-time female work, in which the existing levels of skill are typically low and which has remained untouched by the processes that have elsewhere contributed to skill enrichment.

To some extent, the findings are unexpected; in particular the lack of evidence for the deskilling thesis, although this may be hidden by the extent of 'stagnation' of skills. It is also worth bearing in mind how the research method might have influenced the results: a respondent might be unwilling to say their job has become less skilled because it projects a negative image of their own abilities. Similarly, any new aspect to a job, because of its unfamiliarity, may lead the respondent to overstate the skill required (such problems of measuring skill were examined in detail in Chapter 5).

Beyond the UK, the polarisation of skills is also in evidence. For example, research in the Netherlands (see Excerpt 6.4) and the US reveals the differential impact of technological and organisational change on the work of different employees. Milkman's (1997) case study of the General Motors plant in Linden, New Jersey depicts a complex picture of work transformation but reveals how skilled workers were given opportunities to acquire new skills and retrain, while their semi-skilled counterparts on the production line were denied such opportunities. The consequence is upskilling for one group and deskilling for the other, hence a polarisation effect is occurring.

EXCERPT 6.4

Skill polarisation in the Netherlands

As part of a research programme examining the effects of automation on job content, de Witte and Steijn (2000) analysed the responses of 1022 Dutch employees to a questionnaire survey. The respondents were asked to report on the extent of autonomy in their work, the complexity of their job (both measures being used to assess the skill level of their jobs) and the extent of automation. They were also asked a range of background questions. Their research reveals a wide range of findings, but those of most relevance to us are the following:

- There is a general trend in upskilling associated with increasing automation.
- Professionals and white-collar workers experience the most upskilling.
- The upskilling is most evident among professionals.
- Blue-collar workers are least likely to experience upskilling.
- Some blue-collar workers experience substantial deskilling.

To explain the deskilling amongst blue-collar workers, de Witte and Steijn suggest that *internal differentiation* is occurring. This term means that automation leads to an increase in the complexity of the job but not the autonomy of the job. This internal differentiation is less likely to occur amongst the professional and white-collar workers – in other words, automation brings both an increase in complexity and an increase in autonomy for the employee.

The compensatory theory of skill

The argument put forward by proponents of the compensatory theory (Penn and Scattergood, 1985; Penn, 1990; Penn, Gasteen, Scattergood and Sewel, 1994) is that the general theories of both upskilling and deskilling are inadequate to explain the complexity of skill change, and that empirically-derived, middle-range theory offers a better way forward.

> If the dynamics of skill change are essentially dualistic, then both [upskilling and deskilling theories] can find illustrative examples to support their respective, if incompatible, positions without securing any semblance of an adequate overall analysis. (Penn, 1990: 25)

The compensatory theory is based on the proposition that technological change generates *both* deskilling and upskilling. This can be observed empirically in two respects. First, the effects are international: 'the shift of routine manufacturing from advanced, core economies to less developed, peripheral economies, and the increasing internationalisation of the capital goods (machinery) industry' (Penn, 1990: 25). Second, the effects differ between and within occupations: some groups are advantaged by having a more skilled and central role, while others find themselves deskilled and marginalised. More specifically:

> technological changes tend to deskill *direct productive roles* but put an increased premium on a range of *ancillary skilled tasks* that are associated with the installation, maintenance and programming of automated machinery. This is because modern machinery incorporating micro-electronics tends to simplify many production skills but renders maintenance work far more complex.... [However] within maintenance work itself... there is a far greater need for new electronic based maintenance skills than for traditional mechanical maintenance skills. (Penn, 1990: 25, emphasis in original)

There is a somewhat technologically-determinist undertone to part of this argument: the suggestion that microelectronics have tendencies to impact on certain jobs, independent of the actions and choices of those who design, commission or purchase the technology. Nevertheless, the general thrust of the argument is of interest since it highlights the importance of acknowledging a broader picture of skill change across occupational groups, industries and national contexts.

Automating and informating: the dual impact on skill change

The important role of advanced technology in reconfiguring skills is explored in detail by Zuboff (1988). She argues that a distinction must be drawn between the processes of *automating* and *informating*, since they have impacted upon skills in different ways. The process of automating work operations involves the replacement of living labour with technology, thus it is characterised by a deskilling of work and a reassertion of management control over the work process. Increasingly, however, technological developments also provide an opportunity to generate detailed information about the work operations themselves which, if systematically gathered and analysed, increases the visibility of the productive and administrative work undertaken in an organisation. In other words, technology is informating the work process, and the data require interpretation through the use of cognitive ability. This constitutes an upskilling of work and provides 'a deeper level of transparency to activities that had been either partially or completely opaque' (Zuboff, 1988: 9).

Taken together, the processes of automating and informating lead to a reduction in action-centred skills (doing) but an increase in intellective skills (analysing). At the same time, 'these dual capacities of information technology are not opposites; they are hierarchically integrated. Informating derives from and builds upon automation. Automation is a necessary but not sufficient condition for informating.' (Zuboff, 1988: 11). Moreover, Zuboff argues that although automating displaces human presence, it is not yet clear what the full effects of informating are. While managers can choose either to exploit or to ignore the informating process, her own case study evidence suggests that the tendency has been for managers to stress the automating process and ignore the informating potential. This is not surprising because the informating capacities of advanced technology force managers to rethink traditional structures, work organisation and forms of control.

> The shifting grounds of knowledge invite managers to recognize the emergent demands for intellective skills and develop a learning environment in which such skills can develop. That very recognition contains a threat to managerial authority, which depends in part upon control over the organization's knowledge base ... Managers who must prove and defend their own legitimacy do not easily share knowledge or engage in inquiry. Workers who feel the requirements of subordination are not enthusiastic learners ... Techniques of control that are meant to safeguard authority create suspicion and animosity, which is particularly dysfunctional when an organization needs to apply its human energies to inventing an alternative form of work organization better suited to the new technological context. (Zuboff, 1988: 391–2)

The analysis presented by Zuboff is detailed, so this summary cannot really do justice to the subtlety of her argument. Nevertheless, it illustrates how both the deskilling and upskilling theses are inadequate as single explanations of skill change because while the former concentrates on the process of automating, the latter is focused on the process of informating. As a result, the dual impact of advanced technology is overlooked by both approaches.

TO SUM UP

It is notable that the syntheses above are more firmly based on empirical research than either the deskilling or upskilling thesis, and readily address the complexity of skill change. All three syntheses identify the possibility of deskilling and upskilling occurring

▶

▶ simultaneously, and therefore they reject the notion of an overall general tendency in one direction only. In moving away from general theorising to context-specific understanding of skill change, they can more easily accommodate the diversity of empirical evidence. In spite of their different methodologies – the quantitative survey approach of Gallie (1991), the historical industry studies of Penn (1990), and the qualitative case studies of Zuboff (1988) – they converge in concluding that the overall picture is one of *differing experiences* of skill change.

Learning outcome 8

Use the work categorisation framework to analyse jobs.

Discussion: towards a conceptual framework

The possible trends in work transformation represented by the various approaches explored above can be depicted by developing a simple framework. As with any conceptual schema that seeks to simplify the complexities embedded in work organisation, this is necessarily limited in its explanatory powers, but it does allow us to theorise some analytical distinctions. The framework draws from Fox (1974), Friedmann (1961) and Littler (1982) by proposing that work can be described as varying along two dimensions:

1 *the range of work*: work can vary according to the range of tasks that the employee performs. At one extreme, an employee will perform a very narrow range of tasks, while at the other extreme the employee will be expected to perform a wide range of different tasks;

2 *the discretion in work*: this refers to the extent to which an employee has the ability to exercise choice over how the work is performed, deciding such aspects as the pace, quality, quantity and scheduling of work. At one extreme there will be very little opportunity for employees to use their discretion in this way, while at the other extreme the work will require employees constantly to use discretion in completing the tasks.

By combining these two dimensions as in Figure 6.1, it is possible to visualise the way jobs may vary and to plot four ideal typical cases:

1 *specialist* work: high discretion over a narrow range of work;

2 *specialised* work: a narrow range of prescribed tasks;

3 *generalised* work: a wide range of prescribed tasks;

4 *generalist* work: high discretion over a wide range of work.

The best way of illustrating this typology is to look at a single work setting and assess how different jobs within that setting can be placed in one of these four categories. For example, in a hospital the paramedics and nurses are undertaking generalised work, the doctors perform generalist work, the porters do specialised work and the surgeons are responsible for specialist work. To take another example, consider a nightclub. The manager is doing generalist work, the DJ is doing specialist work, the barstaff are doing generalised work and the bouncers are doing specialised

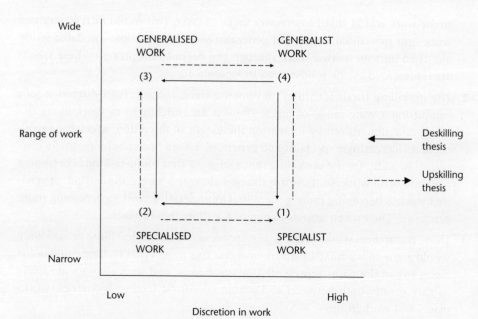

Figure 6.1 Work categorisation framework and trends in skill change

work. This type of categorisation can be undertaken for any workplace. Of course not all jobs will fit neatly into one category, but that is always a limitation of such frameworks. However, if a job does not fit neatly into a category it may well indicate that the work is undergoing a transition – the sort of skill change that we discussed above and which we elaborate below.

EXERCISE 6.5

What do *you* think?

Think of a workplace you are familiar with, list the main jobs and attempt to categorise them using the work categorisation framework. Remember, this framework cannot tell us about the importance of the work. It does not indicate the value of the work, but it helps us to classify the nature of the work.

Mapping the skill changes

In addition to classifying the nature of jobs, the work categorisation framework can be used to show three trends proposed by the skill change theses:

Learning outcome 9

Explain the relationship between skill change and work organisation paradigms.

1 The deskilling thesis is based on the premise that there is a general trend towards low discretion jobs comprising a narrow range of tasks. This manifests itself in the form of a degradation of work along the 'discretion' dimension. In other words, discretion is removed from generalist work (making it more generalised) or from specialist work (making it more specialised). Similarly the deskilling thesis suggests a simplification of work along the 'range' dimension,

so the work would entail a narrower range of tasks. This would turn generalised work into specialised work, and generalist work initially into specialist work, and then into specialised work through the degradation process. These trends are represented by the solid arrows in Figure 6.1.

2   The upskilling thesis identifies an opposite trend towards high discretion jobs comprising a wide range of tasks. There is an enrichment of work along the 'discretion' dimension: by increasing the extent of discretion, specialised work becomes increasingly specialist and generalised work becomes increasingly generalist. In addition, the upskilling thesis suggests that multi-tasking is becoming a feature of all work, so there are changes along the 'range' dimension. Specialised work is becoming more generalised and specialist work is becoming more generalist. The broken arrows in Figure 6.1 show these trends.

3   Those researchers who reject a general tendency of either deskilling or upskilling would argue that a mixed pattern emerges. This means that change could occur along any of the paths represented by the arrows, and such changes are likely to vary greatly both between and within countries, sectors, industries, workplaces and workgroups.

Conclusion: towards a conceptual framework

Finally, we can return to the issue of work organisation with which we began the chapter. We argued that Taylorist and Fordist methods have had a dominant influence on work organisation, so how do these relate to the different theories of skill change? In Figure 6.2, the work categorisation framework is drawn again, but this time we have mapped onto it the dominant forms of work organisation that can be associated with each work category. The term 'paradigm' – which means a distinctive pattern or approach – can be used to describe these forms of work organisation. In other words, it is possible to refer to, for example, the Fordist paradigm or the post-Fordist paradigm. So what do these terms mean and how do they relate to the theories of skill change?

The word Fordism appears in all the paradigms. This is no accident because the Fordist paradigm is considered by most commentators to have had a massive impact on how work was organised during the 20th century – that is why we discussed it so much at the beginning of this chapter. As a result of this dominance, other paradigms of work organisation can be defined in relation to Fordism. Therefore:

- Post-Fordism means 'after Fordism' and refers to types of work organisation that do not rely on the principles of Taylor or the methods of Ford.
- Neo-Fordism means 'new Fordism' and refers to types of work organisation that have *adopted* many of the basic methods of Ford, but have *adapted* them – particularly through more flexible working practices – to fit contemporary circumstances.

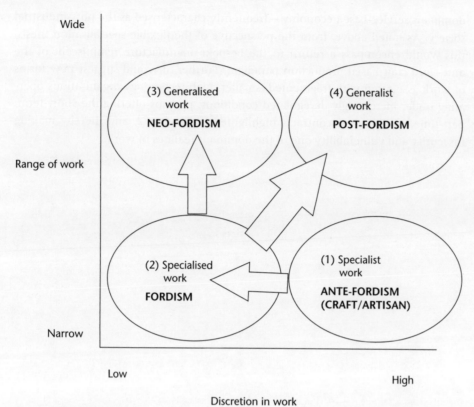

Figure 6.2 Work categorisation framework and paradigms of work organisation

- Ante-Fordism means 'before Fordism' and refers to types of work organisation that are based on methods of craft-based skills, often associated with the independent, self-employed artisan.

Once again the deskilling and upskilling theses offer contrasting interpretations of how work organisation is changing. The deskilling thesis suggests that the dominance of craft/artisan production in the 19th century gave way to Fordism, and this paradigm is continually being renewed as the dominant mode of work organisation under capitalism. The consequent effect is to perpetuate specialised work comprising a narrow range of low discretion tasks. A variant of this deskilling approach comes from commentators who suggest that Fordism has evolved into neo-Fordism (see for example, Harvey, 1989). This perspective contends that by introducing multi-tasking, new management techniques (such as just-in-time, lean production and business process re-engineering) and increasingly automated and internationalised production processes, Fordism enters a new era of capitalism. Thus, proponents of this view (for example, Aglietta, 1979) stress the importance of recognising continuity with the past, rather than characterising change as a quantum leap into a new dimension of capitalism.

In contrast, the upskilling thesis suggests that a dramatic change *has* taken place in advanced capitalist economies. It is suggested that this constitutes a paradigm shift to post-Fordism based on new concepts of work organisation (such as self-managed teams, virtual organisations and teleworking) and an increasingly dominant service-based economy – frequently characterised as the post-industrial society. As noted above, from the perspective of the flexible specialisation thesis, this would encompass a return to the bespoke manufacture reminiscent of the ante-Ford craft-based production paradigm. Further, it would suggest new forms of work associated with fragmented, smaller, high technology organisations operating under increasingly deregulated conditions, perhaps offering the short-term, part-time, employment contracts highlighted in Chapter 2, and thereby making insecurity and vulnerability one of the dominant realities of work.

Emotion work 7

KEY CONCEPTS

- Emotion
- Emotional labour
- Feelings
- Emotional dissonance
- Emotional display

- Surface acting
- Deep acting
- Customer service
- Coping strategies

- Employee well-being
- Alienation
- Emotional exhaustion
- Gender and emotional labour

CHAPTER AIM

To explore the growth of 'emotional labour' in contemporary work organisations and assess its significance for the employees involved.

LEARNING OUTCOMES

By reading and thinking about the material contained in this chapter, you will be able to:

1 define what is meant by emotional labour;

2 demonstrate knowledge of the factors that have brought about the expansion of emotional labour and the reasons for the increased importance attributed to it by management;

3 explain the ways in which employees learn and experience emotional labour;

4 assess employee reactions to emotional labour;

5 identify how managers seek to manage this aspect of employee behaviour;

6 evaluate research on the consequences of emotional labour for employee health and well-being;

7 recognise wider implications of the growth of emotional labour, in particular for the position of women in the labour force.

Introduction

While it has become commonplace to distinguish between jobs involving mainly physical tasks and ones that primarily call for mental performance (utilising know-ledge and information) a growing proportion of the workforce are in fact also engaged in what can be termed the performance of 'emotion' work. For those employed as airline cabin crew, rescue workers, debt collectors, supermarket check-out operators, waiters, bank staff, health care employees and in a host of other occupations, the management of their own – and other people's – emotions represent key aspects of their job. In most service occupations involving direct contact with the public, the *way* in which employees deliver that service has come to represent an increasingly important aspect of the service itself. In some contexts of course, the significance of social interaction as a vital component of service provision has long been recognised. In the restaurant industry, for example, the diner's experience depends not only on the quality of the food consumed but also on the ambience created in the restaurant, which invariably hinges on the disposition and demean-our of the staff waiting on the tables. Thus, as well as performing tasks such as providing information and advice about the menu, taking down orders accurately, and serving and clearing away the meals carefully and efficiently, waiters and waitresses are expected to behave in a manner which contributes to a positive and welcoming atmosphere, irrespective of the pressures they are under or the way they are responded to by their customers. Or, as one waiter succinctly put it, 'I always smile at them...that's part of my uniform' (quoted in Hall, 1993: 460).

In this way, the 'service and its mode of delivery are inextricably combined' (Filby, 1992: 37); to put it another way, 'the emotional style of offering the service is part of the service itself' (Hochschild, 1983: 5). It is clear, however, that in recent years, the range of activities involving emotion work has grown. Thus, for most supermarket check-out operators, for example, it is no longer sufficient to charge up the goods speedily and handle cash, cheques and credit cards accurately; this has also to be a service performed 'with a smile', a friendly greeting, gaining eye contact and a cheery farewell. Moreover, these requirements apply, whatever the circumstances:

> The worst thing is that you are on the till trying to go as fast as you can and you can hear them [the customers] moaning that you are slow...there are times that I just want to look up and say shut up but you have to be busy and keep smiling. (Supermarket check-out operator, quoted in Ogbonna and Wilkinson, 1990: 12)

Similarly, on an airline flight, the expectation is that cabin crew will always display an air of reassurance, even if they fear otherwise:

> Even though I'm a very honest person, I have learned not to allow my face to mirror my alarm or my fright. I feel very protective of my passengers. Above all, I don't want them to be frightened. If we were going down, if we were going to

make a ditching in the water, the chances of our surviving are slim, even though we [the flight attendants] know exactly what to do. But I think I would probably – and I think I can say this for most of my fellow flight attendants – be able to keep them from being too worried about it. (Delta Airlines flight attendant quoted in Hochschild, 1983: 107)

So too, in the High Street banks, management now attach greater importance to the warmth and friendliness of the cashier. As the extract in Excerpt 7.1 relating to a customer service questionnaire distributed by a leading UK bank illustrates, these are aspects of employee behaviour which are now increasingly monitored by their employers.

EXCERPT 7.1

When serving you today

Barclays Bank is one of many companies that uses customer surveys to monitor response not only to banking services, but also to the nature and style of service delivery. The Barclays surveys are distributed twice a year and comprise ten questions relating to a service interaction just completed.

The survey is headed 'When serving you today, how was I at . . .?'. Each of the ten questions has an 11 point response scale, the ends of which are anchored by the words 'Poor' and 'Exceptional'.

- Three questions seek responses to the employee's competence in relation to banking services: 'demonstrating knowledge of our products and services'; 'sorting out any problems or concerns'; 'offering advice'.
- Four questions seek customer judgements on the efficiency of the employee during the interaction: 'making an effort to serve you quickly'; 'carrying out everything competently'; 'explaining things clearly; and 'listening attentively'.
- Three questions are designed to monitor the emotional style of the interaction, ratings being sought for the quality of 'acknowledging/greeting you', 'appearing pleased to see you', and 'making you feel I treated you as an individual'.

Each survey form is individually numbered and is therefore traceable back to individual bank branches and employees.

As social actors we all learn through processes of socialisation in families, schools, and elsewhere how to control and 'manage' emotions in different contexts. Many children, for example, are taught not to be overwhelmed by adversity, but rather to persevere by 'putting on a brave face' or 'grinning and bearing it': that is to say, create an emotional 'mask' behind which real feelings can be hidden. Similarly, in most work situations, individuals are required to suppress some emotions and often, to display others. Thus, doctors are taught to control their emotions towards pain and death, to remain neutral and detached. Similarly, people in authority may regard it as prudent to maintain an emotional distance between themselves and their subordinates, so as to avoid compromising their ability to exercise discipline over those under them. Likewise, those at lower levels within organisations may continue to 'show respect' for those higher up the hierarchy, even if they regard those at more senior levels as incompetent. Thus, in many situations in both work and non-work life, gaps occur between expressed and felt emotions, or what Snyder (1987: 1) refers to as 'the public appearances and private realities of the self'.

Our particular interest in this chapter lies in those jobs where employees are explicitly required to adopt particular sets of 'emotion rules' which define – often in considerable detail – which emotions they must publicly display, and which to suppress, in the performance of their job. Though, implicitly or explicitly, such rules have long represented important elements in many occupations, the coincidence of three developments in recent years makes this aspect of work behaviour particularly worthy of closer attention at this time:

1 It is only comparatively recently that researchers have paid specific and detailed attention to emotional aspects of work performance and their wider significance: most of the studies in this area have been published since 1980.

2 There has been a substantial increase over the last two decades in the proportion of jobs in which employees are 'customer facing', that is, in direct contact with customers of different kinds. In large part, this growth reflects the expansion of the service sector (see Chapter 2). In addition, a significant proportion of manufacturing jobs (such as in sales and purchasing) rely heavily on contact with customers and outside suppliers.

3 There has been greatly increased recognition given to 'customer service' as a vital aspect of competitiveness; this recognition in turn has increased the importance attaching to the emotional performance by employees in direct contact with customers.

The meanings attached by management to customer relations (so-called 'customer care') are examined later in the chapter. So too are the experiences of, and implications for, those delivering that 'care'. Before this, however, it is necessary first to consider briefly what different writers on this subject mean by terms such as emotion and emotional labour.

Emotion and emotional labour

Defining emotional labour

Learning outcome 1

Define what is meant by emotional labour.

Puzzling over what constitutes an emotion has a long pedigree. As Rafaeli and Sutton (1989: 4) comment, though it was more than a century ago that writers such as Charles Darwin and William James wrote on the subject of emotion, those currently seeking to define and interpret human emotions remain baffled by a number of unanswered and seemingly intractable questions. The subject of human emotion, just like the range of emotions a person can express, is a very wide one, and it would delay us unduly to explore the many social, psychological and bioogical avenues of emotion. It is sufficient for the present discussion to note the widespread agreement among those writing on emotions in the workplace that emotions centrally concern an individual's *feelings*. A notable book on the subject, *Emotion in Organization*, for example, described itself as 'a book about feelings' (Fineman, 1993: 1), while other contributions to this area of study similarly make reference in their titles and sub-titles to 'feelings' (James, 1989) 'human feeling' (Hochschild, 1983) and 'real feelings' (Van Maanen and Kunda, 1989).

Even when we narrow the focus to emotions or feelings expressed in the workplace, it remains apparent that the topic is still a potentially enormous one, not least because work represents an important part of social existence, and encapsulates the range of human feelings – the loves, hatreds, fears, compassions, frustrations, joys, guilt and envies – that develop over time wherever any social group interacts. In addition, large areas of research, for instance in relation to job satisfaction and motivation, are concerned with exploring the feelings people have about work. So, in the discussion that follows, the principal focus is narrowed to address those (increasingly common) situations where service employees are required, as part of their job contract, to display specific sets of emotions (by verbal and/or non-verbal means) with the aim, in turn, of inducing particular feelings and responses among those for whom the service is being provided. This can be summed up as *emotional labour*. Hochschild (1983: 7) coined this term to refer to 'the management of feeling to create a publicly observable facial and bodily display' (see Table 7.1). This form of labour, like physical labour, is purchased by employers for a wage; its precise performance can be specified in sets of rules, and its adherence monitored by different forms of supervision and control. Subsequent writers in this area have sought to develop Hochschild's pioneering work. Writers such as Wharton and Erickson (1993), Morris and Feldman (1996) and Abiala (1999), for example, emphasise that emotional labour is not a uniform activity, but varies in both type and intensity: a variability which must be taken into account when assessing the consequences of performing this type of work. The definitions used by writers such as Ashforth and Humphrey (1993: 90) and Morris and Feldman (1996: 987) concentrate attention more on behaviour, rather than (in Hochschild's definition) any presumed management of feelings underlying behaviour.

A number of writers such as Mann (1999: 353) see the dissonance, or gap, between real and displayed emotions as the core characteristic of emotional labour. James (1989), on the other hand, defines emotional labour in a slightly different way, in terms of the work involved in dealing with other people's emotions – the sort of labour, for example, widely performed in hospitals and hospices, where James conducted her research. Pugliesi (1999: 129) draws a similar distinction between the emotional labour centred on managing one's own feelings and the emotional labour which entails managing the feelings of others.

Table 7.1 Some definitions of emotional labour

Author	Definition
Hochschild (1983)	'the management of feeling to create a publicly observable facial and bodily display'
Ashforth and Humphrey (1993)	'the display of expected emotions'
Morris and Feldman (1996)	'the act of expressing organizationally desired emotions during service transactions'
Mann (1999)	[the discrepancy between] 'the emotional demeanor that an individual displays because it is considered appropriate, and the emotions that are genuinely felt but that would be inappropriate to display'
James (1989)	'labour involved in dealing with other people's feelings'
Pugliesi (1999)	distinguishes between 'self-focused' emotional labour (centred on the management of one's own feelings) and 'other-focused' emotional labour (directed towards the management of the feelings of others)

EXERCISE 7.1

What do *you* think?

Read the list of definitions of emotional labour in Table 7.1 and for each one, give an example of a job or occupation where the definition might apply. You should try to give examples other than those already mentioned in the chapter so far.

On closer inspection, it is evident that these definitional positions are in practice closely related. In Hochschild's approach, for example, the employee's emotional display is specifically designed to induce a particular set of feelings (for example, the 'satisfied customer') in the recipient of the labour. Correspondingly, for the nurses in James' study, one of the main ways in which patients' grief and anger is dealt with is by the nurses regulating their own emotions.

TO SUM UP

In placing different emphases on the performer or recipient of emotional labour, the various definitions act to underline the essentially *interactive* nature of this form of labour. It is work performed by employees in direct contact with others (customers, patients, clients) in which the response of those 'others' has a direct bearing on the experience of employees performing emotional labour, and on the attitudes of employers as to how that labour should be performed.

Real vs. displayed emotions

The foregoing discussion raises a key issue: what lies at the heart of emotional labour is not necessarily the expression of real emotions, but *displayed* emotions, which may or may not be truly felt. As the supermarket employee quoted earlier commented, the check-out operators have to smile – and the smile must look authentic – whether or not they feel positively disposed towards the customer. Where employees are required as part of their job to demonstrate feelings they may not share, they are *performing* emotional labour in the sense that the work role involves aspects not unlike those of an actor – for example, adopting the role and the script of the 'happy worker', pleased to be of service (no matter how the customer responds). This has become an influential metaphor not lost on the employee, as demonstrated by the Cathay Pacific flight attendant who commented, 'We say we are all entertainers now because everyone is on stage' (quoted by Linstead, 1995: 198).

A number of sociologists and psychologists have considered social life, including life within work organisations, from a performance or 'dramaturgical' perspective (see for example, Goffman, 1969, 1971; and Mangham and Overington, 1987). This perspective envisages social life as a series of scripted performances in which people act out parts which are consistent with the 'selves' that they wish to present. Individuals are viewed as performing different scripts in different social situations. Goffman (1969: 183) refers to 'the arts of impression management' in relation to how individuals present themselves to the outside world, how different circumstances elicit different performances from the 'actors' involved, and how people 'self-monitor' their performances and adjust these as conditions alter (see also Snyder, 1987, for a discussion of self-monitoring).

The metaphor of the theatre and its component terms such as actor, performance, role, script and being 'on' and 'off' stage, can usefully be applied to an analysis of emotional labour, and the display rules of emotional conduct. At the same time, from a dramaturgical perspective, emotional labour can be seen as a variant of what already occurs in most other social contexts. In jobs requiring emotional labour, employees perform a particular emotion script, just as in other settings individuals perform other emotional displays, some of which are likely to be as inauthentic as those indicated by the check-out operator quoted earlier, who is required to smile even at rude customers. The key difference between these work and other settings, however, lies in the fact that those employees performing emotional labour are *required* to follow what Ekman (1973) and Ashforth and Humphrey (1993: 89) term the 'display rules', as part of their job. Discretion and choice over the nature of displayed feelings is removed or reduced, and the emotional performance forms part of the effort-wage bargain in the same way that physical performance does. As discussed later, for some critics of emotional labour (such as Hochschild, 1983) the problem is that some jobs require employees to undertake 'unacceptable' levels of emotional display, with potentially detrimental effects on the individuals involved. Before examining the effects of emotional labour, however, and the way people learn, experience and cope with this form of labour, it is necessary to consider in a little more detail the factors behind the increase in this aspect of work.

TO SUM UP

Emotional labour entails the performance of certain emotions in line with display rules established by management.

Learning outcome 2

Demonstrate knowledge of the factors that have brought about the expansion of emotional labour and the reasons for the increased importance attributed to it by management.

The expansion of emotional labour

The growth in service activities

In Chapter 2, the degree to which advanced industrial economies have experienced a shift in industrial structure was highlighted, with a diminishing proportion of the total workforce engaged in the primary and secondary sectors, and a growing proportion located in the tertiary, service sector. While an important aspect of service activity involves commercial organisations providing services for one another (for example, management consultancy, specialised maintenance work, and office cleaning) the growth in the service sector has been particularly notable in the area of personal services – the range of services available to the individual citizen. Few of these services are unique to the recent period. What is evident, however, is a growth in consumer choice, either as a result of the multiplication of similar services (such as a proliferation of leisure facilities, financial institutions, or different restaurants in a particular locality) or because of the extension of existing services, in part as a result of advances in technology (for example, travel agents equipped with computer reservation systems enabling them to provide a much extended service, or libraries with access to much greater information via electronic storage systems).

The growth of services to individuals can be categorised in various ways. Lynch (1992) for example, identifies an expansion in:

- financial services (including banks, building societies and insurance companies);
- travel services (such as coach, rail and air services, together with related activities such as car hire);
- leisure services (such as hotels, restaurants, cinemas, theatres, pubs, clubs, sporting facilities);
- provisioning services (different types of retail outlets);
- communication services (such as telephone, media);
- convenience services (such as hairdressing, travel agents).

In addition, in the public (and increasingly, the privatised) sector there has been a growth in competition in, for example:

- educational services;

- health and welfare services;
- environmental services.

Increased emphasis on customer service

This expansion in service activities alone would probably have been sufficient to raise awareness of the significance of how employees interact with customers. However, a major reason why attention has come to focus so strongly on the nature of that interaction reflects not only the fact that such interactions have become more numerous, but that they are also occurring in an increasingly competitive environment, and that the *significance* of those interactions for the customer's overall judgement of the service has increasingly been recognised by management and, as a result, given greater emphasis. The increased competitiveness reflects both a general growth in service choices (for example, different leisure services competing for the customer's free time: should we take the kids to a theme park, the zoo, the swimming pool or the cinema today?) and also the multi-plication of very similar services within a particular locality (shall we take the kids to eat at McDonald's or Burger King?). One effect of this growth of very similar services (and this multiplication is as evident in financial services, supermarkets and a range of other activities as in the fast food industry) is a tendency to even out many of the differences in price and elements of the service 'product': overall the hamburgers are very similar, as are the hotel rooms in the different hotel chains, the airline seats and the various products offered by different estate agents, banks, travel agents and supermarkets.

In such an environment, where the actual services being offered for sale are little differentiated, increased significance becomes attached not to the physical nature of the service being offered, but to its *psychological* nature. The facilities at different banks, for example, may be almost identical, but in which one does the customer feel that they have been 'treated' the best? In this situation, the aim of any particular service provider comes to centre on making the customer feel more positively disposed to that service, such that they return to that particular service provider (be it a shop, restaurant, airline, or hotel) when a repeat service is sought. It is this psychological element which is of particular significance in the recent expansion of emotional labour. The goal of securing a favourable psychological response from the customer has given rise to a much greater emphasis on customer service or 'customer care'. Notions of customer care have long existed of course, embodied in such maxims as 'service with a smile' and 'the customer is always right'. But the growth of a more articulated and extensive customer care philosophy can be traced to the growing importance attributed to customer relations within the 'excellence' movement (Peters and Waterman, 1982; Peters and Austin, 1985) and the spread into the service sector of ideas such as Total Quality Management and 'continuous improvement', originally formulated within manufacturing contexts (Deming 1982; Juran, 1979).

In part, customer care involves simply the efficient delivery of a service – a high quality product, delivered on time and to specification. However, with the duplication of very similar services, customer care manuals have also come to emphasise additional means of securing customer satisfaction. For example, the following comment, by a management writer on the psychology of customer care (Lynch, 1992: 29) is implicit in much of the thinking behind customer care:

> Any action which increases the self-esteem of the customer will raise the level of satisfaction ... Conveying in a sincere manner the message 'You are better than you think you are' is a powerful tool for any service provider.

Thus, boosting the customer's self-esteem is seen to be an important aspect of customer care. There are various ways of achieving this esteem or status enhancement; Lynch (1992), for example, cites the importance of using the customer's name. Indeed, the whole manner in which an employee may be required to deliver a service (smiling, gaining eye contact, giving a friendly greeting) can contribute to putting customers at their ease, showing deference to them, making them feel special, even sexually attractive (Hall, 1993; Linstead, 1995; Wood, 2000). In some situations, attributing status to the customer, and thereby potentially raising their self-esteem, is expressed in ways other than establishing 'friendly' relations. The undertaker's staff, for example, demonstrate a sensitivity to (and thus acknowledge the status of) the bereaved's feelings by performing their duties in a solemn way (at least while in sight of the bereaved). The waiter at a very high class restaurant may also acknowledge a customer's status by being unobtrusive (though remaining attentive and efficient), thereby acknowledging the customer's right to privacy and their status as someone with the ability to eat at such an expensive restaurant (Hall, 1993). In a family friendly restaurant (such as TGI Fridays) on the other hand, status is still attributed to the customer, but in the form of the waiter creating a more openly friendly relationship (see Excerpt 7.2).

EXCERPT 7.2

Performing service at TGI Fridays

In an analysis of empowerment at TGI Fridays, Lashley (1999) reveals how the waiting staff are required to manage their behaviour to reflect the variation in the customers throughout the day. For example, at lunchtime, business customers predominate, in the afternoon there are more families and in the early evening there are mainly couples. Each group will require a different approach, and in this way the staff are performing emotion work.

As Lashley (1999: 797) explains, '"Dub-Dubs", as the waiting staff are called, have to advise customers on the menu and how best to structure their meal. They also have to identify the customer's service requirements and deliver what is needed. In some cases, "having a good laugh with the customers is needed", in others, they need to leave the guests to their own devices, or create the necessary celebratory

▶

atmosphere to match with a birthday or other party occasion. At other times they have to entertain restive children. Employee performance requires, therefore, more than the traditional acts of greeting, seating and serving customers. Employees have to be able to provide both the behaviours and the emotional displays, to match with customer wants and feelings.'

EXERCISE 7.2

What do *you* think?

The argument in this part of the discussion has been that customers are increasingly influenced by the quality of the emotional labour that is performed on them. Given that we are all customers, it is useful to ask ourselves how important emotional labour is to us. And more specifically, how much it influences our patterns of purchasing goods and services.

1 How aware are you of the emotional labour that customer-contact staff are performing on you? (provide specific examples)

2 Do you think the amount of emotional labour that you experience is increasing? In what ways?

3 How important is it to you that people who are delivering a service to you perform emotional labour as part of that service – is it more important to you in some settings (for example, a restaurant), than others (such as a supermarket)?

4 If it is more important to you in some settings than others, why is this the case?

What these various aspects of customer care underline is that in a context of intensifying competition, *how* a service is delivered has come to be defined as central to overall organisational success. As a result, those staff in direct contact with the customer have become increasingly recognised as key representatives of the service organization. Customer-facing staff are situated in crucial 'boundary-spanning' positions which link the organisation to external individuals or groups. One chief executive of a major airline sums up these interactions between organisational members and customers as key 'moments of truth', on which the latter form lasting judgements about the organisation as a whole (Carlzon, 1987).

TO SUM UP

Management have come to pay much greater attention to the manner in which employees perform their interactions with customers. In some settings, highly detailed rules and 'scripts' have been established specifying which emotions must be

▶

▶ displayed, and which suppressed; these display rules are backed up by sanctions (and less frequently, rewards) in an attempt to secure full compliance. However, the fact that systems of punishment and reward exist at all, indicates that compliance with the rules of emotional display remains problematic in many organisations. As the next section examines, in practice many employees experience difficulties in performing this aspect of their job, and resort to various strategies to cope with the exacting demands of emotional labour.

Experiencing emotional labour

Selection and training for emotional labour

Learning outcome 3

Explain the ways in which employees learn and experience emotional labour.

While various situations exist where employees are required to present feelings which are solemn (undertakers), disapproving (debt collectors) or even hostile (night-club bouncers or police interrogators) most consideration has been given to the more common contexts where employees' emotional performance is designed to induce or reinforce positive feelings within the customer. In each of these contexts, the required emotional performance typically involves, 'a complex combination of facial expression, body language, spoken words and tone of voice' (Rafaeli and Sutton, 1987: 33). This combination is secured primarily through the processes of selection, training and monitoring of employee behaviour. Non-verbal elements form an important part of many jobs involving emotional labour, and can be prominent criteria in selection decisions. At Disneyland, for example, the (mainly young) people recruited to work in the park are chosen partly on the basis of their ability to exhibit a fresh, clean-cut, honest appearance – the non-verbal embodiment in fact of the values traditionally espoused in Walt Disney films (Van Maanen and Kunda, 1989). Airline companies too emphasise non-verbal aspects of the work of customer-contact staff, including the importance of a high standard of personal grooming, covering such aspects as weight regulation, uniform, and even colour of eye-shadow (Hochschild, 1983; Williams, 1988). Similarly, at most supermarkets, check-out operators are expected to conform to particular patterns of non-verbal behaviour even when not serving. For example, one check-out operator, Denise (name changed) commented in an interview with the authors that at her store, not only were the check-outs constantly monitored by closed circuit television equipment, but supervisors regularly patrolled behind the check-outs, preventing any of the operators from turning round to talk to fellow operators by whispering the command 'FF', which meant 'Face the Front'. Denise and her colleagues were required not only to 'FF', but also to sit straight at all times; they were strictly forbidden, for example, from putting their elbows on the counter in front of them to relax their backs.

Non-verbal rules of emotional display play an important part in many service organisations, but it is the verbal rules which have been increasingly emphasised in a growing number of settings involving direct contact with customers. While in some contexts, employees receive little or no guidance on the 'correct' verbal behaviour, in others the prescribed verbal repertoire is passed on through detailed training and instruction. At her supermarket, for example, Denise has been instructed to greet the customer, smile and make eye contact, and when the customer pays by cheque or credit card, read the customer's name and return the card using their name ('Thank you Mrs Smith/Mr Jones'). This verbal display of friendliness and deference represents an increasingly common feature not only in supermarkets (Ogbonna and Wilkinson, 1990) but also in other areas of retailing, and service activities involving the public. Those entering the space ride at Disneyland, for example, are met with the words 'Welcome Voyager' by the ride operator (Van Maanen and Kunda, 1989). At McDonald's, counter and window crews are trained in highly routinised scripts, which include a number of verbal and non-verbal emotional labour elements (smiling, being cheerful, polite at all times, and so on) (Leidner, 1991). These scripts are not only designed to create a particular 'tone' for the interaction and a particular 'end' (a sale and customer satisfaction) but their high level of routinisation also allows for dealing with a high volume of customers with a minimum of delay.

EXERCISE 7.3

What do *you* think?

Think about any job you have had that involved a degree of emotional labour. This might have been working for example in a bar, a restaurant, a supermarket, a shop, in a crèche, or as a holiday rep.

1 Overall, did you find the emotional labour part of the job enjoyable or not enjoyable?

2 What were the enjoyable aspects of the emotional labour?

3 What were the aspects that were not enjoyable?

Both verbal and non-verbal emotional labour is prominent in the work of waiters and waitresses (see, for example, Hall, 1993; Mars and Nicod, 1984; and Spradley and Mann, 1975). Those waiting at tables are expected to perform a number of physical tasks but in addition, a warm, friendly and deferential manner is widely seen by employers as a key element in creating a positive ambience. For the waiters and waitresses, there is an additional, instrumental reason for performing their emotional labour effectively, as a significant part of their income derives from tips. Studies have shown that those who smile more do better at attracting larger tips than those who do not (Tidd and Lockard, 1978, cited in Rafaeli and Sutton, 1987). Further, one study found that tips to waitresses were higher where the waitress had made physical contact with the (male) customers by, for example, a fleeting touch of the hand when returning change, or touching the customer's shoulder (Crusco and Wetzel, 1984). Such studies appear to underline further the significance of the service provider boosting the customer's self-esteem by making them feel attractive. This boosting of self-esteem, and the financial implications of doing so effectively, are even more pronounced in parts of the night club industry, as the case in Excerpt 7.3 illustrates.

EXCERPT 7.3

Fantasy labour in the fantasy factory

Several researchers in the United States have studied the labour of dancers working in strip clubs – a setting which Wood (2000) recently termed the 'Fantasy Factory'. These studies provide insights into particularly charged venues where emotional labour is undertaken. The studies also reinforce a number of the points made elsewhere in the chapter, particularly relating to the requirement of the dancers to display some emotions and suppress others, the financial inducements attaching to the 'counterfeiting of intimacy' (Foote, 1954; Boles and Garbin, 1974), and the fact that this is a setting overwhelmingly where women (literally) perform emotional labour for consumption by men, with potential consequences for the status of each.

In some clubs studied, the strippers performed their stage act for tips, these being secured in important part by the women making frequent eye contact with individuals which 'made a customer feel as if a dancer were specially interested in him' (Ronai and Ellis, 1989: 277). In addition, following the staged routines in some of the clubs, the women offered personal dances ('table' or 'lap' dances) to individuals for additional payment. These table dances represent a key source of income for the women, and in efforts to secure them, a variety of emotional labour activities are undertaken.

The essence of these is to make the (usually male) customer feel particularly important, sexy and desirable, which in turn leads the man to buy additional dances. Many of the dancers interviewed by Ronai and Ellis (1989) and Wood (2000) comment that the sexually-charged looks, actions and phrases which make up this 'seduction rhetoric' need to appear genuine – to buy dancers, many individual customers had to feel that the women had 'dropped the routine' and were genuinely interested in, and attracted by, the customer. 'The smile must be convincing. The eye contact must be engaging . . . to make believable their attention and interest in the customers' (Wood, 2000: 24, 28). This is especially the case for regular customers, who can represent an important source of income (and presents, etc.) for individual dancers, but who are also very well placed to judge whether the verbal and non-verbal behaviour of 'their' dancer is repetitive or phoney (Ronai and Ellis, 1989: 287).

As well as expressing 'genuine' emotions, at the same time, in conversations with the customers, the dancers were required to suppress other emotions (like being bored or unattracted to the individual) as well as other aspects of their life. This was particular the case if they were married and had children – attributes which potentially 'jeopardised his [the customer's] ability to see her as a sexy, sensual, and most important, available, woman' (Wood, 2000: 10–11).

▶

> ▶ 'If I tell him I'm married and have a child, he's not going to think I'm sexy any-
> more. Men come in to see sexy, erotic, women who they think are party girls. Moth-
> erhood they can get at home' (dancer quoted in Wood, 2000: 16).
>
> Results of these encounters include an economic exchange (money paid in return
> for a dance provided). In common with several other arenas of emotional labour,
> however, the exchange is also a psychological one, more to the benefit of the male
> customer. 'Strippers increase the status of men through labor aimed at creating a
> designated impression for the men themselves – the impression of being interesting,
> sexy and desirable' (Wood, 2000: 15). The emotional costs of stripping, in terms of
> stigmatisation, rejection by customers, offensive behaviour, as well as physical
> assaults, can be considerable. As Ronai and Ellis (1989: 296) sum it up, 'Stripping, as
> a service occupation, pays well, but costs dearly'.

It is the airline industry, however, which has given rise to one of the path-
breaking studies of emotional labour (Hochschild, 1979 and 1983). In her study of
Delta Airlines flight attendants (elsewhere often referred to as cabin crew, formerly
as air hostesses or stewardesses) Hochschild explores the development, performance and consequences of emotional labour. Selection and training are shown to
play particularly important roles in inculcating particular 'feeling rules' into the
recruits. Selection criteria, for example, included both non-verbal and verbal
aspects. Not only were physical attributes and overall appearance taken into
account in the selection process for flight attendants, but so too was the ability to
'project a warm personality' and display enthusiasm, friendliness and sociability
(Hochschild, 1983: 97). However, while the selection process is used to identify
those who have the predisposition to perform emotional labour effectively,
Hochschild emphasises the training sessions as the place where the flight attendants
are given more precise instruction on how to perform their role. As well as training
in the technical aspects of their job (such as what procedures to follow in an
emergency), instruction is also given on the emotional aspects of the work. At its
simplest, the training affirms the importance of smiling.

Now girls, I want you to go out there and really *smile*. Your smile is your biggest
asset. I want you to go out there and use it. Smile. *Really* smile. Really *lay it on*.
  (Pilot speaking at a Delta Airlines Training Centre, quoted in Hochschild,
  1983: 4, emphasis in original)

The employee's smile and accompanying pleasant and helpful manner are given
considerable emphasis. Flight attendants are encouraged to think of passengers as
'guests in their own home', for whom no request is too much trouble (*ibid*: 105).
The cabin crew member's smile is designed not only to convey a welcome (in the
way the supermarket operator's smile and restaurant worker's smile endeavours to
do) but also to project a confidence and a reassurance that the company in general,

and the plane in particular, can be trusted with the customer's life (*ibid*: 4). The emphasis in the training is on fully identifying with the role, in order to generate a more 'genuine' smile – 'smiling from the inside' – rather than a false looking smile.

It is one thing to be able to smile at friendly, considerate and appreciative customers, but another to smile under pressure such as the bar worker, waitress, or check-out operator faced with large numbers of customers, or service workers in general faced with offensive individuals. It is in these problematic circumstances that management also require compliance with display rules. They seek to achieve this partly by encouraging employees to interpret the situation differently, to suppress any feelings of anger or frustration, and to respond in the manner prescribed by management.

In their study of telephone sales agents, for example, Taylor and Tyler (2000: 84) describe how the (mainly female) agents are trained not to get angry with offensive (often male) customers. As one trainer commented:

> If a man's having a go at you . . . he might even be embarrassing you . . . don't get ruffled, you've got to keep your cool. Remember that you are trying to offer him something and get him to pay for the privilege. He can really talk to you how he wants. Your job is to deal with it . . . *just take a few deep breaths and let your irritation cool down* . . . think to yourself he's not worth it (emphasis in original).

This example matches closely aspects of the emotion training of the Delta flight attendants described by Hochschild (1983), in particular the instructions on how to respond positively to awkward, angry or offensive customers ('irates' as they are known in Delta). A key training device for dealing with such passengers was to re-conceptualise them as people with a problem, who needed sympathy and understanding. Thus, employees were encouraged to think that perhaps the passenger who was drinking too much and being offensive was doing so to mask a fear of flying (or a stressful job, sadness at being away from home, or whatever). Underlying this training is the requirement for attendants to respond positively to such passengers, reflecting the fact that they may be frequent flyers and thus important sources of revenue to the company. Thus, the attendants are required to 'think sales' (*ibid*: 108) no matter how irksome or rude the passenger is being.

Different ways of doing emotional labour

It is evident from the studies undertaken that workers perform a variety of forms of emotional labour and do so in different ways. Hochschild (1983) for example, distinguishes between those who engage in 'surface' acting and those who perform 'deep' acting. Surface acting involves a behavioural compliance with the display rules (facial expression, verbal comments, and so on) without any attempt being made to internalise these rules: the emotions are feigned or faked. Deep acting on the other hand, involves employees internalising their role more thoroughly in an attempt to 'experience' the required emotions. Selection procedures and training programmes such as the ones described by Hochschild are designed to elicit deep acting – that, by developing a set of inner feelings (towards the company, the customer and the attendant's work role), the outward behaviour would follow as a matter of course.

What do *you* think?

Surface and deep acting are two ways of performing emotional labour, and have different implications for how employees approach and perform their work role.

1 What are the advantages and disadvantages of each approach?

2 Overall, if you had to recommend to someone how they should handle their emotional labour, would you advocate a surface acting or a deep acting approach? Why do you say this?

Acting natural

Deep acting of the type described by Hochschild has also been encouraged in more recent years by managers encouraging employees to behave 'naturally' rather than simply stick to a rigid prescribed script. In efforts to create a more 'genuine' interaction, an increasing number of organisations are giving employees the freedom to 'be themselves', to be 'more natural' and 'more authentic' in their interactions with customers.

Rosenthal, Hill and Peccei (1997) for example, report a study of a major UK food retailer which in the mid-1990s moved away from highly scripted forms of service as part of a 'Service Excellence' initiative. These researchers found that many employees preferred being able to be more 'natural' in their dealings with customers, compared to the previous need to adhere to pre-set company scripts (*ibid*: 493).

However, as Taylor (1998: 92) points out in a study of telephone sales staff, in practice the degree of empowerment within this 'emotional autonomy' is very partial. Management at the telephone sales organisation sought a 'naturalness' from employees only in so far as the expression of positive dispositions by staff helped build up a rapport with customers. To put it another way, acting natural was fine in the eyes of management as long as it served the organisation's objectives – to increase sales and improve customer service. The emotional autonomy did not extend to empowering employees to tell rude customers just where to get off.

Ashforth and Humphrey (1993: 94) have subsequently pointed out that these two 'routes' to emotional labour should be supplemented by a third, which takes into account the situation where the expected emotional display is fully consistent with an individual's own inner feelings (see also, Ashforth and Tomiuk, 2000). In such cases, there is no need for the worker to 'act' at all, since the emotion is in harmony with what the individual would have naturally displayed as part of their own identity. An example might be a nurse who has entered that occupation to fulfil a strong desire to care for people who are ill. Other examples in the emotional labour literature include youth shelter workers who identify very closely with the plight of the young people seeking refuge in the shelter (Karabanow, 1999) and highly enthusiastic employees attached to 'high commitment' organisations such as The Body Shop (Martin, Knopoff and Beckman, 1998).

TO SUM UP

Emotional labour involves both extensive verbal and non-verbal behaviour. Both of these form important elements in the selection and training programmes for various occupations. Emotional labour may be performed through surface or deep acting, or in circumstances where the employee so fully identifies with the job that no 'acting' is involved at all.

However, even the person who identifies fully with their job will have their off-days and occasional bad moods. At those times they – like their counterparts who identify with their job less strongly – will be required to manage their emotions to hide their true feelings.

Learning outcome 4

Assess employee reactions to emotional labour.

Reactions to emotional labour

Problematic circumstances for performing emotional labour

For many employees, for much of the time, performing emotional labour is unproblematic. Smiling at customers often elicits a smile in return, and the creation of a friendly interaction. Further, as just noted, there will be those service employees who are very positively disposed to their work, and to smile while doing it is wholly consistent with their general feelings towards the job and the customer. In these latter cases, there is little or no dissonance or 'gap' between the individual's felt and expressed emotions at work: expectation and actuality are closely aligned.

Other circumstances can arise, however, where the performance of emotional labour becomes much more problematic for the individual. One relates to the overall *amount* of emotional labour demanded by the job, especially where the emotional display is required over long periods of time. Cabin crew members aboard inter-continental flights, for example, not only work long duty times, but also suffer from additional fatigue as a result of jet-lag and interrupted sleep patterns. The strain of prolonged emotional display, particularly where customers are being difficult or offensive (see also below) is illustrated in the following extract from Hochschild (1983: 127):

A young businessman said to a flight attendant, 'Why aren't you smiling?' She put her tray back on the food cart, looked him in the eye and said, 'I'll tell you what. You smile first, then I'll smile'. The businessman smiled at her. 'Good', she replied. 'Now freeze and hold that for fifteen hours'.

A second problematic circumstance is where the dissonance between felt and displayed emotions is particularly acute. This may arise if the required emotional display is considered inappropriate by the worker performing the task. The supermarket employee, Denise, quoted earlier, for example, expressed considerable difficulty with using the customer's name when handling cheques or credit cards. To Denise, a shy self-effacing woman, this seemed 'too forward, too familiar' in a situation where she was not acquainted with the individual whose name she was required to use; the result was a continuing unease and embarrassment.

A more commonly reported situation of emotional dissonance is where employees are required to maintain a particular emotional display towards customers who are being rude or offensive. Examples of objectionable behaviour are evidenced in many studies of emotional labour, and occur in all settings from the supermarket check-out, the hospital and the restaurant, to the aircraft cabin, the call centre and the night club. Instances range from verbal abuse to physical assault. To handle these sorts of problematic situations, and generally to reduce the stresses of the emotional aspects of the job, it is clear that performers of this kind of labour adopt a variety of coping strategies.

Monitoring emotional labour

It is one thing for management to issue sets of guide-lines and instructions and run training programmes and refresher courses to perfect and sustain various forms of emotional labour; it is another, however, to be confident that once trained, employees will carry out the emotional labour as specified at all times. That managers recognise the tendency for employees to lapse in their emotional display is reflected in the practices adopted to monitor and modify employee behaviour: disciplining those falling short of the prescribed norms and (less frequently) rewarding unusually high performers. Many of the studies of emotional labour highlight particular supervisory practices, often covertly conducted, to check employee behaviour. Airlines, for example, regularly use 'ghost riders' to check on how employees perform their roles; similarly, supermarkets employ 'mystery shoppers' (people hired by the company and disguised as customers) to monitor performance of check-out operators. At Disneyland, supervisors secrete themselves around the park to check on the behaviour of workers while remaining unobserved themselves (Van Maanen and Kunda, 1989).

Telephone call centre supervisors routinely listen in to calls, and these may be taped for use in appraisal meetings with employees (Taylor, 1998: 93; Taylor and

Learning outcome 5

Identify how managers seek to manage this aspect of employee behaviour.

Tyler, 2000: 83). In their survey of fifty-five call centres in Scotland, Taylor and Bain (1999: 106) identified nine measures used by management in a majority of centres to monitor employee performance. These included quantitative measures such as length of calls and time between calls. However, the most common measure of all – present in more than four out of five call centres – was the monitoring of employee 'politeness towards customer'.

In addition to these various monitoring methods, a growing number of services regularly issue 'customer service' questionnaires (like the banking illustration given earlier) to gain information about the demeanour and emotional style of the employee. Excerpt 7.5 gives another example of such a questionnaire used in the UK in 2000 – this time involving the performance of postal delivery workers.

EXCERPT 7.5

Assessing our performance...in Royal Mail

Royal Mail in the UK distributes questionnaires to customers to measure the service provided by local delivery offices. Various questions ask about time of deliveries, condition of mail received, extent to which letters are delivered to the wrong address, and so on.

In addition, several questions seek information about the postman's/postwoman's demeanour, appearance and emotional style. Not only the questions, but also the response scales used provide insight into employer expectations of postal employees. These questions and response choices include:

Does your postman/postwoman show respect for your property and the neighbourhood?

- shows very little respect
- shows some respect but could be more careful
- always shows respect

Which best describes your postman/postwoman's appearance?

- often looks a bit scruffy
- usually reasonably tidy
- always neat and smart

How friendly is your postman/postwoman?

- never seems cheerful or acknowledges me
- acknowledges me, but only if I greet him/her
- acknowledges me, but doesn't always seem cheerful
- always seems cheerful and acknowledges me

The questionnaire includes the address and postcode of the household completing it, thus allowing identification of individual delivery offices, postal delivery rounds – and specific postal employees.

Emotional labour coping strategies

Despite this level of surveillance, however, it is clear that those required to perform very frequent repetitions of an emotional display and/or perform emotional
labour over long periods, adopt various coping strategies, both in response to the
general pressures, and to handle particular situations such as angry or offensive
customers. At their simplest these strategies involve employees retiring to places,
such as a rest room or canteen ('off-stage' areas where customers are not present)
where they can 'let off steam'. Here, employees can express their anger or frustration
in ways which are denied them when performing their job.

> We do get some very difficult customers . . . when you get too angry you just go
> into the [back] office and have a good swear at them and you come out smiling.
> (Supermarket employee, quoted by Ogbonna and Wilkinson, 1990: 12)

This 'off-stage' area may be as simple as the space created by employees turning
their back on the customer – and the opportunity this provides for gestures such as
face-pulling or eyes-rolling that indicate to other employees a dropping of the
emotional mask. In studies of emotional labour, such strategies are reported in a
wide variety of contexts from High Street retail stores (Martin, Knopoff and Beckman, 1998: 450) to strip clubs (Wood, 2000: 25). As well as 'letting off steam', one
of the additional benefits of these off-stage behaviours is that they may reinforce
the degree of co-worker solidarity: a solidarity which Karabanow (1999) identifies
as an important factor in coping with jobs with high emotional labour demands.

Other strategies for coping with rude customers include engaging in covert activity which at the same time maintains the mask of emotional display: for example,
the waiter who adulterates the offensive customer's food in some way, or the sales
assistant who manages to look in all directions except at the loud customer who is
demanding their attention. Disneyland ride operators deploy a number of covert
activities in response to their situation, and particularly when confronted by
offensive customers; these can include the 'break-up-the-party' ploy of separating
pairs into different rides (despite there being room for both on the same ride), the
'seat-belt squeeze' in which customers are over-tightened into their seats, and
other variants of inflicting physical discomfort (Van Maanen and Kunda, 1989: 67).

Call centre employees also report a variety of covert methods for dealing with
rude or offensive customers. These include limiting the amount of information
provided and responding in a tone of voice which, while officially conforming
to the rules, in practice allows employees to restrict their required emotional
display. One operator in a telecommunications centre described this in the following way:

> Some customers are just a pain in the arse and they treat you like dirt. But I've
> worked out a way of saying things that puts them in their place. If you choose
> your words carefully, there's no way they can pull you in and dig you up for
> what you've said. (Taylor and Bain, 1999: 113)

A telephone sales agent in the study by Taylor and Tyler (2000: 89) makes a similar point:

> If I don't like someone ... it's difficult to explain but I will be efficient with them, giving them what they want and no more, but I will not be really friendly... I sometimes have a really monotone voice, sounding a bit cold...I will not laugh at their jokes, for example.

Resistance in call centres is also facilitated by experienced employees being able to tell when their calls are being monitored by supervisors (*ibid*: 89). This allows for more overt coping strategies such as disconnecting offensive calls.

A more general defence mechanism for coping with the demands of emotional labour is referred to in several studies by phrases such as 'switching off', 'switching to automatic' or 'going robot'. Filby (1992: 39) for example, refers to emotional labourers' ability to 'switch onto autopilot'. These various expressions refer to behaviour involving a continued outward adherence to the basic emotional performance, but an inward escape from the pressures of the job. Many performers of emotional labour, for example, are expected to smile as though they mean it ('smile from the inside') so that customers believe in its sincerity and do not see it as simply part of an act. To switch into automatic may involve limiting this expression of 'sincerity'. Employees may have only limited scope for adopting this strategy, however, if 'sincerity' is also monitored. British Airways passengers arriving at London Heathrow, for example, are regularly canvassed about the service they have just received: did the check-in staff at the departure airport use the passenger's name; did they look them in the eye and smile; and did the smile seem genuine or forced – on a scale of one to four? (Blyton and Turnbull, 1998: 69).

There are also other coping strategies and ways individual employees protest against the pressure of display rules. Hochschild (1983) for example, notes the use of 'slow-downs' among flight attendants and the way some employees enact minor infringements of uniform and appearance codes as a way of not being fully submissive to management instruction. Overall, what such protests and coping strategies indicate is that, in some cases at least, employees experience difficulties in continually performing their role as laid down in training manuals and management instruction.

TO SUM UP

Emotional labour becomes problematic under certain circumstances. Reflecting this, management have established extensive means to monitor employee compliance with particular sets of display rules. Despite this surveillance, employees adopt various strategies to cope with excessive emotional labour.

Some argue, however, that in more extreme cases, the demands of emotional labour have consequences for the workers involved which go significantly beyond the

▶

▶ (relatively) minor irritations of the rude customer. It is to a discussion of these consequences that we now turn, in particular the physical and psychological health implications of performing emotional labour and the argument that emotional labour has particular implications for women's position in the labour force.

Some wider implications of emotional labour

Emotional labour and employee well-being

In principle, just as emotional labour may be a source of job satisfaction for those who gain fulfilment from the work they perform, it is also potentially as significant a source of job dissatisfaction and alienation as other forms of labour (see discussion of alienation in Chapter 8). Indeed, any alienation arising from emotional labour could be particularly acute, since the nature of the task carries the potential for individuals to become self-estranged – detached from their own 'real' feelings – which in turn might threaten their sense of their own identity. Further, where the expressed emotions are not felt, this gap between real and displayed feelings may cause the individual to feel false and create a sense of strain. Various writers have drawn attention to this 'falseness' potentially leading to poor self-esteem, depression, cynicism and alienation from work (Ashforth and Humphrey, 1993: 97). It is this emotional dissonance within which emotional labourers have been described as 'suffer[ing] from a sense of being false, mechanical, no longer a whole integrated self' (Ferguson, 1984: 54, cited in Mumby and Putnam, 1992: 472). Prolonged requirement to conform to emotional display rules, or where these rules require an intensive display of an emotion script, could also contribute to 'emotion overload', particularly where women have to perform a 'second shift' of emotion management in their domestic sphere, once their first shift of emotional labour is completed (Hochschild, 1989; Wharton and Erickson, 1993).

But while in principle there is a potential for emotional labour to be dissatisfying or alienating, how much is this the case in practice? Overall, the evidence on this question remains somewhat inconclusive, though a number of studies in recent years have added significantly to our knowledge in this area.

In her initial study of flight attendants, Hochschild (1983) highlighted a number of negative aspects of the job, leading to 'an estrangement between self and feeling and between self and display' (p. 131). Hochschild identifies such problems as 'feeling phoney' (p. 181) with the flight attendants being unable to express genuine feelings or identify their own needs – inabilities which, for some, resulted in problems of establishing and maintaining close relationships in their private lives (p. 183).

In reviewing Hochschild's work, however, Wouters (1989) argues that the costs of emotional labour should not obscure more positive aspects. For Wouters, the distinction between true and displayed feelings is not as hard and fast as Hochschild implies, for individuals perform all sorts of emotional scripts, outside as

Learning outcome 6

Evaluate research on the consequences of emotional labour for employee health and well-being.

well as inside the workplace – a multiplicity which undermines any distinction between the 'displayed' feelings in emotional labour and 'true' feelings expressed elsewhere. Wouters (1989: 116) also argues that the costs of emotional labour must be offset against the positive side of such jobs, including the pleasure which many derive from serving customers and receiving from them a positive response in return. This argument reiterates the point made earlier: that there are individuals who strongly identify with their work role, and for whom their job and the emotional display rules entailed in that job are fully consistent with their personal values and identity. Indeed, for some employees it is this 'fit' between personal values and job demands that has attracted them into the job in the first place. For such individuals, the performance of the tasks is likely to enhance, rather than reduce, psychological well-being (Ashforth and Humphrey, 1993: 100–1).

EXERCISE 7.5

What do *you* think?

Hochschild (1983) and Wouters (1989) clearly disagree on how we should view emotional labour. For Hochschild, emotional labour is a potentially major problem, while for Wouters, any difficulties entailed in this type of labour are more than offset by the positive aspects of jobs such as those of flight attendants.

Which of these arguments do you think is the more convincing, and why?

In recent years, a number of more quantitative studies have been conducted to measure the effects of emotional labour on employees' health and well-being – notably the impact on job satisfaction, stress levels, degree of 'emotional exhaustion' (or 'burnout') and various physical symptoms. Again, however, these studies do not all point in the same direction, though certain general patterns are identifiable. Among the factors which may be militating against a more consistent picture are:

- a lack of a standard measure of emotional labour (some studies for example simply measure the presence of emotional labour, while others concentrate on the gap between real and displayed emotions as the core measure of emotional labour);
- the diverse range of occupations studied: among others, debt collectors, military recruiting staff, nurses, hairdressers, chauffeurs, travel guides, university employees, shop assistants, waiters, banking staff, and survey research workers: a range which incorporates a wide variety in the type and extent of emotional labour demands.

Several studies identify possible health problems related to emotional labour. In her study of university employees in the United States, for example, Pugliesi (1999) found emotional labour was associated with increased perceptions of job stress, decreased job satisfaction and lower levels of overall worker well-being. Morris and Feldman (1997) similarly found an association between one aspect of emotional labour – the degree of emotional dissonance – and the extent of 'emotional exhaustion' among over five hundred respondents drawn from nursing, recruiting and debt collecting organisations in the United States. Mann (1999) too found a relationship between reported degree of emotional dissonance and higher stress levels among respondents in twelve UK companies.

While Pugliesi found emotional labour to be associated with higher stress and lower well-being regardless of other job factors, a number of other studies have highlighted the importance of certain conditions under which emotional labour has a more marked effect for the people involved. For example, in their study of workers involved in a survey research organisation in the USA, Schaubroeck and Jones (2000) found that overall, emotional labour was associated with the presence of a number of health symptoms. However, this association was mainly present among individuals who reported low levels of job involvement and a low level of identification with the organisation. As the authors conclude (*ibid*: 179), this finding suggests that: 'emotional labour is most unhealthful when one's emotional expressions on the job are not an authentic representation of one's personal beliefs'.

In an earlier study, Wharton (1993) also identified the importance of particular job factors in moderating any effects of emotional labour on employees. In a study of over six hundred banking and health service employees (almost two-thirds of whom were judged to hold jobs which required emotional labour) Wharton found no simple relationship between emotional labour and variables such as the degree of 'emotional exhaustion': as a whole, workers performing emotional labour were no more likely to suffer from emotional exhaustion than others. There was also no evidence of the expected relationship between emotional labour and job satisfaction (indeed, those performing jobs involving emotional labour were slightly *more* satisfied overall than those performing other jobs). What the study found, however, was that people performing emotional labour were less likely to experience emotional exhaustion if they had greater autonomy over how they carried out their work.

TO SUM UP

Despite the variation in results between individual studies, at present the balance of available evidence indicates that emotional labour is associated (in certain circumstances at least) with stress, emotional exhaustion and a lower level of general well-being. This is more likely to be the case where demands for emotional labour are high and/or where emotional dissonance is marked. The latter is likely to be greater among those who identify least with their job or with the organisation they work for. Those with very restricted degrees of control over how they perform their jobs may also find performing emotional labour to be a more negative experience than those with higher levels of job autonomy.

Learning outcome 7

Recognise wider
implications of the
growth of emotional
labour, in particular for
the position of women
in the labour force.

The gender implications of emotional labour

As well as its potential for creating feelings of alienation and emotional exhaustion, several commentators have pointed to possible negative implications of emotional labour for women's position in the labour force: in particular, that it reinforces certain gender stereotypes which in the past have been detrimental to women (see for example, Hochschild, 1983; James, 1989; Mumby and Putnam, 1992). Three aspects of emotional labour are central to this argument:

1   The distribution of emotional labour reflects a gender imbalance: the majority of those doing emotional labour for a living are women. Hochschild (1983) for example, estimates that twice as many women as men occupy jobs which require emotional labour. Moreover, even in single occupations employing both men and women, a number of studies have identified an expectation that the women employees will perform more emotional labour than their male counterparts (Morris and Feldman, 1996: 997; Taylor and Tyler, 2000).

2   Most people performing emotional labour occupy relatively low positions within work hierarchies, with emotional labour rarely being ascribed the status of a skill. Thus, just as women in general are located disproportionately within lower levels of occupational hierarchies, they are similarly disproportionately represented among those lower status jobs requiring emotional labour. For some (see, for example, Ashforth and Humphrey, 1995; Domagalski, 1999; and James, 1989) this reflects the status of 'rationalism' within contemporary capitalism, and also the customary association of rationality and masculinity (Pringle, 1989). In combination, these create a contrast between jobs which are seen to be highly 'rational' and as a result are afforded high status (and are disproportionately occupied by men), and jobs which are more 'emotional' and are accorded much lower status (and are filled disproportionately by women). In hospitals, for example, it is the rational skills of the (mainly male) doctors and hospital managers which are accredited the highest status and rewards, while the emotional well-being of the patient – a key ingredient in their return to full health – is borne largely by the (mainly female) nurses and auxiliaries, and tends to be unrecognised and much more poorly rewarded (James, 1989). This tendency to attribute status to some jobs rather than others is related to the issue of the social construction of skill, discussed in Chapter 5.

3   The main emotions displayed in emotional labour – in particular those involving a display of caring – act to reinforce gender stereotypes, and in particular that 'caring' is an emotion which is more 'natural' in women. Women are widely seen to be not only naturally more caring than men, but also more emotional than men, and more used to dealing with other people's feelings, as part of their domestic caring role. Various studies, for example, have indicated that women are the primary providers of emotional support for their partners and children (see discussion in Wharton and Erickson, 1993: 469). Critics of emotional labour argue that, as a result of this greater responsibility for emotion management in the domestic sphere, this comes to be viewed as a 'natural'

ability in women, or a 'talent' which they have, rather than a skill which has to be acquired. The effect is for management to treat emotional labour as an extension of this natural talent, not a learned skill – with the effect that it is not accorded the status of a skill. It leads management to select women rather than men for many jobs involving emotional labour: see, for example Leidner (1991) on the distribution of work tasks in McDonald's, and Taylor and Tyler (2000) on the selection of candidates for telephone sales positions.

Thus, just as the skills employed (disproportionately by women) in the domestic sphere tend to be under-recognised (see Chapter 10), so too the performance of emotional labour skills in the paid work sphere also tend to go under-recognised and under-rewarded. Filby (1992) correctly points out that it would be misleading to argue that all emotional labour deserves 'skilled' status: indeed, 'much emotion work...is untutored and probably poor' (Filby, 1992: 39). Nevertheless, as the foregoing discussion has illustrated, in a number of different contexts, emotional labour is learned through considerable training, and is performed in far from straightforward circumstances.

An extension of this argument of reinforcing stereotypes is that many front-line service jobs entail the performance of tasks as deferential servants – on aircraft, in hotels and in restaurants and night clubs, for example. It may be argued that, since the majority of emotional labour jobs are performed by women, this potentially acts to reinforce an image of women as servants – an image already reinforced by the unpaid and problematic status of domestic activities. This is particularly pertinent to those settings comprising mainly women performing emotional labour for a largely male customer group; it is mostly men, for example, who fly business class on airlines, eat business lunches, stay at hotels on sales conferences and visit certain types of night club. Further, as well as the nurturing and servant roles, some emotional labour jobs also involve women workers emphasising other aspects of their 'feminine' qualities, in particular applying their sexuality as a way of 'keeping the customers happy'.

As Hochschild (1983: 182) describes, flight attendants are required to play these different roles simultaneously: 'those of the supportive mother and those of the sexually desirable mate, manifesting themselves in 'both "motherly" behavior and a "sexy" look'. Similarly, Linstead (1995: 196) argues that through the nature of their advertising, airlines 'make no secret of their wish to entice a predominantly male clientele on board in the lucrative first and business sectors with gently erotic evocations'. In general, this message may be more subtle now than in the 1970s – when airlines used such advertising slogans as 'I'm Cheryl, Fly Me' (quoted in Lessor, 1984: 42) and 'We really move our tails for you to make your every wish come true' (quoted in Hochschild, 1983: 93) – but the message remains, nevertheless. Sexuality is similarly present in other settings of emotional labour. Filby (1992), for example, in his study of women working in betting shops, notes the sexual banter between cashiers and (mostly male) customers, which forms part of the employees' task of building customer relations and customer loyalty to that branch. Likewise, Hall (1993) notes the existence of the 'obligatory job flirt' which occurs in many restaurants, again as part of a broader management requirement to 'keep the customer happy'. This mix of emotional labour and sexuality reaches its apogee in the strip clubs described by Wood (2000) and others, where much of the income-generating activity for the women dancers is predicated on their ability to flirt and raise the sexual self-esteem of their (overwhelmingly male) customers.

However, the arguments over women and emotional labour are not as clear cut as some of the critics have suggested. For example, as noted above, it is not necessarily the case that women performing emotional labour experience a negative reaction. Indeed, Wharton (1993) in her study found that women performing emotional labour were significantly more satisfied than their male counterparts engaged in similar types of work. As a result of patterns of socialisation, for example, 'women may be better equipped than men for the interpersonal demands of front-line service work and thus experience those jobs more positively than their male counterparts' (Wharton, 1993: 225). Further, in the longer term, other factors may act in favour of changing the position of women performing emotional labour. The growth of jobs requiring emotional labour is resulting in more men needing to manage their emotions as part of the job. As the number of both women and men performing emotional labour rises, this may affect the way emotional labour is delivered, particularly where the clientele is becoming less male dominated. Linstead (1995: 196) notes, for example, the acknowledged need among airline companies to shift the nature of emotional labour in business and first class to attract the growing market in female business travellers.

Further, as the emphasis on effective service increases, employees and groups such as trade unions will potentially be able to use this recognised importance as a lever for improving the status and rewards pertaining to those performing these types of jobs – indeed, at least one writer (Foegen, 1988) has called for workers performing emotional labour to receive separate 'hypocrisy pay' as a recognition of the task involved. More generally, trade unions in Britain have made significant inroads into areas such as call centres: in the survey of call centres by Taylor and Bain (1999: 113–4), more than half had a union or staff association, with unions not only negotiating standard items such as pay, holidays, hours and overtime payments, but also raising such concerns as job stress and levels of employee monitoring and surveillance.

Taking this point further, emotional display does not render women powerless. Indeed, in certain circumstances the 'emotion' could be used as a source of power. Linstead (1995), for example, writing on a strike among Cathay Pacific (CP) flight attendants, points to the attendants' explicit use of emotional display as a means of attracting media attention and public support. The 'perfumed picket line' as it was dubbed by one of the Hong Kong newspapers gained much more coverage than the CP 'managers in suits'. While the attendants did not win the strike (not least because management was successful in hiring outside crews to operate a reduced service) the flight attendants nevertheless indicated their potential power in 'turn[ing] the seductive skills which company training had developed into an effective weapon to mobilize public opinion' (Linstead, 1995: 190).

Several writers have highlighted gender implications of emotional labour, and particularly the way that emotional labour can act to reinforce gender stereotypes in the workplace. The arguments in this area do not all point in the same direction, however, indicating the need for greater clarity on the particular contexts and conditions under which emotional labour acts to the detriment of women's status in the labour market.

Conclusion

Analysing the growth and implications of emotional labour underscores a number of broader developments and issues in contemporary industrial society. It is a growth borne not only out of the expansion of the services available to the general public, but also the competition between those services and the identification of customer relations as a key to business success in a competitive environment. Though long established in various areas of employment, a required emotional display and self-management of feelings has become part of an increasing number of jobs. There is every indication too, that this aspect of work will grow further in coming years, as a public increasingly used to a high level of 'customer care' raises its baseline expectation of what constitutes an appropriate level of that 'care' in an ever widening range of services.

As well as reflecting a growth of, and increased competition between, service providers and the greater significance attaching to customers, emotional labour also underscores certain other issues raised elsewhere in the book. Most notably, emotional labour is an aspect of work which to date has been performed predominantly by women, often while occupying comparatively low positions within their work organisations. It is an aspect of women's work which has also typically been accorded relatively little status. Hence, just as women in general have not typically been the beneficiaries of how the notion of skill has been socially constructed (see Chapter 5), in a similar way emotional labour has not been accorded prestige or skilled status. Rather, the performing of emotional labour has tended to be seen as something that women are 'naturally' good at – an innate talent rather than an acquired skill.

At the same time, as has been noted, it is important not to adopt too simplistic a view of emotional labour. It is an aspect of work which varies considerably in its nature and degree. Its impact on employees will depend on the character of the individuals involved, and some will be far more predisposed to the requirements of emotional labour than others. Further, for many, emotional labour represents a relatively minor part of their job, not unpleasant and often helping to create a more friendly working environment: smiling at others often elicits a smile in return. It is in those cases where emotional labour expectations are excessive that it becomes problematic, potentially giving rise to feelings of alienation, dissonance and emotional exhaustion. Yet, even in these situations it is clear that workers employ various coping strategies to mitigate the excesses of emotional labour. In their use of various 'survival' strategies to make their job more bearable, emotional labourers are not alone. Workers in all types of occupations adopt a whole range of survival strategies to help them to get through the working day. Broader consideration will be given to such strategies in Chapter 9. Meanwhile, we turn to assess the concept of knowledge as a defining feature of contemporary work and society.

Knowledge 8
and work

KEY CONCEPTS

- Knowledge work
- Types of knowledge: embrained, embodied, embedded, encultured and encoded
- Explicit and tacit knowledge

- Knowledge workers
- Professionals
- The entrepreneurial professional
- Knowledge creation
- Continuous improvement (kaizen)

- Knowledge capture
- Expropriation of knowledge
- Information society
- Information age
- Network society

CHAPTER AIM

To assess the concept of knowledge as a defining feature of contemporary work and society.

LEARNING OUTCOMES

By reading and thinking about the material in this chapter, you will be able to:

1 define the meaning of knowledge work based on identifying different types of knowledge;

2 specify the distinctive characteristics of knowledge work by

(a) comparing knowledge workers with routine workers

(b) comparing knowledge workers with professionals;

3 explain the process of knowledge creation and the transformation of tacit into explicit knowledge;

4 recognise the importance of knowledge capture and evaluate how this is achieved through techniques such as continuous improvement;

5 assess whether the need for managers to acquire knowledge places knowledge workers in an advantageous position compared with other employees;

6 explain and evaluate

(a) Bell's thesis of the information society

(b) Castells's thesis of the information age and the network society.

Introduction

> Knowledge and information are becoming the strategic resource and transforming agent of the post-industrial society...just as the combination of energy, resources and machine technology were the transformational agencies of industrial society. (Bell, 1980: 531)

> In an economy where the only certainty is uncertainty, the one sure source of lasting competitive advantage is knowledge. When markets shift, technologies proliferate, competitors multiply, and products become obsolete almost overnight, successful companies are those that consistently create new knowledge, disseminate it widely throughout the organization, and quickly embody it in new technologies and products. (Nonaka, 1991: 96)

> The productivity of knowledge and knowledge workers will not be the only competitive factor in the world economy. It is, however, likely to become the decisive factor, at least for most industries in the developed countries. (Drucker, 1998: 17)

These three quotes have one theme in common: the belief that knowledge is becoming central to organisations and the economies of advanced capitalism. It is an important idea because, if true, it suggests that increasingly work will need to become knowledge intensive and that those people in such knowledge intensive roles ('knowledge workers') will have a central and influential position in the occupational structure of society. Indeed, it has led some commentators to describe the current period as the information age.

In many respects the idea is intuitively appealing – not least for those of us who, as knowledge workers, are allegedly becoming more influential. But does the idea really stand up to scrutiny? Who are these so-called 'knowledge workers'? What role and influence do they have? Is this influence significantly greater than in earlier times? Does it mean that we are now living in an information society?

To explore these issues, the chapter is divided into five sections. First, the concept of knowledge work is examined. Second, knowledge workers are defined, using two different approaches. Third, there is an assessment of knowledge within the workforce, with attention being paid to the processes of knowledge creation and knowledge capture. Fourth, there is a discussion of whether knowledge workers can be considered a special group precisely because their expertise cannot be expropriated by management. Fifth, the concept of the information society is assessed using two theorists: Daniel Bell and Manuel Castells.

Learning outcome 1

Define the meaning of knowledge work based on identifying different types of knowledge.

Knowledge work

One of the central problems when defining knowledge work is establishing whether the term refers to the inputs of that work, the outputs or the work process. For example, the work of a travel agent is based on the input of knowledge (information about the availability of holidays and flights) which the agent processes to produce a service outcome – your holiday. In contrast, as authors, we are processing information (from writers and researchers) to produce *more information* (this book) – so both the input and output might be described as knowledge. While distinctions such as these are possible, the problem is that almost all jobs involve using knowledge in some form. Take the example of taxi drivers: neither the inputs (the driving) nor the outputs (delivering passengers to their destinations) would be described as knowledge work, but the work process itself involves drivers applying their knowledge (of the location, the best route, the local traffic, and so on). Indeed London cabbies refer to their training to get a licence as 'Doing the Knowledge'.

So, the problem with a broad definition of knowledge work is that it is too inclusive to be of any use – everyone is a knowledge worker because everyone's work involves knowledge in some form. Consequently, researchers have sought to find a tighter definition. For example, Winslow and Bramer (1994) suggest that knowledge work is concerned with interpreting and applying information in order to add value to the organisation through creating solutions to problems and making informed recommendations to management. An alternative approach is to think about the type of knowledge being used.

Types of knowledge

Although it is probably accurate to say that almost all jobs entail some aspect of 'knowledge', the *type* of knowledge required differs considerably. In this respect, the work of Blackler (1995) is particularly useful because, from an extensive review of previous writers, he distinguishes between five forms of knowledge. The descriptions below are based on his categories.

1 *Embrained* knowledge: the abstract, conceptual and theoretical information that we have in our heads. It can be applied to solve problems and 'think around' issues in a creative way.

2 *Embodied* knowledge: practical and applied ways of doing things learned from experience. Problems are solved by drawing upon previous experience and a wealth of information about the specific context.

3 *Encultured* knowledge: shared understandings about 'how things are done around here'. This can be an essential part of the organisational culture or the workgroup's culture (see Chapter 9).

4 *Embedded* knowledge: systematic routines that mean a person can perform a task or activity 'without thinking'. The task becomes 'second nature' to the person, to such an extent that the knowledge, learning and skill behind it is submerged from view. This idea has already been encountered (Chapter 5) when discussing tacit skills.

5 *Encoded* knowledge: information conveyed by signs and symbols. This book is a form of encoded knowledge. Information technology has increased the potential for encoding, manipulating and transmitting knowledge.

Blackler observes that these five forms indicate that 'all individuals and all organisations, not just the so-called knowledge workers or knowledge organisations are knowledgeable' (1995: 1026). Further, he suggests that it is not so much that knowledge work is becoming important per se, but that the emphasis is shifting within the forms of knowledge: from embodied and embedded to embrained, encultured and encoded knowledge.

Excerpt 8.1 provides an example of how these concepts can be applied. Read it and then assess your own understanding by attempting Exercise 8.1.

EXCERPT 8.1

Forms of knowledge at Xerox

'Brown's (1991) account of efforts to develop Xerox as a learning organisation provides an example of how the development of each of these different forms of knowledge may contribute to organisational learning. Brown pointed to the advantages for a company like Xerox of undertaking new product development in close association with potential customers (i.e. he identified the relevance of the embedded knowledge of Xerox's customers for an understanding of their reactions to new office machinery). He illustrated how design engineers at Xerox learned from ethnographic studies of how people interact with machines (i.e. from studies of the ways in which encoded knowledge interacts with, and may disrupt, embodied knowledge) and he emphasised too how studies of communications between engineers in Xerox have revealed how essential dialogue is between them (i.e. encultured knowledge) to increase their effectiveness in solving problems. Finally, Brown emphasised the importance of encouraging senior managers to develop new appreciations of their company's established practices (i.e. he pointed to the importance of developing embrained and encultured knowledge at senior management levels).'

Source: Blacker (1995: 1025–6)

EXERCISE 8.1

What do *you* think?

Read the paragraphs below and identify the five types of knowledge.

Maria inserts the photocopy card into the machine but it flashes up a message saying 'P15 error'. However, she removes the card, rubs it on her sleeve, reinserts it and the photocopy machine hums into action.

The photocopy technician had previously told her that when such an error message occurred the only thing to do was to throw away the photocopy card because it had been magnetised. Although she believed him, the next time it occurred she thought

▶

► she'd try to clean it on her sleeve. She tried this because sometimes it worked when her cashpoint card was rejected by the cash machine at the bank, and the two cards looked similar. Sure enough it had solved the problem with the photocopier.

She told the other secretaries in the office about it and so they all now use 'Maria's magic method'. They have even emailed the technician about it. He replied that it was due to the effect of static electricity, and that he would pass the tip on to others who had the same problem.

Criticisms of knowledge work

There are critics of the concept of knowledge work (for example, Collins, 1997; Kumar, 1995; Warhurst and Thompson, 1998). Rather than worry about the different meanings of the term, such critics tend to argue, more fundamentally, that the term is meaningless. In particular they raise two objections:

1 Knowledge work is often routine. Much of the supposed knowledge work involves undertaking tasks that require very little training and offers employees very little discretion.

2 Knowledge work is not a new phenomenon. Employees have always used their knowledge to do their work, and managers have always attempted to make use of their knowledge to improve the effectiveness and efficiency of work. In other words managers have consistently sought to appropriate the employees' knowledge, while employees have often tried to protect it (particularly through trade union regulation, see Chapter 11, and informal work practices, see Chapter 9).

Excerpt 8.2 provides an illustration of the arguments that some of the fiercest critics use to challenge the usefulness of the concept. However, other commentators have suggested that while the term 'knowledge work' can be ambiguous, there is no reason why a precise definition cannot be developed and used to analyse different types of 'knowledge worker'. It is to such an analysis that we now turn with two examples to illustrate this type of approach.

EXCERPT 8.2

A criticism of knowledge work

'Proponents of the knowledge economy fail to appreciate that most tertiary sector growth has occurred not in knowledge work but in the low-paid 'donkey work' of serving, guarding, cleaning, waiting and helping in the private health and care services, as well as hospitality industries.

'We find that much of the "knowledge" work, for example in financial services, requires little more of workers than information transfer...Much of the growth in service work has been in the more explicitly "interactive" categories such as telesales

►

▶

> or call-centres. This type of work has its own routine in that the process is likely to be governed by scripted interactions, and monitored for deviance by supervisors.
>
> 'All workers are, of course, knowledgeable about their work – and always have been . . . It has long been management's job to make capital out of the originality of what labour knows and does . . . The knowledgeable worker is therefore not a post-industrial phenomenon but rather an integral part of the development of industrial capitalism . . .
>
> 'It might be useful to jettison the overly-broad notion of *knowledge workers* in favour of a more realistic appreciation of the growth of *knowledgeablity in work*. The managerial instruments to register and if possible capture employee knowledge have some innovative forms in teamworking and off-line problem-solving groups. But we should not lose sight of the role played by the development of traditional Tayloristic techniques.'
>
> *Source*: Warhurst and Thompson (1998: 5 and 7, italics in original)

Knowledge workers

The 'knowledge worker'

Learning outcome 2a

Specify the distinctive characteristics of knowledge work by comparing knowledge workers with routine workers.

Frenkel, Korczynski, Donoghue and Shire (1995), in reaching a similar conclusion to Blackler, argue that there has been a change in the nature of work so that different kinds of knowledge are increasingly being used in contemporary work: theoretical or abstract knowledge, rather than contextual knowledge. If we put this into the same terms as outlined above, it means an increased emphasis on embrained knowledge rather than embodied and embedded knowledge.

However, Frenkel *et al.* are also aware of the dangers (raised by the critics) of using the term 'knowledge worker' and have developed a clearer definition based on identifying features in the act of work. They theorise that as well as the type of knowledge required, it is important to look at the extent of creativity involved in the work, and the type and level of skills being used. This leads Frenkel *et al.* (1995: 780) to the following definition:

> Knowledge workers rely predominantly on theoretical knowledge, and their work requires a high level of creativity for which they mainly use intellective skills.

Table 8.1 shows how these characteristics of knowledge workers can be contrasted with those of routine workers undertaking the type of work described in Chapter 6. These two types can be seen as the far extremes – many employees will lie somewhere between these two types if the various aspects of their work are analysed according to the dimensions suggested here. It is important to recognise

Table 8.1 A comparison of knowledge and routine workers

Dimension	Knowledge worker	Routine worker
Form of knowledge	Theoretical (embrained)	Contextual (embodied and embedded)
Extent of creativity (generating an original output – response, idea, solution, product, etc.)	High (open-ended, unusual)	Low (rule-based, mundane)
Type of skill	Intellective (reasoning based on abstract cues, inference, synthesis and systematic thinking)	Action-centred (physical sensing and dexterity)

Based on Frenkel *et al.* (1995)

that a particular job can vary between the dimensions, for instance, a landscape gardener could be considered to rely on contextual knowledge and action-centred skill (so closer to a routine worker in these respects) yet also be highly creative (more like a knowledge worker along this dimension). To get a feel for this method of comparing jobs, attempt Exercise 8.3.

EXERCISE 8.2

What do *you* think?

1 Using the three dimensions identified by Frenkel *et al.* (see Table 8.1) evaluate the jobs listed below. You are unlikely to have detailed knowledge of the jobs, but you should have enough general awareness of what each of the jobs entails to be able to arrive at a well-reasoned classification. Remember, the 'knowledge worker' and 'routine worker' are the extremes, so the jobs you are evaluating are likely to fall somewhere between these on one or more of the dimensions.

- Registered nurse
- Customer service representative (in a call centre)
- Architect
- Laboratory technician
- Skilled production worker

2 When you have arrived at a classification for each of these, devise and sketch a diagram that shows the comparison between these jobs. (There are several ways of doing this.)

The entrepreneurial professional

An alternative definition of 'knowledge worker' has been provided by Reed (1996). He rejects the notion of knowledge work being concerned solely with the

Learning outcome 2b

Specify the distinctive characteristics of knowledge work by comparing knowledge workers with professionals.

act of work – in particular information processing and manipulation – which he views as far too inclusive and lacking in theoretical precision. Instead Reed suggests that it is preferable to characterise such work as a form of 'expert work' performed by specialists. In devising this definition he is also keen to distinguish 'knowledge workers' from other types of experts – in particular, professionals (see Excerpt 8.3 for an explanation of the meaning of profession).

Whereas Frenkel, Korczynski, Shire and Tam (1999) argue that knowledge workers can be distinguished from professional workers, Reed prefers to describe 'knowledge workers' as a particular type of professional. He labels this type of worker the 'entrepreneurial professional' and provides the examples of financial and business consultants, project engineers, computer analysts, and media consultants. Drawing upon this description, we can distinguish these knowledge workers by three characteristics:

- they have task-specific, highly specialised cognitive and technical skills;
- they rely on a combination of embrained, embodied and embedded knowledge;
- they aggressively market themselves as purveyors of specialist expertise that can solve complex organisational problems.

To underline their distinctiveness, a contrast can be drawn between knowledge workers and the other two professional groups (1) liberal/independent professionals and (2) organisational professionals (Blackler, Reed and Whitaker, 1993):

1 *Liberal/independent professionals* – for example, doctors, architects and lawyers – can be characterised as follows:
   - they have an occupation-specific knowledge/skill base;
   - they rely on embrained and encoded knowledge;
   - traditionally they have operated autonomously from organisations by controlling the access to the education and training required to qualify and practise. By enacting occupational closure (through the social closure processes described in Chapter 5) they have been able to establish a monopoly position over their work and have gained public recognition of their expertise.

2 *Organisational professionals* – for example, managers, administrators and technicians – can be characterised as follows:
   - they have an organisation-specific (localised) knowledge base;
   - they rely on embedded and encultured knowledge;
   - at best they have built partial occupational closure, through establishing educational and bureaucratic credentials within the organisation. This produces organisational recognition and gives them powerful positions within technical and status hierarchies.

Importantly, Reed suggests that knowledge workers are well suited to the context of globalised capitalism, marketisation and the increasing commercialisation of public sector organisations. In this sense, they are the new face of the professions.

It is a view consistent with that of commentators who have argued that the liberal/ independent professions have, since the 1980s, faced radical challenges as a result of political, economic and technological changes (Abbott, 1988; Burris, 1993; Crompton, 1990, Freidson, 1994). In the words of Reed (1996: 589):

> The predominantly private sector, entrepreneurial professions/knowledge workers have been the real 'winners' in the economic, technological, political and cultural restructuring generated by the shift to a more globalized and flexible regime of capital accumulation. Research suggests that the 'occupationally-owned' assets of the liberal/independent professions and the 'organizationally-controlled' resources of the organizational/managerial professions are both under threat, if not terminal decline. If this is the case, then it offers a golden opportunity to the entrepreneurial professions/knowledge workers to exploit the potential for cognitive expansion, material advancement and socio-political enhancement that these developments present.

Although not using Reed's terminology, a similar distinction between 'knowledge workers' and traditional professionals is made by Scarborough (1999: 7):

> Lacking the demarcations and controls of conventional professional groups, knowledge workers are defined primarily by the work that they do – work which is relatively unstructured and organizationally contingent, and which thus reflects the changing demands of organizations more than occupationally-defined norms and practices.

To elaborate this definition, he highlights three ways that knowledge workers can be distinguished:

1 Unlike traditional professionals, they cannot monopolise specialist knowledge and so cannot derive power from this. However, this does not mean they are powerless. Instead their power derives from their scarcity within a liberal market environment.

2 Knowledge workers are more dependent on employers because 'knowledge work is less a matter of the application of predefined expertise [as with professional work] and more a joint product of human interactions with informational and intellectual assets delivered through information and communication technologies' (*ibid*: 7).

3 Knowledge workers are more instrumental than professionals. They consider the knowledge in terms of its value rather than whether it is good in its own right.

Points 1 and 3 echo Reed's view that knowledge workers are well adapted to the market forces of advanced capitalism. Point 2 underlines the way that knowledge workers are dependent on an appropriate organisational context, rather than being independent professionals. This differs from Reed because it suggests a potential organisational control that he does not consider appropriate for knowledge workers.

The concept of the 'knowledge worker' means different things for our two sets of commentators. For Frenkel *et al.*, it denotes work that requires theoretical knowledge, high creativity and intellective skill. For Reed and Scarborough it denotes a specific type of expertise and professional influence. These two examples demonstrate the importance of clarifying how the concept is being used. As with other concepts explored in the book, it illustrates how a variety of views and approaches can be adopted when exploring aspects of work.

Interestingly, although adopting different meanings of the concept, the commentators arrive at the same conclusion that knowledge work is becoming an increasingly important phenomenon. Frenkel *et al.* point out that change in the content of jobs means more people are becoming knowledge workers, while Reed argues that the expert power of the knowledge workers means that they are becoming influential and dominant among the professional groups. If this is the general trend, then it is clear that managers are going to turn their attention to ways of acquiring this knowledge from the workforce. This is the subject of the next section.

EXCERPT 8.3

Defining and analysing professions

The question of how to define and analyse a profession has been a long-standing concern in the analysis of work. Here we provide a brief overview of the main approaches – although there are numerous variations within each of these broad approaches.

Trait approach

Theoretical perspective: Functionalist

Definition of profession: An occupational group with certain unique characteristics. In particular:

- high proportion of theoretical knowledge;
- lengthy period of education and training;
- peer evaluation of competence;
- professional association;
- code of conduct;
- altruistic service.

Main research concern: How an occupational group attains these features in order to achieve professional status. ▶

Occupational closure approach

Theoretical perspective: Neo-Weberian

Definition of profession: An occupational group with monopolistic control over knowledge.

Main research concern: How an occupational group achieves and protects this monopoly through the process of social closure (see Chapter 5). In particular, the way professionals build power and influence by controlling entry into the occupation, regulating the work processes within the occupation and developing a distinct occupational identity/culture.

Dynamic meaning approach

Theoretical perspective: Relativist/interpretivist

Definition of profession: No general definition is accurate because 'profession' is not a fixed concept. All occupations change and develop, so the term 'profession' means different things in different circumstances.

Main research concern: How occupations change and how the concept of 'profession' is used in specific contexts at different times.

In recent empirically based accounts of professionals (for example, Broadbent, Dietrich and Roberts, 1997) there seems to be:

1 a complete rejection of the trait approach as being static and theoretically sterile;

2 a recognition of the value of the processual features of the occupational closure approach (for example, Fitzgerald and Ferlie, 2000);

3 a preference for the dynamic meaning approach (for example, Hanlon, 1998 and Randle, 1996).

Other terms

'Professionalism' normally means the ideology that underpins these definitions, and thereby directs the behaviour of the professionals.

'Professionalisation' refers to the process through which an occupational group achieves professional recognition and status. Likewise deprofessionalisation means the loss of this recognition and an associated reduction in status and influence.

'Semi-profession' is a term sometimes used to describe an occupation that has some but not all the trappings of a 'true' profession. In particular it is used to describe groups that have a professional body, code of conduct, and regulated training, but have not achieved autonomy in relation to the client or the employing organisation. Recent change in the status and autonomy of professional groups has made the term 'semi-profession' somewhat meaningless, and most contemporary commentators have abandoned it.

▶
Other texts

A thorough analysis of all these concepts and the current approaches to the analysis of the professions can be found in texts such as Abbott (1988), Freidson (1994), Macdonald (1995) and Witz (1992). Good starting points are the articles by Saks (1983) and Crompton (1990).

Knowledge within the workforce

The discussion so far has examined the role of knowledge as a means of distinguishing between groups of employees. Now we turn to the idea that knowledge is present in all forms of work and is a potentially exploitable commodity, which makes it susceptible to management control. In particular, this section explores the importance of knowledge creation and knowledge capture.

Learning outcome 3

Explain the process of knowledge creation and the transformation of tacit into explicit knowledge.

Knowledge creation

The term 'knowledge-creating company' was coined by Ikujiro Nonaka to characterise the way that some Japanese organisations differed from their Western counterparts. He was identifying the way that organisations such as Honda, Canon and Matsushita facilitate the creation of new knowledge by providing an environment in which everyone is encouraged (or even expected) to think and behave creatively and imaginatively in constant pursuit of new ideas, new methods of working and new ways of looking at common problems. In the words of Nonaka (1991: 97):

> To create new knowledge means quite literally to re-create the company and everyone in it in a nonstop process of personal and organizational self-renewal. In the knowledge-creating company, inventing new knowledge is not a specialized activity – the province of the R&D department or marketing or strategic planning. It is a way of behaving, indeed a way of being, in which everyone is a knowledge worker – that is to say, an entrepreneur.

Most important is knowledge that can provide a competitive advantage for an organisation:

> New knowledge always begins with the individual. A brilliant researcher has an insight that leads to a new patent. A middle manager's intuitive sense of market trends becomes the catalyst for an important new product concept. A shop-floor worker draws on years of experience to come up with a new process innovation. In each case, an individual's personal knowledge is transformed into organizational

knowledge valuable to the company as a whole. Making personal knowledge available to others is the central activity of the knowledge-creating company. It takes place continuously and at all levels of the organization. (*ibid*: 97–8)

Nonaka is concerned with the way new knowledge surfaces and gets passed throughout the organisation: in other words how knowledge moves from being *tacit* to *explicit*. We have encountered the notion of tacit knowledge or skill earlier (Chapter 5) when we noted how skill is often embedded in employees, so much so that it can become embedded in their way of working without them recognising its significance or importance. However, according to Nonaka, the importance of recognising the tacit knowledge is the first stage in knowledge creation. Rather than leaving this embedded knowledge in its tacit form, it has to be transformed into explicit knowledge.

Nonaka suggests that the interrelationship between tacit and explicit knowledge can produce a sort of knowledge spiral (see Figure 8.1). The organisation has to encourage individuals to pass on their tacit knowledge to others who then standardise this as explicit knowledge, in the form of procedures, manuals, and so on. This experience in turn enriches the tacit knowledge of the individuals involved and the cycle repeats itself, thereby producing a virtuous spiral of knowledge creation.

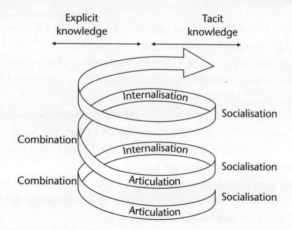

Figure 8.1 Spiral of knowledge creation
Source: Based on description by Nonaka (1991)

However, while Nonaka's analysis is helpful and the term 'knowledge creation' is useful, it does not fully encapsulate the way that the organisation's managers also attempt to acquire the existing knowledge that resides within the workforce. In other words, it does not fully address the ongoing process of capturing knowledge.

Knowledge capture

Knowledge capture is the processes through which managers try to acquire the ideas, judgement and creativity of those intimately involved in the work and develop this as explicit knowledge. The assumption that lies behind this process is that all employees have some knowledge about their job that could be passed on to others and might help improve the effectiveness and efficiency of the organisation. Even an employee doing a fairly menial task will possess knowledge about how to accomplish it. For example, a trolley collector in a supermarket car park possesses knowledge about the best way to push the trolleys, the easiest routes back to the store, hazardous paving, favourite places for trolleys to be abandoned, and so on. Clearly this is not rocket science, but knowledge that it would be useful for the store manager to capture, make explicit (by writing it down) and pass on to new trolley collectors. The gain of doing this is made more apparent when one considers that the labour turnover of trolley collectors is very high.

An example of how knowledge can be captured is provided in Excerpt 8.4. It shows how an attempt has been made to make explicit the knowledge in the heads of the employees. After reading it, attempt Exercise 8.4 which raises some issues about the effects on employees of such attempts to capture knowledge.

EXCERPT 8.4

Knowledge pooling in a law firm

'Law firm McGrigor Donald, which has offices in London and Glasgow employing 52 partners and 150 fee-earning staff with support workers, has shown the courage of its convictions by removing one of its fee-earning partners from the front line and placing her in a backroom role with the 21st-century title of Director of Knowledge Management...

'Christine McLintock, a former specialist in corporate banking law, says that much of the company's information is stored in the minds of the individuals it employs. That information, in most cases gathered by long experience, is a prime asset but not one that all in the company can draw on.

'Her first priority is to release as much of the simpler information as possible and get it on an accessible computer system. In addition she is striving to get more complex ideas exchanged on a face-to-face training level...

'The main basis of McLintock's strategy is to effect a change of culture by concentrating on the more junior employees, but backed by the co-operation of the senior ones. 'It's a two-pronged thing. We are trying to change attitudes and culture: to try to encourage knowledge-sharing and to increase the value of it in people's minds,' says McLintock...

'[One] innovation has been the streamlining of the more simple aspects of the company's work, pooling knowledge to produce a comprehensive document management system and using the company intranet to access previous work that can help prepare documents for current clients.

'This is partly the result of client pressure. With the de-mystification of the law in recent years, a process aided by access to information systems such as the Internet, the company recognises that clients' expectations have increased. ▶

▶ 'Clients don't want to pay a lot of money for what they perceive as mundane tasks. We are trying to keep our edge on competitors,' says McLintock. Furthermore she predicts a time when clients will be able to access the company databases directly on some sort of pay-per-use basis. The knowledge pooling work is laying the foundations of this.

'... She says that by convincing staff to share information, they are freed to do the more complex work which will give a chance for more creativity.'

Source: *Sunday Times* 'Power from the knowledge pool', London 31 Jan, 1999

EXERCISE 8.3

What do *you* think?

Read Excerpt 8.4 entitled 'Knowledge pooling in a law firm'.

1 Why might the employees be resistant to McLintock's plans?

2 If the knowledge-pooling exercise is successful, what are the advantages and disadvantages for:

    (a) the junior employees?

    (b) the senior employees?

3 If all law firms adopted this approach, how might it affect the professional status of the lawyers? To justify your answer, you may need to refer back to Excerpt 8.3 that dealt with defining and analysing professions.

Why try to capture knowledge?

The purpose of capturing knowledge is inextricably linked to the competitive environment. In an increasingly globalised, dynamic and intense competitive environment, companies constantly need to search for a competitive edge. Customers expect quality, variety, value for money and innovation of products and services. Consequently, an organisation's managers must constantly look for improvement in products, processes and service delivery. As well as copying ideas from competitors (to survive) they must look to creativity from within (to gain a competitive advantage). Employees are a valuable source of such creativity. However our concern in this section is not with those people whose job it is to be 'creative', such as those involved in research and development, members of a marketing department or senior management. Instead we are concerned with the way that tacit knowledge of ordinary employees is made explicit.

The importance for managers in being able to capture the knowledge of the workforce is a long standing issue. You might recall from Chapter 6 that Braverman's concern about deskilling centred on the way Tayloristic work organisation and new technology provided opportunities for the conception to be separated from the execution of work. In effect this is the separation of the theoretical knowledge of the work (the thinking) from the practical action (the doing). You will find out from Chapter 9 that this capture of knowledge can never be fully complete because employees who undertake the work will always learn from experience. This allows them to find new ways of working that they might use to the benefit of themselves or their work colleagues. However, since the 1980s, systematic attempts to acquire this knowledge have been put into place by managers. This change in approach is vividly expressed by Dohse, Jurgens and Malsch (1985: 128) as 'mining the gold in the worker's head'. In particular, these techniques have been associated with an increased emphasis on managing quality, and especially important in achieving this is the concept of *continuous improvement*.

Capturing employee knowledge through continuous improvement

Continuous improvement (also known as *kaizen* in Japanese-owned companies) encourages employees and managers to look constantly for ways of making changes to any system or process that will improve performance. The concept stems from Japanese production systems, in particular those of the motor giants such as Toyota. Once an improvement has been suggested, it is evaluated and if found to be of benefit, standardised across the operation. Advocates such as Womack, Jones and Roos (1990) argue that this helps to humanise the workplace and that employees experience the intrinsic reward of seeing their ideas put into practice and getting recognition from management – which in some cases might lead to more favourable appraisals or one-off bonuses.

In contrast, critics argue that such a system is exploitative since it captures the ideas of shopfloor employees, adopts them across the organisation and leads to performance improvements, but does not reward those who came up with the idea in the first place. Researchers have revealed that continuous improvement can have a pernicious effect on the employees because it means that an environment is created whereby individuals and teams are expected to put forward ideas that lead to an intensification of work (Garrahan and Stewart, 1992; Graham, 1995; Lewchuck and Robertson, 1996; Rinehart, Huxley and Robertson, 1997). For example, finding an innovative way of cutting down time in a production process might lead to improved efficiency or output, but for the employee also might remove a period of respite from the production process. Therefore, in many instances it might simply not be in the employee's own interest to find 'improvements'.

Further concerns arise over which groups benefit most from any improvements. As shown in Chapter 4, employees can be very inventive and creative in order to find ways of freeing up time or making informal breaks in the working day. Other ways such creativity can be expressed are explored in Chapter 9. However, the point here is that in such instances it is the employee who benefits directly from his or her creativity – and sometimes this is shared with work colleagues. Under the kaizen system, research suggests that the main beneficiaries of creative improvements are managers. For example, Danford's investigation of Japanese firms in South Wales leads him to argue that:

> Under the cloak of a benign 'one team' ideology, workers become involved in securing for their employer higher levels of capital and labour utilisation, reductions in idle time, an intensification of their labour and a more sophisticated form of worker subordination. They do this by apparently offering to management knowledge of those facets of individual tacit skills and customary practice which provide workers with the means to exert some control over the labour process. (Danford, 1998: 58)

This observation that management gain more from continuous improvement than employees is hardly astonishing. Indeed, as we note throughout the book, commentators frequently refer to the imbalance of the employment relationship – or more forcefully, the exploitative nature of the labour process, exemplified by the analysis of Braverman (Chapter 6). In other words, the possibility that managers will seek to expropriate the knowledge of employees, through techniques like kaizen, is consistent with traditional Taylorist and Fordist management practice and is bad news for employees. Thus Collins (1997: 47) comments:

> All the lessons of history tell us that when management becomes interested in appropriating the knowledge which workers have with regard to work skills and processes, the conditions under which we work tend to deteriorate.

While this is the preferred interpretation of commentators with a labour process orientation (for example, Delbridge and Turnbull, 1992; Dohse, Jurgens and Malsch, 1985; Garrahan and Stewart, 1992) and those of a Foucauldian persuasion (for example, Sewell and Wilkinson, 1992b) others have suggested that a far more complex picture is evident. In particular, commentators are noting how context-specific factors are playing an important role in influencing the employee experience of initiatives designed to improve quality – see Excerpt 8.5. Research such as this reveals that in some organisations employees are not resistant to quality initiatives and techniques such as continuous improvement. Not only do these initiatives increase variety in work but also provide a feeling of involvement, even though the employees realise they are working harder than they used to. Moreover, research also reveals that even continuous improvement regimes are never totally complete – the employee will still find ways of getting around the system in order to gain individually or collectively (Webb and Palmer, 1998; see also the survival strategies discussed in Chapter 9).

EXCERPT 8.5

Employees and quality initiatives

Edwards, Collinson and Rees (1998) advocate a need to find out more about employees' responses to the various initiatives adopted by organisations to improve ▶

▶ quality (Quality Management – QM). They argue that opinion about the effect on employees has tended to fall into two opposite camps of optimists and pessimists:

1 the *optimistic view*: employees like QM because it means involvement and greater responsibility.

2 the *pessimistic view*: employees dislike QM because it means work intensification and increased surveillance.

But this, they suggest, over-simplifies a far more complex picture. An intermediate position, itself having two elements is emerging from research evidence:

3 the *context-dependency view*: whether employees like or dislike QM depends on the specific circumstances of the organisation concerned. Furthermore, employees will like some aspects of QM and dislike others, so their judgement depends on the balance between these aspects.

In order to assess these approaches, Edwards *et al.* surveyed 280 employees in six UK organisations, and analysed a range of variables that might explain their various attitudes towards QM. Their principal findings are as follows:

■ There is evidence of work intensification (as the pessimists predict) – employees say they are working harder due to performance targets and appraisals. However, this is counterbalanced by positive feelings of satisfaction and involvement (as predicted by the optimists).

■ Employees were favourably disposed towards quality where the monitoring of employees (increased surveillance) was most intense. This is in contradiction to the predictions of the pessimistic view.

■ Conditions specific to each organisation promoted or retarded acceptance of quality initiatives, but two features stood out: job security and positive union-management relations.

Overall, Edwards *et al.* (1998: 471) suggest their findings reveal that 'workers have no inherent opposition to the principles of quality management, and acceptance of specific initiatives seems to depend on context'. So they conclude that neither the pessimistic nor optimistic view is adequately supported by their results, and that their findings provide evidence to sustain a context-dependency view.

TO SUM UP

So far our discussion has led us to the conclusion that knowledge creation and capture are important aspects that managers seek to control. Knowledge creation describes the importance of nurturing and developing new ideas while knowledge capture is the process of transforming the tacit knowledge of individuals into explicit knowledge that can be disseminated throughout the organisation. In both senses, the management strategy is expropriation – the acquisition and control of knowledge from within the workforce.

However, there are some commentators who suggest that knowledge workers are distinct because, in general, their knowledge *cannot* be expropriated. It is this viewpoint that the next section evaluates.

Knowledge as an inexpropriable resource

Learning outcome 5

Assess whether the need for managers to acquire knowledge places knowledge workers in an advantageous position compared with other employees.

Potentially, workers whose knowledge cannot be made explicit through the sort of information capture described above are in a strong bargaining position. This is summed up by the well-known management commentator, Peter Drucker:

> Knowledge workers, unlike manual workers in manufacturing, own the means of production. They carry that knowledge in their heads and can therefore take it with them. At the same time, the knowledge needs of organizations are likely to change continually. As a result, in developed countries more and more of the critical work force – and the most highly paid part of it – will increasingly consist of people who cannot be 'managed' in the traditional sense of the word. In many cases, they will not even be employees of the organizations for which they work, but rather contractors, experts, consultants, part-timers, joint-venture partners, and so on. An increasing number of these people will identify themselves by their own knowledge rather than by the organization that pays them. (Drucker, 1998: 18)

In this quote, Drucker is assuming that knowledge does not lend itself to expropriation and is mobile. We have noted in the previous section that expropriation techniques are available to managers, although there may well be situations when managers choose not to use these. On the issue of employees 'carrying knowledge in their heads', we only need to think back to the discussion in Chapter 5 on skill to realise that such knowledge is mobile only if it is valued by other organisations – in other words, as long as it is not firm-specific. In practice, much tacit knowledge is likely to be task-specific (embedded knowledge) or firm-specific (encultured knowledge). This means that even though knowledge may not be expropriable, it is not necessarily mobile, so the range of workers to whom this quote applies is likely to be relatively narrow – most likely Reed's 'entrepreneurial professionals' whom we describe earlier.

In the second part of the quote, Drucker is raising an important issue about the management control of the 'knowledge workers'. He suggests that the relationship with the organisation is indirect. In other words, rather than being full-time employees, knowledge workers are more likely to be external specialists and experts on temporary and part-time contracts. Ironically this means that the value-creating, highly-paid, knowledge workers will form part of an organisation's contingent workforce, alongside the low-skilled, low-paid workers accomplishing various support tasks for an organisation, such as cleaning and security. This type of numerical flexibility delivers performance, but not necessarily organisational commitment or loyalty.

What do *you* think?

Assuming Drucker is correct, would you want to be a knowledge worker? Explain your reasoning, taking into account the risks and opportunities.

The effectiveness of bringing 'knowledge workers' into an organisation on a contingent basis poses a dilemma. On the one hand it allows new and specialist knowledge to be brought into the organisation, but on the other hand it allows firm-specific knowledge to leak out of the organisation (Matusik and Hill, 1998). In other words, the contingent workers who bring external knowledge into an organisation are the same people who can transmit firm-specific knowledge to other organisations. So if, as Drucker argues, knowledge is increasingly the source of a firm's competitive edge, the knowledge workers that are responsible for creating this edge will turn any competitive advantage into a short-lived phenomenon by transferring the knowledge underpinning it (through their contingent work status) to other organisations. This being the case, it is not the contingent (external) knowledge workers who are likely to provide the competitive edge, but the permanent (internal) employees of an organisation. This is a perspective consistent both with the 'resource-based view of the firm' (Barney, 1991) and the concept of 'the knowledge-creating company' (Nonaka and Takeuchi, 1995). But it also suggests that more fundamental change might be occurring within society, in which knowledge workers become central because of their control of information. This societal change has been characterised by some commentators as the information society, and it is to this issue we now turn.

The information society

The concept of the information society has occupied sociologists for several decades, and an excellent analysis of the concept has been undertaken by Webster (1995). Our focus is on two commentators who are central to the debate on the role of knowledge and information in contemporary society: Daniel Bell and Manuel Castells.

Learning outcome 6 (a)

Explain and evaluate Bell's thesis of the information society.

Daniel Bell and the information society

Earlier in the book (Chapter 6), you encountered some of the ideas of Daniel Bell (1973, 1976) in relation to the changing nature of skill. You will recall that his assumption was that society underwent a transformation from industrial to post-industrial, and as a consequence there has been a general trend of upskilling work. We can now return to Bell's work because he was one of the first commentators to suggest that associated with this change was an increasing importance of the role of information.

Bell suggests that pre-industrial society was based on agricultural work, industrial society was based on factory work and post-industrial society (PIS) is based on service work. In this respect the sorts of growth in the service sector that we have noted throughout the chapters is taken by observers like Bell as evidence that we are now in the post-industrial stage of development.

Also important in Bell's analysis is the role of information. He argues that information-based activities are the core of the PIS, and therefore white-collar workers and professionals have become the dominant employee groups. In this respect, he is emphasising the importance of those employees described as knowledge workers above, and of course it explains how he is able to argue a trend towards upskilling (see Chapter 6). He also argues that theoretical, scientific knowledge will drive innovation and policy-making, at organisational and governmental levels, giving rise to a new technical, professional elite – akin to the entrepreneurial professionals described by Reed (see above). Table 8.2 illustrates the main changes envisaged by Bell's thesis.

Table 8.2 Major changes suggested by Bell's thesis

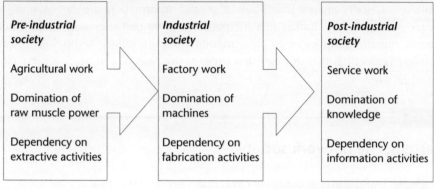

Source: Based on Bell (1973 and 1980)

In his original work published in 1973, Bell was unable to predict the significance of the microprocessor and so the role of information and communication technologies is understated. He later rectifies this (Bell, 1980) and notes the importance of computers, the pricing and the power of information (thereby giving it commodity status), and the significance of advances in telecommunications (see also Lyon, 1986). Consequently, Bell adopts the term 'information society' to represent the social structure of the supposedly post-industrial era.

Bell's analysis is infused with optimism. He assumes that work will increasingly become information intensive (and therefore skilled) and as a result more satisfying. This assumption is questionable in at least two respects:

1 There is an exaggeration in the supposed extent of information-based work – much service sector work is mundane, repetitive and requiring no information processing.

2 Even where service sector work *is* information-intensive, it is not necessarily satisfying or rewarding (for example, working in a call centre).

Elsewhere there are other detailed criticisms of Bell's work (for example, Webster, 1995; Kumar, 1995; Rose, 1991) but this does not detract from the importance of his observations. Indeed, the contribution of Bell is acknowledged by our second theorist, Manuel Castells, who takes a very different perspective on the implications of the growing importance of information in contemporary society.

Learning outcome 6 (b)

Explain and evaluate Castells's thesis of the information age and the network society.

Manuel Castells, the information age and the network society

In the opinion of Manuel Castells (1998, 2000) the information society is not simply a service society – so the evidence of the increasing scale of the service sector cannot be taken as a significant effect in its own right. Instead, Castells introduces us to the idea of the 'network society' being the social structure uniquely characteristic of the current 'information age'. He chooses his terms carefully so as to distinguish his analysis from that of those who use the term 'information society'. He is in agreement with commentators like Bell that knowledge and information have a critical role to play in the development of society. However, Castells argues that knowledge and information are not unique to contemporary society. Rather it is the particular *form* that they take (constituted around microelectronics-based information/communication technologies and genetic engineering) that distinguishes them as the basis of a network society (see Excerpt 8.6).

EXCERPT 8.6

Castells: the network society

'In the last two decades of the twentieth century a related set of social transformations has taken place around the world. While cultures, institutions, and historical trajectories introduce a great deal of diversity in the actual manifestations of each one of these transformations, it can be shown that, overall, the vast majority of societies are affected in a fundamental way by these transformations. All together they constitute a new type of social structure that I call the network society . . .

'We have entered *a new technological paradigm*, centred around microelectronics-based, information/communication technologies, and genetic engineering. In this sense what is characteristic of the network society is not the critical role of knowledge and information, because knowledge and information were central in all societies. Thus, we should abandon the notion of 'Information Society', which I have myself used some times, as unspecific and misleading. What is new in our age is a new set of information technologies. I contend they represent a greater change in the history of technology than the technologies associated with the Industrial Revolution, or with the previous Information Revolution (printing). Furthermore, we are only at the beginning of this technological revolution, as the Internet becomes ▶

> ▶a universal tool of interactive communication, as we shift from computer-centred technologies to network-diffused technologies, as we make progress in nanotechnology (and thus in the diffusion capacity of information devices), and, even more importantly, as we unleash the biology revolution, making possible for the first time, the design and manipulation of living organisms, including human parts. What is also characteristic of this technological paradigm is the use of knowledge-based, information technologies to enhance and accelerate the production of knowledge and information, in a self-expanding, virtuous circle. Because information processing is at the source of life, and of social action, every domain of our eco-social system is thereby transformed.'
>
> *Source*: Castells (2000: 9–10)

To justify his argument, Castells (1998) undertakes an extensive analysis of social, economic and cultural change around the world – which he elaborates in three volumes covering 1,488 pages of text. All we need do here, however, is note some of the key theoretical points he makes that are most relevant to our purposes.

One central concern is with the way economic activity may increasingly be characterised as (1) informational, (2) global and (3) networked.

1 *Informational*: the productivity and competitiveness of all economic units (firms, regions, countries) is determined by their capacity to generate knowledge and manage/process information. Elsewhere, this has been described as the informational mode of development, and it is important to recognise that Castells is not suggesting this replaces capitalism, but that information becomes an essential feature of capitalist development and accumulation.

2 *Global*: the core and strategic activities of capitalism (finance, trade, science and technology, services, production, communication and labour) have the capacity to function on a planetary scale in real or chosen time – they are not constrained by place or time.

> Globalization is highly selective. It proceeds by linking up all that, according to dominant interests, has value anywhere on the planet, and discarding anything (people, firms, territories, resources) which has no value or becomes devalued, in a variable geometry of creative destruction and destructive creation of value. (Castells, 2000: 10)

3 *Networked*: the central mode of organising is the network, in which firms or segments of firms (departments and functions) are temporarily connected together for the purposes of achieving specific business projects, and then are allowed to disintegrate.

> Major corporations work in a strategy of changing alliances and partnerships, specific to a given product, process, time, and space. Furthermore, these co-operations are based increasingly on sharing of information. These are information networks, which, in the limit, link up suppliers and customers

through one firm, with this firm being essentially an intermediary of supply and demand, collecting a fee for its ability to process information. (Castells, 2000: 11)

EXCERPT 8.7

Inequality in the information age

'Long before Francis Bacon coined the phrase "Knowledge is power", quick access to information endowed the recipient with a comparative advantage. The arrival of an information society turns it from an advantage into a necessity. Speed of access to information – whether share prices, new scientific research or news – is more vital than ever.

'And in the information age you need not only knowledge of facts but also knowledge of the skills that produce the knowledge industry, because most new jobs require them.

'Within these trends, subtler changes are taking place. For instance, circles of those with privileged knowledge are widening at the expense of those outside them. In pre-web days, for instance, only an elite circle of people had access to insider knowledge and analysis in the City. Now, thanks to the proliferation of financial web sites with instant (and usually free) access to share prices, charts, analysis and instant gossip, the insider circle has greatly increased.

'But the gap between those in the loop and those outside it is widening, especially as knowledge itself becomes the source of competitive advantage. The digital revolution has opened up a new divide within existing workforces. Older workers (over 40s these days) find that, suddenly, youth is preferred over experience, and stored knowledge is devalued, counting for nothing because of the cultural revolution within the new companies. Suddenly, twenty-somethings are running their own companies instead of being corporate cogs in a bigger machine. [. . .]

'No one is more outside the loop than developing countries. When you read of the amazing electronic markets that are being constructed to harness the deflationary powers of the web and bring down the prices of raw materials and commodities, remember who is at the other end of the chain. Almost certainly it will be a developing country which was already suffering from the decline of its main source of income (commodities), even before the success of the internet. [. . .]

'The fruits of the information revolution are going disproportionately to those who are already in the loop. A new underclass is being created in developing countries – and within developed ones – from which it will be even more difficult to escape.'

Source: Keegan, V. 'If knowledge is power', *The Guardian*, 2000, 7 Sept.

In contrast to Bell's very optimistic analysis, Castells's viewpoint stresses the potential polarising effects of the information age. In particular, he distinguishes between those people who become a strategic and integral part of the networks of capitalism and those who remain outside the network – although still needed by capital (see also, Excerpt 8.7). The distinction hinges on the informational capacity of labour – hence he uses two terms for these primary and secondary groups:

1 *self-programmable* labour: those who are retrainable and adaptive;

2 *generic* labour: those who are exchangeable and disposable.

In some respects this echoes models of labour flexibility – in particular the distinction between the core workforce and the periphery. However, it differs in one important respect: Castells is not concerned with the relationship between employees and organisations, but with the relationship between labour and value chains. This is a key distinction because it means that the position of the employee in the workplace is of less importance than the location of labour in the network. And the essential factor that influences the centrality of that labour is its informational capacity: its ability to add value through information processing.

TO SUM UP

There are two messages in Castells's analysis. The first is that the network society gives rise to connected, valued, individuals who are more in control of their destinies. Yet this is accompanied by a second, bleak message that warns that the network society also discards people leaving them devalued and dispossessed. While this has always happened under capitalism, Castells's thesis acknowledges this downside to the information age – a continuation of the discarding of human potential that has always occurred under capitalism. This contrasts against Bell's thesis of the information society which tends to ignore the possibility that the fate of individuals is not necessarily within their control, or operating under conditions of their own choosing.

EXERCISE 8.5

What do *you* think?

1 Consider the theses of Bell and Castells. Which one are you more convinced by? Justify your answer.

2 Castells arrives at the (for some) controversial conclusion that:

> The networking of relationships of production leads to the blurring of class relationships. This does not preclude exploitation, social differentiation and social resistance. But production-based social classes, as constituted and enacted in the Industrial Age, cease to exist in the network society. (Castells, 2000: 18)

  (a) What does Castells mean by this?

  (b) What evidence is there to substantiate or refute this conclusion?

▶

▶ 3 Bell and Castells (in different ways) are arguing the case for there being 'a paradigm shift in society'.

(a) Explain what this statement means. (Hint: look back to the end of Chapter 6 to refresh your memory about paradigms.)

(b) What is the basis of the supposed paradigm shift?

(c) How would you go about arguing an alternative viewpoint: the case for continuity, rather than a paradigm shift?

Conclusion

Three key themes have surfaced in this chapter. The first is that knowledge work is an increasingly important concept. Contemporary organisations are relying on knowledge and information both to sustain and enhance their competitive position. This means that the knowledge present in all types of work is increasingly being identified by managers as a potentially expropriable commodity. In other words, the knowledgability of employees is a valuable resource to be exploited. One view is that this denotes very little change – merely a continuation of the long-standing exploitative relations between employers and employees within capitalism. An alternative view is that the nature of the expropriation has changed, reflecting greater emphasis being put on knowledge based on theoretical concepts and shared understandings, rather than knowledge based on practice and experience. This is exemplified by the way that tacit knowledge is encoded into explicit knowledge (knowledge creation) and the way techniques such as continuous improvement and quality management establish organisation-wide norms and values (knowledge capture).

A second theme is that 'knowledge workers' are a distinct group who can be distinguished from other types of workers. The main commentators encountered in this chapter – Frenkel *et al.*, Reed, Drucker, Bell and Castells – share this view although they do not agree on exactly which occupations fall into the category. They also share the opinion that 'knowledge workers' are taking an increasingly influential role in contemporary workplaces. Not only is knowledge more important to all organisations, but those employees whose work defines them as mainly 'knowledge workers' are occupying an increasingly central and privileged position.

This links in to the third theme of a fundamental shift in the nature of contemporary society whereby the control and manipulation of information becomes a central organising principle, embodied in the notion of information society or information age. This shift has positive connotations for commentators like Bell and Drucker, while Castells is far more cautious, pointing to the positive effects for some people and the negative impact on others.

Survival strategies 9
at work

KEY CONCEPTS

- Alienation
- Estrangement
- Forced labour
- Voluntary labour
- False consciousness
- Powerlessness

- Meaninglessness
- Isolation
- Self-estrangement
- Making out
- Control versus consent
- Workplace fiddles

- Joking at work
- Sabotage
- Whistle-blowing
- Escaping
- Consent and resistance
- Interpreting workplace behaviour

CHAPTER AIM

To explore how employees survive the alienating tendencies at work by developing various coping strategies.

LEARNING OUTCOMES

After reading and understanding this chapter you will be able to:

1 describe how alienation results from the four types of estrangement originally identi-fied by Marx;

2 explain and assess Blauner's version of alienation;

3 describe the concept of 'making out' and evaluate its role in creating consent within the workplace;

4 classify various types of workplace fiddles and evaluate why they occur within the workplace;

5 explain four functions of joking at work;

6 describe and interpret the importance of workplace sabotage;

7 explain the concept of escaping within a workplace context;

8 assess whether the five survival strategies should be interpreted as forms of consent or resistance.

Introduction

This chapter, perhaps more than any other in the book, illustrates the importance of viewing work as a rich and varied domain of human activity. It is concerned with the ways in which employees get through their working day: how they survive the boredom, tedium, monotony, drudgery and powerlessness that characterise many jobs. In examining this issue, it is necessary to cover a wide range of concepts and research evidence. At the same time, there is one central principle around which the discussion is organised: the notion that in order to 'survive' work, people are obliged to become resourceful and creative in developing strategies that allow them to assert some control over, and construct meanings for, the work activities they are directed by managers to undertake.

In the analysis that follows, we are seeking to access the world of the informal which, although normally hidden from the gaze of the outsider, is no less real for the participants. It is a dynamic world where the subjective experiences of individuals are collectively constructed and reconstructed to create shared understandings and develop norms that guide and pattern behaviour. Yet it is also a regulated world where the structural constraints imposed by power holders (especially managers) limit the actions of individuals and workgroups. The result is a curious mixture of consent and resistance to work.

The analysis begins with a discussion of the extent to which work produces conditions of alienation for employees. This is followed by an examination of the way that alienating tendencies may be countered through various creative strategies by employees. From an assessment of the empirical research on informal work behaviour, five survival strategies are explored: 'making out', fiddling, joking, sabotaging and escaping. Finally, there is an assessment of whether these strategies can be construed as forms of workplace consent or resistance, or both.

Learning outcome 1

Describe how alienation results from the four types of estrangement originally identified by Marx.

Alienation: an objective state or a subjective experience?

The word 'alienation' is freely used in the media (especially in serious late night TV talk shows and Sunday newspapers) and arises in everyday conversation. Yet alienation remains one of the most contested terms in the academic study of work. In fact, in attempting to define and explain 'alienation' fully it would be possible to write a whole chapter on the concept. Here we have restricted the discussion to outlining two different perspectives on alienation. The first views alienation as an objective state and builds on concepts originally defined by Karl Marx, while the second introduces elements of subjectivity into the analysis of alienation and stems from a study by Robert Blauner.

Alienation as an objective state

Marx argues that alienation is an intrinsic part of the capitalist labour process (see Chapter 6 above) and therefore is an unavoidable objective state in which all workers find themselves. It manifests itself because in selling their labour power, employees are relinquishing the right to control their own labour, thus discretion over how and when work should be undertaken becomes the prerogative of employers. This subordination of employees to their employer (or to managers who are acting on behalf of the employer, and sometimes referred to as the 'agents of capital') makes the activity of work a degrading and dehumanising activity.

> [Under capitalism] all the means for developing production are transformed into means of domination over and exploitation of the producer; that they mutilate the worker into a fragment of a human being, degrade him to become a mere appurtenance, make his work such a torment that its essential meaning is destroyed. (Marx, 1930: 713, quoted in Fox, 1974: 224)

As a result of this relationship, according to Marx, employees experience four types of estrangement:

1 self-estrangement;

2 estrangement from the product of their labour;

3 estrangement from their species being;

4 estrangement from others.

Each of these is described in more detail below, and you can see how they are linked together by looking at the top half of the flow chart in Figure 9.1.

1 *Self-estrangement*

Work ought to be a source of satisfaction in its own right, but under capitalism work is merely the means for people to acquire money to satisfy their needs outside of working hours. In other words, people only find *extrinsic* meaning in work. As a consequence, employees experience a sense of 'self-estrangement' because, while they are in work undertaking the activities as instructed by their managers, they cannot be themselves. They are separated from their true selves; they experience a sense of alienation. To get a better idea of how vividly Marx expressed this, see Excerpt 9.1. Also, see Cox (1998).

EXCERPT 9.1

Self-estrangement under the capitalist labour process

'[The worker] does not affirm himself but denies himself, does not feel content but unhappy, does not develop freely his physical and mental energy but mortifies his body and ruins his mind. The worker therefore only feels himself outside his work, and in his work feels outside himself. He is at home when he is not working, and when he is working he is not at home. His labour is therefore not voluntary, but coerced; it is *forced labour*. It is therefore not the satisfaction of a need; it is merely a

▶

> *means* to satisfy needs external to it. Its alien character emerges clearly in the fact that as soon as no physical or other compulsion exists, labour is shunned like the plague. External labour, labour in which man alienates himself, is a labour of self-sacrifice, of mortification. Lastly, the external character of labour for the worker appears in the fact that it is not his own, but someone else's, that it does not belong to him, that in it he belongs, not to himself, but to another. Just as in religion the spontaneous activity of the human imagination, of the human brain and the human heart, operates independently of the individual – that is, operates on him as an alien, divine or diabolical activity – in the same way the worker's activity is not his spontaneous activity. It belongs to another; it is the loss of his self.'
>
> *Source*: Marx (1969: 99–100, emphasis in original)

2   Estrangement from the product of one's labour

The output (the product or object) of one's labour is the physical expression of the effort that has been undertaken and the skills that have been used – a process Marx labels 'objectification'. However, the product of a person's labour is not owned by the employee; it becomes the property of the capitalist (the process of expropriation). As a consequence, the dispossessed employees see the product of their labour as something that is distant and separated from themselves. They become estranged from the product of their labour – in other words, the product becomes an alien object. Or, as Marx expresses it:

> The *alienation* of the worker in his product means not only that his labour becomes an object, an *external* existence, but that it exists *outside him*, independently, as something alien to him, and that it becomes a power on its own confronting him; it means that the life which he has conferred on the object confronts him as something hostile and alien. (Marx, 1969: 97, emphasis in original)

3   Estrangement from one's species being

The alienation caused by self-estrangement and estrangement from the product has wider repercussions for humankind. Marx argues that through work, people express their creativity, produce the means of their own existence and hence realise their humanity. This free, creative endeavour is the very purpose of life, but under capitalism work becomes coercion: forced labour. This means that people become estranged from their very nature; they are left alienated from their 'species being'.

4   Estrangement from others

Due to estrangement from their essential nature, people are left estranged from each other. Marx's argument here stems from a belief that human beings are distinct from animals due to their self-awareness. Thus a person can understand the world through his or her own actions and behaviour, and by appreciating the role and behaviour of others, in relation to one's self. However, the three previous forms of estrangement combine to create conditions in which the unique qualities of humankind are diminished. Under forced labour, people are owned and controlled. They experience this directly and also recognise this estrangement in other people. Consequently, they are both estranged from their own humanity and from others.

Figure 9.1 summarises the above discussion by mapping the relationships between the various concepts in Marx's theory of the labour process and alienation. The top half of the flow chart shows how each of the concepts is linked and leads to alienation at work.

Non-alienating conditions

The bottom half of the flow chart in Figure 9.1 suggests how under non-capitalist conditions the problem of alienation might be avoided. If each of the components are compared with their equivalents in the top half of the diagram, it is clear that while there are similarities, the difference is that the person undertaking the work remains in control of both their labour and the product of their labour. The consequence of self-control over one's labour is that a person is more likely to derive intrinsic meaning from the work being undertaken, rather than *only* seeing

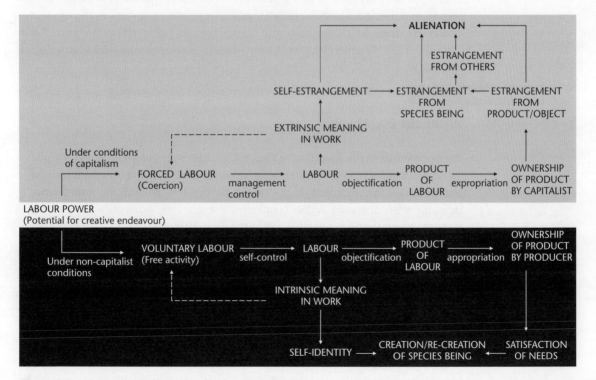

Figure 9.1 Marx's theory of the labour process and alienation

it as a means of getting money. In turn, this might mean that a person's self-esteem and feelings of worth are enhanced – therefore it contributes to their self-identity. Similarly, control over the product of one's labour (appropriation rather then expropriation) means that the outcome of a person's endeavour and effort of work remains in their possession, and they can choose how to use this to satisfy their needs. Overall, there is no alienation because the four features of estrangement do not occur.

The concept of false consciousness

For Marx, the condition of alienation was an objective state under which all employees within capitalist relations suffered. In many ways, this places the concept of alienation beyond empirical investigation because it matters little whether people feel or say they are alienated since the assumption is that the structures of capitalism determine the objective state of alienation. In other words, subjectivity is not part of the analysis, and Marxists are likely to argue that people who claim to be satisfied and fulfilled at work are merely expressing a 'false consciousness': a failure to appreciate the objective reality of their position of subordination and exploitation. Moreover, the Marxist approach to alienation is linked to the work ethic (see Chapter 3) because it rests on the fun-damental assumption that, in an ideal world, work *ought* to be intrinsically rewarding. As Anthony (1977: 141) points out:

> For Marx, alienation represents an imperfection in the purity of the ideal of work, which is the only activity that gives man his identity. The essential paradox of alienation is that it is a pathological state of affairs produced in work as the result of an over-emphasis on a work ethic and on work-based values. It becomes possible to speak of man alienated by his work only when he is asked to take work very seriously.

EXERCISE 9.1

What do *you* think?

The bottom half of the flow chart in Figure 9.1 is idealistic. Indeed, you might argue that it is unrealistic given that the capitalist labour process is the dominant form of work organisation. However, there might be workers around the world who, although often operating within conditions of capitalism, experience *some* of the elements illustrated by the bottom half of the flow chart.

1 To explore this idea, take each of the occupations below and assess their work using the concepts provided in the flow chart:

- a farmer in a small community in a developing country
- a freelance photographer
- a full-time housewife/househusband
- an internet entrepreneur
- a prostitute

(List continues) ▶

▶

- a shopkeeper (self-employed)
- employees in a workers' cooperative
- a drug dealer
- an artist (painter, sculptor, etc)

2 You have probably found evidence of non-alienation in some of these occupations, but how might a Marxist use the concept of 'false consciousness' to suggest your analysis is inadequate?

Alienation as a subjective experience

Learning outcome 2

Explain and assess
Blauner's version of
alienation.

There is an alternative way of looking at alienation that starts from two assumptions that differ from those suggested by Marx.

- Assumption 1: alienation is not inevitable under capitalism.
- Assumption 2: work has different meanings for different people.

Both of these assumptions suggest that it is inadequate to view alienation as an objective condition (the same for all employees under capitalism), but that instead, alienation should be considered a subjective experience (differing from situation to situation, and person to person). One of the most notable attempts to explore the concept in this manner has been undertaken by Blauner (1964). He begins from the proposition that 'alienation is a general syndrome made up of a number of different *objective conditions* and *subjective feelings-states* which emerge from certain relationships between workers and the sociotechnical settings of employment' (Blauner, 1964: 15, emphasis added). He argues that alienation should be divided into four dimensions, each of which can be investigated for different workers to enable a profile of alienation to be drawn up. These dimensions are summarised in Table 9.1.

Blauner, like Marx, focuses on objective conditions which produce alienation, but rather than generalise about the capitalist system as a whole, he differentiates *between* capitalist enterprises according to their technology, and generalises from this.

There is . . . no simple answer to the question: Is the factory worker of today an alienated worker? Inherent in the techniques of modern manufacturing and the principles of bureaucratic industrial organization are general alienating tendencies. But in some cases the distinctive technology, division of labor, economic structure, and social organization – in other words, the factors that differentiate individual industries – intensify these general tendencies, producing a high degree of alienation; in other cases they minimize and counteract them, resulting instead in control, meaning, and integration. (Blauner, 1964: 166–7)

Ultimately, this leads Blauner to a position of technological determinism: he suggests that greater automation will free workers from the drudgery of assembly-lines and machine-minding and will result in decreasing alienation for employees (Blauner,

Table 9.1 Blauner's four dimensions of alienation

Alienation	Definition	Key indicators/measures	Freedom (Non-alienation)

(1) Powerlessness	Employee is controlled and manipulated by others or by an impersonal system (such as technology) and cannot change or modify this domination.	* Extent of control over the conditions of employment
		* Extent of control over the immediate work process:
		  – pace of work
		  – method of work
			Autonomy (empowerment)

(2) Meaninglessness	Employee lacks understanding of the whole work process and lacks a sense of how their own work contributes to the whole.	* Length of work cycle * Range and variety of tasks * Completeness of task	Purposefulness

(3) Isolation	Employee experiences no sense of belonging in the work situation and is unable or unwilling to identify with the organisation and its goals.	* Type and extent of social interaction
		  – formal
		  – informal
			Belonging

(4) Self-estrangement	Employee gains no sense of identity or personal fulfilment from work, and this detachment means that work is not considered a worthwhile activity in its own right.	* Instrumental attitudes * 'Clock-watching' * Expressions of boredom	Self-expression

Source: Summarised from Blauner (1964: 15–35)

1964: 182–3). This is an optimistic projection that suggests the problem of alienation will be resolved within the capitalist framework – a position which, as we have seen in Chapter 6, was vehemently challenged by Braverman (1974) and subsequent labour process theorists.

Criticisms of Blauner's work

Blauner has been criticised for trivialising Marx's notion of alienation 'by conceptualising it in subjective terms' (Watson, 1987: 107). However, while there are numerous points of criticism that can be levelled at Blauner's work, (not least the degree of thoroughness of the empirical data upon which he based his conclusions; see Eldridge, 1971) the problem of being 'overly subjective' is not one of them. Certainly Blauner is accepting the importance of subjectivity because the implication of his thesis is that different employees will have different alienation profiles. But Blauner seems far more interested in using this to generalise about occupational groups, and in particular to assess whether certain types of production technologies led to greater alienation than others. In fact, as his analysis progresses, subjectivity disappears from the discussion. If his thesis was truly examining subjectivity, then his focus would be on individual employees, rather than occupational groups. Moreover, he would probably be more concerned with exploring whether employees doing similar jobs experience the dimensions of alienation differently, and the extent to which this leads to individual, rather than collective profiles of alienation.

Yet, in spite of these criticisms, Blauner's biggest contribution is to reclaim the concept of alienation from Marxist theorists. In re-interpreting the concept and breaking it down into the four separate dimensions, he provides components of alienation which are potentially variable in their intensity and also measurable (or more accurately, comparable). This shifts alienation from being an absolute to a relative concept and allows the theoretical possibility of (objective) conditions of alienation producing (subjective) feelings of non-alienation, as well as (objective) non-alienating conditions leading to (subjective) feelings of being alienated. In other words, allowing subjectivity into the discussion of alienation helps to interpret the complexities and dynamics of employee behaviour and orientations to work. Furthermore, it obliges the observer to recognise that there can be multiple meanings and interpretations of behaviour, even though there may be (shared) structural constraints within the work setting.

EXERCISE 9.2

What do *you* think?

1 Use Blauner's four dimensions of alienation described in Table 9.1 to analyse each of the jobs listed below:

■ supermarket check-out operator
■ lawyer

▶

▶
- assembly-line worker in a factory producing electronic circuit boards
- teacher

(If you prefer, you could use examples of jobs you have done yourself or which you are familiar with)

2 Now use the four dimensions to assess some of the jobs listed in Exercise 9.1. How do your answers compare?

3 What are the difficulties or drawbacks in applying Blauner's four dimensions to particular jobs?

TO SUM UP

So far we have considered two approaches to alienation. The first, based on the original ideas of Marx, views alienation as an objective condition of all work under capitalism. The second, illustrated through the work of Blauner, suggests that alienation varies between occupations and to this extent is experienced subjectively by employees. Although these approaches differ, they both recognise that employees can find themselves in situations of alienation. Therefore the remainder of this chapter is concerned with exploring the question of how (if at all) employees attempt to combat alienating tendencies at work.

Surviving alienation

Our central proposition is that employees develop coping strategies which combat alienation through informal processes and action. In other words, employees take charge of their own destinies by inventing methods of coping that lie outside the formal influence of management. These methods also provide opportunities for employees to counter the prevailing values and beliefs of managers with their own interpretations of the tasks, rules and social interactions that arise at work. In some instances these strategies are collectively negotiated and undertaken by groups of employees; in other instances they represent individual attempts to survive. As we shall see, the meanings and behaviours are dynamic rather than fixed; plural rather than unitary; and creative rather than mundane.

The five main survival strategies that employees engage in are listed below, and in the sections that follow, each is explored in more detail.

1 Making out

2 Fiddling

3 Joking

4 Sabotage

5 Escaping

Making out

Learning outcome 3

Describe the concept of 'making out' and evaluate its role in creating consent within the workplace.

The notion of 'making out' is usually associated with the research undertaken by Michael Burawoy (1979). Like many of the empirical studies discussed in this chapter, Burawoy's method of data collection was based on getting close to the subject under study. It involved participating in the work process in order to experience directly the workplace dynamics and develop an understanding of the meaning and significance of social interaction. With the permission of management, Burawoy began work as an employee in the machine shop of an engine plant which was a division of a multinational company in the United States. From this position of participant observer, Burawoy witnessed an elaborate system of informal behaviour by employees that acted to regulate the work process and ensured that targets were met, yet provided the opportunity for the workers to reassert some control over their working day. He argues that these unofficial shop-floor activities can be seen as a series of games which employees play. These are games concerned with beating the system, finding the angles, working out the dodges or discovering the loopholes – in other words, 'making out'.

> The game of making out provides a framework for evaluating the productive activities and the social relations that arise out of the organization of work. We can look upon making out, therefore, as comprising a sequence of stages – of encounters between machine operators and the social or non-social objects that regulate the conditions of work. The rules of the game are experienced as a set of externally imposed relationships. The art of making out is to manipulate those relationships with the purpose of advancing as quickly as possible from one stage to the next. (Burawoy, 1979: 51)

Burawoy builds on the pioneering work of Roy (1952, 1953 and 1955) to explore how the practice of making out is typically concerned with ways that employees get around the formal rules and regulations laid down by management. At its simplest, making out can be interpreted as the means through which employees secure themselves higher earnings by creatively manipulating the incentive systems (primarily piece-rate payment schemes). However, Burawoy's research led him to argue that economic gain is not the sole motivator for making out. Rather, he suggests (1979: 85) that a range of interlinking motives are at play:

- the reduction of fatigue;
- the desire to pass time;
- the relief of boredom;
- the social and psychological rewards of making out on a tough job;
- the social stigma and frustration of failing to 'make out' on an easy job.

He describes the informal rules and practices that he and his co-workers engaged in as they joined the game of making out. Yet, in so doing they were adapting to the alienating tendencies in the work; they were manipulating the management's rules for their own ends, but they were not fundamentally *challenging* the rules nor undermining management's prerogative to set the rules. In fact, through playing the game of making out they were *consenting* to the formal rules and structures imposed by management.

The issue is: which is logically and empirically prior, playing the game or the legitimacy of the rules? Here I am not arguing that playing the games rests on a broad consensus; on the contrary, consent rests upon – is constructed through – playing the game. The game does not reflect an underlying harmony of interests; on the contrary, it is responsible for and generates that harmony ... The game becomes an end in itself, overshadowing, masking, and even inverting the conditions out of which it emerges. (Burawoy, 1979: 81–2)

EXCERPT 9.2

Making out among refuse collectors

McIntosh and Broderick (1996) evaluate the impact of compulsory competitive tendering (CCT) on the work of a local authority cleansing department. In addition to identifying changes in the organisation of work, they note the impact on the ability of the refuse collectors to 'make out' through a system of 'totting'.

Totting involved sifting through bags and bins in search of 'valuables' or 'sellables' which were then either kept or sold – many refuse collectors regularly took part in car boot sales. The pooling of lead and copper and returned bottles was also an important source of extra income ... Management were often willing to turn a blind eye and saw much of these activities as rewards for doing such a low-status job ... Such activities have not gone completely but the opportunity to tear open bags (a number of households were often identified as being sources of 'tot') has been drastically circumscribed due to the pressures of the workload.' (*ibid*: 424)

In addition, some of the social aspects of the work that made the job bearable have been affected by work intensification, as these quotes from drivers illustrate:
'We had regular people who gave us tea and biscuits, butchers would give us sausages and a bit of meat for doing little jobs for them. Most of that is gone now, we don't have time to stop and do odd jobs.' (*ibid*: 424)
'We used to have time to chat to the old folks and stop a couple of times a day for tea round people's houses. We used to have customer care. Now you are lucky if you see anyone, let alone talk to them.' (*ibid*: 425)

Manufacturing consent

Theorists such as Crozier (1964), Mayo (1933) and Roethlisberger and Dickson (1966) have argued that games undermine management objectives because they are the expression of a counter-control by the shopfloor. But Burawoy concludes

Table 9.2 Fundamental contradictions in managing the labour process

	Control		*Consent*
Management aim:	To secure employee compliance	vs	To enlist employee cooperation
Contradiction 1:	Limiting discretion	vs	Harnessing discretion
Contradiction 2:	Close supervision (direct control) (low trust)	vs	Employee autonomy (responsible autonomy) (high trust)
Contradiction 3:	Disposable labour (numerical flexibility)	vs	Dependable labour (commitment)
Contradiction 4:	Cohesive workforce	vs	Collective solidarity

Source: Based on Hyman (1987: 39–43)

that far from representing a threat to capitalism, games 'manufacture consent' towards the extant social relations of production and help secure the creation of surplus value. By challenging the periphery of the rules, the core of those rules – to produce for the employer – goes uncontested. In this way Burawoy shifts the focus of analysis away from control towards consent. He argues that the labour process under advanced capitalism should not be seen solely in terms of management's control over employees, but must also be viewed as a means through which employees are persuaded to consent to their own subordination, thereby co-operating with management's overall objectives (Burawoy, 1985: 126). This counter-balancing of control with consent helps to address some of the criticisms levelled at Braverman's (1974) analysis of the labour process which dwelt upon the centrality of the labour control objectives of management (see Chapter 6).

Control versus consent

The tensions between control and consent have been subsequently brought into sharper focus by Hyman (1987). Table 9.2 illustrates the contradictions embedded in the labour process which emerge from Hyman's discussion (1987: 39–43). The argument starts from the premise that management is faced with two competing pressures. On the one hand, there is a need to control and direct employees to ensure that production and performance targets are met. On the other hand, there is a requirement to enlist the skill and co-operation of employees in meeting those targets. These competing pressures lead to four key contradictions.

Contradiction 1: Management must simultaneously limit and harness discretion: limit the discretion which employees might apply against management's interests and harness those aspects of their discretion which aid profitable production.

> For even though capital owns (and therefore has the right to 'control') both means of production and the worker, in practice capital must surrender the means of production to the 'control' of the workers for their actual use in the production process. All adequate analysis of the contradictory relationship of labour to capital in the workplace depends on grasping this point. (Cressey and MacInnes, 1980: 14)

Contradiction 2: Management must impose systems of close supervision to ensure that their objectives are complied with, yet also provide the space and freedom for employees to exercise creative discretion. Friedman (1977b) argues that managers are therefore faced with a choice between two broad supervision strategies of either trying to establish 'direct control' (involving the simplification of work and close supervision) or 'responsible autonomy' (wider discretion over how work is completed, with consequently less supervision). These strategies do not resolve the contradiction – not least because they are mutually exclusive. Direct control might be the best way to guarantee compliance, but at the cost of commitment; responsible autonomy may enlist commitment, but does not guarantee compliance with management wishes. Some managers might recognise the possibility of placing a different emphasis on control or consent depending on the group of employees: responsible autonomy for highly skilled, core employees in scarce supply but direct control over low skilled, peripheral workers who are easily replaced. But even responsible autonomy might need to be moderated with some direct control given that 'there are few (if any) workers whose voluntary commitment requires no external reinforcement' (Hyman, 1987: 42). More cynically, however, it might be argued that responsible autonomy is a ploy by managers to disguise their dependency on the workforce. By emphasising autonomy, empowerment, discretion and an absence of close supervision, they can engage in a more subtle attempt to obscure the exploitative nature of the labour process, and particularly the commodity status of labour.

Contradiction 3: Management requires labour to be both disposable and dependable. If labour power is considered a commodity, employees can be hired or fired according to the changing requirements of the business (reflecting seasonal, weekly or even daily fluctuations in demand). Managers can therefore seek to maximise the disposability of labour. However, operating a hire-and-fire policy is likely to (a) undermine the commitment of employees to the organisation, and (b) alert those workers whose skills are in scarce supply, or who are strategically placed, to their centrality to the success of the organisation. Conversely, to implement policies of dependability, such as employment security and the development of an internal labour market, acts to reduce the ability of managers to adapt the labour force to match fluctuations in demand. Indeed, this trade-off between commitment and flexibility has become one of the central problems for contemporary human resource management (for fuller discussion see Noon, 1992: 23–4).

Contradiction 4: Management recognises the need to create a co-operative, cohesive workforce for the benefit of profitable production, but the problem for management is that such a cohesive workforce may develop a collective solidarity that could be used against management's interests. In other words, the workforce cohesion necessary to meet management objectives potentially also provides the conditions for collective solidarity, which may lead workers to challenge those objectives. In a similar way, policies aimed at individualising the workforce and controlling the individual worker (through, for example, performance-related pay, appraisal and promotion) potentially undermine the basis of co-operation between employees that management invariably requires to meet performance targets.

Overall, Burawoy's proposition that, within the workplace 'coercion must be supplemented by the organisation of consent' (1979: 27) helps to synthesise the above contradictions embedded in the capitalist labour process. Essentially, the contradictions reflect the fundamental differences of interest between employers and employees. It is in the employer's interest to secure as much surplus value as possible from the labour of their employees, while it is in the employees' interest to limit the exploitation and extract full payment for their effort. Consequently, employers and managers seek to obscure the appropriation of surplus value, and it is precisely because the game of making out aids this process of obscuring the exploitation that managers are generally content to go along with it. It is only when making out becomes counter-productive that managers seek to suppress it.

The participation [of workers] in games has the effect of concealing relations of production while co-ordinating the interests of workers and management . . . It is through their common interest in the preservation of work games that the interests of workers and shop management are co-ordinated. The workers are interested in the relative satisfactions games can offer while management, from supervisors to departmental superintendents, is concerned with securing co-operation and surplus . . . The *day-to-day adaptations of workers create their own ideological effects that become focal elements in the operation of capitalist control.* (Burawoy, 1985: 38–9, emphasis in original)

Criticisms of Burawoy

While Burawoy's analysis is persuasive and helps to explain why alienating work is endured more often than it is challenged, two important criticisms can be levelled at his thesis.

1 Burawoy's analysis ignores gender

The workplace he studied was composed entirely of men, so he had no opportunity to explore the importance and effect of gender on the social organisation of production. It could be argued that gender could have an important impact upon several of the features that Burawoy characterised as being critical to the manufacture of consent: the shopfloor culture encouraging competition, game playing as an end in itself, the structure of work, the social hierarchy and workgroup dynamics (for a fuller discussion, see Davies, 1990). Of course a similar point may be made about ethnicity and other ways in which employees are stratified.

2 Burawoy overstates the role of consent

Burawoy's eagerness to explain consent blinds him to the possibility that there remains a subversive element in some of the making out he describes. While being incorporated into the system, the employees are still challenging it through constantly subverting the capitalist control of the labour process by continually inventing new ways of making out. As Clawson and Fantasia (1983: 676) comment:

Over and over again, Burawoy takes some feature of the workplace which had generally been identified as evidence of workers' progressive potential, and argues that it actually serves to reinforce the system. He does not seem to understand that a phenomenon can do both things at the same time, that something can be itself and its opposite. In other words, Burawoy's Marxist argument lacks a dialectical analysis.

TO SUM UP

Burawoy argues that employees creatively find time and space to pursue their own objectives within the broad rules set by managers. This process of making out provides them with both extrinsic and intrinsic rewards, thereby creating an incentive to perpetuate the behaviour and consent to the regime established by management. Managers tolerate the making out activities of employees because such activities help to obscure the ultimately exploitative nature of the capitalist labour process. However, critics have suggested that Burawoy too readily interprets employee behaviour as consent and disregards the extent to which many of the behaviours represent a form of resistance, through informal actions which subvert management's intentions.

This last point needs further emphasis because it has important implications for the analysis in the rest of the chapter. What seems to have happened is that in presenting a case for the importance of consent on the shopfloor, Burawoy has allowed the role of resistance to slip from view. Making out is not just about consent: it may also represent a form of resistance. In other words, in considering making out as a survival strategy, we should be aware of its dual impact. Moreover, this is a cautionary note to bear in mind as we turn to the next survival strategy: workplace fiddling.

Learning outcome 4

Classify various types of workplace fiddles and evaluate why they occur within the workplace.

Fiddling

Fiddling is not an exceptional activity: almost everyone is at it. Indeed, it has been estimated that between 75 and 92 per cent of people regularly add to their incomes in ways that are technically against the law (Mars, 1982: 1). As discussed in Chapter 12, for some people this will entail earning income which is not declared to the Inland Revenue, thereby attempting to evade tax payments. For others, fiddling involves adding to their total income by theft from the workplace, for example, taking office stationery for private use, surfing the internet in office hours, doing repairs to personal items using the company's equipment and materials, or artificially inflating expense claims. The list of fiddles at work is as extensive and varied as human ingenuity, and for many it represents an important additional (albeit covert) element in their total rewards, and an important way of altering the balance of the effort-reward bargain.

Various researchers have unearthed the fiddles that are endemic in particular occupations (see for example, Ditton, 1977 on fiddling among bread salesmen and a discussion of other studies of fiddling), but it is Mars (1982) who has perhaps gone furthest in analysing the practice and significance of workplace fiddles. It is useful to summarise his work briefly here for it reveals not only the relationship between forms of fiddling and the occupational structure, but also illustrates how for many, the motive for fiddling goes far beyond any anticipated financial benefit – indeed the frequently small financial gain would often not seem to justify the risks involved unless other contributory factors were influencing the decision to fiddle.

Mars (1982) has developed a typology of fiddling and linked this to distinctive characteristics of different occupations. He uses two dimensions to categories jobs: (1) whether the jobs are subject to extensive rules and close supervision, and (2) whether the jobs involve group activity and are characterised by strong workgroup controls. The presence or absence of these characteristics translates into four different occupational categories each of which provide different opportunities for fiddling. He labels those people who choose to exploit this opportunity to fiddle as 'hawks', 'donkeys', 'wolves' and 'vultures' – each label denoting the characteristics of the way they fiddle, as explained below.

HAWKS: People who work as individuals rather than as part of a group and also are not subject to close supervision; examples include journalists, entrepreneurial managers, waiters and taxi drivers. Someone owning and operating a small business would also fit into this category.

DONKEYS: People in jobs that are highly constrained by rules and who work in relative isolation from others – such as shop assistants and many assembly-line workers.

WOLVES: People who 'work – and steal – in packs' (Mars, 1982: 2), with groups operating according to clearly defined rules, controls and hierarchies governing their fiddling activity. Examples here might include airport baggage-handlers and dock gangs.

VULTURES: People who need the support of a group in order to fiddle, but who act alone. Mars includes such occupations as travelling salesmen and bread roundsmen in this category where group support may be needed to collude with a fiddle (for example, the delivery drivers who share the knowledge about which places they can deliver short to, where checks are unlikely to be carried out, and where to sell the extra goods afterwards).

In drawing such distinctions, Mars usefully points to the different opportunities and constraints for fiddling which characterise different jobs. It reveals that fiddling of one form or another is possible in (and endemic to) almost all occupations. Thus, for a large part of the workforce, the rewards from their job comprise not only the visible element (their wage or salary, paid holidays, pension, and so on) but also an invisible element, reflecting fiddled goods and/or fiddled time. Even in jobs which at first sight appear very highly constrained by close supervision and/or detailed rules governing behaviour, fiddling still takes place. Moreover, it occurs even when penalties are severe and where the possible amounts to be fiddled are small in comparison to the gravity of the sanctions applicable if the person is caught. This leads to the conclusion that any financial benefit from fiddling at work is only one motive, and, for many people, not necessarily the most important one. For some, fiddling provides the only interest in an otherwise monotonous work day – a survival strategy. Indeed, the risk element of getting caught may add a *frisson* of excitement. For others, fiddling may be an expression of frustration or resentment, 'a way of hitting out at the boss, the company, the system or the state' (Mars, 1982: 23).

EXCERPT 9.3

Fiddling at the supermarket

One of the common fiddles amongst shopfloor employees at a large UK supermarket chain is 'grazing'. This is when a shelf-stacker consumes some of the products while they work, for example, crisps, sweets, biscuits and pieces of fruit. This grazing activity is particularly prevalent during the night-shift when there are no customers around and fewer managers. In the words of one store manager:

'Grazing is frowned upon but it is difficult to catch the culprits. We know it is occurring because we find empty packets hidden at the back of shelves. During the summer months strawberries are a particular attraction for grazers. We frequently find a pile of strawberry stalks and a half empty carton of cream.'

Another problem the store has is with van drivers who deliver the orders that customers place through the internet shopping service. The store manager explained: 'We find that van drivers will regularly stop for breaks when they are on their deliveries. They are not supposed to because they are given proper scheduled breaks as part of their shift. They ought to do the deliveries as efficiently as possible, and then return to the store. We also know that some of them do private errands for friends and family on their rounds – picking things up and dropping them off at other houses.

'Worst of all, is when the drivers cut corners in giving good customer service. They are supposed to spend time with the customer explaining whether any items have been substituted and checking whether these are acceptable. If they don't do this, then the customer might ring the store to complain about the item when they unpack their shopping. We will then have to refund them for the item and collect it, or else give the customer the item free of charge.'

Why managers tolerate fiddling

Although the types, motives and outcomes of worker-initiated fiddles are many and varied, this picture is made even more complex when management's approach to fiddling is taken into account. One might expect that fiddling is something which is carried out by workers, *in spite of* the best endeavours by management to prevent it. However, managers frequently 'turn a blind eye' to fiddling activity, provided that it does not rise above a certain level, and particularly where it involves fiddling a third party (for example, the customer) rather than the employing organisation. A survey of 813 UK managers conducted by *Management Today* (2000) revealed that 50 per cent were aware of fiddling in their workplace, but only 4 in 10 would be prepared to take action to stop it occurring. This toleration varies according to the type of fiddle involved, as Figure 9.2 illustrates.

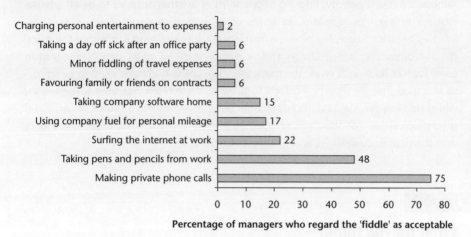

Figure 9.2
Acceptability of workplace fiddles
Source: Management Today (2000)

Percentage of managers who regard the 'fiddle' as acceptable

There are several possible motives for managers to collude with fiddling:

1 It might reflect management's awareness of the near impossibility of stamping out fiddling entirely and if one form of fiddling is suppressed, another is likely to develop to take its place.

2 It might help management maintain a co-operative workforce – if all fiddling was heavily policed by management this might increase workforce discontent and reduce the degree of worker consent to other management objectives.

3 It might enable management to pay lower wages. The availability of fiddles to those working in hotels and restaurants, for example – ranging from not declaring income from tips to the tax authorities to fiddles related to the food and drink served – helps to subsidise low wages. Similarly, among Ditton's (1977: 17) bread salesmen (generally low paid and working long hours) morale was sustained by sales supervisors indicating a 'solution' to the threat of the salesmen having to make up shortages in takings: over-charging customers.

4 It might be because managers themselves are also involved in fiddling, either for their own monetary gain or to protect their position. Mars (1982: 68) for example, recounts the case of a check-out operator in a supermarket where, to balance stocks against stock records, operators were asked to fiddle the customers:

> Every now and then one of the managers will come up to you, usually with a packet of tea, and put it close to the till, near the sweets and chocolates so

that it can be taken as a purchase, and say 'put that through a couple of hundred times will you'. There's never any explanation of *why* you're to do it, what it's for – but it's to sort out their stocks. It is usually done just before and just after stock-taking and it'll just be for a day. (Quoted in Mars, 1982: 68, emphasis in original)

TO SUM UP

Although a covert activity, fiddling of one form or another appears to be an integral element of most occupations. In terms of a 'survival strategy', fiddling normally involves breaking the rules, whereas making out involves working within the rules. But the distinction is not always clear cut. However, for most people involved in some form of fiddling at work, the monetary value of the fiddling is likely to be small – so much so that the efforts required to prevent it are often not seen to be worthwhile. Fiddling can yield additional income but also represents a source of social and psychological gain to individuals responding to aspects of their job, those in authority over them, their co-workers and/or their customers.

EXERCISE 9.3

What do *you* think?

Read Excerpt 9.3 about 'fiddling at the supermarket', then answer the following questions:

1 Using Mars' typology, into which category would you put (a) the shelf-stackers and (b) the delivery drivers?

2 Evaluate each of the fiddles at the supermarket. Are some more detrimental to the organisation than others? Are some more acceptable than others? Explain your answers.

3 Put yourself in the position of the employees. How might they justify their fiddling?

4 What advice would you give the store manager about dealing with these fiddles?

Learning outcome 5

Explain four functions of joking at work.

Joking

The most disappointing aspect of examining the role of humour in work organisations is that when the humour is taken out of the context in which it emerged, it usually ceases to be funny. It is rather like having to explain a joke – it ruins it. Consequently, at the risk of ruining some good jokes, this section explores the significance of humour at work. It is important to begin the analysis by acknowledging the pioneering work of the anthropologist Radcliffe-Brown (1952) who identified the significance of the 'joking relationship' between people.

What is meant by the term 'joking relationship' is a relationship between two persons in which one is by custom permitted, and in some instances, required to tease or to make fun of the other, who, in turn, is required to take no offence... The joking relationship is a peculiar combination of friendliness and antagonism. The behaviour is such that in any other social context it would express and arouse hostility, but it is not meant seriously and must not be taken seriously. There is a pretence of hostility and real friendliness. To put it another way, the relation is one of permitted disrespect. (Radcliffe-Brown, 1952: 90–1)

Subsequent studies of joking and humour have argued that these activities are a natural part of work organisations and also perform four important functions:

1 joking maintains social order and releases tension;

2 joking challenges authority;

3 joking forges group identities;

4 joking alleviates monotony and makes work tolerable.

Each of these is explained in the following sections.

1 *Joking maintains social order and releases tension*

A primary function of the joking relationship is the prevention or reduction of antagonism; typically it develops between people who are required to be in close contact for long periods of time, yet who have some divergence of interests. Not surprisingly, therefore, the concept can be applied to work settings where teasing and banter are part of the daily routine of organisational life. For example, Bradney (1957) used the concept of the joking relationship to explain how sales staff in a large department store regulated their interpersonal relations. She argued that joking helped to mitigate the intrinsic antagonisms caused by the formal work roles and structures.

There is clearly a divergence of interests among sales assistants... as a result of their formal relationship. Each wants to increase her own sales – to earn both a better living and the approval of her employer – and is in competition with the others to do this. There is also every likelihood of hostility and conflict between them when they interrupt and hinder each other just at a time when this interferes most with selling. (Bradney, 1957: 183)

The 'joking relationship' provides the employees with an informal structure through which differences of interest and status are negotiated through playful insults and teasing ('permitted disrespect') rather than with open hostility. Bradney concludes:

By means of a tradition of joking behaviour between its members, which is quite unknown to the management, this store is able to avoid considerable tension and disagreement that would be likely to occur as a result of the difficulties inherent in its formal structure. In so doing it gives the employees a source of positive enjoyment in carrying out their routine activities and incidentally, by means of this, renews their energy to cope even more adequately with their routine problems. (Bradney, 1957: 186–7)

To take another example, Spradley and Mann (1975) used participant observation to explore the working lives of cocktail waitresses, and demonstrate how humour reinforces the gender division of labour within the cocktail bar. The waitresses worked closely with the male bartenders and strong bonds developed between them. Yet there was a clear status differential, with the waitresses in a subordinate position. Waitresses quickly learned that the needs of the bartenders came first because they had the power to make the waitresses' work comfortable or difficult. The joking relationship between the barmen and the waitresses was one means by which any conflict caused by this power imbalance was mediated. The bartenders would use humour to assert their status, cover their own mistakes and to reprimand a waitress. On the other hand, the waitresses employed humour to assert themselves, particularly as a response to feelings of unfairness and powerlessness. Thus, conclude Spradley and Mann (1975: 100):

> Anger and frustration are dissipated and feelings of inequality felt by the waitresses are deflected . . . It creates a buffer between the waitress and bartender in potential conflict situations and provides a means for handling inadequate role performances that occur in full public view . . . But the joking relationship also maintains the status inequality of female waitresses and reinforces masculine values. By providing a kind of 'safety valve' for the frustrations created for women in this small society, joking behaviour insures that the role of female waitresses remains unchanged.

This suggests that humour plays an important role in enabling an employee to cope with the inevitable frustrations and tensions of working life. As a form of safety valve, it allows an individual to let off steam, without challenging the power structures and inequalities that have led to the frustration in the first instance (Wilson, 1979). Spradley and Mann's (1975) cocktail waitresses enjoyed moments where they asserted themselves through humour, but the gendered power structure remained intact. Similarly, Boland and Hoffman (1983) in a study of a small machine shop, noted how the machinists would frequently put cartoons into the steel drums containing the finished pieces for the quality inspectors at the customer's plant. The jokes poked fun at the competence of the inspectors and management, compared with the skill and judgement of employees in the machine shop.

2 Joking challenges authority

Joking at work is a way of challenging authority structures. In other words, jokes are an expression of the informal triumphing over the formal (Douglas, 1975). This raises the question of whether humour may be construed as a subversive activity at work. Empirical studies of humour in fact reveal very few examples where humour is used in a subversive manner. One such example can be found in Westwood's (1984) study of a clothing factory. As participant observer, she cites a 'prank' that resulted in the end of day buzzer being set off ten minutes early and the women fleeing the building with glee, fully aware that it was not the official leaving time.

> The next day management instituted an investigation into what was termed 'the incident'. The shopfloor was absolutely delighted that their speedy exodus had caused such obvious pain to management. Everyone who was asked about it shook their heads wisely, at once 'agreeing' with management's view that this was a very serious matter, while keeping quiet about the identity of the buzzer-pusher. (Westwood, 1984: 91)

Incidents such as these are few and far between, however, and tend to represent occasions where the humour has 'got out of hand'. What is striking from the case evidence is the extent to which humour is highly regulated and ritualised by the workgroups. Far from subverting authority, humour merely issues a mild challenge, which seems more about preserving the status quo than overturning it. Indeed, it could be argued that jokes provide an outlet for the expression of frustration and discontent which might otherwise build up unchecked, and eventually become channelled into activities that have more serious consequences for the organisation (see the discussion on sabotage below).

3 Joking forges group identities

It is also apparent from the examples cited so far that humour seems to be playing a role in establishing a shared group identity. This occurs through a process of social regulation whereby the members of a work setting use humour as one of a range of cultural devices to establish group norms and perpetuate the group's existing dominant values. Humour thereby reinforces the existing social structure and is performing a boundary function (Linstead, 1985b: 744) by protecting the group from outsiders. For example, in a vivid description of the role of humour among engineering workers in a vehicle plant, Collinson (1988) reveals how the supervisors and white-collar staff became the butt of jokes for the engineers: jokes which explicitly denigrated them as being stupid, manipulative and effeminate, and hence different from the hardworking, proudly masculine 'fellas' on the shopfloor.

Newcomers and deviants were also controlled by humour. For example, the apprentices were subjected to initiations which ranged from embarrassing (being sent for a 'long stand') to the degrading: 'Pancake Tuesday is always celebrated by "greasing the bollocks" of the apprentices with emulsion then "locking them in the shithouse, bollock naked"' (Collinson, 1988: 189). These practical jokes 'not only instructed new members on how to act and react, but also constituted a test of the willingness of initiates to be part of the male group and to accept its rules' (*ibid*: 188). It was all about bringing people into line; for example, Collinson was told in reference to a lad who entered the company with 'diplomas galore':

> They had a French letter on his back by ten o'clock. They had him singing and dancing in the loo with the pretext of practising for a pantomime . . . we soon brought him round to our way of thinking. (*ibid*: 189)

In some instances this can have a pernicious effect, resulting in employees feeling excluded or victimised. In particular it can become a form of harassment, creating severe difficulties for women in male-dominated environments or ethnic minorities (see Chapter 10 and Excerpt 9.4).

In Collinson's study humour was also used by the engineers to control their colleagues who were considered not to be working hard enough under the collective bonus scheme. Humour was a way of bringing co-workers into line in order to maximise earnings. The effect of all this was eloquently summed up by the engineer who commented that:

> The men are the gaffers now. They watch each other like hawks. The nature of the blokes is such that they turn on each other . . . You're more worried about what the men think than the gaffers . . . I'm just as bad if there's someone not working. (Collinson, 1988: 197)

EXCERPT 9.4

Just light-hearted banter and horse-play?

A broker at a London firm is suing his former employers for racial discrimination and unfair dismissal.

He claims that he was subjected to anti-Semitic abuse, including the names 'Yiddo' and 'Jew Boy'. He also objected to the way a Jewish skull-cap was placed on top of the office television whenever a Jewish person was giving the financial bulletins. On one occasion he was told to put on a Nazi uniform (hired by the company) as punishment for turning up late. He refused to put on the costume, not least because his grandmother had died in Auschwitz.

The company claims that the culture of the office meant that 'banter' was a way of relieving stress in such a high-pressured job. They said that it was applied to everyone, and that the broker himself had engaged in it, calling his manager a 'big nosed tosser', his colleague a 'fat Jock' and non-Jewish people in the office 'Yoks' (Yiddish slang for Gentiles). Furthermore they said there was a 'bad taste costume' ritual whereby brokers who arrived late had to dress up in humiliating outfits, so, for example, a Welsh broker had to wear a Bo Peep costume.

Source: Based on reports in *The Guardian*, 'Skull cap used by "race jokers"', 1 February 2001; and *The Times*, 'Brokers "used racial abuse to relieve stress"', 1 February 2001

4 Joking alleviates monotony and makes work tolerable

Conformity and compliance at work can also be encouraged by humour in another way: by obscuring the monotony of the work process. This is vividly demonstrated by Roy's (1960) participant observation as a machine operator in a factory (examined in more detail in Chapter 4 above). When Roy first joined the factory he became acutely aware of how tedious the work was, but as he became embroiled in the jokes and pranks on the shopfloor, he found himself distracted from the boredom. Many of the jokes became predictable daily events – 'banana time', 'peach time', 'window time' and so on – and these rituals suppressed some of the drudgery of the 12-hour working day by punctuating it with moments of humour. Indeed, it was only after a serious argument had broken out causing the social cohesion of the workgroup to break up and all interaction to be 'strictly business', that Roy was reminded of the tedium of the work process and began to experience fatigue. In other words, it was humour that provided a means of coping with the boredom and the hard work.

Humour allows people to distance themselves from the unpleasant and boring aspects of work (Cohen and Taylor, 1976: 34), as exemplified by the engineering worker from Collinson's study (1988: 185) who commented that, 'Some days it feels like a fortnight...I had to stop myself getting bored so I increased the number of pranks at work.' Or the women in Westwood's study (1984) who used jokes, often related to sex, to spice up the drudgery of the day. A favourite joke of some of the women in the factory she studied was to:

> Draw lewd pictures of penises and naked men and women, give them captions and send them around the units hoping that they would embarrass some of the other women and provoke a response ... Written jokes were passed around and sniggered at through the working day. It all added excitement and 'a bit of a laff' to the factory days. Sex, of course, was a crucial ingredient and always managed to spice up the end of the day. (Westwood, 1984: 91)

From this point of view, the practical joking and the repartee revealed by the studies cited above are merely examples of employees taking a break from work by indulging in a pleasurable activity. To think about this and the other functions of joking, attempt Exercise 9.4.

EXERCISE 9.4

What do *you* think?

Using your knowledge of the four functions of joking, interpret the events described in Excerpt 9.4.

TO SUM UP

A difficulty facing any attempt to generalise about the significance of humour in work organisations is assessing the impact of subjectivity. The meaning of 'a joke' is negotiated by the participants of a work setting, but its significance may vary from individual to individual. The same humorous incident can be perceived in various ways and may have alternate meanings for different participants. However, irrespective of the specific interpretation an individual puts on a humorous event, the empirical evidence suggests a common theme: joking at work plays an important regulatory function by providing a means of expression that assists group cohesion and deflecting attention from the dehumanising aspects of work. On occasion it is used to challenge authority, but rarely does it undermine the existing power hierarchy. In this way joking is a vital factor in obscuring the social relations of production, and suppressing the alienating tendencies of work.

Learning outcome 6

Describe and interpret the importance of workplace sabotage.

Sabotage

The notion of sabotage often conjures up the image of people engaged in wilful acts of destruction, as retribution for some felt injustice: from the Luddites in the 1820s who destroyed the machinery that was progressively replacing their jobs, to the more contemporary examples of the sacked accounts clerk whose last act is to reformat the computer's hard disk, erasing all the pay-roll information. Or the newspaper sub-editor whose anger with management led him to reword a news story so that the initial letter of each paragraph formed the word 'bollocks' when read vertically. However, studies (for example, Dubois, 1979; Edwards and Scullion, 1982; Taylor and Walton, 1971) suggest that this popular image of sabotage fails to account for the complexity and subtlety of motivation and method. In particular, Linstead (1985a) identifies two key problems in the analysis of sabotage: first, the difficulty of trying to interpret the action, especially whether it represents an intentional, malicious attempt to destroy or disrupt the work process or the product; second, the problem of whether or not to designate the action as rational behaviour. Should all acts of sabotage be attributed to a logical cause, even in the absence of a specific declaration of intent? Both of these problems highlight the need for specific contextual information before it is possible to understand the meanings and motives of sabotage behaviour.

These problems make any generalisation about sabotage fraught with difficulties, not least the danger of understating the importance of the subjective experience of the supposed saboteur. Nevertheless, it is possible to classify acts of sabotage into two broad categories (loosely based on Taylor and Walton, 1971):

1 *A temporary expression of frustration* with the work process, rules, managers, co-workers, or indeed any aspect of the organisation. In such circumstances sabotage is likely to be the wilful malicious act of a frustrated individual. The

anger is placated and the tension dissipated through, for example, kicking the photocopier or being intentionally rude to a customer. Although undesirable in the eyes of management, the consequences of such sabotage are transient and generally offer no serious threat to the functioning of the organisation. Such incidents may even be seen as tolerable and necessary expressions of dissent which act as a kind of safety valve.

2 *An attempt to assert control* over the work process, thus presenting a direct challenge to authority, and consequently far more serious for management. In some circumstances such sabotage may be expressed as individual action (for example, halting a machine by, quite literally, 'putting a spanner in the works'); in others, a meaningful challenge can only be orchestrated through collective action (for example, customs officers at an airport 'working to rule' by checking every passenger, thus causing enormous disruption).

As with the case of humour, acts of sabotage may simultaneously have different meanings for different people involved, so in practice there is far more complexity than this simple typology might suggest.

A further problem is that in practice many acts of sabotage do not easily fit these categories, but are located in a grey area between the two. Consider the following example cited by Taylor and Walton (1971: 228):

When 600 shipyard workers employed on the new Cunarder QE2 finished on schedule they were promptly sacked by John Brown's, the contractors involved. With what looked like a conciliatory gesture they were invited to a party in the ship's luxurious new bar, which was specially opened for the occasion. The men became drunk, damaged several cabins, and smashed the Royal Suite to pieces.

One interpretation might be that this was a rational act of reasserting control by a group of workers reflecting their alienation from the product of their labour. Another interpretation: the frustration of the sacking, linked to the indignity of being invited to 'celebrate' this, unleashed a temporary destructive urge. Then again, perhaps the men were just so drunk that they lost any sense of rational intent and would have gone on the rampage irrespective of where they were drinking. All three interpretations might be correct. Indeed, each might be applicable to different workers: the behaviour may have been the same, but the reasons behind it may have differed. If questioned, the workers might have attributed different meanings and significance to their behaviour – provided, of course, they could remember the incident once they had sobered up.

Virtuous sabotage? The case of whistleblowing

Finally, there might be instances where the supposed sabotage is perpetrated by someone who believes that they have a duty to bring out into the open malpractice or misconduct occurring within the organisation. This is usually called whistle-blowing. The bad publicity that ensues is clearly disadvantageous for the organisation, but is the whistleblower really a saboteur? If they believe they are performing a public service by the disclosure of information about an unlawful or unethical practice, they have virtuous rather than malicious motives. For example:

> Joy Cawthorne resigned as an instructor at an outdoor activity centre in protest over its safety standards. Subsequently, she gave evidence against her former employer after four children died in a canoeing accident in Lyme Bay. The managing director was convicted of manslaughter and sentenced to three years' imprisonment. (Lewis, 1997: 6)

An alternative interpretation is that a whistleblower is an aggrieved or disgruntled employee seeking revenge on the organisation. This means they are acting with malicious intent, so whistleblowing constitutes a form of sabotage. While this might be the case in some instances, it is also clear that whistleblowing is costly for an individual's career. They often face harassment or retaliation (Micelli and Near, 1992), get sidelined in career terms, lose their jobs and find it difficult to get alternative employment. For example, Glazer and Glazer (1989) found that over two-thirds of the 64 whistleblowers they interviewed had become unemployed as a result. So, according to Perry (1998: 240–1) 'whistle-blowing might well be classified as a form of occupational suicide – or perhaps accidental career death.'

Unintentional sabotage?

Analysing sabotage becomes even more confusing because some actions may have destructive or damaging results without there being any malevolence in the minds of the perpetrators. Indeed, there are numerous instances when attempts to adjust the work process to achieve productivity targets, and thus 'make out', carry the risk of potential negative, long term consequences. For example, Taylor and Walton (1971: 232) cite the practice in aircraft assembly of using an instrument called a 'tap' which allows the wing bolts to be more easily inserted but potentially weakens the overall structure. Using the tap is strictly prohibited by factory rules, yet its use continues covertly because without it production cannot function effectively. So, should the workers who use 'taps' be described as saboteurs? Or are they merely irresponsible workers?

In the following example there is little evidence of malicious intent behind the worker's actions; he is easing the work, making out as best he can within the rules set by management.

> The engines passed the [worker] rapidly on a conveyor. His instructions were to test all the nuts and if he found *one* or *two* loose to tighten them, but if three or

more were loose he was not expected to have time to tighten that many. In such cases he marked the engine with chalk and it was later set aside from the conveyor and given special attention. The superintendent found that the number of engines so set aside reached an annoying total in the day's work. He made several unsuccessful attempts to locate the trouble. Finally, by carefully watching all the men on the conveyor line, he discovered that the [worker] was unscrewing a *third* nut whenever he found two already loose. It was easier to loosen *one* nut than to tighten two. (Mathewson, 1931: 238, emphasis in original, cited in Hodson, 1991: 281)

Similarly, in the next example the employee's behaviour reflects a frustration with the conditions of work imposed by management. It is irresponsible behaviour, but is it sabotage?

One of the young male workers [in the brewery] took a bottle in his hand and made a throwing motion with it. Later, on break, I asked him what he was throwing at. He replied that he was not throwing at anything in particular . . . He said that he didn't want to do any damage, that he was just bored and that it would be fun to lob bottles out like grenades and watch them crash and blow up . . . He added, 'It's so dull out there I'd just like to make something happen, to have something interesting to do or see'. (Molstad, 1986: 231)

Moreover, there may be occasions where the consequence of an act of sabotage is separated in time and space from the saboteur. For example, devising and intentionally spreading computer viruses is a malicious act of sabotage, yet the perpetrators may have no specific organisational target for their actions. Their motives seem to be the challenge of creating something that frequently destroys the work of others, but the consequences of their actions may never be known to the perpetrators as they remain unaware of how extensively and to whom the virus spreads.

TO SUM UP

In trying to generalise about sabotage, as in the case of joking, we are faced with the difficulty of interpreting the behaviour of individuals and understanding the meanings that they attribute to it. It is impossible to interpret all acts that have destructive consequences as being planned, rational behaviour with malicious intent. Indeed, stupidity, thoughtlessness and irrationality may better explain the behaviour in some circumstances. However, while making out, joking and, to some extent, fiddling are widely tolerated by management, sabotage is not. It is viewed as a negative activity, perhaps because it presents a direct challenge to authority, and carries a more easily quantifiable cost: the damage and loss of production, customers, and so on. Nevertheless, consistent with the other forms of informal behaviour, sabotage can also be interpreted as a way that employees (individually and collectively) respond to alienating tendencies at work.

Learning outcome 7

Explain the concept of escaping.

Escaping

The term 'escape' can be applied in two ways that are relevant to our present discussion:

1 *Physical escape*, by quitting the job (temporarily through absence, or permanently through exiting the organisation). This is relatively easy to identify as it can be represented in job turnover figures and levels of absence. A high labour turnover indicates some dissatisfaction with the job – although sources of this dissatisfaction may be diverse and difficult to pinpoint: pay, conditions, job content, promotion opportunities, superordinates, co-workers, recognition, equity, or some combination of these. Similarly, as noted in Chapter 4, voluntary absence (taking a day off) is used by a significant proportion of people as a temporary respite from the pressures and frustrations contained within many work settings.

2 *Mental escape*, by withdrawing into one's own thoughts. This is more complex to analyse because it is harder to detect and can take a variety of forms. One way of coping with boredom, for example, is to retreat from conscious activity into the realms of daydream. The work is performed in an automaton-like fashion, relying on internalised routines (as discussed in Chapter 5) which act to free the person to concentrate on thoughts outside of work. In this sense, the person can 'escape' into a world of their own. Indeed, this can be the only way of coping for some service sector workers (such as flight attendants) who are obliged to maintain a cheerful façade for hours on end (discussed further in Chapter 7).

Physical and mental withdrawal are not mutually exclusive categories. For example, a person may drift into a daydream, planning how to escape from their particular job, and subsequently enact this plan, perhaps by gaining qualifications at night school, or securing a small business grant, or playing the lottery. So the daydream may be an outlandish fantasy or an attainable goal. Others might want escape not for themselves but for their family, so people find themselves engaging in stoic tolerance of their particular work circumstances in the hope that this will secure a better future for daughters and sons. As Westwood (1984: 235) observes from her study of hosiery workers:

> [The] women wanted their daughters to have the opportunity to pursue education and training as a means to a life which would be more autonomous. There was a strong sense from the women that they did not want their daughters to be undervalued or wasted in the way they had been.

A similar attitude is evident among male workers, particularly for their sons. To take an example from Collinson's (1992: 185) study of engineering workers:

> [Alf, 30 years old] feels imprisoned on the shopfloor with little possibility of promotion . . . Investing in the self-sacrificing role of parental breadwinner, Alf

holds on to a belief in 'personal success' and dignity . . . He insists, 'I've not done too bad, I keep me family. But it's too late for me. I've been telling the lad I want him to do better than I've done. He'll have every opportunity I didn't have. I'm probably more ambitious for the kids than I am for me. If I could give them my ambition, I'd consider myself a success then. Some, if they got a lad in here [the factory] would think it were a success, me, I'd consider it a failure.'

These views represent a type of deferred gratification or success by proxy, and bring together the two parts of escaping: the mental escape of oneself through dreaming of, and planning for, the physical escape of one's offspring from similar future conditions of boredom and oppression.

The instances of withdrawal contained in these examples reflect a way of coping with work that accommodates the existing circumstances that face employees – a coping strategy based on resigned acceptance of the status quo. While it is likely that such employees would display neither a very high commitment to the organisation nor an enthusiasm for their work, it does not automatically follow that they would perform their tasks inefficiently or carelessly. Indeed it may be a method of coping with the repetitive and boring work that characterises low-skilled, routine jobs (see Chapter 6).

TO SUM UP

Physical escape presents a problem for management either in the form of the need to address absence or revise recruitment and retention policies – in this sense it represents a challenge. Mental escape does not necessarily present a problem for management: unlike making out, fiddling, joking, sabotage and physical escape, the mental escape from work does not raise an alternative discourse, and in this sense offers no challenge. It is the most passive of the informal behaviours explored, yet, more poignantly than any of the others, suggests accommodation with the various aspects of estrangement that constitute alienation.

Conclusion: surviving by consent and resistance

Learning outcome 8

Assess whether the five survival strategies should be interpreted as a form of consent or resistance.

The discussion has highlighted five principal strategies that employees can adopt to deal with the alienating tendencies of work: making out, fiddling, joking, sabotage and escaping. It is clear that these represent 'unofficial' or 'informal' behaviours at work: they demonstrate the importance of looking below the surface into the depths of the workplace where other, complex patterns of action and meaning can be found. To explore this domain, it is necessary to use research methods based on getting close to the subject, either through direct involvement (participative observation, sometimes covert) or detailed case-study analysis (semi-structured interviews and close observation). Such methods were employed by all the researchers cited in this chapter, and their subsequent analyses have helped to illuminate a side of work previously shaded by management rhetoric. In other words, alternative behaviours are being enacted on a daily basis by employees in a bid to survive the worst aspects of their working days.

But caution needs to be exercised: to explain work as 'a struggle for survival' may be melodramatic. Moreover, to characterise the five survival strategies as *always* problematic for management is, as has been noted already, an untenable proposition. What seems to be occurring is that each of the strategies can represent (and be interpreted as) consent *or* resistance to management. This warrants some explanation, so to assist in this, Table 9.3 summarises the different behaviours that could be interpreted as representing consent or resistance for each of the five survival strategies.

The problem of different interpretations

Table 9.3 is designed to show how each of the survival strategies could be interpreted in different ways:

- There can be different interpretations of *different* survival strategies. For example, some people might consider making out, joking and escaping as forms of consent, while viewing fiddling and sabotage as forms of resistance.
- There can be different interpretations of the *same* survival strategy. For example, some people might see making out as a form of consent, while others would view it as a form of resistance.

Table 9.3 Interpretation of the five survival strategies

Survival strategy	Interpreted as a form of consent	Interpreted as a form of resistance
Making out	Acts of 'game playing' within the organisation's rules, which result in mutual benefit for employees and managers.	Acts that undermine management control by bending the rules to satisfy the self-interest of employees.
Fiddling	'Deserved' perks that help subsidise wages and confer status on employees.	Theft that affects profitability and undermines the integrity of everyone in the organisation.
Joking	Forms of group self-regulation that preserve the status quo and provide a way of letting off steam.	Challenges to management authority that undermine the status and policies of managers and make them appear foolish.
Sabotage	(a) Expressions of frustration or irresponsible behaviour (letting off steam). (b) Well-meaning actions that have unintended negative consequences.	(a) Malicious acts against property and people, intended to 'get even' with the organisation. (b) Well-meaning actions intended to 'expose' the organisation (whistleblowing).
Escaping	Acts of withdrawal that result in the employee passively accepting the status quo, even though they disagree with management policy or objectives.	Acts that result in withdrawal of goodwill or mental and physical effort, thereby reducing organisational performance and undermining management objectives.

- There can be different interpretations from situation to situation. In other words, a particular piece of behaviour associated with a survival strategy might be considered a form of consent in one situation but a form of resistance in another, because of the different circumstances that surround it.

To illustrate how there might legitimately be different interpretations, consider the following example:

A builder employed on a new housing development has taken a few bags of cement. He might consider this a permissible 'perk', but the site manager might interpret it as theft from the company (a sackable offence). On the other hand, the builder might be stealing the cement to 'get back at' his employer, while the site manager simply turns a blind eye believing it to be a way of circumventing demands for better pay. So, the *same* fiddling behaviour might represent an expression of either consent or resistance (by the builder); equally, it may be interpreted (by the site manager) as either an expression of resistance (therefore a problem) or consent (no problem). Furthermore, the interpretations by the builder and site manager might coincide or differ, thus potentially adding greater complexity to the situation.

EXERCISE 9.5

What do *you* think?

If you currently have a part-time job (or have taken a vacation job in the past) think about the various strategies that you and your work colleagues have used to get through the working day.

1 Provide examples for each of the five strategies: making out, fiddling, joking, sabotage and escaping.

2 Take each example in turn and decide whether it should be viewed as a form of consent or resistance. Justify your decision.

Interpretation is complex

Even where a particular behaviour seems clearly to fall into one category or the other, there are frequently alternative interpretations. Take, for example, the escape strategy of absence from work. It has been noted how regularly taking days off is generally seen as unacceptable by management and is often viewed with disdain by fellow employees (especially those with a strong work ethic). However, suppose a secretary was absent from the office the first Monday in every month in order to take an elderly parent to the hospital for a regular check-up. Should these extra 12 days paid unofficial leave be construed as resistance; or might such regular absences enhance the secretary's consent to managerial authority when in work? Similarly, are all jokes innocuous ways of coping by letting off steam, or might the pointed humorous comments aimed at the supervisor slowly erode the latter's status and authority? Even sabotage poses problems of interpretation: for instance, does the photocopier fail to work because it has been kicked by an employee, or does an employee kick the photocopier because it fails to work?

Once again, as in previous chapters, a complex picture emerges which requires the analysis of work to incorporate a plurality of interpretations, experiences and behaviours. It forces us to question unreflective, supposedly 'common sense' understandings that frequently litter management textbooks and the popular press. The foregoing analysis puts us in a position to challenge the dogmatic viewpoints of those who state that all rule-bending is problematic; all fiddling is costly; all sabotage is destructive; all joking is fun; or all absence is simply laziness.

Unfair discrimination 10 at work

KEY CONCEPTS

- Fair and unfair discrimination
- Criteria of discrimination
- Stereotypes
- Race and ethnicity
- Exclusion from employment
- Harassment
- Institutional racism

- Liberal perspective on equal opportunities
- Radical perspective on equal opportunities
- Reactionary perspective on equal opportunities
- Positive action and positive discrimination
- Sameness and difference
- Equal treatment and special treatment

CHAPTER AIM

To assess the process of discrimination and its impact on employees.

LEARNING OUTCOMES

After reading and understanding this chapter you will be able to:

1 define and apply the concept of discrimination;

2 assess the type of disadvantage that occurs in getting work, with particular reference to race and ethnicity;

3 assess the type of disadvantage that occurs within the workplace, with particular reference to race and ethnicity;

4 critically evaluate three different perspectives on equal opportunities;

5 explain how perceptions of fairness depend on assumptions made about the principles of sameness and difference;

6 map the process of discrimination and explain why consensus about fairness differs between individuals and social groups.

Learning outcome 1

Define and apply the
concept of
discrimination.

Introduction

Imagine you are scanning the appointments section of a newspaper and come across the following advert. As you read it, ask yourself the question: what aspects of the advert are discriminatory?

> Sales executive required for a medium-sized electronics firm wanting to expand its customer base into Japan. Applicants must have at least five years previous experience of international sales and be aged between 28 and 35. Fluency in Japanese is essential. The job requires energy, dedication, and adaptability, as considerable periods of time will be spent outside the UK. Starting salary will be commensurate with age and experience, and a mixed benefits packet will be offered in line with personal requirements.

The answer is: all of it! The company's management is seeking to discriminate between people on the basis of whether or not they have the appropriate attributes to carry out the job. The important issue, however, is not whether discrimination is occurring (it certainly is) but whether the discrimination is based on *fair criteria*. For example, the requirement of fluency in Japanese is obviously a criterion which discriminates in favour of people who can speak the language; if you cannot speak Japanese you will not get the job and there-fore will be discriminated against. Yet, the company managers who have made 'fluency in Japanese' a criterion for choosing between people are likely to argue that this is fair because it is an essential requirement for the job. How-ever, if you are of the opinion that 'fluency in Japanese' is *not* a necessary requirement to do the job, then you could argue that this is an unfair criterion on which to discriminate between people. Similarly, the advert stipulates that the applicants must be aged between 28 and 35, therefore people are being discriminated against on the basis of age; as indeed they are on 'previous experience' and less tangible qualities, such as 'drive and adaptability'. Judge-ments about whether any of these are justifiable criteria upon which to dis-criminate between potential applicants will influence opinions about the overall fairness of the recruitment.

At issue, therefore, is not the question of discrimination itself (selecting suitable from non-suitable applicants) but the *fairness* of the discrimination (whether the grounds for discriminating between the applicants are legitimate and justifiable). The problem is, of course, that when people talk of 'discrimination' they invari-ably mean *unfair* discrimination. Typically, therefore, if someone described the advert as 'discriminatory', they are likely to mean that they consider it unfair in the ways in which it discriminates between people. In this respect, the word 'discrimination' has lost its literal meaning and is more normally used to imply criticism. Try Exercise 10.1 to assess your own opinions about fairness of discrimination.

What do *you* think?

For each of the situations described below, decide whether you would consider them to be justifiable or unjustifiable forms of discrimination. In each case explain your reasoning.

1 A Sikh bricklayer is denied a job on a building site because the hard hat would not fit over his turban.

2 He is also denied a job as a security guard because all staff are required to wear a uniform which includes a peaked cap.

3 A Muslim office worker is sacked for taking long lunch breaks every Friday. Instead of taking lunch he has a five mile journey to the Mosque for prayers.

4 Workers in an open-plan office vote in favour of a smoking ban. The three workers who smoke must now go outside for a cigarette.

5 A bearded man is refused a job in a large Scandinavian furniture store because it has a 'no facial hair' policy.

6 You are not allowed into a night-club because you are wearing jeans.

Victims of discrimination

Commentators on discrimination have identified six criteria that represent the main bases of discrimination and lead to accusations of unfairness:

- sex/gender;
- race/ethnicity;
- disability;
- sexual orientation;
- religion;
- age.

Clearly, these are not mutually exclusive categories, so some people find themselves experiencing unfair discrimination from several different directions. The extent to which different individuals experience one or several sources of disadvantage serves to underline a central theme running through the book: the plurality of human work experience. Nevertheless, the experience of discrimination also has some common manifestations which transcend these individual categories.

Definition of stereotyping

Stereotyping is the act of judging people according to your assumptions about the group to which they belong. It is based on the belief that people from a specific

▶

▶ group share similar traits and behave in a similar manner. Rather than looking at a person's individual qualities, stereotyping leads us to jump to conclusions about what someone is like. This might act against the person concerned (negative stereotype) or in their favour (positive stereotype). For example, the negative stereotype of an accountant is someone who is dull, uninteresting and shy – which of course, is a slur on all the exciting, adventurous accountants in the world. A positive stereotype is that accountants are intelligent, conscientious and trustworthy – which is equally an inaccurate description of some of the accountants you are likely to encounter. The problem with stereotypes is that they are generalizations (so there are always exceptions) and can be based on ignorance and prejudice (so are often inaccurate). It is vital for managers to resist resorting to stereotyping when managing people otherwise they run the risk of treating employees unfairly and making poor quality decisions that are detrimental to the organization.

Source: Heery and Noon (2001: 347)

Negative stereotypes

At the heart of most discrimination lies a stereotype about a particular group of people, which means that an individual is not judged according to his or her own qualities (see Excerpt 10.1). This process acts in two directions: the object group (ethnic minorities, the disabled, women, travellers, asylum seekers, and so on) tend to be attributed a negative stereotype, while the subject group (those doing the judging) tend to give themselves a positive stereotype. To illustrate the effects of such stereotypes, consider the quotes below from ethnic minorities working in the construction sector, published in the trade journal *Construction* (1999). Each shows the way prior assumptions of other people impact on the experiences of these employees.

Architect:
If you're black, you're expected to be holding a shovel and digging, not in management. When I turn up and ask to see drawings, people look at me as if to say, "What do you want them for?" and direct me to the site entrance.

Site Manager:
When I was promoted to foreman, they sent me down to a new job and some bloke said to me: "Two things son. I ain't taking orders from you because (a) you're younger than me and (b) you're black."

Chargehand:
I'll be standing there and one of my lads will be standing next to me and the delivery man will naturally walk up to him because he assumes he's the boss. Sometimes I have a little smirk about it . . . Sure, there is some graffiti in the toilet that says Les is a black bastard – it is normal, I'm the boss.

Negative stereotyping is particularly experienced by people with disabilities. A study by Reynolds, Nicholls and Alferoff (2001) reveals how a stereotypical image of 'the disabled employee' having lower productivity, higher absence and greater dependency on others, leads to a general perception of disabled people being 'hard to employ'. Not only does this reduce access to jobs, it also perpetuates a general tendency to marginalise disabled people: 'a process by which disabled people find themselves, in various ways, on the edges of social life, only being considered as a "side" issue, or as a necessary "extra" problem' (Reynolds, Nicholls and Alferoff, 2001: 193). Further effects of the stereotyping and exclusion of disabled people can be found in Oliver (1996).

Similarly, age-typing of jobs is revealed in a study by Oswick and Rosenthal (2001). Their survey of managers shows how certain jobs are deemed best suited to certain age groups and how age discrimination is then justified on these grounds. So, according to the respondents it was seen as legitimate to discriminate in favour of older workers when the job demanded stability, loyalty and maturity, and against them when fitness, energy and innovation were required. In many respects this is reminiscent of the sex-typing of jobs discussed in Chapter 5. The result is a pernicious process:

> the stereotyping of a person according to their social group and irrespective of their individual attributes; the association of a particular job with the need for certain attributes; and the matching of the stereotype to the job rather than the individual. As well as being morally questionable, it is also bad personnel practice, assuming the objective is to get the best person for the job. (Noon and Ogbonna, 2001: 11)

TO SUM UP

Discrimination is about applying various criteria to choose between people, so the key issue becomes the fairness of the criteria upon which the discrimination is based. Fair criteria lead to discrimination that is justifiable (fair discrimination), whereas unfair criteria lead to unfair discrimination (more usually simply labelled discrimination), which is unjustifiable and about which something needs to be done. At the heart of discrimination is the stereotyping of a person according to assumptions about the group to which they belong.

Experiencing discrimination

This section explores the key features of how discrimination is experienced by drawing on examples of race and ethnicity. This is not to imply that this category of discrimination is more important than the others – indeed, later in the chapter gender is brought into the analysis – but the focus allows the key concepts to be illustrated by concentrating on one criterion of discrimination.

Defining race and ethnicity

It is important to clarify what is meant by race and ethnicity. As noted in other chapters, many of the concepts encountered when studying work can be identified as being socially constructed, and in this way changeable and negotiable – the most vivid example of this being 'skill' (see Chapter 5). It can be argued that race and ethnicity are in many ways similarly socially constructed: they are concepts used by a particular group to define themselves and thereby identify their difference from 'the other'. In this case, the process of social construction involves a dominant group focusing on elements of a person's behaviour, appearance, attitude, belief or biography which identify them as in some way different from the dominant group and belonging to a separate group (usually a minority). Of course, people differ from each other in many ways but only certain differences are perceived to be relevant – these 'relevant' differences have been arrived at through common agreement and understandings by members of the group, and reinforced through its values, beliefs and norms.

- *Racial* differences are related to physical features, the most obvious example being skin colour.
- *Ethnic* differences are related to cultural features such as language, customs, and religion.

A particular group of people (from a country's population to a small team of workers in a factory) will therefore come to some common understanding as to what racial and/or ethnic differences are of relevance in distinguishing themselves from others. From context to context, and group to group, racial and ethnic boundaries are drawn differently and have varying relevance.

There is considerable debate about the concept of 'race' because it has been discredited by biological science: everyone is of mixed 'race'. Recent analysis of DNA has led geneticists to conclude that there is more genetic variation within supposed racial groups than between racial groups. Politically, however, it remains important because, as Mason (1994) points out, some people behave as though clearly identifiable groups do exist, hence racism (for a fuller review of this detailed debate see Anthias, 1992; Anthias and Yuval-Davis, 1992; Miles, 1993).

The controversy over race has led to increasing focus by social scientists on the utility of 'ethnicity' as a way of defining difference. But the concept of ethnicity is not without problems (for a full discussion see Yinger, 1986). It has led to some anomalous legalistic distinctions in the UK: for example, 'gypsies' constitute an ethnic group but Rastafarians do not (Forbes and Mead, 1992). The current situation is that the law recognises an ethnic group as one which has a long shared history and a cultural tradition of its own, and that this might be identified through characteristics such as: a common geographical origin; a common language; a common literature; a common religion; and the characteristic of being a minority in a larger community (Forbes and Mead, 1992: 23). However, much of the categorisation of 'ethnicity' tends to rely on a mixture of physical differences (primarily skin colour) and geographical origin. For example, Table 10.1 shows the categories used in the 2001 Census of Great Britain.

Table 10.1 Ethnic categories used in the 2001 Census of Great Britain

White	Mixed	Asian or Asian British	Black or Black British	Chinese or other ethnic group
British	White and Black Caribbean	Indian	Caribbean	Chinese
Irish	White and Black African	Pakistani	African	Other ethnic group
Other White	White and Asian	Bangladeshi	Other Black	
	Other Mixed	Other Asian		

In addition, it is important to recognise that race and ethnicity, like gender, deserve increased status as an analytical construct central to understanding work in organisations (Nkomo, 1992), but this has been limited (up to now) by the ethnocentric tendency of most academics in framing theoretical and research questions. However, there is a richness of empirical enquiry that we can draw upon to explore the disadvantages faced by ethnic minorities.

Disadvantage in getting work

A principal way that ethnic minorities experience discrimination at work is through a lack of equality of opportunity in getting jobs. In the UK, the rate of unemployment for the ethnic minority population is higher than for the white population, although there are important differences between and within ethnic groups (Modood *et al.* 1997; Pilkington, 2001). It has also been observed that in times of recession, when competition for jobs intensifies, the ethnic minority population tends to suffer more: a faster rising rate of unemployment, reaching a higher peak than the white population. In periods of recovery, the rate falls more quickly than among the white population. Therefore, when comparing rates of unemployment between ethnic minorities and whites, the broader cyclical pattern of unemployment has to be taken into account, as the difference will vary according to economic peaks and troughs. (Brah, 1986; Dex, 1983; Jones, 1993; Modood *et al.*, 1997; Rhodes and Braham, 1986; Smith, 1981).

Training opportunities

Exclusion from employment is also a reflection of the relevance of the skills possessed by an individual, so access into jobs is likely to be related to the extent of training and retraining undertaken. Access to training schemes is particularly important for people from ethnic minority backgrounds because it provides a vital means of improving employment prospects in a labour market already biased against them through unfair discrimination. However, research reveals that just as there are barriers

Learning outcome 2

Assess the type of disadvantage that occurs in getting work, with particular reference to race and ethnicity.

to employment, there are also barriers for ethnic minorities within UK Government training schemes designed to improve employment prospects. For example, an analysis of the provision of training schemes for unemployed adults (Ogbonna and Noon, 1995; Noon and Ogbonna, 1998) revealed that ethnic minorities were joining the scheme in representative proportions, yet they did not enjoy the positive outcomes (jobs and qualifications) to the same extent as experienced by their white counterparts. Through detailed interviews with the providers of the training and the trainees themselves, two types of disadvantage were revealed:

1 *Discrimination among the training providers* (private firms providing off-the-job instruction). Here, unfair discrimination was experienced in terms of the time spent with each trainee (ethnic minorities receiving less attention), the stereotyping of ability and, in a few cases, verbal abuse.

2 *Discrimination among the placement providers* (local organisations who provided hands-on experience). (a) Placements were generally difficult to secure for all trainees, and faced with direct competition from white trainees, ethnic minorities were less successful (the providers could pick and choose, and some were found to be using overtly racist criteria) (Ogbonna and Noon, 1995: 551–6). (b) When placements were secured, ethnic minority trainees were less likely to be placed in major institutions like banks, insurance companies and department stores. Instead, there was a tendency for them to be sent to (or only be accepted by) small companies (many of whom saw this as useful 'free labour') and voluntary organisations. While at least providing some work experience, both of these types of organisation had neither the resources to provide adequate on-the-job training to back up the skills learned in the classroom, nor the staffing vacancies to offer employment following the completion of the placement period.

These findings echo earlier studies that have similarly revealed unfair discrimination in training (see, for example, Cross, 1987; Cross, Wrench and Barnett, 1990; Lee and Wrench, 1987).

Recruitment and selection

Another key area where disadvantage is experienced by ethnic minorities is in the process of recruitment and selection. Studies have revealed discriminatory practices in both the private and public sectors (Brown and Gay, 1985; Jenkins, 1986; Jewson, Waters and Harvey, 1990), in white-collar and professional occupations (Firth, 1981; Hubbuck and Carter, 1980), and among graduate recruiters (Brennan and McGeevor, 1987; Noon, 1993). The problem for researchers, however, is how to identify discrimination in recruitment and selection, particularly if, as Jenkins (1986: 240) argues, the majority of discrimination among employers 'is neither strikingly visible nor necessarily self-consciously prejudiced'. One way of tackling this problem is by undertaking research using covert methods. See an example of this approach in Excerpt 10.2 and then attempt Exercise 10.2.

EXCERPT 10.2

A covert experiment on racial discrimination

An experiment was conducted by one of the authors (Noon, 1993, and then repeated six years later, (Hoque and Noon, 1999) in which speculative letters of application were sent to personnel managers in the UK's top 100 companies from two fictitious MBA students – one whose name identified him as Asian, and the other as most likely white. The purpose of the research was to test how effective the equal opportunity practices were in the companies. In theory, the applicants should have been treated the same because the factual content of the letters was identical and the 'candidates' were equally qualified. The experiment also controlled for other factors that might affect the results, such as the time the letters were sent and the person replying.

Through a statistical analysis of the responses to the letters it was possible to examine three issues:

- whether the applicants were equally likely to receive a reply;
- whether the quality of the replies was the same for both candidates;
- whether there were differences in the quality of response from companies with and without equal opportunity statements in their annual reports.

The findings for the two studies are summarised in the table below.

Issue	Main findings of 1992 study	Main findings of 1998 study
1 Likelihood of response	Both applicants were equally likely to receive a reply.	Both applicants were equally likely to receive a reply.
2 Quality of response	Better quality (more encouraging) replies were sent to the white applicant.	No statistically significant evidence of unequal treatment in terms of quality of reply.
		The disappearance of unequal treatment is explained by those companies moving into the top 100 rather than by improvement from those companies remaining within the top 100.
3 Effects of equal opportunity statement	Companies with equal opportunity statements were more likely to treat both applicants the same.	Having an equal opportunity statement made no difference to the treatment of the applicants.
	When discrimination occurred amongst companies with equal opportunity statements, it was *against* the ethnic minority applicant.	Companies with specific mention of equal opportnities for ethnic minorities were more likely to discriminate *against* the ethnic minority applicant.

What do *you* think?

Read Excerpt 10.2 and then answer the following questions:

1 What do the findings suggest about the state of equal opportunities in the UK's top 100 companies in 1998 compared with 1992?

2 How might you explain the findings relating to the equal opportunity statements?

3 This research is based on the use of covert methods: those answering the letters did not know they were subjects of research.

   (a) In your opinion, is this ethical? Explain your reasoning.

   (b) How might the researchers in this case justify their choice of methods?

   (c) What alternative methods could have been used?

Case study research based on interviews has similarly found evidence of racial and ethnic discrimination. Frequently this appears to be the result of negative stereotypes held by managers in charge of the selection process (see for example, Hubbuck and Carter, 1980; Jenkins, 1986; Jewson *et al.*, 1990). Indeed, Ram (1992) found that the necessity to access the white-dominated business society has led even some Asian employers to discriminate against ethnic minorities in favour of whites. However, unfair discrimination can also occur unintentionally as a result of bad or inappropriate selection methods. A particularly notable example (Labour Research Department, 1990) is the case of British Rail where, as part of the selection process for train drivers, personality questionnaires were used which were supposed to reveal strengths in terms of 'relationships with people', 'thinking style' and 'feelings and emotions'. The results were controversial, however, because they profiled all the white candidates positively and all the black candidates negatively. The reason for this is that personality tests are culturally bound because they rely on values, beliefs and norms that are reflected in the dominant culture; so people from a different cultural background are more likely to fall outside the acceptable profile. Although the managers at British Rail had no intention of discriminating against ethnic minority candidates, the use of the personality test produced that effect. This problem of unintentional indirect discrimination is returned to when the liberal perspective on equal opportunities is examined.

Learning outcome 3

Assess the type of disadvantage that occurs within the workplace, with particular reference to race and ethnicity.

Disadvantage in the workplace

Having secured a job, people from ethnic minority backgrounds can experience further unfair discrimination in terms of full recognition of achievement and promotion. Jones' (1993) analysis of occupational structure, for example, revealed that ethnic minorities were disproportionately clustered in jobs deemed lower skilled, and were notably under-represented in senior management grades in large organisations – a situation similarly experienced by women. The pattern remains broadly the same in a later survey (Modood *et al.*, 1997) although the authors make important distinctions between ethnic groups – in particular the notably disadvantaged position of Caribbean and Bangladeshi respondents compared with the more favourable position of Chinese respondents.

Harassment

Irrespective of the type of work being undertaken, it is evident that many ethnic minorities experience discrimination from their co-workers on a regular basis. Some of the harassment becomes so severe that it is brought to public attention – such as the disturbing case of the UK postal worker whose suicide note explained that he had been racially harassed at work (*The Guardian*, 2001, 9 January). However, much racial abuse remains hidden and perniciously erodes the morale and self-worth of its victims, similar to the way persistent bullying can break the spirit of a child.

A particularly vivid example is the case of the UK fire service where a confidential Home Office report in 1994 revealed an alarming amount of racial and sexual harassment, ranging from verbal abuse and being ostracised, to physical attacks. For instance, it highlighted the experience of an Afro-Caribbean fire-fighter: 'The first day, the blokes tricked us...They threw a bucket of water over us. We laughed our heads off and I thought "I've been accepted". (*The Observer*, 10 April 1994). Clearly this could be construed as an initiation ritual (the sort of event explored when analysing humour in Chapter 9) but whereas the 'ragging' continued for this particular fire-fighter, it stopped for his white colleague. He goes on to explain how the attacks increased in severity:

> They dragged me out of my bed, put me under the shower. They tied me up, they put me under the water tower and filled it with water. I nearly drowned. They grabbed me and set me head-first in a fire bin. They set my shoes on fire, whacked me in the head. They'd tell me to do things to test my strength, and then while I was exercising try and trip me up, knock my hands away. (*The Observer*, 10 April 1994)

Instances such as this led to an investigation of the Fire Service and a further Home Office report 'Equality and Fairness in the Fire Service' (published in 1999) labelled the Service racist, sexist and homophobic.

> In one of the most damning indictments of a public sector body, the report found the fire service to be one of the last bastions of white, male, laddish culture. Stronger leadership and cultural changes were needed to improve equality and fairness for staff, said the report, which found prejudice was rife among the overwhelmingly white male officers in the service. Women regularly suffered sexual harassment from colleagues, while gay and lesbian fire-fighters risked vilification if they were open about their sexuality, the report

concluded. Firefighters from ethnic minorities faced routine name calling, were forced to fit in with the prevailing white culture, and often felt they were passed over for promotion because of their skin colour. (*The Guardian*, 17 September 1999)

Similar dramatic cases can be found in the private sector. For instance in October 1999, 800 workers at Ford UK's Dagenham factory staged a walk-out in protest against alleged 'entrenched racism', which included harassment by foremen and racial taunts (*Financial Times*, 7 October 1999). This followed an earlier industrial tribunal case against the company (which admitted liability) where it was revealed that an Asian employee had experienced persistent abuse:

> Mr Parma suffered years of routine abuse by his foreman and his team leader. Once, he opened his sealed pay packet to find the word "Paki" scrawled inside. In another incident, he saw graffiti threatening to throw him to his death. [...] On one occasion he was ordered into the "punishment cell", a small booth in which oil is sprayed over engines, but he was not allowed to wear protective clothing. He became ill and needed medical attention.
>
> On another occasion Mr Parma had his lunch kicked out of his hands and was told: "We're not having any of that Indian shit in here." He was also warned that he would have his legs broken if he ever named any of his tormentors. The police were called in at one stage, but the Crown Prosecution Service decided to drop charges. (*The Independent*, September 24, 1999)

Examples such as this illustrate the way that certain groups are exposed through work to hostile social environments. For many people, the harsh reality is that work becomes a domain of unpleasant social interaction: harassment, in its various guises and manifestations, is entrenched as part of everyday life.

Institutionalised disadvantage

When discrimination is deeply embedded in an organisation, it is popularly described as 'institutional ' – hence institutional racism, sexism, homophobia and so on. This suggests that the institution itself embodies values, structures and processes that deny equal opportunities for certain groups of employees. In this sense it replaces the notion of discrimination being the attitude and actions of one person towards another, with the concept of discrimination being a pervasive process across the whole organisation. This excuses individuals, but blames the entire (impersonal) system. It is therefore a devastating indictment of an organisation, suggesting something rotten at its core. Within the UK there has been a particular upsurge in the use of the term 'institutional racism' to explain racist attitudes and behaviour following investigation into public sector organisations such as the Metropolitan Police, the Fire Service and the Prison Service (see Excerpt 10.3).

EXCERPT 10.3

'Malicious racism' in youth prison

'A confidential prison service report following the murder of an Asian inmate by a white prisoner at Feltham [youth prison] West London, has concluded that the youth jail is guilty of institutional racism, with ethnic minority staff and inmates enduring overt racist abuse by warders and failures by senior management...

'The report [. . .] brands Feltham as "institutionally racist", and found a "damning indictment of how staff are failing in their duty of care towards prisoners".

'It concludes: "There is evidence that racism exists at Feltham, both overtly and by more subtle methods. Minority ethnic staff should not have to tolerate the level of harassment that exists in order to feel accepted as part of the team. Similarly, prisoners should be able to live free from racist abuse by staff." [. . .]

'The report says: "Evidence found by the team suggests that a small number of staff sustained and promoted overtly racist behaviour as well as more subtle methods and that there are issues surrounding both staff and prisoners.

"Staff from all ethnic groups told of an underlying culture that suggests the only way minority ethnic group staff can be accepted as part of the team of Feltham is by enduring racist comments and racist banter/jokes. Senior managers know what they should be doing but have not done it. This leads the inquiry team to form the conclusion that Feltham is institutionally racist."

'The report, stamped as confidential on each of its 30 pages, found a "failure by staff at all levels to take complaints of racist incidents seriously". It said some of those responsible for race training believed racist jokes could be acceptable.

'Half of Feltham's 717 inmates are from Asian or Afro-Caribbean backgrounds, as are 11% of its 654 staff. The senior management is entirely white.'

Source: Abridged from Dodd, V. '"Malicious racism" in youth prison', *The Guardian*, 22 Jan 2001

As noted in the previous section, the culture of an organisation may perpetuate values and attitudes that exclude certain ethnic groups. In addition, however, institutional racism implies that processes within the organisation are deficient:

> The strength of [the concept of] institutional racism is in capturing the manner in which whole societies, or sections of society, are affected by racism, or perhaps racist legacies, long after racist individuals have disappeared. The racism that remains may be unrecognised and unintentional, but, if never disclosed, it continues uninterrupted. (Cashmore, 1996: 170)

This means that processes within organisations may be embedded within structures, policy and practices that disadvantage employees, even though individual managers may not be making overtly racist decisions. There can be legislative attempts to prevent this (for example, laws on indirect discrimination, see below) but disadvantage persists within organisational processes such as:

- word of mouth methods for internal recruitment;
- dress codes that prevent people practising their religious beliefs;
- promotions based on informal recommendations, rather than open competition;
- informal assessments rather than formal appraisals;
- assumptions about training capabilities;
- assumptions about language difficulties and attitudes.

This structural, institutionalised disadvantage serves to perpetuate the situation because those most likely to change policies within organisations regarding equal opportunities are denied access to decision-making processes. For instance, Modood *et al.* (1997: 104–5) conclude from their survey that:

> both men and women in nearly all the minority groups shared one fundamental difference from white men and women. They were much less likely to be in the top occupational category [managers and employers] and when they were, they were much less likely to work in large establishments. The explanations for this are likely to be complex. There may be some direct discrimination, but part of the explanation could lie in the continued importance of social-educational networks.

A prime example of this comes from a hospital in the UK which was taken to an industrial tribunal. It was found to have a macho culture that tolerated and encouraged racist and sexist language among the senior medical staff and managers. The strong social networks meant that women and ethnic minorities were excluded from important groups and decisions, most notably the payment of merit awards (financial bonuses) (*The Guardian*, 2000, 4 December).

Instances such as this illustrate the important point that many of those who control policy – predominantly white, able-bodied, men – have little incentive to change a system (albeit unfair) from which they benefit. Moreover, it suggests that there is a role for outside intervention to coax reluctant organisations into action. The type of intervention depends upon the particular perspective taken on equal opportunities – which shall be explored in the next section.

EXERCISE 10.3

What do *you* think?

1 'The concept of "institutional racism" rather than individual racism absolves those within the organisation of any responsibility for the unfair discrimination'.

   (a) What is meant by this statement? ▶

▶

    (b)   Do you agree or disagree with it? Explain your viewpoint.

2 Is it legitimate to describe an institution as racist? (Think about whether the institution can take action or whether it is the people within the institution)

3 What action would you recommend to tackle the problems of the Youth Prison in Excerpt 10.3?

TO SUM UP

Ethnic minorities suffer disadvantage in access to work and within the workplace. The former can occur through procedures that deny impartial treatment in training opportunities or the processes of recruitment and selection. The latter typically manifests itself in blatant harassment or more subtle forms of institutional racism.

Three perspectives on equal opportunities

Learning outcome 4

Critically evaluate three different perspectives on equal opportunities.

Devising policy to ensure equal opportunities is rife with controversy, due to the inevitable way it is entwined with political and moral beliefs. The notion of what constitutes fairness, and how policy can be constructed to enhance this, will differ from person to person. It is possible, however, to identify three broad perspectives on equality. The first two perspectives, *liberal* and *radical*, are based on concepts developed by Jewson and Mason (1986); the third perspective, *reactionary*, is an attempt to complete the spectrum by briefly assessing the view that rejects interference by policy-makers. Each perspective is examined in turn. Further critical analysis can be found in Cockburn (1989 and 1991), Miller (1996) and Richards (2001).

The liberal perspective

From this perspective, 'equal opportunity exists when all individuals are enabled freely and equally to compete for social rewards' (Jewson and Mason, 1986: 313). The role of policy-makers is therefore to ensure that the rules are fair. 'It is not their job to determine who are the winners and losers, but to ensure only that the social mechanisms by which winners and losers select themselves are based on principles of fairness and justice' (*ibid.*). Policy is therefore concerned with devising *fair procedures*, so that justice is seen to be done.

In the UK, this liberal perspective has informed legislation which requires employers to act according to certain guidelines, a breach of which might make them liable to prosecution for unfair practice (see Dickens, 2000, for a useful summary of the legislative provision). While this legal framework sets some boundaries, it would be misleading to suggest that it clearly establishes fair rules. As with any legalistic solution, interpretation of the rules becomes a problem – not least because it may depend on defining the type of discrimination occurring (see Excerpt 10.4).

Direct and indirect discrimination

The legislation in the UK identifies two types of discrimination.

Direct discrimination occurs when the treatment of, or attitude towards, a person is less favourable because of their sex, race, or disability. For example, if the advert at the beginning of this chapter had asked for a salesman or implied that only male applicants would be considered, then the company would have been in breach of the Sex Discrimination Act 1975 because it directly discriminates against women. Direct discrimination is therefore relatively easy to detect, and so relatively easy for employers to avoid, providing they are well-informed about their legal requirements.

Indirect discrimination occurs when a requirement or condition is applied equally but has the consequence of disadvantaging a particular group (sex or race, but not disability). This means that there does not necessarily have to be an *intention* to discriminate – it is not the action itself, but the *effect* of the action that matters. The example of British Rail's personality tests cited earlier illustrates the problem. However, in practice the law tends to favour the employer because, as Jenkins (1986: 250) argues, 'for particular policies or conditions to be indirectly discriminatory, it is necessary that they cannot be shown to be justifiable'. Consequently, selection criteria such as labour market history or relevant experience, or practices such as word-of-mouth recruitment, may fall outside the definition, in spite of the fact that they are likely to disadvantage ethnic minorities. Furthermore, Jenkins suggests that white managers, in a white-dominated business, may make ethnocentric judgements about who will 'fit in', which may be legally justifiable in terms of the 'business necessity' to employ manageable workers (*ibid*: 78).

As well as setting the legalistic framework, the liberal perspective on equal opportunities has made it permissible in the UK for organisations to embark upon *positive action* programmes. These are initiatives designed to counteract the effects of past discrimination and seek to redress the gender and ethnic profile of the workforce. This is frequently confused with positive discrimination (preferential treatment for disadvantaged groups, discussed below), but it is vital to recognise the difference: in the UK, positive action is lawful whereas positive discrimination is not. The most typical examples of positive action initiatives are the provision of company crèches, advertising campaigns aimed at specific groups, career-break schemes, and awareness training for managers.

An important feature, critical to the success of positive action initiatives, is *equal opportunity monitoring*. Essentially, monitoring is a process of data collection and analysis (particularly with regard to the composition of the workforce, recruitment and promotion) which can be used as part of the policy formation process (for example, see *Industrial Relations Review and Report*, 1990; Jewson *et al.*, 1992). Although monitoring is voluntary at present, groups like the UK's Commission for Racial Equality are increasingly convinced that the way forward is to make monitoring compulsory. Those commentators who remain sceptical about monitoring tend to argue that it is costly, highly bureaucratic and unworkable. Webb and Liff (1988: 550) suggest that 'Merely processing the numbers of applications generated by the use of such procedures in the current climate is likely to be beyond the resources of many employers. The result is that the policy is circumvented and derided.' More cynically, it can be argued that monitoring can become 'a smoke-screen behind which discrimination continues to flourish' (Jenkins, 1987: 118).

Criticism of the liberal approach

In a critique of the liberal approach to equal opportunities, Webb and Liff (1988) argue that it is not enough to view unfair discrimination as an essentially technical problem that can be rectified through fair procedures. They suggest that because inequality is deeply embedded, it is insufficient to see the solution lying with simply rectifying unfair discrimination in recruitment, selection, training and promotion:

> Women fail not because they are less able to carry out the tasks; they are excluded because of the way that necessary qualifications are defined. The competition is structured against women because the job is perceived as requiring skills, experiences and working patterns far more likely to be found amongst men, or indeed seen as inherently male. (Webb and Liff, 1988: 549)

This resonates with the discussion in Chapter 5 concerning how notions of skill are often constructed to the disadvantage of women. Managers in organisations need to reassess job requirements which may have been historically developed and bear little relation to current needs. This, argue Webb and Liff, would include the structuring and grading of jobs and the terms on which they are offered. 'What should be asked of employers is not that they accept less qualified, less able women in preference to men but that they rethink what the job requires in ways that do not rule out competent women' (Webb and Liff, 1988: 549). Therefore, this 'job audit' approach goes much further than the typical positive action programmes of the liberal perspective, yet as we shall see, rejects the solution proposed by the radical approach.

The radical perspective

The dilemma for more radically-minded policy-makers in addressing equal opportunities was eloquently summed up by US President Lyndon Johnson in 1965, with the following analogy:

> Imagine a hundred yard dash in which one of the two runners has his legs shackled together. He has progressed 10 yards, while the unshackled runner has gone 50 yards. At that point the judges decide that the race is unfair. How do they rectify the situation? Do they merely remove the shackles and allow the race to proceed? Then they could say that 'equal opportunity' now prevailed. But one of the runners would still be forty yards ahead of the other. Would it not be the better part of justice to allow the previously shackled runner to make up the forty yard gap; or to start the race all over again? (Quoted in Bell, 1973: 429)

As has been noted, the liberal perspective would suggest that it is enough to remove the shackles, and ensure that henceforth there is no unfair advantage. However, as President Johnson pointed out, this does not rectify the existing situation of inequality. In other words, policy should address any extant structural disadvantage as well as ensure greater equality of opportunity in the future. This represents a more radical approach because it suggests that policy-makers should be concerned with the *outcome*, rather than the *process*, and should therefore be seeking to ensure a *fair distribution of rewards*. Consequently, there is a requirement to intervene directly through policies of *positive discrimination* (known as affirmative action in the US). A common example of this is setting quotas for disadvantaged groups, which organisations must achieve or face legal penalties. For example, there could be a requirement for an organisation to have 30 per cent of its workforce from a particular ethnic minority group in line with the ethnic profile of the local community from which it recruits its employees. This means that the recruiters can discriminate in favour of someone *because* they are from an ethnic minority.

Criticism of the radical approach

Obviously the policy of positive discrimination is not without its critics. First, there are those who argue that it merely shifts the unfairness from one group to another. In particular, it means that white, able-bodied, heterosexual men may find themselves victims of discrimination. This has led to a backlash in the US, with right-wing politicians seeking to revoke the affirmative action legislation.

A second group of critics of affirmative action are members of disadvantaged groups themselves who condemn the policy because it devalues their achievements by raising the suspicion that they did not really deserve the job, promotion or whatever. For example, even if positive discrimination played no part in the selection process, and the female candidate genuinely was the best qualified for the job, she will always be faced with those who begrudgingly mutter, 'She only got the job because she's a woman and it helps achieve the quota'. Moreover, in the UK, positive discrimination is unlawful, and policy suggestions towards it have been condemned by the Chartered Institute of Personnel and Development, who label it 'reverse discrimination'.

The reactionary perspective

This third perspective is concerned less with equality than inequality. It emanates from notions of biological essentialism, and postulates the natural inequality of people due to genetic differences. Proponents of this view tend to argue that 'natural selection' will prevail, and such phrases as 'the law of the jungle' and 'the survival of the fittest' are evoked as explanations as to why policy-makers should *not* intervene. This perspective, in practice, covers a broad range of opinion, from the backlash 'victims' noted above, to the most abhorrent racists, and is therefore a melting pot of stereotypical views, prejudice and arbitrary judgements. A contemporary expression of this perspective is embraced by the 'New Right', the generic term for an ideology that reflects a 'curious and unstable combination of the market mechanism, moral authoritarianism and the racially based theory of national identity' (Parekh, 1986, quoted in Allen and Macey, 1990: 385). In the United States, this has found expression most vividly among the fundamentalist, cable TV preachers, but as Allen and Macey (1990: 385–7) note, the ideology has achieved a ready outlet in the press and among some academics within Europe, especially in Britain, France and Germany.

This perspective need not detain us further, but it is perhaps the one that most vividly highlights the moral and political dimension of equal opportunities. The question of whether and how to rectify unfair discrimination is one that impassions people. Understanding a person's perspective on equality is, therefore, an important stage in predicting their opinions on the fairness of policies. Almost everyone has an opinion; most are willing to state it. Exercise 10.4 is designed to encourage you to think about different opinions and reflect on your own viewpoint.

EXERCISE 10.4

What do *you* think?

1 Which of the three perspectives is most closely aligned with your views on equal opportunities?

2 What are the strengths of your perspective?

3 What are the weaknesses?

Role play exercise

You could role play a debate between proponents of the radical and liberal perspectives. This can be done as two teams, with a chairperson to keep order. In preparation, each team should make notes of their arguments and counter-arguments, and attempt to be both logical and consistent in presenting their case.

▶

▶

Toss a coin to decide who starts the debate. The winner presents their case first, speaking for no more than five minutes. This is followed by a five minute presentation of the case from the other side. The debate then opens up with questions and responses. Set a time limit for the debate.

Debrief afterwards, highlighting the strong and weak arguments. If numbers allow it, there could be a panel of observers who provide feedback on the quality, logic and consistency of the arguments.

Remember, when role playing you need to adopt a given viewpoint for the purpose of the exercise – even though you may not hold this view yourself.

TO SUM UP

The liberal and radical perspectives emphasise the importance of intervention in order to achieve equality of opportunity, but differ on the type of intervention necessary. The former tends to have a process focus, while the latter is focused on outcomes. The reactionary perspective considers too much intervention has already taken place and believes market forces should prevail. Understanding a person's perspective goes some way to revealing their likely approach to the issue of discrimination. But this can be taken a step further by exploring how discrimination decisions are enacted and evaluated within organisations.

Learning outcome 5

Explain how perceptions of fairness depend on assumptions made about the principles of sameness and difference.

Theorising discrimination

Fairness is, as discussed at the start of this chapter, a subjective concept. At its root are moral assumptions about how people ought to be treated so that equal opportunity prevails. Two key questions present themselves:

■ To ensure equality of opportunity, should people be treated the same, or should they be treated differently?
■ On which criteria should they be treated the same or differently?

The answers are not straightforward. A person can be the victim of unfair discrimination through receiving the same treatment or different treatment, depending on the circumstances. To illustrate this point, consider the criteria of age and sex in the job advertisement at the start of this chapter.

■ Applicants are treated *differently* according to age. In other words, age is used to discriminate between people, so applicants older than 35 could be rejected, even if they satisfied the other criteria, such as previous work experience.
■ Applicants are treated the *same* regardless of sex. In other words, sex is not used as a criterion to discriminate, so (theoretically) applicants will be treated the same regardless of their sex.

The problem is as follows: by ignoring gender differences, women applicants that have taken time out from work to have children are likely to have accumulated less previous work experience than men of an equivalent age. Indeed, it could transpire that many potential women applicants who meet the (legitimate) previous work experience criteria are older than 35, and therefore fall outside the age band required. Thus, by treating applicants *differently* with regard to age, and the *same* with regard to sex, the advert may well be unfairly discriminating against potential women applicants who satisfy all the other criteria.

This issue of recognising how unfair discrimination can emerge from the concepts of 'sameness' and 'difference' is addressed by Liff and Wajcman (1996) in an analysis of equal opportunity policy and gender. They reach the conclusion that attention must be paid to both because they reflect different forms of disadvantage:

> Sometimes women are disadvantaged by being treated differently when in fact they are the same (e.g. denied a job for which they are perfectly well qualified) and at other times by being treated the same when their difference needs to be taken into account (e.g. having their absence to look after a sick child treated the same way as a man who is absent with a hangover). (Liff and Wajcman, 1996: 86)

Recognising the way that the dominant group (in this case, male employers) selectively use the concepts of sameness and difference to construct disadvantage against women, Liff and Wajcman (following Bacchi, 1990, and Cockburn, 1991) suggest that the arguments can be turned back on the dominant group using a similar logic of selectivity, but with the purpose of eliminating disadvantage for women:

> [Equal treatment] is entirely appropriate for tackling some types of discrimination and can be expected to have brought benefits. Here the best way forward is for women to be treated the same as men, for example by ensuring that selection and appraisal methods are free from bias. In other cases, where women have been excluded from certain types of experience or qualification, or where they have specific demands placed on them from the home which impinge on their work, this difference should be acknowledged. Appropriate equality initiatives [special treatment] in this context would include targeted training courses, childcare or the opportunity for men and women to work different hours. (Liff and Wajcman, 1996: 86)

To summarise the problem: unfair discrimination can occur by ignoring differences and giving people equal treatment, *or* by identifying differences and giving (some) people special treatment. As a further illustration, Excerpt 10.5 highlights the differential impact of children on the careers of men and women, by contrasting two viewpoints. Read it and then attempt Exercise 10.5.

EXCERPT 10.5

Do women lose out at work because of maternity leave?

YES

'It is a quarter of a century since the Equal Pay Act, but women still earn only 80 pence for every pound pocketed by men. There have been scores of initiatives to help women break through the corporate glass ceiling, but just 3% of directors are female [. . .]

It is not because women are less educated or skilled, or because employers think women aren't up to the job, or because women are uninterested in jobs or money. Twentysomething female graduates earn as much as their male counterparts. Women continue to lose at work because they have children, and so their career paths are broken. Men have children and continue working as if nothing had happened. We either accept the resulting gap in pay and promotion, as conservatives do, or level the playing field. My view is that we have to give men the same rights to paid time off for childcare as women (44 weeks, with the first six paid at 90% wages).

Only when men bear equal responsibility for parenting will women have a shot at equality. Not before.'

(Richard Reeves, The Industrial Society)

NO

'Richard Reeves' statement that women continue to lose at work because they have career breaks, while true, implies that all women define their success in life mainly in terms of careers and not in terms of motherhood. For many women this is not true. Many of my friends were only too pleased to give up work and look after their children.

'They feel insulted when this is seen as less important or prestigious than having a job, which can be tedious, unrewarding and unglamorous. They regard bringing up their children as the finest thing they have ever done.

'Men are different from women and women are on the whole psychologically and biologically better equipped to be the principal child nurturers. A recent report by a Lancaster University psychology professor concluded that most fathers saw their parental role as protector and breadwinner and preferred to leave nurturing to their womenfolk. This may be a non-PC view. But men should be given an opportunity to behave as they feel in this matter without being criticised. If men took as much leave as women over the birth of a baby, the disruption to many firms (especially small ones) would be horrendous and increase the resentment by the childless towards those, especially women, with children.'

(Ruth Lea, Head of the Policy Unit, Institute of Directors)

Source: Extracts from *The Guardian*, 'Do women lose out at work because of maternity leave?'
8 August, 2000

What do *you* think?

Read Excerpt 10.5 about the effects of maternity leave.

1 Which one of the two commentators is arguing for

   (a) 'same treatment'? Explain their reasoning.

   (b) 'different treatment'? Explain their reasoning.

2 Whose view do you most agree with? Explain why you find it convincing.

3 Continue the discussion by:

   (a) writing a short response on behalf of Reeves to the comments made by Lea;

   (b) writing Lea's possible counter-response.

Mapping the process

As can be seen, the issue of discrimination becomes more complex when it is applied to work organisations. Conceptually it is confusing because similar and different treatment can both ensure and deny fairness. To help clarify this, it is possible to map the theoretical process behind discrimination decisions within organisations. Thus the flowchart in Figure 10.1 shows the relationships between the concepts discussed in this section so far. The critical group are the decision-makers (typically managers at all levels) who have the power to exercise choices in line with their own beliefs and their own political agenda, although within constraints set by external pressures (for example, legislation, public opinion and labour supply) and internal pressures (for example, other managers, employees, trade unions, and key individuals such as the manager's own boss). This is very similar to the strategic choice thesis suggested by Child (1972, 1997) which emphasised the political and ideological aspects of decision-making by managers. Figure 10.1 is only concerned with the range of management decisions that directly affect other people (usually subordinates): for example, deciding whom to appoint; whom to allocate to a particular shopfloor task or team; whom to promote; whether to give someone a pay rise; who needs training; whom to make redundant; and so on. In decisions such as these, important choices are made in two respects:

■ a choice about the criteria on which to discriminate between people (age, race, qualifications, experience, performance, gender, personality, physical appearance, or whatever):

■ a choice about how to apply each selected criterion, that is, whether to adopt a policy of sameness (equal treatment) or difference (special treatment).

As the earlier discussion highlighted, managers tend to identify a particular criterion and decide whether there should be equal treatment or special treatment; in other words, whether their policy is to be based on the principle of sameness or

Learning outcome 6

Map the process of discrimination and explain why consensus about fairness differs between individuals and social groups.

difference for that particular criterion. To illustrate: in promoting someone, senior managers might decide that work experience with the firm is important whereas educational qualifications are not. In this case employees who have given many years of service to the firm will be looked on more favourably than newcomers (a policy based on difference leading to special treatment with regard to work experience). Conversely, employees with a university degree will not be looked upon more favourably than those without a degree (a policy based on sameness leading to equal treatment with regard to educational qualification). It can be seen, therefore, that a policy based on sameness or difference can be applied to any criterion, and the decision-makers are the key actors in both identifying the criteria and relating a policy of sameness or difference to them.

These choices made over criteria and policy are judged by other members of the organisation: people will be assessing whether the discrimination is fair or unfair. If a person feels there were justifiable criteria with an appropriate policy, then the perception is likely to be of fairness. Alternatively, if it is felt that there were unjustifiable criteria or that a justifiable criterion had been distorted through an inappropriate policy, then the perception of unfairness is likely to prevail. Such interpretations can be made by individuals or may be negotiated by groups (for example, work teams, trade unions, professionals, informal social cliques). Thus, for any policy or action associated with any criterion of discrimination there is likely to be a plurality of responses: some individuals and groups will interpret it as fair and others as unfair. As a result, competing interpretations can occur. The extent to which people concern themselves with issues of fairness will vary according to the circumstances and is likely to reflect whether they are directly involved with, or affected by, the outcome. Similarly, the diagram cannot reflect the power or the will of individuals and groups to take action. However, when unfairness is perceived, this might lead to greater internal and/or external pressure in an attempt to influence future decisions (shown by the feedback loop in Figure 10.1).

This flowchart of the process of discrimination indicates the relationships between various concepts that have been explored in this chapter so far. It is descriptive in that it attempts to encapsulate the importance of structural constraints, agency (through the choices of decision-makers) and subjectivity (especially through interpretation of discrimination). It is not normative, and cannot be used as a diagnostic tool because it does not show *how* choice or action can affect the direction of interpretation (that is, whether a policy is fair or unfair). Indeed, the subjectivity of the process militates against theorising in such a way. This is an important point because it suggests that policy initiatives aimed at eliminating interpretations of unfair discrimination will need to address the structural, moral and political issues embedded in the process of discrimination.

Emerging from this analysis is a clear message with a fuzzy response. The message is that where discrimination is perceived as unfair, discontent is bound to occur. But the response is that the perception of unfairness depends on several factors, most notably: the perspective of the individuals concerned, the perceived appropriateness of the criterion of discrimination, and the individual and social acceptability of the type of treatment (special or equal).

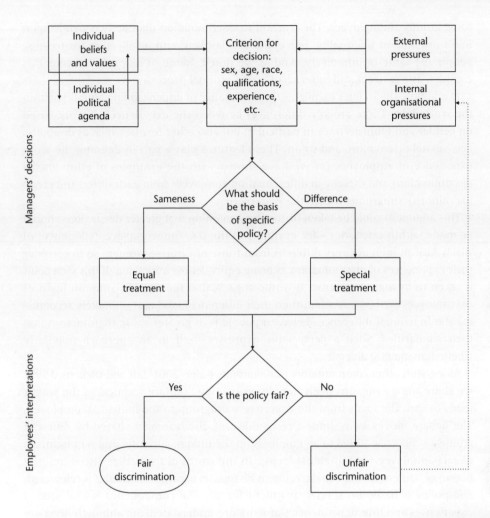

Figure 10.1 The process of discrimination in an organisation

TO SUM UP

On the one hand, fairness may be said to prevail when people are treated in a similar way (equal treatment), but in some circumstances equal treatment undermines fairness. On the other hand, treating some people differently (special treatment) in certain circumstances might ensure fairness, but can lead to perceptions of unfairness or privilege. The interpretation of fairness depends on whether the criterion is considered justifiable by individuals and social groups within the organisation.

Conclusion

This chapter has explored the nature and form of discrimination. It has sought to explain how the concept of discrimination differentiates between people and leads to varied experiences within the workplace – most notably the disadvantage of some groups of employees. The reaction to discrimination ultimately depends upon one's orientation to equality, perceptions of fairness, and justification for treating people the same or differently. And as we noted, 'same or different treatment' is complex as a concept and in terms of organisational processes.

In addition, the chapter highlights the importance of understanding plurality within the workplace. There are key differences between the experiences of work based on gender and ethnicity/race in particular, but also other features such as disability, age, sexual orientation, and so on. These features play a part in defining the work experience of employees (as we have shown with the examples of ethnic/racial discrimination) and thereby in differentiating employees from each other, and creating minority subgroups within the workplace.

This argument could be taken further by suggesting that greater distinctions should be made within categories – for example, in the UK, the workplace experiences of Black African men are very different from those of Chinese women, so to consider their experiences of discrimination as being equivalent is misguided. If this viewpoint is taken to its logical extreme, it would suggest that the shared, common features of employees are less important than their differences, and that ultimately recognising the individual differences between people is of greater value than focusing on their similarities. Such a perspective expresses itself in an approach popularly labelled 'managing diversity'.

Along with other commentators (for example, Kaler, 2001; Liff and Dickens, 1999) we share some sympathy with the 'diversity' view, but are sceptical of the way it tends to shift the focus from the collective workgroup to the individual employee. The debate moves away from a recognition of disadvantages shared by different groups (a collective focus) to an emphasis on the unique attributes and requirements of each employee (an individual focus). In the words of the earlier discussion: the notion of 'sameness' and equal treatment disappears because 'difference' is celebrated, and policy is based on special treatment for all. The consequence is that shared experiences and interdependencies at work are understated. So, although diversity and plurality are closely-linked concepts, plurality encourages a focus both on differences between people, and commonalities that cluster people into groups with shared experiences and common goals.

Representation 11
at work

KEY CONCEPTS

- Collective representation
- Employee interests
- Asymmetry of power
- Frontier of control
- Contested terrain
- Trade unions

- Union membership
- Dual allegiance
- Instrumentality
- Solidarity
- Union strategies

CHAPTER AIM

To explore the nature of workers' collective representation and assess its significance for the employees involved.

LEARNING OUTCOMES

After reading and thinking about the material contained in this chapter, you will be able to:

1 understand the logic behind employees seeking representation by a collective body;

2 identify the main factors accounting for union membership patterns, and how these operate at societal, organisational, workplace and individual levels;

3 recognise the primary influence of instrumentality in employees' decision to become a union member;

4 identify the different priorities that union members have in relation to their representative organisation;

5 assess the question of whether union members are able to hold dual commitment to work organisation and union;

6 evaluate the extent to which members think that trade unions are effective on behalf of their members.

Introduction

Up to now we have considered the realities of work for employees either as individuals or as members of work groups. But, in addition to being members of work teams, sections, departments and establishments in large or small organisations, workers combine into other collectives as part of their everyday work experience. The most common form that this collectivism takes is membership of a trade union. Other collectives include professional associations, staff associations and various work-based clubs and societies. Attention in this chapter, however, is particularly focused on trade union membership, primarily reflecting not only the greater prominence of these organisations in industrial society, compared to other employee collective organisations, but also (reflecting this prominence) the more detailed enquiry that has been undertaken on aspects of trade union membership. The purpose of this chapter is to examine the nature of this membership more closely to see how it casts further light on the different ways in which employees experience their working lives.

To accomplish this, we begin by briefly examining the rationale for trade unions, and in particular the reasoning underpinning workpeople's decisions to become and/or remain a union member – and indeed their reasons for terminating their union membership. Following this, the various factors influencing employees' decision to join a union are considered: the main factors which encourage or inhibit union membership and which help to explain the actual patterns of union membership. What becomes evident from this discussion is the way in which several different levels of explanation can be identified – that patterns of union membership can be understood by reference to factors operating at the individual, workgroup, organisation and societal levels.

Once we have identified the main variables influencing the employee's decision to join a trade union, we turn briefly to the related question of what priorities union members have in relation to their representative body and how (and why) these priorities can change over time. An associated question here that we also explore is whether workers think that trade unions deliver on these priority areas and whether overall they effectively represent their members' interests at work. It is arguable, for example, that a perceived failure by trade unions to deliver on member priorities in recent times is one explanation for the marked decline in union membership and union influence that has been evident in many (though not all) industrial countries since the early 1980s.

In addition to issues relating to member views on their trade union, another question that has periodically been raised in studies of union membership is whether or not commitment to a union can co-exist with, or acts to diminish, commitment to the work organisation. The evidence on this question is mixed and we review the different arguments and findings.

Following examination of these issues surrounding current patterns of membership and representation, we then turn to consider the question of the future of employee representation: what the future may hold for individuals and their representative organisations, what trade unions are currently doing to try to shape a future that includes a more secure and influential union presence, and to what extent this mirrors employee views on representation. In the concluding section we reflect on what this analysis of representation contributes to our overall assessment of the realities of work – and in particular how it further underlines the inadequacy of the portrayal of a single reality of work.

Joining a collective

Learning outcome 1

Understand the logic behind employees seeking representation by a collective body.

Why should an employee consider joining a collective organisation? The answer to this in part depends on the nature of that collective group:

- Individual employees may join and remain members of a *professional association*, for example, because it is only through membership that they retain their professional registration. All practising clinical psychologists in Britain for example must be members of the British Psychological Association.
- Employees may become members of a *staff association* automatically if their employing organisation supports such an association. Thus, when an individual is recruited by an organisation, he or she also becomes a member of the staff association. The staff association may represent employee opinion on joint committees with management, as well as organising social and other events for employees.
- Joining a *trade union* – our main focus in this chapter – more explicitly reflects a decision to become part of a body that provides collective and independent representation of employee interests.

The decision to seek collective representation by joining a trade union may be seen to reflect three key features about a worker's identification of their interests at work.

1 *A recognition that the interests of employer and employees are not identical.* If the interests of the two were seen by the employee to be wholly synonymous, there would be no basis or need for separate representation to that offered by the employing organisation. Employees would rest comfortably in the knowledge that because their interests were commonly shared with the employer, the latter would always and inevitably act in the interests of the employee – there could be no possibility of any alternative.

In practice, however, while employer and employee can be seen to share various interests in common (such as, in most circumstances, the survival of the organisation) they also hold a number of distinct interests. This separation of interests can be identified, for example, in relation to the distribution of rewards, with management and workforce likely to hold differing views on the way that any surplus (profit) should be distributed among shareholders, managers and non-managerial grades. A similar separation of interests may be identified in relation to the expenditure of effort or total adherence to the designated work time periods. It is clear that from an employer's point of view, their interest lies in employees expending effort consistently over the whole of the working period, and defining that working period as the entire time that the individual is contracted to work. As we discussed in Chapters 4 and 9, however, employees may pursue a separate interest by covertly creating spells of reduced effort or unofficial rest periods, in order to survive more comfortably a monotonous or arduous work regime – or even in some cases to protect the very job itself, where greater effort might lead to the work being divided between fewer staff. Thus, part of the rationale for joining a trade union springs from a desire among employees to challenge the management rationality and give expression to aspects of a workers' counter-rationality.

In aspects such as work pace, work allocation and the way in which work tasks are performed, we can refer to the notion of a 'frontier of control' between management and employee rationalities. Like other frontiers or borders throughout history, this frontier in the workplace is periodically subject to challenge by management or union, in which ground is gained and conceded, and where the two parties use power, strategy and tactics to seek territorial advantage. The fact that this frontier exists, and that it represents what Edwards (1979) terms a 'contested terrain' between management and workforce in the ways we have discussed in many of the foregoing chapters, symbolises both the existence and salience of distinct interests in the workplace.

EXCERPT 11.1

Shared interests?

In a recent study of workers in four sites manufacturing tinplate, two in the UK (at Ebbw Vale and Trostre, both in South Wales), one in the Netherlands (at Ijmuiden west of Amsterdam) and a smaller plant in Norway (in Bergen on the Norwegian west coast), a representative sample of employees (a 20 per cent sample at each plant) were asked whether they agreed or disagreed with the statement that managers and workers in their organisation shared the same interests. As the table below shows, in each case only a minority of workers thought that the interests of the two groups were shared. Less than one in four of the Dutch sample thought so, compared to just over a third of the Welsh respondents and two in five of the Norwegian employees.

Identification of shared interests with management

	UK	Netherlands	Norway
	n = 154	n = 150	n = 38
Respondents who agreed that...	36%	24%	42%
'Management have the same interests as workers in the business'			

Source: P. Blyton and N. Bacon, Unpublished report of findings of Corus Packaging Plus Values Survey, 2001

What do *you* think?

1 Place the issues listed below on the following continuum of whether you think managers and workers share a common interest over the issue, or hold partially or wholly separate interests. Assign one of the numbers from the continuum to each of the issues.

1	2	3	4	5
Share identical interests				Have completely separate interests

- Health and safety standards
- Basic pay
- Introducing new technology
- Levels of overtime working
- Bonus payments
- Flexible working hours
- Equal opportunities
- Company share price
- Developing new products/services

2 Briefly explain the basis for your positioning of each issue on the continuum.

2 *Joining a trade union signals a recognition of an asymmetry of power between employer and employee.* This lack of symmetry is sufficient to make it worthwhile in the eyes of the employee to seek additional power through combining with other employees. If the employee saw her or his interests as distinct from those of the employer, but power to be approximately equally distributed between employer and employee, then the rationale for collective representation would be reduced, or at least altered:

- *reduced* because the employee may be more likely to view the possibility of effectively representing himself or herself in dealings with management;
- *altered* in so far as union membership would then be seen as a strategy of gaining dominant power over the employer (rather than an equality of power), thereby creating considerable advantage in determining the distribution of rewards.

However, in practice most appear to recognise that the opposite condition is normally the case, that an asymmetry of power exists in favour of the employer – and is expressed in the employer's ultimate power to hire and fire. Thus, for individual employees, the decision to combine with others in a trade union is an attempt to augment their minority power in dealings with the employer, over those areas where the interests of employer and employee do not coincide.

3 *Joining together in a trade union indicates a recognition by employees that they hold sufficient interests in common as to make membership of a common organisation both*

feasible and desirable. This is not to say that employees will view all interests as shared with the rest of the union membership, but that they judge their interests to overlap sufficiently to allow common membership and a joint pursuit of objectives. Membership thus involves a voluntary alliance of employees who recognise the benefits of having their interests represented collectively.

TO SUM UP

Becoming a member of a trade union is simultaneously a recognition of differing interests from those of the employer, a shared interest with other employees, and the identification of the trade union as an appropriate vehicle to pursue those shared interests.

Learning outcome 2

Identify the main factors accounting for union membership patterns, and how these operate at societal, organisational, workplace and individual levels.

Reasons for membership

Explaining the factors that influence whether or not employees become and remain trade union members has long been an area of interest for economists, industrial relations researchers, sociologists and social psychologists. Typically, economists have dealt more with more macro, economy-level factors, industrial relations researchers have considered particularly the organisational and workplace-level contexts, and sociologists and social psychologists the work group and individual-level reasons for joining (see Figure 11.1).

Societal-level factors

Our main concern in this chapter will lie with employees and their immediate work context, for it is these levels that are the most informative about the individual's own experience of work. Before considering these, however, it is useful to note broader, macro-level influences on union membership patterns. These point, for example, to the influence of business cycles, levels of unemployment and longer term economic 'waves' on levels of union membership (Bain and Elsheikh, 1976; Booth, 1983; Carruth and Disney, 1988; Kelly and Waddington, 1995). Also significant are the effects of government policies and laws favourable or unfavourable to trade unions (Freeman and Pelletier, 1990) and the role of broad shifts in industrial and occupational structures on union membership patterns (Green, 1992).

Much discussion has been focused on the last of these, and in particular on the impact of a decline in employment in those industries where trade unionism has traditionally been strong (coal, steel, shipbuilding and other parts of manufacturing, for example) and the rise of other industries, notably private sector service activities, where trade unionism has not been well established. This account of union membership decline has been referred to as the 'mountain gorilla hypothesis': that

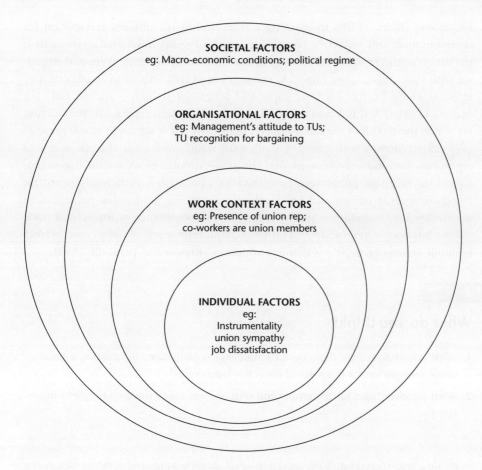

Figure 11.1 Levels of influence on trade union (TU) membership decisions

the reduction in the natural habitat of trade unions (traditional manufacturing industries) has led to a decline in the species (trade union members) in the same way that the natural habitat of the mountain gorilla has brought about a marked reduction in its population (Blyton and Turnbull, 1998: 113). At the same time, as various writers have pointed out, this argument about changes in industrial structure does more to *describe* what has happened to union membership than to *explain* it: there is no *inevitable* reason why union membership will automatically decline with the growth of service employment and the decline in manufacturing jobs (Kelly, 1990; Blyton and Turnbull, 1998: 113–4). What the industrial structure analysis does is to highlight the extent to which union membership has been concentrated in some quarters (manufacturing, public sector) far more than in others and that overall, trade unions have not yet managed to rectify this by large-scale expansion in the growing private sector service industries.

Organisation-level factors

Among industrial relations researchers, a key influence on union membership patterns is management's attitude to trade unionism, reflected particularly in their willingness to grant 'recognition' to a union for purposes of representation and bargaining (Bain, 1970). In granting a trade union (or unions) recognition for representation and collective bargaining, employing organisations agree to treat the union as the representative voice of specified groups of employees and negotiate with that union, for example over changes in overall terms and conditions (pay rates, working hours, overtime rates and length of holidays, and so on). For Metcalf (1991: 19) this union recognition by management represents 'the fulcrum on which the health of the labour movement turns' for it signals to employees not only management's willingness to work with trade unions but also the access to representation and involvement that the trade union enjoys within the organisation. In the past, public sector organisations have been particularly noted for recognising trade unions and for developing extensive joint union-management machinery for consultation and negotiation. This acceptance of the role of trade unions has been a key variable in bringing about high levels of union membership in public sector organisations in many countries (Blyton and Turnbull, 1998).

EXERCISE 11.2

What do *you* think?

1 What advantages may there be for employing organisations in granting a trade union recognition for purposes of collective bargaining?

2 What disadvantages for the employing organisation could there be in taking this step?

While these societal and organisation-level analyses are useful when discussing overall trends in union membership and union density (that is, the proportion of the potential membership that are actual union members) they are less useful in explaining the decisions of individual employees to join or not join, to remain in or to leave a trade union. For those concerned with these aspects of behaviour, their analysis is concentrated on the immediate work context in which people are situated and on individual attitudes towards trade unions.

Local work context factors

Within the immediate work context, the two key variables that appear to be particularly influential on union-joining decisions are first, whether there is a trade union representative present and second, whether or not other work colleagues are union members. The finding on the first of these is that one of the main reasons why employees do not join unions is that they have not been asked to join. If asked, many join. Thus, contact by a trade union representative appears crucial to many employees' decision to join. The Workplace Employee Relations Survey (WERS) 1998 data (Cully, Woodland, O'Reilly and Dix, 2000: 204) for example, show that in those workplaces where union representatives were both present and devoted more time to union activities (and thus were presumably more visible in their union role) they were more likely to have recruited new members than representatives who spent less time performing their union duties. Waddington and Whitston (1997: 529) in a wide-ranging membership survey of twelve UK unions, similarly identify the important role of local union representatives in recruitment. Likewise, Peetz (1998: 36) cites a number of Australian and other studies where lack of contact by the union was found to be a factor in low union recruitment.

In relation to the second work context factor – whether or not work colleagues are union members – British Social Attitudes Survey data discussed by Millward (1990) show that the reason of 'most of my colleagues are members' was expressed by over half of the sample as an important factor in joining a union. In practice, this relationship between work colleagues' membership and the employee's own decision to join may have two aspects to it:

1 Employees in unionised environments may feel uncomfortable being 'free riders' – that is people who enjoy many of the benefits of trade unionism such as negotiated pay increases without actually joining the union. In these circumstances, the non-members may feel under some pressure to join the union themselves. Peetz (1998: 34) in his analysis of factors accounting for why people join unions in Australia for example, notes 'peer pressure' acting in some settings as an influence on why people join.

2 Individuals may wish to become a union member like the others as a way of expressing solidarity and a common interest with their fellow workers.

Individual factors

In terms of individual factors, most attention has been given to explaining why people join unions rather than why they remain members or terminate their membership – though somewhat paradoxically rather than look explicitly at joining behaviour, many of the studies in this area have studied people already belonging to trade unions and attempt to establish what factors led them to join. Following Klandermans (1986), Guest and Dewe (1988) and others, we can divide the most common sets of individual reasons for joining into three categories. We will outline these and then consider the evidence for the relative importance of each.

1 *Job dissatisfaction reasons.* Various studies have identified a relationship between job dissatisfaction and union membership (see for example, the discussion in Wheeler and McClendon, 1991). Overall, most emphasis has tended to be placed on dissatisfaction with pay and benefits as associated with a decision to join a union (Wheeler and McClendon, 1991: 61). In addition, however, some studies have pointed to a broader range of areas of dissatisfaction which may be associated with union membership; for example, Guest and Dewe (1988) found an association between membership and dissatisfaction with opportunities for involvement in decision-making.

2 *Instrumental reasons.* These involve calculations by individual employees that the benefits of union membership will outweigh any costs associated with that

membership. Benefits centre on aspects such as improved job protection as a result of union membership; negotiated improvements in pay and conditions; access to union representation and advice if disciplinary cases or threat of redundancy arise; and the benefit of access to other union services which may range from financial advice to discounts on a variety of goods and services. Thus, the anticipated benefits are of two kinds – actual benefits such as the access to union services, and potential or 'insurance' benefits such as that the union can be called upon, if needed, for advice or representation. These actual and potential benefits must be weighed against the costs of membership – most directly the costs of subscriptions, but also potentially other, indirect costs such as might be incurred where the employer is hostile or unsympathetic to trade union activity, or where the union is also campaigning on issues that the individual member does not favour.

3 *Solidaristic or union sympathy reasons.* These centre on the individual becoming a trade union member through 'a belief that joining a union is…a natural thing to do' (Guest and Dewe, 1988: 180). This positive orientation to trade unionism may be the result of aspects of socialisation, such as growing up in a household where union membership was valued and the norm, or a subsequent ideological orientation in favour of trade unions. This latter orientation may derive from the experience of work itself – for example, recognising the value of trade unions by witnessing their activities first hand within the workplace.

The significance of different individual factors

Learning outcome 3

Recognise the primary influence of instrumentality in employees' decision to become a union member.

Given these three different categories of individual reasons why employees might join a union, what does the evidence show to be the most important of these reasons? We have the benefit of data on this question from several countries and most of these data point to the primacy of instrumental reasons. Looking at the UK first, Millward (1990: 34) for example, reports British Social Attitudes Survey data which show that in a list of reasons given for joining a union, instrumental reasons – 'protection' and 'negotiating better pay and conditions' – held first and second positions. These were followed by union sympathy reasons, such as belief in unions in principle and support for colleagues. Similarly, a plant-based study in the UK which explicitly examined the relative importance of the three categories (job dissatisfaction, instrumentality and belief in unions) also found that instrumental reasons were the most influential in employees' decision to belong to a union (Guest and Dewe, 1988). Job dissatisfaction was identified as a secondary influence, while solidarity with unionism accounted for only a very small element in employees' decision. Further, in their study of new members in twelve UK trade unions, Waddington and Whitston (1997: 521) found instrumental reasons for joining to be the most prominent, much ahead of union sympathy reasons. Of the minority who did identify union sympathy reasons, these were more likely to be older rather than younger workers and full-time rather than part-time workers (*ibid*: 527–8).

This general pattern of findings is mirrored in Australian survey data reported by Peetz (1998: 32–5) which similarly identify instrumental reasons (in the form of protection, and advice offered by unions) as the most commonly-stated reasons for belonging to a union. Ideological reasons on the other hand, were expressed by only a small proportion (less than one in ten) of the Australian sample (job dissatisfaction reasons were not measured in the survey). A further significant reason for belonging to a union in Australia was given as union membership being compulsory at the employee's workplace (Peetz, 1998: 32). Formerly, this was also a factor significant in a proportion of UK organisations until a series of legislative changes, and in particular the 1990 Employment Act, removed any compulsory, 'closed shop' element from union membership.

Reviewing studies undertaken both in the United States and elsewhere on this question of union membership decisions, Wheeler and McClendon (1991) also identify instrumentality as a key factor. This was particularly evident in studies outside the United States, while inside the US instrumentality appears to represent one of several influential variables (others including job dissatisfaction, belief in unions and nature of job). Summarising their review by quoting Adams (1974), the authors conclude that outside the US in particular, 'self interest is more in evidence than is solidarity' and if anything 'this tendency would appear to be on the rise' (Wheeler and McClendon, 1991: 73).

EXERCISE 11.3

What do *you* think?

1 The evidence from different countries indicates the dominance of instrumental reasons in union joining decisions. Why do you think this is?

2 Wheeler and McClendon (1991) quote Adams (1974) in saying that self-interest reasons for joining a trade union may be on the rise. Why do you think that this may be the case?

3 Why do you think only minorities of people appear to join trade unions for solidaristic reasons?

Just as we can gain insight into this topic by asking why people join a union, we can also achieve an impression of the importance of different reasons by asking employees why they have *not* joined a union. Here, both individual and workplace factors are again evident. In the Australian data discussed by Peetz (1998: 35–8) for example, the most frequent reason given for not joining a union was an instrumental one: specifically, a perceived lack of gain from becoming a member, due to the absence of union influence or effectiveness. Likewise, in the British Social Attitudes Survey data, while many of those asked were unable to identify any strong reason for not having joined a union, of those who could state a reason, the instrumental response of 'I can't see any advantage in joining' was the most prominent (cited by 28 per cent of non-members as a 'fairly important' or 'very important' reason for not having joined) (Millward, 1990).

TO SUM UP

Factors influencing union membership patterns can be identified at societal, organisational, workgroup and individual levels. For individuals, the decision to join appears particularly affected by whether their work colleagues are members, whether they have been asked to join by a union representative, and whether they recognise a net practical benefit from being a union member.

Learning outcome 4

Identify the different priorities that union members have in relation to their representative organisation.

What do employees want from their union membership?

If union members predominantly hold an instrumental orientation towards union membership, this raises the question of what instrumental priorities they have in relation to their representative organisation. A useful source of information on member priorities in the UK is again the British Social Attitudes Survey. Questions in this annual survey provide not only an indication of the main priorities, but also how these indicate a pattern of continuity and change over time. For example, in the later 1980s, trade union members were emphasising the primacy of economic concerns in their priorities for unions – in particular, improving pay and conditions and protecting jobs – with a secondary priority being given to areas such as equity issues and having more say in decision-making within the work organisation (Millward, 1990: 37). However, by the early and mid-1990s, the relative weight attached to these priorities had shifted somewhat due to changes in the economic context and increased threats of redundancy. Thus, by the later date, union members were placing much greater emphasis on the need for unions to protect jobs, as a result pushing other issues such as improving pay and conditions down the list of priorities (Bryson and McKay, 1997: 37; see also Chapter 2).

Further insight into the question of member priorities for unions can be obtained by considering their views on the type of issues that unions should be involved in, compared with those perceived as better left for employees themselves to deal with. In the WERS 1998 survey, for example, employees were asked about who they thought should deal with a series of different issues (Cully, Woodland, O'Reilly and Dix, 2000: 211). Members were most strongly in favour of their union being involved with pay issues, together with disciplinary issues. When it came to 'dealing with complaints about work' however, union members were equally split between viewing the union as the best means of pursuing the issue, or dealing with it themselves. Thus, whereas union members appeared to see pay and disciplinary questions as ones where collective representation was appropriate, many perceived work-related complaints as more of an individual issue.

What do *you* think?

1 If you have been a member of a trade union in the past (or are currently a member) what were the main things that you wanted from your union membership? List up to three in their order of priority.

2 Overall, how well did (does) your union satisfy these priorities? If the union has not fully satisfied your priorities, what do you think are the main reasons for this?

▌ Dual commitment to company and union?

Learning outcome 5

Assess the question of whether union members are able to hold dual commitment to work organisation and union.

One question that has periodically come to the fore in relation to union membership is whether or not union members are able to maintain a 'dual allegiance' to company and union – that is, whether they can be committed and loyal to both organisations simultaneously, or whether the two have a zero-sum relationship with commitment to one existing at the expense of commitment to the other. This question was the subject of a number of studies in the 1950s (for example Dean, 1954; Kerr, 1954; Purcell, 1954) when unionism was expanding in the United States. It was returned to in the UK in the late 1970s, a period of considerable increase in white-collar unionism (Blyton, Nicholson and Ursell, 1981; Nicholson, Ursell and Blyton, 1981). Subsequently, this question attracted further interest in North America in the 1980s (for example, Angle and Perry, 1986) and elsewhere in the 1990s (Deery, Iverson and Erwin, 1994; Guest and Dewe, 1991). In part, the more recent interest reflects the debate on whether trade unionism and the pursuit of human resource management are compatible (Guest, 1989).

The early studies indicated that dual allegiance was indeed possible, with workers clearly able to express commitment to both union and company. This was found to be particularly the case where industrial relations were pursued in an atmosphere of co-operation (Rosen, 1954). Similarly in the UK studies of white-collar workers, dual allegiance was also evident, with employees holding senior positions within local authorities appearing to experience little difficulty in simultaneously undertaking active union roles (Blyton, Nicholson and Ursell, 1981). Subsequently however, while studies in the United States have continued to show evidence of dual commitment (for example, Angle and Perry, 1986; Beauvais, Scholl and Cooper, 1990; Margenau, Martin and Peterson, 1988) later studies both in Australia and the UK have found somewhat different results. In a study of white-collar public service workers in Australia for example, Deery, Iverson and Erwin (1994) found no evidence of dual commitment. While they identified commitment to the work organisation as being associated with such factors as job satisfaction and feelings of autonomy, these factors were unrelated to union commitment. In Guest and Dewe's (1991) study of UK electronic engineering workers, a majority appeared to identify with *neither* company nor union – a finding which the authors explain partly in terms of employee dissatisfaction with both organisations.

Other evidence would seem to lend support to the Guest and Dewe finding, suggesting that earlier writers may have made too much of the issue of dual allegiance. For there is plenty of evidence to indicate that, on average, membership commitment to their union is generally weak. This is reflected, for example, in the low average attendance at union branch meetings, and the difficulty that unions frequently have in securing enough candidates to hold elections for union representative posts. In general, union members do not demonstrate a high level of union consciousness or what Blackburn and Prandy (1965) term 'unionateness' (see also, Prandy, Blackburn and Stewart, 1974). Indeed, the level of commitment to the union that can be identified tends usually to be what Hartley (1992) refers to as 'passive commitment' (for example, loyalty and general belief in unions) rather than 'active commitment' (expressed for example, in a willingness to work for the union). One reason why levels of member commitment may be low is if trade unions are not seen as effective organisations. It is to this question that we now turn.

TO SUM UP

Most union members appear to experience little difficulty in simultaneously maintaining their role of union member and employee. In the past this has been identified as evidence of employees' ability to maintain a dual allegiance to union and employer. However, it may also reflect a low level of commitment to one or both of these organisations.

Learning outcome 6

Evaluate the extent to which members think that trade unions are effective on behalf of their members.

Do members think that trade unions deliver?

The finding that other things being equal, terms and conditions of employment are higher in unionised than non-unionised establishments suggests that trade unions deliver in terms of effectively representing members' interests on key elements of the employment contract (Freeman and Medoff, 1984). The fact too that many employees retain membership of a trade union throughout their working lives is also suggestive of a widespread perception of the net benefit of union membership. However, other evidence reveals a more varied picture of employees' assessment of trade union representation. Most notably, there is the stark evidence of the widespread decline in trade union membership in many industrial societies over the last two decades. Traxler, Blaschke and Kittel (2001: 82) for example, note marked falls in membership density between 1980 and 1995 in countries such as New Zealand, Australia, the UK, Ireland, Italy and Portugal, with smaller falls in density levels in many other countries including Belgium, France, Germany, Japan, the Netherlands, Switzerland and the USA. There are a variety of reasons that account for the decline, but whatever the contributory factors, the fact remains that a diminishing proportion of employees have seen fit to hold membership of a trade union. It is not the case that trade unions have failed to recruit over this period – it is simply that they have not recruited at a rate sufficient to overcome membership turnover (estimated in the UK to be around twelve per cent per annum though in some sectors such as retail, union turnover rates are significantly higher; see Cully and Woodland, 1998; also Metcalf, 1991: 22).

From a variety of sources, it is possible to piece together a picture of whether the unions are seen to be doing a good job, on what issues, and overall, whether their presence in the workplace makes a difference. In general (and not surprisingly perhaps) those who are members of trade unions are more positive about the overall effect of trade unions than those who are not members, or those who formerly were members but have given up their membership. Yet, even union members are far from overwhelmingly positive about the effect of unions. In the WERS 1998 sample, for example, approaching half (46 per cent) of union members thought that trade unions made a difference to what it is like at work, compared to three out of ten (30 per cent) of non-union members and just over one-quarter (26 per cent) of ex-union members (Cully, Woodland, O'Reilly and Dix, 2000: 212–3). Significantly, those working in establishments where union density was highest were more likely to believe that unions made a difference, compared to those where fewer employees were in unions (we return to this below).

A generally similar picture is given in the British Social Attitudes Survey (Bryson, 1999) in which employees in unionised (and non-unionised) workplaces were asked if their workplace would be better or worse if the union ceased to exist (or if a union was introduced). In the unionised workplaces, while almost half (49 per cent) of employees thought that removal of the union would make the workplace worse, a substantial minority (40 per cent) thought that the union's removal would make no difference. Further, in nonunion workplaces, a clear majority (65 per cent) thought that the introduction of a union would make no difference. Findings such as these would not be surprising for commentators who argue that trade unions traditionally have not had policies that serve the interests of women (Colling and Dickens, 2001) or ethnic minorities (Hoque and Noon, 2001; Wrench, 1987) – see Excerpt 11.2 for some contemporary evidence of this.

EXCERPT 11.2

Are trade unions failing ethnic minorities?

The question of whether unions are delivering effective interest representation for ethnic minority employees was addressed by Noon and Hoque (2001) in an analysis of the findings from the UK 1998 Workplace Employee Relations Survey. Responses from 23,853 employees covering 1880 workplaces were compared statistically to

▶

▶

assess whether there were significant differences between white and ethnic minority employees in terms of training, promotion, job performance and pay. The results show some notable differences suggesting inequality is occurring, and of particular concern is the apparent ineffectiveness of trade unions:

■ There is evidence of inequality between whites and ethnic minorities in workplaces with recognised trade unions.

■ There is less evidence of inequality between whites and ethnic minorities in workplaces without recognised trade unions.

■ Ethnic minorities in unionised workplaces do not receive better treatment than ethnic minorities in non-unionised workplaces.

■ Whites in unionised workplace receive better treatment than whites in non-unionised workplaces.

The analysis also includes a comparison of men and women, and reveals that ethnic minority women suffer the greatest inequality. Not only do they receive less favourable treatment than white men and women, in some instances they also receive poorer treatment than ethnic minority men.

The authors conclude that the results, 'add to the criticisms sometimes made of trade unions that equal opportunities for ethnic minorities are not high on their list of priorities. For union policy-makers [such findings] should raise questions about the appropriateness and inclusiveness of their current representation of ethnic minorities. The implication must be that the relevance of trade unionism to ethnic minorities diminishes if unions cannot ensure equal treatment.' (Noon and Hoque, 2001: 114)

One of the factors that might explain why union members (and even more non-members) fail to identify the union as making a difference in the workplace could be their perception of unions lacking power in dealings with management. In the WERS sample for example, only just over half (52 per cent) of union members thought that unions were taken seriously by management, and smaller proportions of non-members and ex-members thought so (Cully, Woodland, O'Reilly and Dix, 2000: 213). This perception of a lack of influence has heightened as a result of the decline in membership levels in the 1980s and 1990s. In the British Social Attitudes survey, for example, the proportion indicating that 'unions have too little power' more than doubled between the mid-1980s (when one in ten thought unions had too little power) and the mid-1990s (when one in four held this view) (Bryson and McKay, 1997: 35).

Also relevant here is the question of the extent to which members think that the union effectively represents their interests. In their study of employees in the electronics industry, for example, Guest and Dewe (1991) found that union members were clear that the union was the best representative of their interests on wage-related matters. Yet, on other traditional issues for unions such as job security and working conditions, a higher proportion of union members thought that senior management or their immediate boss better represented their interests than the union (*ibid*: 82). This tendency was even more pronounced in relation to other areas such as staffing levels, overtime, introduction of new equipment, work transfer and work organisation. In these areas, only small proportions of union members saw their union representatives as best representing their interests, compared to their immediate boss or senior management.

Hence, the assessment of representation by trade unions is a mixed one. While those in unions are more likely to view union presence as making a difference, even among this group there is a substantial proportion who disagree. If one of the factors influencing these attitudes is a perceived weakness of unions in their dealings with management, then a 'vicious circle' of union presence is evident (see Figure 11.2). For, in the WERS respondents, where there were fewer union members, these members were less likely to view the union as influential, compared to where there were more members (Cully, Woodland, O'Reilly and Dix, 2000: 212). So, a decision to quit the union because of a perceived lack of influence is likely to have the effect of driving down perceived union influence even further, potentially leading to further membership losses.

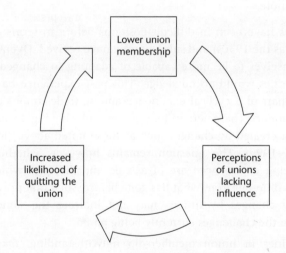

Figure 11.2 The vicious circle of union presence

TO SUM UP

The picture of whether members think that their union effectively represents the member's interest is a mixed one. While members are more likely than not to think that unions effectively represent them on issues such as pay and job security,

▶

▶ substantial minorities (and a majority of non-members) think that the union is not effective in representing members on a wide variety of issues. Partly, this reflects a perceived weakness of trade unions vis-à-vis management, resulting in many seeing the union as making little difference in the workplace.

The future of union representation

The question of what the future holds for trade unions has been the focus of much conjecture in recent years. Widespread declines in union membership, a marked shift in the nature of workforce composition, changes in management's approach to dealing with its 'human resources' directly rather than through union represen-tatives, and even the question of whether society is becoming more individualistic and less communal or collective in character, have all led to the question being posed as to whether unions are 'withering away' – organisations that are past their 'sell-by' date and are terminally in decline.

Yet at the same time, there is counter-evidence which suggests that pronounce-ments on the death of trade unions may be premature. Three factors are particu-larly worthy of note.

1 Trade unions have been in difficult positions before in terms of membership losses (such as the 1930s) and subsequently have revived. Overall, unions have shown themselves to be more capable of adapting to changed circumstances than their critics would acknowledge. This past experience has been seen by some to be part of a cyclical experience among trade unions and illustrating their evolutionary character: unions periodically having to adapt to a new environment created by changes such as those noted above (for a discussion, see Hyman, 1999). The question remains however, whether the changes currently being experienced are of a scale and diversity which make them qualitatively different from what has gone before, such that previous successful evolutionary changes by unions may not indicate the same potential for adaptation to the challenges currently being posed.

2 Recent declines in union membership notwithstanding, many millions of employees in industrial economies (as well as industrialising countries) continue to be members of unions. What is more, the decline that has taken place has not occurred uniformly across all countries and sectors. Indeed, not only have some countries not recorded a decline in union membership, but have actually registered a counter-trend, with increases in union membership levels. The Nordic countries – Denmark, Finland, Norway and Sweden – for example, all recorded increases in union density levels between 1980 and 1995 (Traxler, Blaschke and Kittel, 2001: 82).

3 As well as these counter-trends, there is evidence that a more general revival of trade union membership levels may be occurring. In Britain, for example, the

overall level of union membership rose in the late 1990s, reversing a twenty-year pattern of decline in membership totals (Hicks, 2000). Increased union organising and membership campaigns have played a significant part in this. Further, in the UK, recent statutory union recognition procedures look set to reinforce this more concerted recruitment activity.

Union strategies

Currently the academic debate on trade union revival is taking place along two dimensions, relating separately to questions of union strategy towards employers and towards actual and potential members.

1 In relation to employers, a central issue revolves around:

■ whether unions should develop their influence by entering more partnership relations with employers, eschewing adversarial relations in favour of more consensual relations designed to produce 'mutual gains' for both parties (Kochan and Osterman, 1994), or

■ whether unions would be better placed by adopting a more adversarial, militant approach to employers – protecting member interests by a more explicit recognition of the separation of those interests from those of the employer (Kelly, 1996).

EXERCISE 11.5

What do *you* think?

Those favouring closer social partnership for unions in their dealings with management argue that this represents a feasible way for trade unions to recover their position and gain greater involvement in the workplace. Such involvement is seen, in turn, as a way of demonstrating to members and potential members the relevance of the union within the work organisation – and thus the value of joining or retaining union membership.

Those favouring a more militant approach by unions argue in contrast that the social partnership route is likely to create weak and ineffective unions by eroding their capacity to resist management and adopt an independent position. As a result of this weakness, members are anticipated to become apathetic, reducing the capacity of unions to mobilise the membership for any form of concerted action.

1 Overall, which strategy do you think trade unions should follow to expand their influence and membership appeal: partnership or militancy? Explain your reasoning.

2 Are there circumstances where one strategy would be more appropriate than the other? What circumstances for example might be more appropriate for pursuing (a) a partnership approach, and (b) a more militant approach?

For more discussion of the partnership and militancy strategies for trade unions, see Kochan and Osterman (1994) and Kelly (1996).

2 Towards actual and potential members, the debate is whether unions would be more appealing if they:

- offered a more individualistic service, perhaps one stressing the benefits of membership in terms of individual services, advice and so on, or
- emphasised more explicitly the collective aspects of trade unionism and the benefits to members deriving from being part of a collective body.

EXCERPT 11.3

Organising the unorganised

'The contrast between an organising and a servicing model of trade unionism has become an established feature of debate on trade union strategy in the USA, Britain and other countries in recent years [...]. At its most basic the distinction refers to the difference between a form of unionism in which the union as an institution acts on behalf of its members who are conceived of as clients or customers, and one in which members actively participate and 'become' the union through their collective organisation and activity.

'The distinction is important [...] because it has been used to launch a programme for the revitalization of organised labour that is deemed equally applicable to all national cases and for all types of union. This programme originated in the United States – the term 'organising model' was first coined in 1988 in a manual for US labour organisers [...] – and has attracted adherents elsewhere.

'Among the broad principles, the most basic is that unions must commit themselves to organising the unorganised as their first priority. Applying the organising model, in the first instance, means committing greater effort and resource to the task of recruiting workers into membership.

'Membership is to be created and sustained, however, through the development of self-sustaining collective organisation among workers. In the US organisers speak of identifying workplace leaders, while in the UK they refer to activists and the need to attract and retain membership around an activist core.

'A feature of this emphasis on mobilization is the use of a particular moral discourse to frame union activity, which uses the language of "dignity, justice and respect" at work. This framing language not only legitimates union joining and activity it also presents the union as a counter to the employer. Organising unionism is generally adversarial or militant in its assumptions and seeks to organise workers against the employer. Indeed the emphasis on collective representation arises from a conviction that workers must generate their own power resources if they are to secure concessions from employers...'.

Source: Heery, Delbridge, Salmon, Simms and Simpson (2001)

Both of these aspects of union strategy – in their relations with employers and members – are concerned with increasing union influence and their appeal to prospective members. However, what tends to be absent from a surprising amount of this discussion is an explicit reference back to what encourages employees to join a union and what central purposes they see in membership. What we have seen from the earlier discussion is that employees are encouraged to join particularly by the presence of a union representative in their vicinity and/or whether their co-workers are already members. In deciding to join, members have a predominantly instrumental attitude to their representative body. What these two factors indicate for those unions seeking to recover their former membership levels is first, the importance of a local presence and local activists, and second, the need to emphasise the union's role in advancing member interests, both by collective means and by dealing with individual concerns. The protective function offered by the union, and the ability of unions to improve pay, security and so on were shown earlier to be the key to individual member joining decisions, and their decision to retain their membership once having joined.

As new members join, several things happen:

1 Others also join, because their peers have.

2 Where union density is higher, it is more likely that unions will be seen by members and potential members as influential and making a difference.

3 Where potential members see the union as making a difference, they in turn are more likely to join – thus reinforcing the 'virtuous circle' of events (see Figure 11.3).

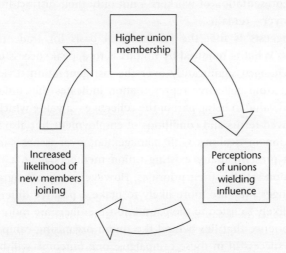

Figure 11.3 The virtuous circle of union presence

Waddington and Whitston (1997: 518) cite studies showing that only around one in seven non-members object in principle to trade unions. So, the growth of unionism is being prevented by other factors: non-availability (perhaps also reflecting management hostility), and a perceived lack of influence. Successfully addressing these aspects in the coming years could result in a cycle of growth, restoring much of the position lost by the past twenty-year cycle of decline.

TO SUM UP

Though the future of union representation is far from certain, what is more certain is the likely importance of local activity in any future influence wielded by trade unions within the workplace. Whether this activity, and any ensuing increases in union membership that stem from it, will be better encouraged through partnership relations with employers, or by emphasising the differences in interests between employees and employers, is likely to vary depending on particular circumstances within individual work organisations and individual trade unions.

Conclusion

This discussion of the collective representation of employee interests has served to underline one of the main themes running through the book: that the interests of employees and management are not identical and these translate into competing rationalities within the workplace. Despite the decline in membership that many unions have experienced during the past twenty years, this distinction between management and worker interests remains, as does the asymmetry of power between employer and individual employee. Thus, whatever the recent experience of union movements in many countries around the world, the rationale for the collective representation of workers – not only their distinct interests but also their weaker power – remains.

What this suggests is that the fundamental basis for trade union recovery remains present. What is required by unions is to appeal successfully to a labour force that has changed significantly over the last generation. Evidence on what employees want from collective representation indicates that unions must stress the instrumental value in being part of the collective – a value which translates not only into improved terms and conditions of employment but also into protection and representation in dealings with management over issues such as threat of redundancy. At present, many existing union members have a mixed view on whether the union satisfies their priorities. However, most are agreed that where unions are stronger they are more likely to make a positive difference, management are more likely to listen to them, and non-members are more likely to join.

It is this experience that lies behind the union organising campaigns currently taking place. If successful in these campaigns, one outcome will be the need for management to rethink many current human resource management (HRM) approaches which have tended to marginalise trade unions and collective forms of representation in favour of direct communication with individual employees. The HRM thinking highlights the difficulties that much contemporary management has in accepting the existence of multiple realities of work and the unsuitability of a single (managerial) perspective on the workplace.

Hidden work 12

KEY CONCEPTS

- Hidden work
- Concealed work
- Unrecognised work
- Deviant work
- Non-declared work

- Domestic work
- Foregone expense
- Foregone wage
- Voluntary work

CHAPTER AIM

This chapter explores the size and character of the 'hidden work' sector and examines the different ways in which hidden work relates to work in the formal or visible work sector.

LEARNING OUTCOMES

After reading and thinking about this chapter, you will be able to:

1 explain why work that lies outside the formal work sector may be considered 'hidden' work;

2 distinguish between different categories of hidden work and recognise the bases on which the categories are formed;

3 assess the measurement problems associated with quantifying the size of the hidden work sector;

4 assess the problems associated with predicting future trends in hidden work;

5 distinguish between different forms of concealed work and how these relate to the pattern of work in the formal work sector;

6 distinguish between different types of unrecognised work and how these relate to patterns of work in the formal work sector.

Introduction

Up to now, our examination of the realities of work has concentrated on those activities taking place within what might be termed the 'formal' or 'visible' work sector. This is where the goods and services produced are included in official statistics, such as the calculation of a country's Gross National Product (GNP) and where workers involved in the production of those goods and services receive a wage, which in turn is subject to tax. Yet, to focus all our attention here would be to misrepresent the totality of work and work experience. For as well as productive activity taking place within the formal economy, there are other contexts in which productive activity also occurs but which do not figure in national accounts of production or earnings. Thus, for example, while a joiner working for a firm producing windows creates output and earns a wage, both of which are 'visible' in terms of production and earnings accounts, if that same individual repairs a window in their own home or voluntarily assists in making a new door for a local youth club, none of this work will be 'visible' in terms of it being included in any national accounts. Similarly, if someone minds a friend's child for a day, who pays cash in return, which is not declared to the tax authorities, this income and the work for which the payment was received will not figure in national accounts. Each of these aspects of work – in the domestic and voluntary spheres, and receiving payment for work which is not declared for tax – are hidden, but they are unquestionably work, nonetheless.

Work that occurs outside the formal work sector can be 'hidden' from public gaze in one of two ways.

Learning outcome 1

Explain why work that lies outside the formal work sector may be considered 'hidden' work.

■ It might be *concealed* from the State authorities because it involves illegal activity. Either the activity itself is a crime such as drug dealing, or the income deriving from a legal activity is not declared for tax, thereby representing the illegal act of tax evasion. In this general category too is work activity, such as prostitution, which involves some activities that are illegal (such as soliciting) but which is also hidden because of its widespread social status as stigmatised work.

■ Work may be 'hidden' by being *unrecognised* as 'real' work, primarily because those performing the tasks do not receive payment; the archetypal case here is housework.

Each of these two general categories of hidden work is comprised of a range of individual activities. Yet, at the same time, these various activities hold certain key elements in common. For example, as well as each being 'hidden' for one reason or another, they all exhibit significant (albeit different) links with the formal or visible work sector. To explore these different aspects and implications of hidden work, the chapter is divided into three further sections. The first examines the main dimensions of hidden work and considers some of the attempts to measure the size of, and trends within the hidden work sector. Sections two and three then consider the two main areas of hidden work – concealed work and unrecognised work – in more detail, in order to establish the basis for an overall assessment of the significance of hidden work in the totality of work experience.

Defining and measuring hidden work

Consider this scenario and as you read it, think about the different aspects of hidden work involved. Imagine a household where Jeremy, an employee at a firm of estate agents, had decided to build an extension to his house. The additional space would provide an extra bedroom to house his elderly mother, Doris, who had suffered a stroke and was no longer able to look after herself in her own home. Faced with this situation, Jeremy and his wife Joanne, had decided that the best thing would be for Doris to live with them so they could be on hand to give her the care she needed.

Given the urgency of the situation and the inevitable delays of 'red tape', Jeremy decided to try and get the plans for the extension through the local authority Planning Committee more quickly than was usual. Fortunately, his membership of the local golf club had helped him to develop a number of 'useful' contacts, one of which was the local government officer in the Planning Department whose job it was to draw up the lists of property development for consideration by the Planning Committee. After an informal chat and a gift of a couple of bottles of whisky, the plans were put forward for consideration (and passed) very speedily.

Lacking the finances to pay a firm of builders to do the extension, Jeremy started on the work himself at weekends. However, he soon fell behind his schedule, not least because every other weekend he had custody of the two children by his first marriage, which occupied most of his time. To free up some of these weekends, Joanne (a nursery nurse by training) would spend a good part of her time amusing the children. She also kept Jeremy supplied with numerous cups of tea and a cooked lunch, as well as completing various other domestic chores (such as the ironing and cleaning) that were usually left until the weekend.

Even though Jeremy was freed from the child care and domestic chores, he still found himself making little headway with the work at weekends and soon began to put in an hour or two on the building work during the week, by pretending to his boss that he was leaving the office early to do a house evaluation, or have a meeting with a prospective vendor. However, after a few weeks it was clear that not even this extra time was progressing the work fast enough, so one evening Jeremy called up various contacts in the building trade to try to find someone to help. He was put in touch with a building labourer, Ron, who agreed to give him a hand, working at weekends. Ron made it clear that he would want to be paid in cash, with no receipts, but that in return he would 'borrow' the equipment they would need from his employer – an excavator to dig the trench for the foundations and a concrete mixer – provided that any equipment was back on his firm's premises before Monday morning.

With the added help of Ron, the extension was soon finished and Doris duly moved in. Yet, while the arrangement of having Doris under the same roof meant that there was now less travelling involved in visiting her, Joanne soon found that the combination of tasks of keeping her own household going, looking after her mother-in-law and doing her job at a local nursery school, was getting too much for her. As a result, she gave up her job at the nursery, although to keep some interest outside the home, she carried on doing some voluntary work in the evenings which involved organising fund-raising activities for a local hospital.

The most remarkable aspect of this account is that although there is a large amount of 'work' being done, only two of the activities figure as part of the formal economy: Jeremy's job at the estate agents, and Joanne's job at the nursery school. The remaining work all takes place within the domains of hidden work. For example, as well as Jeremy's DIY building activities, there is the care dispensed by Joanne to her mother-in-law and to her husband's children, together with the work involved in her keeping the men supplied with food and drink as well as undertaking the other domestic tasks of cleaning and ironing, not to mention the voluntary work. In addition, the work done by Ron is also hidden in that his requirement for cash-in-hand payments with no receipts suggests an intention not to declare some or all of this income to the tax authorities. The account also contains examples of some of the fiddles which are often associated with the hidden work sphere: for example, the planning officer taking a 'backhander' to push Jeremy's application up the queue, Jeremy's use of office hours to work on the extension, and Ron's unauthorised 'borrowing' of his employer's equipment (see Chapter 9 for a more detailed discussion of workplace fiddling). This account also underlines the need for some means of categorising the diverse activities which fall under the general heading of hidden work.

Categorising hidden work

Learning outcome 2

Distinguish between different categories of hidden work and recognise the bases on which the categories are formed.

There are various ways in which the hidden work sphere might be categorised. The preference here is for one based on the distinction made earlier:

- Activities that are 'concealed' because they are illegal, because they contain illegal aspects and attract social stigma, or because the income deriving from legal activities is not declared to the tax authorities.
- A variety of 'unrecognised' work which is hidden as a result of not generally being performed for payment, thus placing those work activities not only outside market relations but also outside the range of activity widely considered to constitute 'real' work.

As Figure 12.1 indicates, under each of the two main categories, different individual work activities may be located. The examples given do not represent an exhaustive list but are indicative of the sorts of activity to be found within each of the general areas of hidden work. Further, the distinction between different activities and categories will, in practice, often be blurred by individuals simultaneously pursuing more than one aspect of hidden work: for example, by performing work activities which benefit both the household and a wider group (for example by gardening and growing flowers which are used to decorate both the home and the local church). However, while recognising the existence of overlaps, this does not invalidate the main distinction between concealed and unrecognised work, since this distinction is based on the fundamentally different *causes* of their hiddenness.

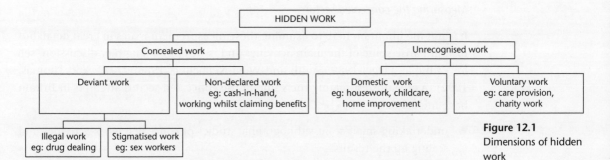

Figure 12.1
Dimensions of hidden work

Other commentators have drawn broadly similar distinctions between the main categories of hidden work, though there is some variation in the labels used and the degree to which some of the categories (notably the domestic and voluntary spheres) are treated separately or as elements of a single category. For example, while Gershuny (1983) distinguishes between the 'household', 'communal' and 'underground' economies, and Handy (1984) refers to the 'household', 'voluntary' and 'black' economies, Smith and Wied-Nebbeling (1986) in their work on Britain and Germany make a distinction only between the 'black' and the 'self-service' economies in the two countries, while Rose (1985) distinguishes between the 'unofficial' and 'domestic' economies. Following writers such as Felt and Sinclair (1992: 45) the terminology preferred here is concealed and unrecognised *sectors* rather than 'economies' to emphasise that these areas do not represent activities completely separate from a formal, visible economy. Indeed, in various ways (discussed below) the hidden work sector is inextricably tied in various ways to the formal work sector and many people are, to a greater or lesser extent, active in both visible and hidden sectors.

Problems in measuring the scale of hidden work

As most researchers in this area have acknowledged, there are several inherent measurement problems that exist in relation to hidden work, so much so that anything approaching an accurate quantification of the overall scale of hidden work is virtually impossible.

Three distinct measurement problems become immediately apparent:

1 *What is to be included?* Most measurement attempts, for example, have been undertaken with a view to estimating how much revenue is lost to the State as a result of concealed market activities. By definition, those seeking to calculate such estimates are not interested in non-market activities which make up the unrecognised work sector. As a result, the latter has been the subject of far fewer attempts to quantify and measure.

2 *How can non-market activities be quantified?* In the few attempts that have been made to measure both the concealed and the unrecognised work sectors, a key problem has been how to put a monetary value on activities which are not paid for.

3 *How can work activities be measured accurately that are concealed because they are illegal?* The very act of concealment creates major obstacles for the quantification and measurement of those activities.

Learning outcome 3

Assess the measurement problems associated with quantifying the size of the hidden work sector.

Measuring the concealed sector

It is not the intention here to examine these measurement issues in great detail but to summarise some of the main activities and issues (for a lengthier discussion, see for example, Fiege, 1989; Smith and Wied-Nebbeling, 1986: 27–42; and Thomas, 1992). As regards estimating the value of the concealed sector, attempts in Britain have included:

- undertaking small-scale, ethnographic studies of concealed work activities and scaling up the results;
- aggregating up from the results of investigations of single cases by the Inland Revenue where discrepancies are revealed between declared and actual income;
- seeking to establish differences between levels of income and expenditure in the economy as a whole, or among samples of households (using surveys such as the Family Expenditure Survey). The working assumption here is that if total expenditure is greater than declared income, the additional income required for this expenditure will have been acquired through concealed activities;
- attempting to measure the concealed sector by the amount of cash in circulation. This is based on an assumption that transactions in the concealed sector are conducted in cash. Particular attention has been given to the amount of large denomination bank notes in circulation, on an assumption that these figure disproportionately in concealed transactions.

EXERCISE 12.1

What you *you* think?

1 Outline the strengths and weaknesses of each of the four methods of estimating the value of the concealed sector described in this section.

2 On the basis of your assessment, which do you think is likely to yield the most accurate results, and why?

3 Are there any other methods that you can suggest to obtain a better measure of concealed work?

Despite the variety and ingenuity of these attempts to measure the concealed work sector, it remains the case that 'a considerable margin of error surrounds all estimates of the scale of concealed transactions' (Smith and Wied-Nebbeling, 1986: 40). This is probably putting it mildly: all the measurement instruments applied to the concealed sector are extremely blunt, making the practice of estimation highly unreliable, if not altogether impossible. As a result, it is difficult to challenge (or improve upon) estimates such as the much-quoted one by the Inland Revenue (1981) which estimated in the late 1970s that the value of non-declared work in the UK was around 7.5 per cent of GNP. Over the intervening period, others have concluded fairly similar estimates; Rose (1985: 125), for example, estimates that between 4 and 7.2 per cent of total labour time may be spent in concealed work. Similarly, calculating the average of nine studies identified by Rose (*ibid*: 126) gives a mean estimate of the value of undeclared work of just under 6.5 per cent of Gross Domestic Product (GDP).

Measuring unrecognised work

As noted above, while the core problem of measuring concealed work is the reluctance of those taking part to having their activities made visible, the main difficulty in measuring the unrecognised work sector is one of establishing an accurate valuation. Since those performing household and voluntary work do not normally receive payment, these activities do not have a readily calculable monetary value. There are, of course, ways in which a money value can be conferred on these tasks. In relation to household-based work activities, for example, these fall into two general approaches: measuring the foregone expense or the foregone wage (Chadeau, 1985: 242):

- *The foregone expense* involves calculating the cost of purchasing the various tasks from the formal or visible work sector. In terms of domestic work activities, for example, this may be calculated either on the basis of the cost of employing a general housekeeper, or the cost of hiring the specialist services of a cook, cleaner, gardener, and so on.
- *The foregone wage* involves estimating the lost income incurred by the person who is undertaking the domestic work, who could otherwise devote an equivalent amount of time to paid work.

While both these methods of calculation produce a monetary value for household domestic work, both suffer from measurement problems. The most prominent of these is that the alternative methods of calculation are likely to yield quite different valuations (the foregone expense likely to indicate a significantly higher valuation of household tasks). Yet, while such problems signal the need to treat any calculations with caution, it remains equally clear that *irrespective of the method of calculation, the monetary value of work activities in the unrecognised work sector is very high*. Chadeau (1985: 245–6), for example, reviews over thirty studies undertaken in various countries mainly between 1960 and 1980 which adopted a variety of bases on which to estimate the value of domestic work. She calculates that the combined average estimate from these studies is that domestic work is equivalent to over one third (34.7 per cent) of GNP.

EXERCISE 12.2

What do *you* think?

1 Why should measuring the foregone expense result in a higher estimate for the value of domestic work than measuring the foregone wage?

▶

▶

2 What does this tell us about the nature of employment experience and opportunities for many women?

Other estimates have put the value of the unrecognised work sector even higher. Handy (1984: 19) for example, comments that over half the country's total labour time is devoted to productive activity in or around the household and that if this work were charged, it could amount to 40 per cent of the formal economy (see also Rose, 1985: 133). As Handy (1984) also points out, when combined with the extent of voluntary work that is undertaken this would make the size of the unrecognised work sector as much as *one half* of the total economy.

TO SUM UP

Whatever the measurement problems and the range of estimates that these generate, the value of unrecognised work is vast. Further, given the number of people involved and the time spent on domestic and other non-market activities, the monetary value of the unrecognised work sector almost certainly dwarfs the value of activities in the concealed sector by a large margin.

Learning outcome 4

Assess the problems associated with predicting future trends in hidden work.

Problems of predicting trends in hidden work

Just as it is almost impossible to establish an accurate valuation of hidden work, it is also difficult to draw definitive conclusions about likely overall trends:

- Is the size of the hidden work sphere changing over time?
- Are some aspects changing more or less rapidly?
- Are aspects of hidden work changing in the same or different direction to one another?

The problem here is more than one of establishing reliable benchmarks from which to estimate change. Other problems include the diversity of the hidden work sector, the range of possible influencing variables and the possibility that single variables will have contrasting effects on different aspects of hidden work.

Hidden work and the economic cycle

Consider the relationship between the amount of hidden work and the state of the economy. It has been argued, for example, that during periods of strong economic growth, the scope for concealed work activity will tend to rise as people have more money to purchase goods and services, and the formal economy is less able to keep up with the total level of demand. Correspondingly, it is argued that economic recession will tend to dampen concealed work activities, as the amount of money to spend on goods and services diminishes (O'Higgins, 1989: 175). Yet, an opposite argument would seem to be equally plausible. In periods of economic recession when levels of disposable income are depressed, people could conceivably increase their efforts to obtain the goods and services they require more cheaply by entering into more 'cash-in-hand' transactions. Also, if unemployment rises as a result of recession, this could increase the amount of time spent on domestic and voluntary activities (MacDonald, 1996).

It may also be the case that while some aspects of concealed work decline during recessions, others – such as 'earning while claiming' (claiming welfare payments while concealing additional income being earned from cash-in-hand activity) – increase during periods when unemployment is greater (though the overall import-ance of earning while claiming has been exaggerated in the past, particularly in comparison to other undeclared income fraud). Further, as writers such as Thomas (1992) have pointed out, if one of the outcomes of recession and a lack of employ-ment opportunities is to stimulate a growth in self-employment, this may stimulate an increase in concealed work since it is the self-employed sector which accounts for a high proportion of concealed work through failing to declare all the income earned.

Similarly, while it is arguable that a growth in participation rates in the formal work sector could act to limit the amount of time available for activity in the unrecognised work sphere (such as voluntary work), at the same time it is evident that some aspects of concealed work thrive on the income, contacts, opportunities and skills deriving from paid employment (Pahl, 1984 and 1988). Hence, the problem of identifying a relationship between the economic cycle and hidden work is not just one concerning the overall relationship between the two, but is also compounded by the fact that some elements of hidden work may increase (or decrease) in response to different economic conditions.

Trends in hidden work

Another example of the difficulties in projecting possible trends in hidden work is that while some long term factors may have stimulated a *growth* in hidden work during the last century, others may have acted in favour of a *decline* in aspects of hidden work.

- In terms of growth, an overall rise in levels of taxation over a long period for example, potentially acts to increase the incentive for undertaking non-declared work. Further, the long term decline in the basic working week in the visible work sector has potentially increased opportunities for workers to devote more time to additional activities in the hidden sector. And, following Gershuny's (1983) argument, the decline in the total number of domestic servants in the early decades of the twentieth century was accompanied by a growth in the proportion of households performing their own domestic tasks.

- In terms of decline, long term developments such as a rise in women's labour market participation and the growth in the welfare state (the latter providing care in the formal sector to augment existing family and communal care of the elderly, sick and disabled) have potentially acted, over a long period, in favour of reducing the total time devoted to domestic and voluntary activities.

These countervailing influences on hidden work, however, are yet further complicated if shorter time horizons are taken into account. For example, while the development of the welfare state in the UK over the last fifty years may have altered the balance between care being provided in the formal or the domestic and voluntary work spheres, more recent legislation in the UK (notably the National Health Service and Community Care Act 1990) has resulted, in latter years, in a shift of emphasis back towards more care being dispensed in the domestic and voluntary spheres, rather than in the formal work sector. As a result of this policy, local authorities are now required both to take account of caring provision already being given in their assessments of individuals' care needs, and to promote the development of domiciliary care rather than residential care (see also below).

TO SUM UP

The different measurement problems and the variety of possible influences on the scale and development of hidden work as a whole, indicate that any general conclusion cannot safely go beyond saying that though overall trends cannot clearly be defined, it is evident that the amount of hidden work performed remains very substantial and is unlikely to be declining significantly (nor will do so in the foreseeable future) and could grow further beyond its current size.

Learning outcome 5

Distinguish between different forms of concealed work and how these relate to the pattern of work in the formal work sector.

Exploring hidden work I: concealed work

'Concealed' work is one of many labels that have been applied to that aspect of hidden work which directly or indirectly involves illegal activities. Other terms that have been used include the 'black', 'shadow', 'submerged', 'irregular', 'underground', 'unobserved', 'unofficial', 'illicit', 'subterranean' and 'informal' sector or economy (see, for example, Feige, 1989; Gershuny, 1983; Rose, 1985; Smith and Wied-Nebbeling, 1986; and Thomas, 1992). Our choice of the 'concealed' sector reflects the fact that this aspect of hidden work involves market transactions that are purposely concealed from view, either because they are illegal in themselves, because they contain illegal aspects and are subject to a social stigma, or because they are associated with fraudulent behaviour, such as the evasion of taxes or working while claiming State unemployment benefit (Smith and Wied-Nebbeling, 1986: 2). Though relatively simple, even this categorisation is not problem-free, however, partly because it covers such a wide scale of activities (for example from small-scale, cash-in-hand transactions to multi-million pound drug-dealing) but also, by ring-fencing behaviours and applying particular labels to denote them, this conveys an impression that it is possible to draw a clear and definite distinction between the 'concealed' and the 'visible' sectors. In reality, however, this distinction tends to be much more blurred.

Deviant work

One of the main reasons why some people conceal the work they are engaged in is because it is illegal. Some of the categories more commonly used to describe aspects of visible work, however, also apply to deviant work. For example, for some people, criminal activity is a part-time pursuit, a supplement to other income acquired through legal channels. For others, however, crime is their full-time 'occupation'. Indeed, references are commonly made to individuals who are 'professional' criminals, pursuing a criminal 'career' (for a discussion of crime as alternative work behaviour, see Ferman, 1983: 217).

Not all deviant work is wholly illegal. The very large (see excerpt 12.1 below) but mainly hidden sex industry, for example, comprises various forms of work (for example, prostitution and the production of pornography), some aspects of which are legal, others not. As regards prostitution, for example, in the UK it is illegal 'to loiter or solicit in a street or public place for the purpose of prostitution' (Street Offences Act 1959, quoted in Lacey, Wells and Meure, 1990: 362) just as it is to live off the immoral earnings of someone else; however, it is not illegal to work as a prostitute in a private place.

In the case of the sex industry, the label of deviant work reflects not only those aspects which are illegal, but also the degree to which sex workers are stigmatised by the rest of society (Goffman, 1963; Woollacott, 1980). This may be slowly changing as collectives of sex workers continue to campaign for greater legal protection and employment rights, and as police and other authorities (in at least some countries and localities) begin to move in the direction of exercising greater control of the sex industry through registration and licensing procedures, rather than by continued prohibition and suppression (West, 2000; O'Connell Davidson, 1998). However, the stigmatisation of sex workers remains widespread, exemplified by the continued resistance of residents' groups and others to prevent the growth of sex work – particularly on the streets – in their locality. Thus, any gains stemming from collective representation and any changes in approach by police authorities and judiciaries notwithstanding, the social stigma and legal pressures continue to combine to cast prostitutes (and other sex workers) as 'outsiders' in the world of work (Becker, 1963). At the same time, this shared experience as outsiders helps to generate a supportive work culture among many of the workers themselves (Woollacott, 1980: 198), a work group culture further strengthened by the danger of abuse, disease and injury which sex workers constantly face (see also Adkins, 1995; Brewis and Linstead, 2000a, 2000b).

EXCERPT 12.1

A growth industry

The sex industry is huge. Ranging from pornography to lap-dancing to prostitution, the industry has been estimated to be worth $56 billion per annum worldwide, and £2 billion per year in the UK (Devi, 2000). The industry has grown

▶

▶ substantially as a result of the internet. Sex sites are by far the most commonly sites visited, and account for most of the sales and profits in the industry. In 1998, for example, over seventy per cent of Playboy's $318 million sales were accounted for by the internet.

As well as the growth of the sex industry on the internet, the 'live' sex industry is also growing. One study, for example has estimated that 80,000 men visit a prostitute in London every week (quoted in Devi, 2000: 16). There are now upwards of 40 table or lap-dancing clubs across London, and in the US, the Inland Revenue Service estimates that the table-dancing club sector is worth $8 billion per annum.

EXERCISE 12.3

What do *you* think?

1 Can you think of other work sectors that are hidden because the work conducted is stigmatised by society in some way?

2 What are the aspects of the work that have brought about the stigmatisation?

Non-declared work

For many people, their main experience of concealed work will be work undertaken for payment but which is hidden from the tax authorities. It is widely believed that the biggest source of untaxed income is that accruing to the self-employed, whose income is not subject to tax collection through Pay-As-You-Earn (PAYE) arrangements. On the basis of the findings of individual investigations by the Inland Revenue in the UK, it is evident that a significant proportion of the self-employed fail to declare all their income to the tax authorities (see Chapter 2 for discussion of the growth of self-employment).

Aside from the self-employed population, however, in recent periods of high unemployment, undeclared income deriving from 'working and claiming' has regularly become a *cause célèbre* of governments, with clamp-downs on the 'benefit fraud' stemming from those claiming unemployment and/or other welfare payments while also acquiring income from work which is not declared to the authorities. This governmental selective attention – pursuing the small-scale frauds of the unemployed with a vigour hardly shown towards their richer counterparts engaging in large-scale tax evasion – probably reflects not only a class bias and the political appeal of lowering the social security bill by removing those caught 'fiddling benefit', but also a *realpolitik* of the benefit fiddlers being much easier to catch than their larger-scale and more sophisticated tax-dodging counterparts. In this endeavour, governments have also been assisted by the periodic involvement of sections of the press (such as *The Sun* newspaper's 'Split on a Scrounger' campaign, with a telephone hotline for anonymous callers) and by a willingness among some to 'shop' neighbours whom they suspect of benefit offences, to the local social security office (see also Pahl, 1984: 95). What these Government and press campaigns reflect too, is a perception that unemployed people are particularly the ones involved in cash-in-hand activities: that they are available for such work by virtue of not having a formal job, and are successful in obtaining cash-in-hand work because they can afford to take jobs at a lower payment than would be offered in the visible work sector, because any wage is supplemented by the welfare benefits also being claimed.

Clearly, a proportion of the total cash-in-hand work *is* undertaken by the unemployed, though often for very small payment (see excerpt 12.2 below; also MacDonald, 1994 and 1997). The growth of small sub-contracting firms in both manufacturing and services has probably extended the availability of cash-in-hand work into a wider range of sectors over the past two decades. What Pahl (1984) and others have shown, however, is that it is a far from accurate picture to portray most cash-in-hand work activities as being undertaken by the unemployed. On the contrary, much of this work is carried out by people who are already in employment and are undertaking additional work in their spare time (like Ron in our earlier example). For Pahl (1984) and others, it is the extra resources available to those in employment which increases their access to additional work. Employment provides contacts as well as sufficient financial resources to acquire the equipment and materials necessary for undertaking other work (garden machinery, power tools, transport, and so on), together with the skills necessary for conducting other activity.

Unemployment, on the other hand, is for many not only an intensely isolating experience (whatever contacts that might have been made while in employment are soon lost) but also that the (low) level of unemployment income restricts the unemployed in extending their own concealed activity, other than in those areas requiring little or no capital expenditure, such as labouring for others or cleaning windows (Pahl, 1984: 97). What this also indicates is that just as the distinction between employed and unemployed confers income and status on the former rather than the latter, in the same way, employment – and the benefits stemming from employment – provides access to more highly rewarded areas of concealed work than those available to the unemployed, who are largely restricted to lower paying activities.

TO SUM UP

Work may be concealed because it is illegal, undeclared or stigmatised in some way. The total volume of concealed work is very large and probably growing. While much attention has been given to the extent of concealed work undertaken by the unemployed, in practice this probably accounts for only a small proportion of the total monetary value of concealed work activities.

EXCERPT 12.2

Fiddly jobs

'Fiddly jobs' is one of the expressions referring to work for payment that is under-taken whilst claiming social security and unemployment benefits. Estimates differ on the extent of working whilst claiming. MacDonald (1994: 509) quotes studies which found variation in undeclared working ranging from one in seven families to up to two-thirds of poor households. In MacDonald's own sample of over two hundred people in the North East of England, just under one-third had done fiddly jobs.

Most of the jobs that MacDonald investigated were short-term (typically a day or two), irregular, infrequent and poorly rewarded. The most common jobs were as sub-contract labour (particularly doing cleaning or maintenance jobs) in the nearby steelworks, and construction work, car mechanics, taxi driving, window cleaning and bar work. The people engaging in fiddly work were disproportionately white, working class males in their twenties and thirties who had skills and/or a reputation for reliability, and who moved in the social circles through which fiddly work was distributed.

The people undertaking the fiddly work viewed it as an accepted survival strategy, reflecting the low level of State benefit they received. It was also seen as risky (because of the possibility of being caught by the benefit authorities), hard work, unsociable (often involving long and irregular hours) and low paid.

The fiddly jobs, despite their irregularity and infrequency, nevertheless provided some beneficial work routine for the individuals. As MacDonald comments (1997: 119), 'For this sample of poor and long-term unemployed people fiddly work became a necessary way of maintaining individual self respect and household incomes.'

Learning outcome 6

Distinguish between different types of unrecognised work and how these relate to patterns of work in the formal work sector.

▌ Exploring hidden work II: unrecognised work

Domestic work

The hidden work sphere is dominated by domestic labour within the household. This is the case however its magnitude is measured – in volume of activity, number of people involved, total time spent or overall value of activities. It is domestic work too, and the way that it is organised and performed, which has particularly significant implications for the pattern and experience of work in the visible work sector. Here, there is space to explore only certain aspects of domestic work, but even a brief examination provides ample indication of the various points at which work in the domestic sphere touches upon and shapes the broader realities and experiences of paid work, and more generally underlines the continued promin-ence of domestic work in overall work experience.

Domestic work and paid employment

A number of these points of contact between domestic work and paid employment have already been highlighted in earlier chapters:

■ In the discussion of attitudes towards time discipline in Chapter 4, for example, it was noted how the household, together with schools and other institutions has played an important part in the development and internalisation of values towards regularity, punctuality and time thrift.

■ More broadly, the domestic sphere represents a key location for childhood socialisation, including socialisation relating to work values (see Chapter 3).

■ The domestic sphere also represents an important source of material support for those working in paid employment. The household acts to deliver labour to the work place in a condition fit for work: clothed, fed, rested.

■ Over and above these physical contributions, the domestic sphere also provides an important source of psychological support for those in paid work: a context in which they can relax, 'wind down', and 'switch off' from the pressures of their job.

■ The desire for comfort and well-being in the domestic sphere also acts as a motivation for continuing to value the financial benefits of paid work.

In addition to these different support roles vis-à-vis the formal work sector, the domestic sphere also exerts a major influence on the overall pattern of labour market participation. At its simplest, the large amount of time expended on housework and child-care limits the time available for other activities, including paid employment. But of course, the main point here is that domestic work has not simply limited the labour market participation of people in general: it has especially limited the participation of women in paid work. For it is women who disproportionately continue to shoulder the responsibilities for domestic work. As industrialism developed, the increased prominence of the male 'breadwinner' left women with the large part of the domestic responsibilities. And, even though the participation rates of women in the labour market have risen considerably since the post-1945 period, and especially since the 1960s (see Chapter 2), this has not been matched by a corresponding sharing of the burden of household work between men and women, or an equalising of the overall responsibility for the domestic sphere (Horrell, 1994).

Table 12.1 highlights the unequal distribution of household activities among both working and non-working men and women. What is evident is that women in each category undertake a much greater amount of household tasks than men. Even in the category where men devote more time than women – gardening and DIY – this additional time does little to restore any balance to the total time that men and women spend on domestic work. The overwhelming difference between men and women lies in the area of cooking and routine housework – a differentiation of time especially marked among working men and women. As one commentator reviewing the overall evidence on domestic work puts it, 'none of the data seems to warrant any suggestion that the traditional female responsibility for household work has been substantially eroded' (Morris, 1990: 102).

Table 12.1 Time use relating to domestic work in Britain (hours and minutes per day)

Activity	In paid employment		Not in paid employment	
	Women	Men	Women	Men
Cooking, routine housework	2:02	0:32	2:45	0:58
Gardening and DIY	0:19	0:37	0:31	1:20
Care of children and adults	0:36	0:19	1:23	0:18
Shopping	0:37	0:20	0:55	0:34
Total	3:34	1:48	5:34	3:10

Figures for 1995
Source: Adapted from Equal Opportunities Commission (1998: 64)

EXERCISE 12.4

What do *you* think?

Consider the pattern of results in Table 12.1.

1 What do you think are the main factors influencing the distribution of domestic work activities?

2 It is generally agreed that the relative proportions of domestic work undertaken by men and women have changed only marginally over the past two decades, despite the increasing proportion of women in the labour market (see Chapter 2). What factors do you think account for this lack of change?

As writers such as Duncombe and Marsden (1995) point out, this continuing inequality spans not only the distribution of physical work tasks, but also the emotion work that takes place in the household. Women continue to shoulder a disproportionate amount of the emotion caring work, with their male partners giving priority to their paid work roles (see also the discussion of emotional labour in Chapter 7). For many women, therefore, taking on paid employment has added to their sum of total work, rather than brought about any equalising of work responsibilities with their male partners. 'Married women in employment bear a disproportionate "dual burden" of paid and unpaid work' (Gershuny, Godwin and Jones, 1994: 152). Comparing time-budget surveys conducted in the UK in 1974/75 and 1987, Gershuny and his colleagues (1994: 176–7) do in fact suggest that husbands' proportion of the household's work had risen by 1987 compared with 1975, particularly where their wives were in full-time employment. However, overall a significant gap still remains, particularly where women have not been in paid employment for a long period. Gershuny and colleagues (1994: 179) argue that this may reflect a process of 'lagged adaptation' with husbands (and wives) moving only slowly away from their former assumptions about domestic responsibilities (see also Horrell, 1994, and for an examination of male perspectives on household work activities, see Goodwin, 1999).

Grateful slaves?

An Australian study by Baxter and Western (1998) has explored an apparent paradox in domestic work: that, despite shouldering responsibility for most household tasks, a large percentage of women are satisfied with the division of household labour. Possible reasons that the authors identify for this include: women accepting that there is little alternative to the prevailing situation; holding a traditional attitude towards the role of men and women which encourages them to accept the bulk of household tasks; women working fewer hours in paid work, creating a feeling of having primary responsibility for household tasks; and the possibility that women enjoy doing housework tasks more than men.

Drawing on a national survey of over 1700 men and women, Baxter and Western found that women in Australia spent far longer on domestic labour than men: an overall average of 43 hours per week for women, compared to 16 hours for men.

However, only around one in seven women reported any dissatisfaction with the way they and their partners divided childcare or household tasks. Perhaps not surprisingly given the distribution of hours, very few of the men (only around one in thirty) indicated any dissatisfaction with the way the tasks were divided.

Looking further at the attitudes to housework, the authors found that if husbands participated in certain household chores conventionally the responsibility of women – such as preparing meals, cleaning the house, doing the washing or ironing – women were more satisfied, even if in practice the men did not spend long on any of the activities, compared to their partners. The authors comment that 'This finding implies that for most women the key issue is having "help" with some specific activities rather than an equal division of time on housework' (p. 117).

Other factors positively correlated with women's satisfaction with housework included whether they held more traditional gender role attitudes, and whether they were satisfied with their paid employment. In addition, more educated and younger women tended to be less satisfied than their less educated and older counterparts.

Note: The term 'grateful slaves' is taken from Hakim (1991)

Women, household work and labour market participation

The shouldering of a disproportionate share of responsibilities for household tasks and child-care has various implications for women's position in the labour market. For example:

■ Women are more likely to exhibit a greater discontinuity in labour market activity, with periods of employment interspersed with periods of child-care.

This in turn contributes both towards a lower rate of progression within internal career hierarchies and a resulting disproportionate occupancy by women of lower level and more poorly paid jobs (see also, Chapter 10).

■ With women more likely to be occupying less well paid jobs than their male partners, this tends to lead to any mobility among many couples being male driven: couples relocate on the basis of the labour market for the male's job. Such mobility patterns in turn potentially further exacerbate women's position in the labour market, since they are forced to seek employment in labour markets that have been chosen more to suit the job requirements of their male partners rather than themselves.

■ The ways in which women's domestic work responsibilities influence their pattern of labour market participation is particularly represented by the nature and growth of part-time working. Over four-fifths of part-time workers are women and more than two-thirds of female employees work part-time (see Chapter 2). One of the reasons why employers seeking to expand part-time working have been successful in securing an adequate supply of available labour, has been the requirement of many women to combine a desire or need for paid employment with their continuing domestic responsibilities. For many, this combination can best or only be achieved by engaging in part-time, rather than full-time employment.

Several factors make women's disproportionate involvement in household work problematic. For example, much of the activity which comprises household work is both highly repetitive (cooking, cleaning, washing, and ironing, for example) and immensely time-consuming. Indeed, as Oakley (1974: 45) points out, the virtually continuous nature of domestic work experienced by many women is summed up in such traditional phrases as 'a woman's work is never done'. The housewives in Oakley's own study worked, on average, 77 hours per week – double the working week of many workers in full-time paid employment (Oakley, 1974: 93). Further, for much of the time, housework activities are performed in isolation, and at times under considerable time pressures. The combined effect of these factors is that many find housework a source of frustration, dissatisfaction and low self-esteem. The strength of these negative feelings is, for many, seemingly stronger than any positive aspects of domestic work deriving from, for example, a degree of autonomy, or involvement with child development.

However, what exacerbates and encapsulates the problematic nature and status of domestic work is that it is work which is unpaid. As noted earlier, it is this absence of payment which is key to making this aspect of work 'hidden'. In addition, the fact that most domestic work remains practically as well as metaphorically hidden (since much of it takes place 'behind closed doors') adds to the 'invisible' nature of this aspect of work.

TO SUM UP

Domestic work is hidden not only in terms of its status and social recognition, but also in terms of national accounts of total work output, as well as by the private nature of much of household life.

Voluntary work

Like unpaid domestic labour, voluntary work – which has also been referred to by such terms as 'communal' work (Gershuny, 1983) and 'gift work' (Handy, 1984) – is generally (though not exclusively) characterised by an absence of money payment for work undertaken. It is also work normally undertaken outside the family and as the name implies, is work that is voluntary rather than 'forced' in any way. A definition of voluntary work adopted by the Volunteer Centre UK (now the National Centre for Volunteering) for example, is 'work undertaken with benefit to others outside the immediate family, not directly in return for wages, undertaken by free choice, not required by the state or its agencies' (Davis Smith, 1992: xi).

The scale of voluntary work

For Gershuny (1983) one of the long-term factors stimulating the growth of voluntary work has been the rising cost of buying in services from the formal economy, leading to an increased self-provisioning from within the community. However, it is important not to overlook the fact that the exchange of unpaid work has always been a basis on which communities, particularly rural communities, have functioned (see, for example, Felt and Sinclair, 1992). And, like other aspects of hidden work, voluntary work is characterised by its large scale and broad diversity. A survey of volunteering conducted in the UK in the early 1990s, for example, indicated that up to 23 million adults are involved in voluntary work of one sort or another each year, and that as many as 100 million hours may be spent on organised and unorganised voluntary activity every week (Joseph Rowntree Foundation, 1991; see also Davis Smith, 1992: 3). Women are slightly more likely to be involved in voluntary activities than men, and those in paid work (or recently in a paid job) more likely to be involved in voluntary work than those who have been out of the labour market for some time (Davis Smith, 1992: 6,8).

The range of activities which constitute voluntary work is vast and incorporates informal activities (such as doing an elderly neighbour's shopping) and various social exchange or mutual self-help activities (such as participating in a babysitting circle) as well as work in the more 'organised' voluntary work sector which itself is composed of an almost endless range of activities: from the St John's Ambulance to prison visiting, from voluntary fire services to charity shops, from trade union activity to environmental work, and from canvassing during elections to serving on the local Neighbourhood Watch committee. As Harding and Jenkins (1989: 119) point out, the nature of voluntary work is also diversified in terms of the levels at which activities take place: while some voluntary activities are local in character, others are part of national or even multinational voluntary organisations. Studies of voluntary activity in the UK have found that the most common activities within the organised voluntary work sector include fundraising, running an event, serving on a committee and providing transport, while the most common areas for voluntary activity relate to sports and exercise, children's education, and health and welfare (Joseph Rowntree Foundation, 1991).

Voluntary work and paid work

Voluntary work has numerous connecting points with the paid work sector. The two are in fact often undertaken side by side (as in aspects of social service provision; see below). And, as MacDonald (1997: 113) discusses, working in the voluntary sector can provide the experience, skills, contacts and references necessary for voluntary workers to gain paid employment. Further, many voluntary jobs give rise to very similar feelings to those experienced in paid work: voluntary jobs can provide structure to people's lives just as paid work does and are sources of job satisfaction and individual fulfilment; at the same time, working voluntarily frequently leads to a time commitment that creates fatigue and stress among the volunteer workgroup akin to those felt among groups of workers in the paid work sector. Likewise, many voluntary jobs (like working as a volunteer for the Samaritans, for example) entail a great deal of emotion work, with the various outcomes that this can give rise to (see Chapter 7).

However, rather than attempt to consider all the many facets of the intersection between voluntary work and the paid work sector, it is possible to take one example to illustrate the broader argument concerning the relevance of this aspect of hidden work for the visible work sphere. Given its growing prominence in public debate in recent years, a useful example is that of the voluntary provision of care for someone who is elderly, sick or disabled. Historically, tending the sick and elderly has represented a major aspect of voluntary activity. Prior to the introduction of a welfare state, much of the tending of the old and infirm took place within the household and the community. The rise of State-funded care reduced (but by no means totally eliminated) this reliance on care from within the community.

In more recent years, however, various factors have once again increased the significance being placed on care provided within the community rather than by the State. One of these factors is the general increase in life expectancy which has taken place, resulting in a larger proportion of the population living into very old age. Estimates relating to Britain, for example, suggest that the proportion of the population over the age of 85 years may be 50 per cent higher by the year 2031 than it was in the early 1990s (Corti and Dex, 1995: 101). Second, as mentioned earlier, at the same time as the proportion of elderly people in the population is rising, the State (through legislation such as the NHS Community Care Act) has increased the emphasis placed on the self-provisioning of care needs by the families and others close to those requiring care, and by voluntary organisations, rather than care being dispensed directly by State-funded professional care facilities (Means and Smith, 1994: 118–20). A Department of Health report summed up its view on the importance of voluntary work in this area thus: 'The Department of Health believes that volunteers working alongside social service departments bring vital added value to the implementation of community care policies, supporting people to live independently in their own homes and participate in their local communities' (Department of Health, 1996: 1).

Clearly, caring for someone who is old, disabled or ill could, depending on the circumstances, be categorised as either domestic work or voluntary work. Attending to an infirm spouse in one's own home, for example, is part of many individuals' everyday domestic routine. On the other hand, many people provide care for someone in the latter's home, for example by paying regular visits to an elderly neighbour. This overlap of categories should not delay us unduly; as noted earlier, in practice many activities straddle boundaries within the overall hidden work sector. What is more important here is the relevance of caring for a broader understanding of work as a whole.

There are several issues arising from the relationship between the voluntary dispensing of care and the formal work sector. These include, for example, whether or not voluntary care activity undermines the role and status of those performing a care function as part of their paid employment, or whether a willingness among the public to perform some tasks voluntarily has restricted the growth of occupations which otherwise would have expanded to meet a greater demand for care provision. Probably the most important aspect of the interaction between caring and employment, however, is the potential impact which providing care has on the carer's own access to the labour market and their employment experience. It is clear that, in many cases, looking after a sick or elderly person is very time-consuming and significantly influences a carer's activity and career in the formal work sector. According to data from the British Household Panel Study (a regular survey of over five thousand households in Britain) in the early 1990s, almost one in seven adults was providing informal care for someone sick, disabled or elderly (Corti, Laurie and Dex, 1994; Corti and Dex, 1995: 101). Just under one-third of the carers were looking after someone in their own home, while two-thirds provided care for someone living elsewhere. While a higher proportion of carers were women (17 per cent of the female adult population), the proportion of men (12 per cent of the male adult population) providing care was nevertheless significant. Over a third (35 per cent) of all co-resident carers (those looking after someone in their own home) spent at least 50 hours per week on caring. Women spent more time on care than men, both inside and outside the household.

Given the amount of time devoted to providing care, it is only to be expected that this will impact significantly on carers' patterns of paid employment. This is indeed what Corti and her colleagues found (Corti, Laurie and Dex, 1994). For example, overall participation rates of women and men carers in the formal work sector were significantly lower than their counterparts not involved in caring. Further, among those carers in employment, the likelihood of working part-time rather than full-time was significantly higher. Carers were also more likely to occupy lower level jobs than their counterparts not involved in caring. Many involved in co-resident care in particular, indicated that family responsibilities had prevented them from either looking for a job, accepting a full-time job, or changing jobs. Caring responsibilities had also required many to leave paid employment altogether, or work fewer hours (Corti, Laurie and Dex, 1994: 28, 38). Such effects are not surprising given the time spent on caring. In the study by Corti and colleagues (1994: 37) for example, two-fifths of the male and female co-resident carers who held full-time jobs, also spent 20 hours or more a week on caring.

It is clear from studies of carers (see also for example, Arber and Ginn, 1995) the extent to which they are forced to forego employment opportunities, or change their working patterns to fit in with their caring responsibilities. In this respect, caring activity provides another illustration of the way in which hidden work impacts upon the nature and experience of work in the visible work sector.

Conclusion

Overall, probably as much work activity takes place outside the formal work sector as inside. This albeit brief examination of the dimensions of hidden work indicates how, for many, the realities of work are shaped by experiences away from 'visible' employment. What is more, these hidden work realities are clearly highly diverse: the woman at home caring for a young family; the unemployed person working voluntarily to maintain some routine and a sense of purpose; the older individual discouraged from seeking paid employment, using time available for house repairs and DIY; the daughter or son working part-time while at the same time caring for an elderly parent; the individual who secures an income through illegal activity of one sort or another. The range of activities is as great, if not greater than the diversity of work experiences in the visible work sector.

Each of these areas of hidden work deserves greater recognition and more careful analysis to reflect their significance in many people's lives. In this chapter, it has been possible only to touch upon the diverse realities of hidden work. What is clear even from this brief examination, however, is not only the scale and importance of hidden work *per se*, but also the degree to which the hidden and visible work spheres interrelate. Indeed, so extensive is this degree of inter-relatedness that any analysis of one sphere cannot be satisfactorily undertaken without due recognition being given to the significance of the other. Further, the diversity of hidden work adds considerably to the overall diversity in work experiences and work realities. This theme of diversity is one that has been evident throughout the book and is a theme we comment upon further in the concluding chapter.

What do *you* think?

This chapter has highlighted a number of types of hidden work.

From your own experience, either of jobs that you have undertaken yourself or have personal knowledge of, give an example of each of the forms of hidden work discussed, preferably using examples that have not already been discussed in the

▶

▶ chapter. To remind you, the different categories of hidden work that have been discussed are:

- Concealed work   – deviant work
                    – non-declared work
- Unrecognised work – domestic work
                    – voluntary work

13 Conclusion

KEY CONCEPTS

- Change
- Continuity
- Informality
- Sub-cultures

- Rationality
- Counter-rationalities
- Complexity

CHAPTER AIM

To bring together the main themes from the earlier chapters and draw some broader conclusions about the realities of work.

LEARNING OUTCOMES

After reading and thinking about the material contained in this chapter, you will be able to:

1 identify the importance of both change and continuity in the nature of work;

2 recognise the importance of sub-cultures that exist alongside formal management structures;

3 understand the dual existence of management rationalities and employee counter-rationalities within the workplace;

4 appreciate the complexity of work behaviour and the variety of work experience.

Introduction

This exploration of the realities of work has taken us through a century of industrial history and fifty years of empirical research, a variety of sectors in differing economic and political contexts, a range of work settings and processes, and a plethora of experiences and understandings of working. The constant finding has been one of plurality: in theories, research methods and analyses as well as results, observations and understandings. This is a valuable conclusion in its own right. It alerts us to the importance of acknowledging that different explanations are possible for the same phenomenon, because it is experienced and interpreted differently. In turn, this allows us to draw conclusions about four themes that have emerged from foregoing chapters:

- change and continuity;
- informality and sub-cultures;
- managerial rationalities and employee counter-rationalities;
- analytical complexity.

Change and continuity

Learning outcome 1

Identify the importance of both change and continuity in the nature of work.

An abiding theme in the study of work is the extent to which there has been a change from, or continuity with the past. It has already been observed how some commentators have delineated one stage of societal development from another: for example, the theories of industrial and post-industrial society (Chapters 3 and 8) or Fordist, neo-Fordist and post-Fordist production (Chapter 6). Others have argued that the changes are in fact so great as to require a new paradigm that represents not only a marked economic, political, institutional, cultural and social shift, but a quantum leap in the way we understand the world: a leap from modernist to postmodernist conceptions of the world (for a full discussion see Harvey, 1989; Lyon, 1994; also, for an analysis linked to human resource management, see Legge, 1995: 286–328).

In all the preceding chapters, however, what has been evident has been a mixture of both change *and* continuity. It has been shown that in the workplace there have been new theories, ideas, technologies, and practices to replace the old ones. But these have developed alongside patterns and work arrangements that continue to reflect important resonance with the past. Table 13.1 illustrates some of the principal areas of change and continuity that have been explored in the preceding chapters. It suggests how change in one aspect of work can produce continuity in another. Indeed, the overall extent to which work in contemporary society can be characterised as being radically different from, or fundamentally similar to, what has gone before depends largely upon which themes are being addressed:

- a focus on the features illustrated by the left-hand side of Table 13.1 would lead to the conclusion that work has undergone notable change;
- a focus on the right-hand side would suggest a pattern of continuity.

Table 13.1 Change and continuity in work

Notable CHANGE	but also CONTINUITY
New patterns of production and consumption	Persistence of the work ethic
Rise of the service sector	Continued existence of routine, boring jobs
Technological change with some growth of high-skilled jobs	New types of low-skill, low-discretion jobs
Increase of emotion work	Undervaluing of social abilities as skill
More women in the labour market (feminisation)	Gendered division of labour and unfair discrimination
New forms of work (flexibility) and working time patterns	Traditional working methods and forms of control
New management initiatives for work intensification	Traditional methods of control and reliance on employee consent
Emergence of post-Fordist organisations	Taylorist/Fordist organisations remain
Decline in trade union density	Desire for collective representation
Increasing importance of knowledge workers	Management techniques for appropriating 'knowledge'
Increasing globalisation and the emergence of an information society	Social division between the economically advantaged and disadvantaged

It seems to us that one of the important realities of work that has changed significantly is the growing fragmentation and uncertainty of much work experience, with an increasing proportion of jobs subject to greater job insecurity, less permanent contracts, and more variable work arrangements. A weakening of trade union influence and a widespread political reluctance to offset this by greater statutory protection of the employed workforce, have acted to bolster the power of employers. In turn, this has allowed the latter to shift a greater share of the burden of market risk, and requirements for flexibility, onto the shoulders of employees. Thus, when faced with competing expectations of shareholders and workforce, the strength of one and the lessening power of the other have meant that management have increasingly been able to respond to market and financial pressures through redundancies, plant closures and increased work demands, rather than through longer-term market and innovation strategies (see Chapter 2).

Just as increasing employment fragmentation, insecurity and greater work pressures constitute significant changes, there are equally important realities that demonstrate continuity: among the most notable is continued unfair discrimination within labour markets and employing organisations. This discrimination manifests itself in a number of ways but it particularly means that some groups have greater access to higher-level, more prestigious, better-paid jobs, than others. It is evident that for many in the workforce, the reality of their work experience is one of inequitable treatment, compared with groups which have been more favoured in the labour market. The question of discrimination was addressed directly in Chapter 10, but at other points in the book too, the way that social arrangements have favoured some groups rather than others, has been clear. Three of these points were the discussion of:

- how the notion of skill is, in important part, socially constructed (Chapter 5);
- the comparative lack of skill attributed to jobs involving emotional labour, particularly in comparison with jobs perceived as more 'rational' in character (Chapter 7);
- the ways that the work performed in households importantly influences access to, and success within, the paid employment sector (Chapter 12).

In each of these, the different realities for women, compared to their male counterparts, have been emphasised. Women are the ones holding skills which have disproportionately failed to be recognised as deserving skilled status; women are disproportionately involved in emotional labour jobs, where the content of those jobs tends to receive only limited recognition; and it remains women who carry a disproportionate share of responsibility for household tasks, to the detriment of the nature of their involvement in paid employment. This continuing difference in the realities of work of men and women is made more salient by the increasing feminisation of the workforce (see Chapter 2).

EXERCISE 13.1

What do *you* think?

Find an example of a theorist or commentator in any of the previous chapters who is arguing:

(a) the case for change; or

(b) the case for continuity.

For each example, summarise their arguments in a few sentences, and explain whether you find their ideas convincing.

Informality and sub-cultures

A common theme that emerges from various chapters is how employees cope with the realities of work by developing informal rules and a shared identity. Although work can require individual as well as collective behaviours, there exist underpinning

Learning outcome 2

Recognise the importance of sub-cultures that exist alongside formal management structures.

values, which are shared and negotiated collectively, and from which norms of informal behaviour develop. In other words, the broad patterns of behaviour are framed within negotiated orders which constitute workplace sub-cultures. In part, this negotiated order is accomplished through forms of collective representation (Chapter 11) but the notion also encapsulates a range of informal workplace experience. A sub-culture is characterised by sets of meanings that are shared by a particular group, and reinforced through beliefs, values and norms. Newcomers must learn the norms of behaviour and in so doing begin to understand the meanings and become imbued with the values and beliefs, eventually internalising them. This concept of sub-culture is important because it highlights the need to treat organisations as pluralist rather than unitary entities: a collection of sub-cultures rather than a single culture. In this sense, there may be a formal organisational culture proclaiming common values and beliefs, but behind this façade, there are likely to be different informal sub-cultures reflecting varying values and beliefs.

Over a period of time, strong sub-cultures may become embedded into the work organisation. It was noted in Chapter 5 the impact this has on conceptions of skill, particularly perpetuating assumptions about what constitutes men's and women's work. Similarly, sub-cultures may have a powerful impact (either positive or negative) on the process of discrimination at work (explored in Chapter 10) by promoting a collective understanding of fairness and unfairness in the treatment of various individuals and groups by managers. More generally, it was noted how the economic necessity of both visible work (Chapter 3) and hidden work (Chapter 12) was guided by a moral dimension, which itself often reflects dominant cultural values and beliefs.

Sub-cultures represent collective interests that are *different* from the formal management ideology and structures within an organisation. This arises from the pluralistic nature of all organisations. However, the types of informal, unofficial behaviours associated with coping with alienation (Chapter 9), time-discipline (Chapter 4) and stress from emotional labour (Chapter 7), are themselves often regulated by the sub-culture; in turn, this assists in the production of consent, thus helping to obscure the exploitative nature of the capitalist labour process. The sub-culture provides the mechanism for this informal regulation, so cannot really be construed as acting against profitable production; in this sense such sub-cultures are not usually counter-capitalism. They may perhaps be seen as counter-managerial in that they challenge aspects of control, but even then management prerogative is not opposed.

Learning outcome 3

Understand the dual existence of management rationalities and employee counter-rationalities within the workplace.

Rationalities and counter-rationalities

Modern texts on managing tend to paint too uniform a view of work and workers, and by extension, too uniform a view of what constitutes 'effective' management. This view, we believe, in turn reflects an over-developed sense of the omnipotence of managerial rationality pervading the workplace: that is, an assumption that the rules as defined by management are the ones strictly adhered to by the workforce. What has been demonstrated throughout the book, however, is the simultaneous existence of a strong workers' counter-rationality, reflecting the different interests which management and workforce bring to the workplace. Put simply, for management it is the *output* from work which is the central issue, while for the workforce the *process* of working is an end in itself, as well as the main means of gaining income. As discussed in Chapter 3, notwithstanding any increased emphasis on consumerism and the construction of identity around consumption rather than production ('I am what I buy', rather than 'I am what I do') workers continue to go to work for more than just money. The sheer amount of time spent working, and thus the centrality of work in the majority of adults' waking hours, means that the experience of work, and the process of working, remain important. What this reinforces is how the strategies that workers adopt contribute in various ways towards a counter-rationality, and towards making work as 'humane' as possible: by easing workloads, breaking up a monotonous day, creating fun, generating interaction, building up group identities, maintaining self-esteem.

As we have also seen, in the main these counter-rationalities function not only for workers but also indirectly for management, and for the maintenance of capitalist wage relations. For in ways much discussed in industrial sociology, by challenging and subverting the margins of managerial rationality, workers maintain a broader consent to the core of that rationality. Rarely is there evidence of counter-rationalities going beyond fairly confined boundaries: the occasional unauthorised absence, the limited time taken up by practical jokes, the minor deviations from management's requirements over emotional labour. These do not add up to a fundamental challenge to, or rejection of, a system. They represent a way of making that system more acceptable and creating a feeling that workers can exercise a measure of control over managerial definitions of work reality. Therefore, workers' counter-rationality does not typically represent a fundamental challenge to managerial authority. Workers may 'misbehave', but they do so, for the most part, within tacitly agreed, and narrow limits.

This is not to say that such behaviour remains unproblematic for management. We can see how, for example, in various ways management are seeking to increase the utilisation of working time (see Chapter 4). But, we can also see the *limited* nature of these managerial attempts to tighten up organisational regimes. Such a limitation is born partly out of a recognition that the costs (for example, in terms of worker morale) of suppressing all 'indulgences' are probably greater than the sum of any ensuing benefits. The limited assault on employees' counter-strategies is probably also born out of an awareness that a complete suppression is simply not possible.

The foregoing comments diverge from a view of the workplace as a site where surveillance and compliance have reached near total levels. For the most part, such workplaces would seem to remain a small minority. Most workplaces appear to operate not on a basis of management seeking total and continuous conformity with detailed sets of prescribed rules governing all aspects of behaviour at work, but rather more of a system of negotiated order, whereby tacit agreements are established as to what levels of deviation from formal rules are allowed. These levels are not fixed or immutable – customs and practices are subject to modification over time – and periodically give rise to tension, as each side attempts to shift the boundary or respond to the other's attempts to shift it. But the complex requirement that capital has from wage labour – the need for consent as well as control, for active co-operation rather than merely passive compliance in translating labour power into productive labour – gives rise to a management-workforce relationship based on negotiation and a tension between the two different interest groups and their twin rationalities, rather than the uniform imposition of a dominant rationality.

EXERCISE 13.2

What do *you* think?

Drawing on the arguments and issues raised in earlier chapters:

1 Justify why is it important to take into account the perspective of the employee when trying to understand work.

2 Explain how the management of employees could be made more effective by taking closer account of employee experiences of, and attitudes towards, work.

Learning outcome 4

Appreciate the complexity of work behaviour.

Analytical complexity

It is a truism that life is complex, so why should it be presumed that working life is simple? Why do so many managers continue to believe in the quick-fix or the latest buzz-word? Why do students seek neatly-packaged answers? Why do management texts produce six-step solutions to ubiquitous problems? Why do lecturers resort to key-word acronyms to explain a multitude of varied human behaviour? It is because they are all in search of 'the simple answer', when the real answer is: there is no simple answer. Engaging with complexity is time-consuming, costly, confusing and frequently disillusioning, yet it is the only satisfactory way of exploring work.

If there are no simple solutions to complex problems, then either the complexity must be confronted, or the problem redefined to simplify the challenge. Frequently, academics employ the latter method, but with varying degrees of success. To analyse helps to understand the problem, but not necessarily to find a solution. For example, Chapter 5 revealed how different ways of 'measuring' skill were used by different researchers. None of the methods was without its limitations, and each led to different conclusions about how the concept of skill should be understood. The solution (if it can be described as such) was to examine the complexity of the concept, and an attempt to integrate all the approaches in an effort to arrive at a multi-faceted 'measure' of skill: and ultimately, an explanation so complex that it would be of virtually no 'practical' use in the workplace. It is this last point that alerts us to a particular problem with accepting complexity: it does not provide what the market wants. Because people (managers especially) want simple solutions and explanations there is a pressure to produce them. Complexity is simplified, the nostrum emerges and the quick-fix solution is invented. So, it is of little wonder that the realities of work invariably fail to match up to the descriptions included or implied in many management texts.

Engaging with complexity also requires a more open-minded approach to the nature of problems. If a person is looking for 'the logical solution', in the same way as, for example, Taylor (Chapter 6) believed that scientific management was the answer to all productivity problems, then the mind is closed to the equally logical possibility that there is no single solution. Indeed, the emergent picture is that the realities of work are characterised by contradiction, dilemma and paradox. For example, it was discussed in Chapter 9 how the contradictions embedded in the capitalist labour process produce the dilemma of control for managers, and how, through the process of 'making out', employees paradoxically consent to their own subordination and exploitation. Throughout the analysis, the importance of contradictory theories and interpretation has surfaced: for example, the question of the demise or survival of the work ethic (Chapter 3); the theses of deskilling, upskilling or reskilling work (Chapter 6); the significance of emotion work (Chapter 7); the forms of survival strategy to cope with alienation (Chapter 9); and the liberal, radical and reactionary perspectives on equal opportunities (Chapter 10).

By acknowledging and confronting complexity throughout the chapters, it has been possible to demonstrate the richness and variety of the experience of work. Moreover, the pluralist approach we have taken has meant that these complex realities can be explored without the discussion flitting through a postmodern carnival or being constrained by a structuralist prison.

EXERCISE 13.3

What do *you* think?

1 How does a pluralist approach help in analysing the complexity of contemporary work? Use examples from previous chapters to support your arguments.

2 What are the limitations of such an approach?

A final word

The different chapters have revealed the diversity of work experience. It is a diversity born partly out of the multitude of different contexts within which work takes place, together with the very many occupations and tasks that people perform at work, and the different work schedules and contractual arrangements that employees are engaged on. However, at the same time, the diversity also derives from the different ways that people construct meaning and identity in their roles as workers: the different values they attach to work, the ways they behave and interact at work, and the different strategies they employ to adjust to, and ameliorate the pressures of work in contemporary industrial society.

There are no signs that this diversity is set to diminish. On the contrary, the continued introduction of more varied employment contracts and work schedules, the expanding technological base of many economic sectors, the changing knowledge intensity and skill requirements of work, and the range of activities that comprise particularly the expanding service sector, all point to the continued prominence of diversity in the experience of work. Identifying and analysing this complexity will thus remain a central task in the study and understanding of the future realities of work.

Bibliography

Abbott, A. (1988) *The System of Professions*, Chicago: University of Chicago Press.

Abiala, K. (1999) 'Customer orientation and sales situations: variations in interactive service work', *Acta Sociologica*, 42 (3): 207–22.

Adam, B. (1990) *Time and Social Theory*, Cambridge: Polity.

Adams, R. J. (1974) 'Solidarity, self-interest and the unionisation differential between Europe and North America', *Relations Industrielles*, 29 (3): 497–512.

Adkins, L. (1995) *Gendered Work: Sexuality, Family and the Labour Market*, Milton Keynes: Open University Press.

Aglietta, M. (1979) *A Theory of Capitalist Regulation*, London: New Left Books.

Ali, A. (1988) 'Scaling an Islamic work ethic', *The Journal of Social Psychology*, 128 (5): 575–83.

Allen, J. and Henry, N. (1996) 'Fragments of industry and employment', in R. Crompton, D. Gallie and K. Purcell (eds) *Changing Forms of Employment*, London: Routledge, pp. 65–82.

Allen, S. and Macey, M. (1990) 'Race and ethnicity in the European context', *British Journal of Sociology*, 41 (3): 375–93.

Angle, H. L. and Perry, J. L. (1986) 'Dual commitment and labor-management relationship climates', *Academy of Management Journal*, 29: 31–50.

Anthias, F. (1992) 'Connecting "race" and ethnic phenomena', *Sociology*, 26 (3): 421–38.

Anthias, F. and Yuval-Davis, N. (1992) *Racialized Boundaries*, London: Routledge.

Anthony, P. D. (1977) *The Ideology of Work*, London: Tavistock.

Applebaum, H. A. (1981) *Royal Blue: The Culture of Construction Workers*, New York: Holt, Rinehart and Winston.

Arber, S. and Ginn, J. (1995) 'Gender differences in the relationship between paid employment and informal care', *Work, Employment and Society*, 9 (3): 445–7.

Armstrong, P. (1988) 'Labour and monopoly capital', in R. Hyman and W. Streeck (eds) *New Technology and Industrial Relations*, Oxford: Blackwell, pp. 143–59.

Arrowsmith, J. and Sisson, K. (2000) 'Managing working time', in S. Bach and K. Sisson (eds) *Personnel Management*, Third edition, Oxford: Blackwell, pp. 287–313.

Ashforth, B. and Humphrey, R. (1993) 'Emotional labour in service roles: the influence of identity', *Academy of Management Review*, 18 (1): 88–115.

Ashforth, B. E. and Tomiuk, M. (2000) 'Emotional labour and authenticity: views from service agents', in S. Fineman (ed.) *Emotion in Organizations*, Second edition, London: Sage, pp. 184–203.

Atkinson, J. (1984) 'Manpower strategies for flexible organisation', *Personnel Management*, August: 28–31.

Attewell, P. (1990) 'What is skill?', *Work and Occupations*, 17 (4): 422–48.

Bacchi, C. (1990) *Same Difference: Feminism and Sexual Difference*, Sydney: Allen & Unwin.

Bach, S. and Sisson, K. (2000) 'Personnel management in perspective', in S. Bach and K. Sisson (eds) *Personnel Management*, Third edition, Oxford: Blackwell, pp. 3–42.

Bacon N. and Blyton, P. (2001) 'Exploring employee responses to 'deadly combinations' of HRM initiatives', mimeo, Cardiff Business School.

Bain, G. S. (1970) *The Growth of White Collar Unionism*, Oxford: Clarendon.

Bain, G. S. and Elsheikh, F. (1976) *Union Growth and the Business Cycle*, Oxford: Blackwell.

Baltes, B. B., Briggs, T. E., Huff, J. W., Wright, J. A. and Neuman, G. A. (1999) 'Flexible and compressed workweek schedules: a meta-analysis of their effects on work-related criteria', *Journal of Applied Psychology*, 84 (4): 496–513.

Bank of England (2000) 'The international environment', *Bank of England Quarterly Bulletin*, August: 233–46.

Bargaining Report (2001) 'Teleworking: who wants to telework?' *Bargaining Report*, No. 212, January: 7–10.

Barley, S. R. (1996) 'Technicians in the workplace: ethnographic evidence for bringing work into organization studies' *Administrative Science Quarterly*, 41 (3): 404–41.

Barney, J. (1991) 'Firm resources and sustained competitive advantage', *Journal of Management*, 17 (1): 99–120.

Batstone, E., Gourlay, S., Levie, H. and Moore, R. (1987) *New Technology and the Process of Labour Regulation*, Oxford: Clarendon.

Baxter, J. and Western, M. (1998) 'Satisfaction with housework: examining the paradox', *Sociology*, 32 (1): 101–20.

Beauvais, L. L., Scholl, R. W., and Cooper, E. A. (1990) 'Dual commitment among unionised faculty: a longitudinal investigation', *Human Relations*, 44: 175–92.

Becker, G. (1964) *Human Capital*, New York: National Bureau of Economic Research.

Becker, H. (1963) *Outsiders: Studies in the Sociology of Deviance*, New York: The Free Press.

Beechey, V. (1982) 'The sexual division of labour and the labour process: a critical assessment of Braverman', in S. Wood (ed.) *The Degradation of Work?*, London: Hutchinson, pp. 54–73.

Bell, D. (1973) *The Coming of Post-Industrial Society*, New York: Basic Books.

Bell, D. (1976) *The Cultural Contradictions of Capitalism*, London: Heinemann.

Bell, D. (1980) 'The social framework of the information society', in T. Forester (ed.) *The Microelectronics Revolution*, Oxford: Blackwell, pp. 500–49.

Berg, P. (1999) 'The effects of high performance work practices on job satisfaction in the United States steel industry', *Relations Industrielles*, 54 (1): 111–35.

Beynon, H. (1973) *Working for Ford*, Harmondsworth: Penguin.

Blackburn, R. and Prandy, K. (1965) 'White-collar unionisation: a conceptual framework', *British Journal of Sociology*, 16: 111–22.

Blackler, F. (1995) 'Knowledge, knowledge work and organizations: an overview and interpretation', *Organization Studies*, 16 (6): 1021–46.

Blackler, F., Reed, M. and Whitaker, A. (1993) 'Editorial introduction: knowledge workers and contemporary organizations', *Journal of Management Studies*, 30 (6): 851–62.

Blauner, R. (1964) *Alienation and Freedom*, Chicago: University of Chicago Press.

Blyton, P. (1985) *Changes in Working Time: An International Review*, London: Croom Helm.

Blyton, P. (1989) 'Working population and employment', in R. Bean (ed.) *International Labour Statistics*, London: Routledge, pp. 18–51.

Blyton, P. (1992) 'The search for workforce flexibility', in B. Towers (ed.) *Handbook of Human Resource Management*, Oxford: Blackwell, pp. 295–318.

Blyton, P. (1994) 'Working hours', in K. Sisson (ed.) *Personnel Management*, 2nd edition, Oxford: Blackwell, pp. 495–526.

Blyton, P. (1995) *The Development of Annual Working Hours in the United Kingdom*, Geneva: International Labour Organization.

Blyton, P., Martinez Lucio, M., McGurk, J. and Turnbull, P. (2001) 'Globalization and trade union strategy: industrial restructuring and human resource management in the international civil aviation industry', *International Journal of Human Resource Management*, 12 (3): 445–63.

Blyton, P., Nicholson, N. and Ursell (1981) 'Job status and white collar members' union activity', *Journal of Occupational Psychology*, 54 (1): 33–45.

Blyton, P. and Trinczek, R. (1995) 'Working time flexibility and annual hours', *European Industrial Relations Review*, No. 260, September: 13–14.

Blyton, P. and Turnbull, P. (1998) *The Dynamics of Employee Relations*, Second edition, Basingstoke: Macmillan.

Boland, R. J. and Hoffman, R. (1983) 'Humor in a machine shop', in L. Pondy, P. Frost, G. Morgan and T. Dandridge (eds) *Organizational Symbolism*, Greenwich, CT: JAI Press, pp. 187–98.

Boles, J. and Garbin, A. P. (1974) 'The strip club and stripper-customer patterns of interaction', *Sociology and Social Research*, 58 (1): 136–44.

Booth, A. (1983) 'A reconsideration of trade union growth in the United Kingdom', *British Journal of Industrial Relations*, 21 (3): 379–91.

Bosworth, D. (1994) 'Shiftwork in the UK: evidence from the LFS', *Applied Economics*, 26 (6): 617–26.

Boyer, R. (ed.) (1988) *The Search For Labour Market Flexibility*, Oxford: Clarendon.

Bradley, H. (1989) *Men's Work, Women's Work*, Oxford: Blackwell.

Bradley, H., Erickson, M., Stephenson, C. and Williams, S. (2000) *Myths at Work*, Cambridge: Polity.

Bradney, P. (1957) 'The joking relationship in industry', *Human Relations*, 10 (2): 179–87.

Brah, A. (1986) 'Unemployment and racism: Asian youth on the dole', in S. Allen, A. Watson, K. Purcell and S. Wood (eds) *The Experience of Unemployment*, London: Macmillan, pp. 61–78.

Bratton, J. (1992) *Japanization at Work*, London: Macmillan.

Braverman, H. (1974) *Labor and Monopoly Capital*, New York: Monthly Review Press.

Brennan, J. and McGeevor, P. (1987) *Employment of Graduates from Ethnic Minorities*, London: Commission for Racial Equality.

Brewis, J. and Linstead, S. (2000a) *Sex, Work and Sex Work: Eroticizing Organization*, London: Routledge.

Brewis, J. and Linstead, S. (2000b) 'The worst thing is the screwing (1): consumption and the management of identity in sex work', *Gender, Work and Organization*, 7 (2): 84–97.

Broadbent, J., Dietrich, M. and Roberts, J. (1997) *The End of the Professions? The Restructuring of Professional Work*, London: Routledge.

Brown, C. and Gay, P. (1985) *Racial Discrimination: 17 Years after the Act*, London: Policy Studies Institute.

Brown, J. S. (1991) 'Research that invents the corporation', *Harvard Business Review*, January-February: 102–111.

Browning, H. L. and Singelmann, J. (1978) 'The transformation of the US labour force', *Politics and Society*, 8 (3): 481–509.

Brunhes, B. (1989) 'Labour flexibility in enterprises: a comparison of firms in four European countries' in Organisation for Economic Cooperation and Development (ed.) *Labour Market Flexibility: Trends in Enterprises*, Paris: OECD, pp. 11–36.

Bryson, A. (1999) 'Are unions good for industrial relations?', in R. Jowell, J. Curtice, A. Park and K. Thomson (eds) *British Social Attitudes: The 16th Report*, Aldershot: Dartmouth.

Bryson, A. and McKay, S. (1997) 'What about the workers?', in R. Jowell, J. Curtice, A. Park, L. Brook, K. Thomson and C. Bryson (eds) *British Social Attitudes: the 14th Report. The End of Conservative Values?*, Aldershot: Ashgate, pp. 23–48.

Buchanan, D. A. (1986) 'Management objectives in technical change', in D. Knights and H. Willmott (eds) *Managing the Labour Process*, Aldershot: Gower, pp. 67–84.

Buchanan, D. and Boddy. D. (1983) *Organisations in the Computer Age: Technological Imperatives and Strategic Choice*, Aldershot: Gower.

Burawoy, M. (1979) *Manufacturing Consent*, Chicago: University of Chicago Press.

Burawoy, M. (1985) *The Politics of Production*, London: Verso.

Burchell, B., Elliott, J., Rubery, J. and Wilkinson, F. (1994) 'Management and employee perceptions of skill', in R. Penn, M. Rose and J. Rubery (eds) *Skill and Occupational Change*, Oxford: Oxford University Press, pp. 159–89.

Burchell, B. J., Day, D., Hudson, M., Lapido, D., Mankelow, R., Nolan, J. P., Reed, H., Wichert, I. C. and Wilkinson, F. (1999) *Job Insecurity and Work Intensification: Flexibility and the Changing Boundaries of Work*, York: Joseph Rowntree Foundation.

Burris, B. H. (1993) *Technocracy at Work*, Albany: State University of New York Press.

Butcher, S. and Hart, D. (1995) 'An analysis of working time 1979–1994', *Employment Gazette*, May: 211–22.

Cappelli, P. (1995) 'Rethinking employment', *British Journal of Industrial Relations*, 33 (4): 563–602.

Cappelli, P. (1999) 'Career jobs are dead', *California Management Review*, 42: 146–67.

Carlzon, J. (1987) *Moments of Truth*, New York: Harper and Row.

Carpentier, J. and Cazamian, P. (1977) *Nightwork*, Geneva: International Labour Organisation.

Carruth, A. and Disney, R. (1988) 'Where have two million trade union members gone?', *Economica*, 55 (1): 1–19.

Cashmore, E. (1996) *Dictionary of Race and Ethnic Relations*, London: Routledge.

Castells, M. (1998) *The Information Age: Economy, Society and Culture* (Three volumes) Oxford: Blackwell.

Castells, M. (2000) 'Materials for an exploratory theory of the network society', *British Journal of Sociology*, 51 (1): 5–24.

Cavendish, R. (1982) *Women on the Line*, London: Routledge.

Chadeau, A. (1985) 'Measuring household activities: some international comparisons', *Review of Income* and Wealth, 31 (3): 237–53.

Charles, N. (1986) 'Women and trade unions' in Feminist Review (ed.) *Waged Work*, London: Virago, pp. 160–85.

Child, J. (1972) 'Organisation structure, environment and performance: the role of strategic choice', *Sociology*, 6 (1): 1–22.

Child, J. (1984) *Organisation: A Guide to Problems and Practice*, Second edition, London: Harper and Row.

Child, J. (1985) 'Managerial strategies, new technology and the labour process', in D. Knights, H. Willmott and D. Collinson (eds) *Job Redesign*, Aldershot: Gower, pp. 107–41.

Child, J. (1997) 'Strategic choice in the analysis of action, structure, organizations and environment: retrospect and prospect', *Organization Studies*, 18 (1): 43–76.

Clarke, T. (1989) 'Imaginative flexibility in production engineering: the Volvo Uddevalla plant', paper presented to Employment Research Unit Conference, Cardiff Business School.

Clausing, K. A. (2000) 'Does multinational activity displace trade?', *Economic Inquiry*, 38 (2): 190–206.

Clawson, D. and Fantasia, R. (1983) 'Beyond Burawoy: the dialectics of conflict and consent on the shop floor', *Theory and Society*, 12: 671–80.

Cockburn, C. (1983) *Brothers: Male Dominance and Technological Change*, London: Pluto Press.

Cockburn, C. (1985) *Machinery of Dominance*, London: Pluto.

Cockburn, C. (1986) 'The material of male power' in Feminist Review (ed.) *Waged Work*, London: Virago, pp. 93–113.

Cockburn, C. (1989) 'Equal opportunities: the short and long agenda', *Industrial Relations Journal*, 20 (3): 213–25.

Cockburn, C. (1991) *In the Way of Women*, Basingstoke: Macmillan.

Cohen, S. and Taylor, L. (1976) *Escape Attempts*, Harmondsworth: Penguin.

Colling, T. and Dickens, L. (2001) 'Gender equality and trade unions: a new basis for mobilisation' in M. Noon and E. Ogbonna (eds) *Equality, Diversity and Disadvantage in Employment*, Basingstoke: Palgrave, pp. 136–55.

Collins, D. (1997) 'Knowledge work or working knowledge? Ambiguity and confusion in the analysis of the "knowledge age"', *Employee Relations*, 19 (1): 38–50.

Collinson, D. (1988) '"Engineering humour": masculinity, joking and conflict in shop-floor relations', *Organization Studies*, 9 (2): 181–99.

Collinson, D. (1992) *Managing the Shopfloor*, Berlin: de Gruyter.

Collinson, D. and Knights, D. (1986) '"Men only": theories and practices of job segregation in insurance' in D. Knights and H. Willmott (eds) *Gender and the Labour Process*, London: Sage, pp. 140–78.

Construction (1999) 'Building: purging the industry of racism', May.

Cooper, C. (1996) 'Hot under the collar', *The Times Higher Education Supplement*, 21 June: 12.

Corti, L. and Dex, S. (1995) 'Informal carers and employment' *Employment Gazette*, March: 101–7.

Corti, L., Laurie, H. and Dex, S. (1994) *Caring and Employment*, Employment Department Research Series No. 39, London: HMSO.

Cox, J. (1998) 'An introduction to Marx's theory of alienation', *International Socialism Journal*, 79: 41–62.

Cressey, P. and MacInnes, J. (1980) 'Voting for Ford: industrial democracy and the control of labour', *Capital and Class*, 11: 5–33.

Crompton, R. (1990) 'Professions in the current context', *Work, Employment and Society*, Special issue: 147–66.

Cross, M. (1987) 'Equality of opportunity and inequality of outcome: the MSC, ethnic minorities and training policy', in R. Jenkins and J. Solomos (eds) *Racism and Equal Opportunity Policies in the 1980s*, Cambridge: Cambridge University Press, pp. 73–92.

Cross, M. (1988) 'Changes in working practices in UK manufacturing 1981–88', *Industrial Relations Review and Report*, no. 415: 2–10.

Cross, M., Wrench, J. and Barnett, S. (1990) *Ethnic Minorities and the Careers Service*, Research paper no. 73, London: Department of Employment.

Crowther, S. and Garrahan, P. (1988) 'Corporate power and the local economy', *Industrial Relations Journal*, 19 (1): 51–9.

Crozier, M. (1964) *The Bureaucratic Phenomenon*, London: Tavistock.

Crusco, A. H. and Wetzel, C. G. (1984) 'The Midas touch: the effects of interpersonal touch on restaurant tipping', *Personality and Social Psychology Bulletin*, 10 (4): 512–17.

Cully, M. and Woodland, S. (1998) 'Trade union membership and recognition 1996–7', *Labour Market Trends*, 106 (7): 353–64.

Cully, M., Woodland, S., O'Reilly, A. and Dix, G. (2000) *Britain at Work*, London: Routledge.

Cunnison, S. and Stageman, J. (1995) *Feminizing the Unions*, Aldershot: Avebury.

Dale, I. and Kerr, J. (1995) 'Small and medium sized enterprises: their numbers and importance to employment', *Labour Market Trends*, December: 461–5.

Danford, A. (1998) 'Work organisation inside Japanese firms in South Wales: a break from Taylorism?' in P. Thompson and C. Warhurst (eds) *Workplaces of the Future*, Basingstoke: Macmillan, pp. 40–64.

Davies, S. (1990) 'Inserting gender into Burawoy's theory of the labour process', *Work, Employment and Society*, 4 (3): 391–406.

Davis Smith, J. (1992) *Volunteering: Widening Horizons in the Third Age*, Dunfermline: The Carnegie UK Trust.

de Witte, M. and Steijn, B. (2000) 'Automation, job content and underemployment', *Work, Employment and Society*, 14 (2): 245–64.

Dean, L. R. (1954) 'Union activity and dual loyalty', *Industrial and Labor Relations Review*, 12: 526–36.

Deery, S. J. and Mahony, A. (1994) 'Temporal flexibility: management strategies and employee preferences in the retail industry', *Journal of Industrial Relations*, 36 (3): 332–52.

Deery, S. J., Iverson, R. D. and Erwin, P. J. (1994) 'Predicting organizational and union commitment: the effect of industrial relations climate', *British Journal of Industrial Relations*, 32 (4): 581–97.

Delbridge, R. (1998) *Life on the Line in Contemporary Manufacturing*, Oxford: OUP.

Delbridge, R. and Turnbull, P. (1992) 'Human resource maximisation: the management of labour in just-in-time manufacturing systems', in P. Blyton and P. Turnbull (eds) *Reassessing Human Resource Management*, London: Sage, pp. 56–73.

Delbridge, R., Turnbull, P. and Wilkinson, B. (1992) 'Pushing back the frontiers: management control and work intensification under JIT/TQM factory regimes', *New Technology, Work and Employment*, 7 (2): 97–106.

Deming, W. E. (1982) *Quality, Productivity and Competitive Position*, Cambridge, MA: MIT Press.

Denman, J. and McDonald, P. (1996) 'Unemployment statistics from 1881 to the present day', *Labour Market Trends*, January: 5–18.

Department for Education and Employment (1995a) 'Changes to the coverage of the monthly count of claimant unemployment', *Labour Market Trends*, November: 398–400.

Department for Education and Employment (1995b) 'New developments in the pattern of claimant unemployment in the United Kingdom', *Employment Gazette*, September: 351–8.

Department of Health (1996) *Working Alongside Volunteers: Promoting the Role of Volunteers in Community Care*, London: Department of Health.

Devi, S. (2000) 'Sex in the City' *The Business FT Weekend Magazine*, 8 January: pp. 14–18.

Dex, S. (1983) 'Recurrent unemployment in young black and white males', *Industrial Relations Journal*, 14 (1): 41–9.

Dickens, L. (1995) 'UK part-time employees and the law – recent and potential developments', *Gender, Work and Organization*, 2 (4): 207–15.

Dickens, L. (2000) 'Still wasting resources? Equality in employment', in S. Bach and K. Sisson (eds) *Personnel Management*, Third edition, Oxford: Blackwell, pp. 137–69.

Ditton, J. (1977) *Part-Time Crime: An Ethnography of Fiddling and Pilferage*, London: Macmillan.

Ditton, J. (1979) 'Baking time', *Sociological Review* 27 (1): 157–67.

Doganis, R. (1994) 'The impact of liberalization on European airline strategies and operations', *Journal of Air Transport Management*, 1 (1): 15–25.

Dohse, K., Jurgens, U. and Malsch, T. (1985) 'From Fordism to Toyotism? The social organization of the labour process in the Japanese automobile industry', *Politics and Society*, 14 (2): 115–46.

Domagalski, T. A. (1999) 'Emotion in organizations: main currents', *Human Relations*, 52 (6): 833–52.

Douglas, M. (1975) *Implicit Meanings: Essays in Anthropology*, London: Routledge and Kegan Paul.

Drucker, P. (1998) 'The future that has already happened', *The Futurist*, 32 (8): 16–18.

Dubois, P. (1979) *Sabotage in Industry*, Harmondsworth: Pelican.

Duncombe, J. and Marsden, D. (1995) '"Workaholics" and "whingeing women": theorising intimacy and emotion work – the last frontier of gender inequality?', *Sociological Review*, 43 (1): 150–69.

Edwards, P. K. and Scullion, H. (1982) *The Social Organisation of Industrial Conflict*, Oxford: Blackwell.

Edwards, P. K. and Whitston, C. (1991) 'Workers are working harder: effort and shop-floor relations in the 1980s', *British Journal of Industrial Relations*, 29 (4): 593–601.

Edwards, P. K. and Whitston, C. (1993) *Attending to Work: The Management of Attendance and Shopfloor Order*, Oxford: Blackwell.

Edwards, P., Collinson, M. and Rees, C. (1998) 'The determinants of employee responses to total quality management: six case studies', *Organization Studies*, 19 (3): 449–75.

Edwards, R. (1979) *Contested Terrain: The Transformation of the Workplace in the Twentieth Century*, London: Heinemann.

Ekman, P. (1973) 'Cross culture studies of facial expression', in P. Ekman (ed.) *Darwin and Facial Expression*, New York: Academic Press, pp. 169–222.

Eldridge, J. E. T. (1971) *Sociology and Industrial Life*, Middlesex: Nelson.

Elger, T. (1990) 'Technical innovation and work reorganization in British manufacturing in the 1980s: continuity, intensification or transformation?', *Work, Employment and Society*, Special Issue, May: 67–102.

Elger, T. (1991) 'Task flexibility and the intensification of labour in UK manufacturing in the 1980s', in A. Pollert (ed.) *Farewell to Flexibility?*, Oxford: Blackwell, pp. 46–66.

Equal Opportunities Commission (1998) *Social Focus on Women and Men*, London: Office for National Statistics.

Evans, S. (1990) 'Free labour and economic performance: evidence from the construction industry', *Work, Employment and Society*, 4 (2): 239–52.

Featherstone, M. (1990) *Consumer Culture and Postmodernism*, London: Sage.

Felstead, A. and Jewson, N. (1995) 'Working at home: estimates from the 1991 census', *Employment Gazette*, March: 95–9.

Felstead, A. and Jewson, N. (2000) *In Work, At Home*, London: Routledge.

Felt, L. F. and Sinclair, P. R. (1992) 'Everyone does it: unpaid work in a rural peripheral region', *Work, Employment and Society*, 6 (1): 43–64.

Ferguson, K. (1984) *The Feminist Case Against Bureaucracy*, Philadelphia: Temple University Press.

Ferman, L. A. (1983) 'The work ethic in the world of informal work', in J. Barbash, R. J. Lampman, S. A. Levitan and G. Tyler (eds) *The Work Ethic – A Critical Analysis*, Wisconsin: Industrial Relations Research Association.

Ferrie, E. and Smith, K. (1996) *Parenting in the 1990s*, London: Family Policy Studies Centre.

Fiege, E. L. (1989) 'The meaning and measurement of the underground economy', in E. L. Fiege (ed.) *The Underground Economies*, Cambridge: Cambridge University Press, pp. 175–96.

Filby, M. P. (1992) '"The figures, the personality and the bums": service work and sexuality', *Work, Employment and Society*, 6 (1): 23–42.

Financial Times (1999) 'Ford chief to meet unions over Dagenham race row', 7 October.

Fineman, S. (ed.) (1993) *Emotion in Organizations*, London: Sage.

Firth, M. (1981) 'Racial discrimination in the British labor market', *Industrial and Labor Relations Review*, 34 (2): 265–72.

Fitzgerald, L. and Ferlie, E. (2000) 'Professionals: back to the future?', *Human Relations*, 53 (3): 713–39.

Foegen, J. H. (1988) 'Hypocrisy pay', *Employee Responsibilities and Rights Journal*, 1 (1): 85–7.

Foote, N. N. (1954) 'Sex as play', *Social Problems*, 1: 159–63.

Forbes, I. and Mead, G. (1992) *Measure for Measure: A Comparative Analysis of Measures to Combat Racial Discrimination in the Member Countries of the European Community*, Research Series no. 1, Sheffield: Employment Department.

Fox, A. (1966) *Industrial Sociology and Industrial Relations*, Research paper 3, Royal Commission on Trade Unions and Employers' Associations, London: HMSO.

Fox, A. (1974) *Beyond Contract*, London: Faber and Faber.

Francis, B. and Penn, R. (1994) 'Towards a phenomenology of skill' in R. Penn, M. Rose and J. Rubery (eds) *Skill and Occupational Change*, Oxford: Oxford University Press, pp. 223–43.

Freeman, R. B. and Medoff, J. L. (1984) *What Do Unions Do?*, New York: Basic Books.

Freeman, R. and Pelletier, J. (1990) 'The impact of industrial relations legislation on British union density', *British Journal of Industrial Relations*, 28 (2): 141–64.

Freidson, E. (1994) *Professionalism Reborn: Theory, Prophecy and Policy*, Cambridge: Polity.

Frenkel, S., Korczynski, M., Donoghue, L. and Shire, K. (1995) 'Re-constituting work: trends towards knowledge work and info-normative control', *Work, Employment and Society*, 9 (4): 773–96.

Frenkel, S. J., Korczynski, M., Shire, K. A. and Tam, M. (1999) *On the Front Line: Organization of Work in the Information Economy*, New York: Cornell University Press.

Friedman, A. (1977a) *Industry and Labour: Class Struggle at Work and Monopoly Capitalism*, London: Macmillan.

Friedman, A. (1977b) 'Responsible autonomy versus direct control over the labour process', *Capital and Class*, 1 (Spring): 43–57.

Friedman, A. (1990) 'Managerial activities, techniques and technology: towards a complex theory of the labour process', in D. Knights and H. Willmott (eds) *Labour Process Theory*, London: Macmillan, pp. 177–208.

Friedmann, G. (1961) *The Anatomy of Work*, London: Heinemann.

Fuchs Epstein, C. and Kalleberg, A. L. (2001) 'Time and the sociology of work: issues and implications', *Work and Occupations*, 28 (1): 5–16.

Fuchs, V. (1968) *The Service Economy*, New York: Basic Books.

Gallie, D. (1991) 'Patterns of skill change: upskilling, deskilling or the polarization of skills?', *Work, Employment and Society*, 5 (3): 319–51.

Gallie, D. and White, M. (1993) *Employee Commitment and the Skills Revolution*, London: Policy Studies Institute.

Garrahan, P. and Stewart, P. (1992) *The Nissan Enigma: Flexibility at Work in a Local Economy*, London: Mansell.

Gershuny, J. (1978) *After Industrial Society? The Emerging Self-Service Economy*, London: Macmillan.

Gershuny, J. (1983) *Social Innovation and the Division of Labour*, Oxford: Oxford University Press.

Gershuny, J. and Miles, I. (1983) *The New Service Economy: The Transformation of Employment in Industrial Societies*, London: Pinter.

Gershuny, J., Godwin, M. and Jones, S. (1994) 'The domestic labour revolution: a process of lagged adaptation', in M. Anderson, F. Bechhofer and J. Gershuny (eds) *The Social and Political Economy of the Household*, Oxford: Oxford University Press, pp. 151–97.

Gill, J. and Johnson, P. (1997) *Research Methods for Managers*, Second edition, London: Paul Chapman.

Glaser, B. G. and Strauss, A. L. (1967) *The Discovery of Grounded Theory: Strategies for Qualitative Research*, Chicago: Aldine.

Glazer, M. P. and Glazer, P. M. (1989) *The Whistleblowers*, New York: Basic Books.

Goffman, E. (1963) *Stigma*, Harmondsworth: Penguin.

Goffman, E. (1969) *The Presentation of Self in Everyday Life*, London: Allen Lane.

Goffman, E. (1971) *Relations in Public*, New York: Basic Books.

Goodwin, M. and Duncan, S. (1986) 'The local state and local economic policy: political mobilisation or economic regeneration', *Capital and Class*, 27: 14–36.

Gorz, A. (1982) *Farewell to the Working Class*, London: Pluto.

Gorz, A. (1985) *Paths to Paradise: On the Liberation from Work*, London: Pluto.

Graham, L. (1995) *On the Line at Subaru-Isuzu*, Ithaca, NY: ILR/Cornell.

Grant, D. (1999) 'HRM, rhetoric and the psychological contract: a case of "easier said than done"', *International Journal of Human Resource Management*, 10 (2): 327–50.

Green, F. (1992) 'Recent trends in British trade union density: how much of a compositional effect?', *British Journal of Industrial Relations*, 30 (3): 445–58.

Green, F. (2001) 'It's been a hard day's night: the concentration and intensification of work in late twentieth century Britain', *British Journal of Industrial Relations*, 39 (1): 53–80.

Guest, D. (1989) 'Human resource management: its implications for industrial relations and trade unions', in J. Storey (ed.) *New Perspectives on Human Resource Management*, London: Routledge, pp. 41–55.

Guest, D. (1990) 'Have British workers been working harder in Thatcher's Britain? – a re-consideration of the concept of effort', *British Journal of Industrial Relations*, 28 (3): 293–312.

Guest, D., Conway, N., Briner, R. and Dickman, M. (1996) 'The state of the psychological contract', *Issues in People Management*, No. 21, London: IPD.

Guest, D. E. and Dewe, P. (1988) 'Why do workers belong to a trade union? A social psychological study in the UK electronics industry', *British Journal of Industrial Relations*, 26 (2): 178–93.

Guest, D. E. and Dewe, P. (1991) 'Company or trade union: which wins workers' allegiance? A study of commitment in the UK electronics industry', *British Journal of Industrial Relations*, 29: 81–97.

Hacket, R. D. and Bycio, P. (1996) 'An evaluation of employee absenteeism as a coping mechanism among hospital nurses', *Journal of Occupational and Organizational Psychology*, 69: 327–38.

Hakim, C. (1991) 'Grateful slaves and self-made women: fact and fantasy in women's work orientations', *European Sociological Review*, 7 (2): 101–21.

Hall, E. (1993) 'Smiling, deferring and flirting: doing gender by giving good service', *Work and Occupations*, 20 (4): 452–71.

Handy, C. (1984) *The Future of Work*, Oxford: Blackwell.

Hanlon, G. (1998) 'Professionalism as enterprise: service class politics and the redefinition of professionalism', *Sociology*, 32 (1): 43–63.

Harding, P. and Jenkins, R. (1989) *The Myth of the Hidden Economy*, Milton Keynes: Open University Press.

Hartley, J. F. (1992) 'The psychology of industrial relations', in C. Cooper and I. Robertson (eds) *International Review of Industrial and Organizational Psychology*, Chichester: John Wiley.

Hartmann, H. (1979) 'Capitalism, patriarchy and job segregation', in Z. Eisenstein (ed.) *Capitalist Patriarchy and the Case for Socialist Feminism*, New York: Monthly Review Press, pp. 206–47.

Harvey, D. (1989) *The Condition of Postmodernity*, Oxford: Blackwell.

Hassard, J. (1989) 'Time and industrial sociology', in P. Blyton, J. Hassard, S. Hill and K. Starkey (eds) *Time, Work and Organization*, London: Routledge, pp. 13–34.

Heery, E. and Noon, M. (2001) *A Dictionary of Human Resource Management*, Oxford: Oxford University Press.

Heery, E. and Salmon, J. (eds) (2000) *The Insecure Workforce*, London: Routledge.

Heery, E., Delbridge, R., Salmon, J., Simms, M., and Simpson, D. (2001) 'Global labour? The transfer of the organising model to the United Kingdom', in Y. Debrah and I. Smith (eds) *Globalisation, Employment and the Workplace: Patterns of Diversity*, London: Routledge, pp. 41–68.

Herriot, P. (1998) 'The role of the HR function in building a new proposition for staff', in P. R. Sparrow and M. Marchington (eds) *Human Resource Management – The New Agenda*, London: FT/Pitman, pp. 106–16.

Herriot, P., Manning, W. E. G. and Kidd, J. M. (1997) 'The content of the psychological contract', *British Journal of Management*, 8: 151–62.

Hewitt, P. (1993) *About Time: The Revolution in Work and Family Life*, London: Rivers Oram.

Heyes, J. (1997) 'Annualised hours and the "knock": the organisation of working time in a chemicals plant', *Work, Employment and Society*, 11 (1): 65–81.

Hicks, S. (2000) 'Trade union membership 1998–99: an analysis of data from the Certification Officer and Labour Force Survey', *Labour Market Trends*, July: 329–38.

Hill, R. (2000) 'New Labour Force Survey questions on working hours', *Labour Market Trends*, January: 39–47.

Hill, S. (1991) 'Why quality circles failed but Total Quality Management might succeed', *British Journal of Industrial Relations*, 29 (4): 541–68.

Hirst, P. and Thompson, G. (1996) *Globalization in Question*, London: Polity.

Hochschild, A. R. (1979) 'Emotion work, feeling rules and social structure', *American Journal of Sociology*, 85 (3): 551–75.

Hochschild, A. R. (1983) *The Managed Heart: Commercialization of Human Feeling*, Berkeley: University of California Press.

Hodson, R. (1991) 'Workplace behaviors', *Work and Occupations*, 18 (3): 271–90.

Hoggett, P. (1996) 'New modes of control in the public services', *Public Administration* 74 (1): 9–36.

Hoque, K. and Noon, M. (1999) 'Racial discrimination in speculative applications: new optimism six years on?', *Human Resource Management Journal*, 9 (3): 71–82.

Horrell, S. (1994) 'Household time allocation and women's labour force participation', in M. Anderson, F. Bechhofer and J. Gershuny (eds) *The Social and Political Economy of the Household*, Oxford: Oxford University Press, pp. 198–224.

Horrell, S. and Rubery, J. (1991) *Employers' Working Time Policies and Women's Employment*, London: HMSO.

Horrell, S., Rubery, J. and Burchell, B. (1994) 'Gender and skills' in R. Penn, M. Rose and J. Rubery (eds) *Skill and Occupational Change*, Oxford: Oxford University Press, pp. 189–222.

Hubbuck, J. and Carter, S. (1980) *Half a Chance? A Report on Job Discrimination Against Young Blacks in Nottingham*, London: Commission for Racial Equality.

Hutton, W. (1995) *The State We're In*, London: Cape.

Hyman, R. (1987) 'Strategy or structure? Capital, labour and control', *Work, Employment and Society*, 1 (1): 25–55.

Hyman, R. (1991) 'Plus ça change? The theory of production and the production of theory', in A. Pollert (ed.) *Farewell to Flexibility?*, Oxford: Blackwell, pp. 259–83.

Hyman, R. (1999) 'Imagined solidarities: can trade unions resist globalization?', in P. Leisink (ed.) *Globalization and Labour Relations*, Cheltenham: Edward Elgar.

Incomes Data Services (1996) 'UK to toe the line on working time limits', *Employment Europe*, no. 413: 26–8.

Industrial Relations Review and Report (1990) 'Ethnic monitoring – policy and practice', *IRS Employment Trends*, 478: 4–11.

Inglehart, R. (1997) *Modernization and Postmodernization: Cultural, Economic and Political Change in 43 Societies*, Princeton, NJ: Princeton University Press.

Ingram, A. and Sloane, P. (1984) 'The growth of shiftwork in the British food, drink and tobacco industries', *Managerial and Decision Economics*, 5 (3): 168–76.

Inland Revenue (1981) *Annual Report*, No. 123, London: HMSO.

Jacobs, J. A. and Gerson, K. (2001) 'Overworked individuals or overworked families?', *Work and Occupations*, 28 (1): 40–63.

Jacoby, S. M. (1999) 'Are career jobs heading for extinction?', *California Management Review*, 42: 123–45.

Jahoda, M. (1979) 'The impact of unemployment in the 1930s and the 1970s', *Bulletin of the British Psychological Society*, 32: 309–14.

Jahoda, M. (1982) *Employment and Unemployment*, Cambridge: Cambridge University Press.

James, N. (1989) 'Emotional labour: skill and work in the social regulation of feelings', *Sociological Review*, 37 (1): 15–42.

Jaques, E. (1956) *Measurement of Responsibility*, London: Tavistock.

Jaques, E. (1967) *Equitable Payment* (revised edition), Harmondsworth: Penguin.

Jenkins, R. (1986) *Racism and Recruitment*, Cambridge: Cambridge University Press.

Jenkins, R. (1987) 'Equal opportunities in the private sector: the limits of voluntarism', in R. Jenkins and J. Solomos (eds) *Racism and Equal Opportunity Policies in the 1980s*, Cambridge: Cambridge University Press, pp. 110–24.

Jenson, J. (1989) 'The talents of women, the skills of men', in S. Wood (ed.) *The Transformation of Work?*, London: Unwin Hyman, pp. 141–55.

Jewson, N. and Mason, D. (1986) 'The theory and practice of equal opportunity policies: liberal and radical approaches', *Sociological Review*, 34 (2): 307–34.

Jewson, N., Mason, D., Waters, S. and Harvey, J. (1990) *Ethnic Minorities and Employment Practice: A Study of Six Employers*, Research Paper No. 76, Sheffield: Employment Department.

Jewson, N., Mason, D., Lambkin, C. and Taylor, F. (1992) *Ethnic Monitoring Policy and Practice: A Study of Employers' Experiences*, Research paper no.89, London: Department of Employment.

Jones, T. (1993) *Britain's Ethnic Minorities*, London: Policy Studies Institute.

Joseph Rowntree Foundation (1991) *National Survey of Volunteering*, Social Survey Research Findings No. 22, York: Joseph Rowntree Foundation.

Juran, J. M. (1979) *Quality Control Handbook*, New York: McGraw-Hill.

Kaler, J. (2001) 'Diversity, equality, morality', in M. Noon and E. Ogbonna (eds) *Equality, Diversity and Disadvantage in Employment*, Basingstoke: Palgrave, pp. 51–64.

Karabanow, J. (1999) 'When caring is not enough: emotional labor and youth shelter workers', *Social Service Review*, 73 (3): 340–57.

Keep, E. (1989) 'Corporate training strategies: the vital component?', in J. Storey (ed.) *New Perspectives on Human Resource Management*, London: Routledge, pp. 109–25.

Keep, E. (1994) 'Vocational education and training for the young', in K. Sisson (ed.) *Personnel Management*, Second edition, Oxford: Blackwell, pp. 299–333.

Kelly, J. (1982) *Scientific Management, Job Redesign and Work Performance*, London: Academic Press.

Kelly, J. (1985) 'Management's redesign of work: labour process, labour markets and product markets', in D. Knights, H. Willmott and D. Collinson (eds) *Job Redesign*, Aldershot: Gower, pp. 30–51.

Kelly, J. (1990) 'British trade unionism 1979–89: change, continuity and contradictions', *Work, Employment and Society*, 4 (Special issue): 29–65.

Kelly, J. (1996) 'Union militancy and social partnership'. In P. Ackers, C. Smith and P. Smith (eds) *The New Workplace and Trade Unionism*, London: Routledge, pp. 41–76.

Kelly, J. and Waddington. J. (1995) 'New prospects for British labour', *Organization*, 2 (3/4): 415–26.

Kerr, C., Dunlop, J. T., Harbison, F. H. and Myers, C. A. (1960) *Industrialism and Industrial Man*, London: Heinemann.

Kerr, W. (1954) 'Dual allegiance and emotional acceptance – recognition in industry', *Personnel Psychology*, 2: 59–66.

Klandermans, P. G. (1986) 'Psychology and trade union participation: joining, acting, quitting', *Journal of Occupational Psychology*, 59: 189–204.

Kleinknecht, A. and ter Wengel, J. (1998) 'The myth of economic globalization', *Cambridge Journal of Economics*, 22 (5): 637–67.

Knights, D. and Willmott, H. (eds) (1990) *Labour Process Theory*, London: Macmillan.

Knights, D., Willmott, H. and Collinson, D. (eds) (1985) *Job Redesign: Critical Perspectives on the Labour Process*, Aldershot: Gower.

Kochan, T. and Osterman, P. (1994) *The Mutual Gains Enterprise*, Cambridge, Mass: Harvard Business School Press.

Koestler, A. (1976) *The Ghost in the Machine*, London: Picador.

Korczynski, M., Shire, K., Frenkel, S. and Tam, M. (1996) 'Front line work in the "new model service firm": Australian and Japanese comparisons', *Human Resource Management Journal*, 6 (2): 72–87.

Kreckel, R. (1980) 'Unequal opportunity structure and labour market segmentation', *Sociology*, 14 (4): 525–50.

Kumar, K. (1995) *From Post-Industrial to Post-Modern Society*, Oxford: Blackwell.

Kusterer, K. (1978) *Know How on the Job*, Boulder, Colorado: Westview Press.

Labour Market Trends (2001) 'Labour market spotlight', *Labour Market Trends*, January: 9–12.

Labour Research Department (1990) 'The right personality for the job?', *Labour Research*, September: 15–16.

Lacey, N., Wells, C. and Meure, D. (1990) *Reconstructing Criminal Law*, London: Weidenfeld and Nicolson.

Lashley, C. (1999) 'Empowerment through involvement: a case study of TGI Fridays restaurants', *Personnel Review*, 29 (6): 791–811.

Lazonick, W. (1978) 'The subjection of labour to capital: the rise of the capitalist system', *Review of Radical Political Economics*, 10 (1): 1–31.

Lee, D. (1982) 'Beyond deskilling: skill, craft and class', in S. Wood (ed.) *The Degradation of Work?*, London: Hutchinson, pp. 146–62.

Lee, G. and Wrench, J. (1987) 'Race and gender dimensions of the youth labour market: from apprenticeship to YTS', in G. Lee and R. Loveridge (eds) *The Manufacture of Disadvantage*, Milton Keynes: Open University Press, pp. 83–99.

Legge, K. (1995) *Human Resource Management: Rhetorics and Realities*, Basingstoke: Macmillan.

Leidner, R. (1991) 'Serving hamburgers and selling insurance: gender, work and identity in interactive service jobs', *Gender and Society*, 5 (2):154–77.

Lessor, R. (1984) 'Social movements, the occupational arena and changes in career consciousness: the case of women flight attendants', *Journal of Occupational Behaviour*, 5: 37–51.

Lewchuck, W. and Robertson, D. (1996) 'Working conditions under lean production: a worker-based benchmarking study', in P. Stewart (ed.) *Beyond Japanese Management: the End of Modern Times?*, London: Frank Cass.

Lewis, A. (1995) 'The deskilling thesis revisited: on Peter Armstrong's defence of Braverman', *Sociological Review*, 43 (3): 478–500.

Lewis, D. (1997) 'Whistleblowing at work: ingredients for an effective procedure', *Human Resource Management Journal*, 7 (4): 5–11.

Liff, S. and Dickens, L. (1999) 'Ethics and equality: reconciling false dilemmas', in J. Marshall and D. Winstanley (eds) *Ethical Issues in Contemporary Human Resource Management*, London: Macmillan, pp. 85–101.

Liff, S. and Wajcman, J. (1996) '"Sameness" and "difference" revisited: which way forward for equal opportunity initiatives?', *Journal of Management Studies*, 33 (1): 79–94.

Linhart, R. (1981) *The Assembly Line*, London: Calder.

Linstead, S. (1985a) 'Breaking the "purity rule": industrial sabotage and the symbolic process', *Personnel Review*, 14 (3): 12–19.

Linstead, S. (1985b) 'Jokers wild: the importance of humour in the maintenance of organizational culture', *Sociological Review*, 33 (4): 741–67.

Linstead, S. (1995) 'Averting the gaze: gender and power on the perfumed picket line', *Gender, Work and Organization*, 2 (4): 190–206.

Littler, C. R. (1982) *The Development of the Labour Process in Capitalist Societies*, Aldershot: Gower.

Littler, C. R. (1985) 'Taylorism, Fordism and job design' in D. Knights, H. Willmott and D. Collinson (eds) *Job Redesign*, Aldershot: Gower, pp. 10–29.

Littler, C. R. and Salaman, G. (1982) 'Bravermania and beyond: recent theories of the labour process', *Sociology*, 16 (2): 251–69.

Livingstone, D. W. (1998) *The Education-Jobs Gap. Underemployment or Economic Democracy*, Boulder, Colorado: Westview Press.

Lynch, J. J. (1992) *The Psychology of Customer Care*, London: Macmillan.

Lyon, D. (1986) 'From "post-industrialism" to "information society": a new social transformation?', *Sociology*, 20 (4): 577–88.

Lyon, D. (1994) *Postmodernity*, Buckingham: Open University Press.

Macan, T. H. (1994) 'Time management: test of a process model', *Journal of Applied Psychology*, 79 (3): 381–91.

Macdonald, K. M. (1995) *The Sociology of Professions*, London: Sage.

MacDonald, R. (1994) 'Fiddly jobs, undeclared working and the "something for nothing" society', *Work, Employment and Society*, 8 (4): 507–30.

MacDonald, R. (1996) 'Labours of love: voluntary working in a depressed local economy', *Journal of Social Policy*, 25 (1): 1–21.

MacDonald, R. (1997) 'Informal working, survival strategies and the idea of an "underclass"', in R. K. Brown (ed.) *The Changing Shape of Work*, Basingstoke: Macmillan, pp. 103–24.

Management Today and KPMG Forensic Accounting (2000), *Business Ethics Survey*, October.

Mangham, I. L. and Overington, M. A. (1987) *Organizations as Theatre*, Chichester: Wiley.

Mann, S. (1999) 'Emotion at work: to what extent are we expressing, suppressing or faking it?', *European Journal of Work and Organizational Psychology*, 8 (3): 347–69.

Manwaring, T. and Wood, S. (1985) 'The ghost in the labour process' in D. Knights, H. Willmott and D. Collinson (eds) *Job Redesign*, Aldershot: Gower, pp. 171–96.

Margenau, J. M., Martin, J. E. and Peterson, M. M. (1988) 'Dual and unilateral commitment among stewards and rank and file union members', *Academy of Management Journal*, 31: 359–76.

Mars, G. (1982) *Cheats at Work: An Anthropology of Workplace Crime*, London: Allen and Unwin.

Mars, G. and Nicod, M. (1984) *The World of Waiters*, Boston, MA: George Allen and Unwin.

Marsh, C. (1991) *Hours of Work of Women and Men in Britain*, London: HMSO.

Martin, G., Staines, H. and Pate, J. (1998) 'Linking job security and career development in a new psychological contract', *Human Resource Management Journal*, 8 (3): 20–40.

Martin, J., Knopoff, K. and Beckman, C. (1998) 'An alternative to bureaucratic impersonality: bounded emotionality at The Body Shop', *Administrative Science Quarterly*, 43: 429–69.

Marx, K. (1930) *Capital*, London: Dent.

Marx, K. (1969) 'Alienated labour', in T. Burns (ed.) *Industrial Man: Selected Readings*, Harmondsworth: Penguin, pp. 95–109.

Marx, K. (1976) *Capital*, Vol. 1, Harmondsworth: Penguin.

Mason, D. (1994) 'On the dangers of disconnecting race and racism', *Sociology*, 28 (4): 845–58.

Massey, D. (1988) 'What's happening to UK manufacturing?', in J. Allen and D. Massey (eds) *The Economy in Question*, London: Sage, pp. 45–90.

Mathewson, S. B. (1931) *Restriction of Output Among Unorganized Workers*, New York: McGraw-Hill.

Matthaei, J. (1982) *An Economic History of Women in America*, Brighton: Harvester.

Matusik, S. F. and Hill, C. W. L. (1998) 'The utilization of contingent work, knowledge creation and competitive advantage', *Academy of Management Review*, 23 (4): 680–97.

Mayo, E. (1933) *The Human Problems of an Industrial Civilisation*, New York: Macmillan.

McClelland, K. (1987) 'Time to work, time to live: some aspects of work and the reformation of class in Britain 1850–1880', in P. Joyce (ed.) *The Historical Meanings of Work*, Cambridge: Cambridge University Press, pp. 180–209.

McCormick, B. J. (1979) *Industrial Relations in the Coal Industry*, London: Macmillan.

McIntosh, I. and Broderick, J. (1996) 'Neither one thing nor the other: compulsory competitive tendering and Southburg cleansing services', *Work, Employment and Society*, 10 (3): 413–30.

McKee, L. and Bell, C. (1986) 'His unemployment, her problem: the domestic and marital consequences of male unemployment', in S. Allen, A. Waton, K. Purcell and S. Wood (eds) *The Experience of Unemployment*, Basingstoke: Macmillan, pp. 134–49.

McLennan, G. (1995) *Pluralism*, Buckingham: Open University Press.

McLoughlin, I. and Clark, J. (1994) *Technological Change at Work*, Second edition, Milton Keynes: Open University Press.

Means, R. and Smith, R. (1994) *Community Care: Policy and Practice*, Basingstoke: Macmillan.

Metcalf, D. (1989) 'Water notes dry up: the impact of the Donovan reform proposals and Thatcherism at work on labour productivity in British manufacturing industry', *British Journal of Industrial Relations*, 27 (1): 1–31.

Metcalf, D. (1991) 'British unions: dissolution or resurgence?', *Oxford Review of Economic Policy*, 7 (1): 18–32.

Meyer, S. (1981) *The Five-Dollar Day: Labor Management and Social Control in the Ford Motor Co., 1908–21*, Albany: SUNY Press.

Milberg, W. S. (1998) 'Globalization and its limits', in R. Kozul-Wright and R. Rowthorn (eds) *Transnational Corporations and the Global Economy*, Basingstoke: Macmillan, pp. 69–94.

Micelli, Z. and Near, J. (1992) *Blowing the Whistle*, New York: Lexington Books.

Miles, R. (1993) *Racism after 'Race Relations'*, London: Routledge.

Milkman, R. (1997) *Farewell to the Factory: Auto Workers in the Late Twentieth Century*, Berkley: University of California Press.

Miller, D. (1996) 'Equality management – towards a materialist approach', *Gender, Work and Organization*, 3 (4): 202–214.

Millward, N. (1990) 'The state of the unions', in R. Jowell, S. Witherspoon, L. Brook and B. Taylor (eds) *British Social Attitudes: The 7th Report*, Aldershot: Gower, pp. 27–50.

Modood, T., Berthoud, R., Lakey, J., Nazroo, J., Smith, P., Virdee, S. and Beishon, S. (1997) *Ethnic Minorities in Britain: Diversity and Disadvantage*, London: Policy Studies Institute.

Molstad, C. (1986) 'Choosing and coping with boring work', *Urban Life*, 15 (2): 215–36.

Moorhouse, H. F. (1984) 'American automobiles and workers' dreams', in K. Thompson (ed.) *Work, Employment and Unemployment*, Milton Keynes: Open University Press, pp. 246–60.

Moorhouse, H. F. (1987) 'The "work" ethic and "leisure" activity: the hot rod in post-war America', in P. Joyce (ed.) *The Historical Meanings of Work*, Cambridge: Cambridge University Press. pp. 237–57.

More, C. (1980) *Skill and the English Working Class 1840–1914*, London: Croom Helm.

More, C. (1982) 'Skill and the survival of apprenticeship' in S. Wood (ed.) *The Degradation of Work?*, London: Hutchinson, pp. 109–22.

Morgan, G. (1986) *Images of Organization*, London: Sage.

Morris, J. A. and Feldman, D. C. (1996) 'The dimensions, antecedents and consequences of emotional labor', *Academy of Management Review*, 21 (4): 986–1010.

Morris, L. (1990) *The Workings of the Household*, Cambridge: Polity.

Mott, P. E., Mann, F. C., McLoughlin, Q. and Warwick, D. (1965) *Shiftwork: Social, Psychological, and Physical Consequences*, Ann Arbor: University of Michigan Press.

MOW International Research Team (1987) *The Meaning of Working*, London: Academic Press.

Mumby, D. and Putnam, L. (1992) 'The politics of emotion: a feminist reading of bounded rationality', *Academy of Management Review*, 17 (3): 465–86.

Mumford, L. (1934) *Technics and Civilisation*, New York: Harcourt, Brace and World.

Nanayakkara, S. (1992) *Ethics of Material Progress: the Buddhist Attitude*, Colombo: The World Fellowship of Buddhist Dhammaduta Activities Committee.

Naylor, K. (1994) 'Part-time working in Great Britain – an historical analysis', *Employment Gazette*, December: 473–84.

Neathey, F. (1992) 'Job assessment, job evaluation and equal value' in P. Kahn and E. Meehan (eds) *Equal Value/Comparable Worth in the UK and the USA*, Basingstoke: Macmillan, pp. 65–81.

New Earnings Survey (2001) *New Earnings Survey 2000*, London: Office for National Statistics.

Nicholson, N. (1977) Absence behaviour and attendance motivation: a conceptual synthesis', *Journal of Management Studies*, 14 (3): 231–52.

Nicholson, N. and Johns, G. (1985) 'The absence culture and the psychological contract – who's in control of absence', *Academy of Management Review*, 10 (3): 397–407.

Nicholson, N., Ursell, G. and Blyton, P. (1981) *The Dynamics of White-Collar Unionism*, London: Academic Press.

Niles, F. S. (1999) 'Towards a cross-cultural understanding of work-related beliefs', *Human Relations*, 52 (7): 855–67.

Nkomo, S. (1992) 'The emperor has no clothes: rewriting "race in organizations"', *Academy of Management Review*, 17 (3): 487–513.

Nolan, P. (1989) 'Walking on water? performance and industrial relations under Thatcher', *Industrial Relations Journal*, 20 (2): 81–92.

Nonaka, I. (1991) 'The knowledge-creating company', *Harvard Business Review*, November–December: 96–104.

Nonaka, I. and Takeuchi, H. (1995) *The Knowledge-Creating Company*, New York: Oxford University Press.

Noon, M. (1992) 'HRM: a map, model or theory', in P. Blyton and P. Turnbull (eds) *Reassessing Human Resource Management*, London: Sage, pp. 16–32.

Noon, M. (1993) 'Racial discrimination in speculative application: evidence from the UK's top 100 firms', *Human Resource Management Journal*, 3 (4): 35–47.

Noon, M. (1994) 'From apathy to alacrity: managers and new technology in provincial newspapers', *Journal of Management Studies*, 31 (1): 19–32.

Noon, M. and Delbridge, R. (1993) 'News from behind my hand: gossip in organizations', *Organization Studies*, 14 (1): 23–36.

Noon, M. and Hoque, K. (2001) 'Ethnic minorities and equal treatment: the impact of gender, equal opportunities policies and trade unions', *National Institute Economic Review*, 176: 105–16.

Noon, M. and Ogbonna, E. (1998) 'Unequal provision? Ethnic minorities and employment training policy', *Journal of Education and Work*, 11 (1): 23–39.

Noon, M. and Ogbonna, E. (2001) 'Introduction: the key analytical themes', in M. Noon and E. Ogbonna (eds) *Equality, Diversity and Disadvantage in Employment*, Basingstoke: Palgrave, pp. 1–14.

O'Connell Davidson, J. (1998) *Prostitution, Power and Freedom*, Oxford, Polity Press.

O'Higgins, M. (1989) 'Assessing the underground economy in the United Kingdom', in E. L. Fiege (ed.) *The Underground Economies*, Cambridge: Cambridge University Press, pp. 175–96.

Oakland, J. S. (1989) *Total Quality Management*, Oxford: Butterworth-Heinemann.

Oakley, A. (1974) *The Sociology of Housework*, London: Martin Robertson.

Oakley, A. (1982) *Subject Woman*, London: Fontana.

OECD (1995) *Employment Outlook 1995*, Paris: Organisation for Economic Cooperation and Development.

OECD (1996) *Employment Outlook 1996*, Paris: Organization for Economic Cooperation and Development.

OECD (1999) 'Privatisation trends', *Financial Market Trends*, No. 72: 129–45.

OECD (2000a) *OECD Economic Outlook*, No. 67, Paris: Organisation for Economic Cooperation and Development.

OECD (2000b) *OECD Employment Outlook 2000*, Paris: Organisation for Economic Cooperation and Development.

OECD (2000c) *OECD in Figures 2000*, Paris: Organisation for Economic Cooperation and Development.

Offe, C. (1985) *Disorganised Capitalism*, Cambridge: Polity Press.

Office for National Statistics (2000) *Social Trends 30*, London: The Stationery Office.

Office for National Statistics (2001a) *Social Trends*, No. 31, London: The Stationery Office.

Office for National Statistics (2001b) *User Manual for the National Statistics Socio-economic Classification*, London: Office for National Statistics.

Ogbonna, E. and Noon, M. (1995) 'Experiencing inequality: ethnic minorities and the Employment Training scheme', *Work, Employment and Society*, 9 (3): 537–58.

Ogbonna, E. and Wilkinson, B. (1990) 'Corporate strategy and corporate culture: the view from the checkout', *Personnel Review*, 19 (4): 9–15.

Oliver, M. (1996) *Understanding Disability: From Theory to Practice*, London: Macmillan.

Oswick, C. and Rosenthal, P. (2001) 'Towards a relevant theory of age discrimination in employment', in M. Noon and E. Ogbonna (eds) *Equality, Diversity and Disadvantage in Employment*, Basingstoke: Palgrave, pp. 156–71.

Pahl, R. (1984) *Divisions of Labour*, Oxford: Blackwell.

Pahl, R. (1988) 'Some remarks on informal work, social polarization and the social structure', *International Journal of Urban and Regional Research*, 12: 247–67.

Pain, N., Ashworth, P., Holland, D., Hubert, F., and te Velde, D. W. (2000) 'The world economy', *National Institute Economic Review*, No. 172: 33–61.

Palmer, B. (1975) 'Class, conception and conflict', *Review of Radical Political Economics*, 7 (2): 31–49.

Parekh, B. (1986) 'The New Right and the politics of nationhood', in G. Cohen (ed.) *The New Right: Image and Reality*, London: Runnymead Trust.

Parkin, F. (1979) *Marxism and Class Theory: A Bourgeois Critique*, London: Tavistock.

Peetz, D. (1998) *Unions in a Contrary World*, Cambridge: Cambridge University Press.

Penn, R. (1982) 'Skilled manual workers in the labour process, 1856–1964', in S. Wood (ed.) *The Degradation of Work?*, London: Hutchinson, pp. 90–108.

Penn, R. (1983) 'Theories of skill and class structure', *Sociological Review*, 31 (1): 22–38.

Penn, R. (1985) *Skilled Workers in the Class Structure*, Cambridge: Cambridge University Press.

Penn, R. (1990) *Class, Power and Technology*, Cambridge: Polity Press.

Penn, R. and Scattergood, H. (1985) 'Deskilling or enskilling? An empirical investigation of recent theories of the labour process', *British Journal of Sociology*, 36 (4): 611–30.

Penn, R., Gasteen, A., Scattergood, H. and Sewel, J. (1994) 'Technical change and the division of labour in Rochdale and Aberdeen', in R. Penn, M. Rose and J. Rubery (eds) *Skill and Occupational Change*, Oxford: Oxford University Press, pp. 130–56.

Penn, R., Rose, M. and Rubery, J. (eds) (1994) *Skill and Occupational Change*, Oxford: Oxford University Press.

Perlow, L. A. (1999) 'The time famine: toward a sociology of work time', *Administrative Science Quarterly*, 44: 57–81.

Perlow, L. A. (2001) 'Time to co-ordinate: towards an understanding of work-time standards and norms in a multicountry study of software engineers', *Work and Occupations*, 28 (1): 91–111.

Perry, N. (1998) 'Indecent exposures: theorizing whistleblowing', *Organization Studies*, 19 (2): 235–57.

Peters, T. and Austin, N. (1985) *A Passion for Excellence*, New York: Random House.

Peters, T. and Waterman, R. H. (1982) *In Search of Excellence*, New York: Harper and Row.

Phillips, A. and Taylor, B. (1986) 'Sex and skill', in Feminist Review (ed.) *Waged Work – A Reader*, London: Virago, pp. 54–66.

Pickard, J. (1991) 'Annual hours: a year of living dangerously', *Personnel Management*, August: 38–43.

Pilkington, A. (2001) 'Beyond racial dualism: racial disadvantage and ethnic diversity in the labour market', in M. Noon and E. Ogbonna (eds) *Equality, Diversity and Disadvantage in Employment*, Basingstoke: Palgrave, pp.171–89.

Piore, M. J. and Sabel, C. F. (1984) *The Second Industrial Divide*, New York: Basic Books.

Polanyi, M. and Prosch, H. (1975) *Meaning*, Chicago: University of Chicago Press.

Pollard, S. (1963) 'Factory discipline and the industrial revolution', *The Economic History Review*, 16: 254–71.

Pollard, S. (1965) *The Genesis of Modern Management: A Study of the Industrial Revolution in Great Britain*, Harmondsworth: Penguin.

Pollert, A. (1981) *Girls, Wives, Factory Lives*, London: Macmillan.

Pollert, A. (1988) 'The "flexible firm": fixation or fact?', *Work, Employment and Society*, 2 (3): 281–316.

Pollert, A. (ed.) (1991) *Farewell to Flexibility?*, Oxford: Blackwell.

Pollitt, H. (1940) *Serving My Time: An Apprenticeship to Politics*, London: Lawrence and Wishart.

Poor, R. (ed.) (1972) *4 Days, 40 Hours*, London: Pan.

Prandy, K., Blackburn, R. M. and Stewart, A. (1974) 'Concepts and measures: the example of unionateness', *Sociology*, 8: 427–46.

Pringle, R. (1989) 'Bureaucracy, rationality and sexuality: the case of secretaries', in J. Hearn, D. L. Sheppard, P. Tancred-Sheriff and G. Burrell (eds) *The Sexuality of Organization*, London: Sage, pp. 158–77.

Prins, R. and de Graaf, A. (1986) 'Comparison of sickness absence in Belgian, German and Dutch firms', *British Journal of Industrial Medicine*, 43: 529–36.

Procter, S. and Mueller, F (eds) (2000) *Teamworking*, Basingstoke: Macmillan.

Pugliesi, K. (1999) 'The consequences of emotional labor: effects on work stress, job satisfaction and well-being', *Motivation and Emotion*, 23 (2): 125–54.

Purcell, J. (1989) 'The impact of corporate strategy on human resource management', in J. Storey (ed.) *New Perspectives on Human Resource Management*, London: Routledge. pp. 67–91.

Purcell, J. (1995) 'Corporate strategy and its link with human resource management strategy', in J. Storey (ed.) *Human Resource Management: A Critical Text*, London: Routledge. pp. 63–86.

Purcell, T. V. (1954) 'Dual allegiance to company and union: packinghouse workers', *Personnel Psychology*, 7: 48–58.

Radcliffe-Brown, A. R. (1952) *Structure and Function in Primitive Society*, London: Cohen and West.

Rafaeli, A. and Sutton, R. I. (1987) 'Expression of emotion as part of the work role', *Academy of Management Review*, 12 (1): 23–37.

Rafaeli, A. and Sutton, R. I. (1989) 'The expression of emotion in organizational life', in L. L. Cummings and B. M. Staw (eds) *Research in Organizational Behaviour*, Greenwich, CT: JAI Press, pp. 1–42.

Ram, M. (1992) 'Coping with racism: Asian employers in the inner city', *Work, Employment and Society*, 6 (4): 601–18.

Randle, K. (1996) 'The white-coated worker: professional autonomy in a period of change', *Work, Employment and Society*, 10 (4): 737–53.

Reed, M. (1996) ' Expert power and control in late modernity: an empirical review and theoretical synthesis', *Organization Studies*, 17 (4): 573–97.

Reid, D. A. (1976) 'The decline of Saint Monday', *Past and Present*, no. 71: 76–101.

Reynolds, G., Nicholls, P. and Alferoff, C. (2001) 'Disabled people, (re)training and employment: a qualitative exploration of exclusion', in M. Noon and E. Ogbonna (eds) *Equality, Diversity and Disadvantage in Employment*, Basingstoke: Palgrave, pp. 172–89.

Rhodes, E. and Braham, P. (1986) 'Equal opportunity in the context of high levels of unemployment', in R. Jenkins and J. Solomos (eds) *Racism and Equal Opportunity Policies in the 1980s*, Cambridge: Cambridge University Press, pp. 189–209.

Richards, W. (2001) 'Evaluating equal opportunity initiatives: the case for a "transformative" agenda', in M. Noon and E. Ogbonna (eds) *Equality, Diversity and Disadvantage in Employment*, Basingstoke: Palgrave, pp. 15–31.

Riemer, J. W. (1977) *Hard Hats: The Working World of Construction Workers*, Beverly Hills, CA: Sage.

Rinehart, J., Huxley, C. and Robertson, D. (1997) *Just Another Car Factory? Lean Production and its Discontents*, Ithaca, NY: ILR Press.

Ritzer, G. (1993) *The McDonaldization of Society*, Thousand Oaks, CA: Pine Forge Press.

Ritzer, G. (1998) *The McDonaldization Thesis*, London: Sage.

Robbins, S. P. (1998) *Organizational Behaviour*, Eigth edition, New Jersey: Prentice Hall.

Rodgers, D. (1978) *The Work Ethic in Industrial America 1850–1920*, Chicago: University of Chicago Press.

Roethlisberger, F. J. and Dickson, W. J. (1966) *Management and the Worker*, Harvard: Harvard University Press.

Rogoff, B. and Lave, J. (eds) (1984) *Everyday Cognition: Its Development in Social Context*, Cambridge MA: Harvard University Press.

Rolfe, H. (1986) 'Skill, deskilling and new technology in the non-manual labour process', *New Technology, Work and Employment*, 1 (1): 37–49.

Rolfe, H. (1990) 'In the name of progress? Skill and attitudes towards technological change', *New Technology, Work and Employment*, 5 (2): 107–21.

Ronai, C. R. and Ellis, C. (1989) 'Turn-ons for money: interactional strategies of the table dancer', *Journal of Contemporary Ethnography*, 18 (3): 271–98.

Rosa, R. R. (1995) 'Extended workshifts and excessive fatigue', *Journal of Sleep Research*, 4 (2): 51–6.

Rose, M. (1985) *Re-Working the Work Ethic*, London: Batsford.

Rose, M. (1988) *Industrial Behaviour*, Second edition, Harmondsworth: Penguin.

Rose, M. (1991) *The Post-Modern and the Post-Industrial*, Cambridge: Cambridge University Press.

Rose, M. (1994) 'Skill and Samuel Smiles: changing the British work ethic', in R. Penn, M. Rose and J. Rubery (eds) *Skill and Occupational Change*, Oxford: Oxford University Press, pp. 281–335.

Rose, R. (1985) 'Getting by in three economies: the resources of the official, unofficial and domestic economies', in J.-E. Lane (ed.) *State and Market*, London: Sage, pp. 103–41.

Rosen, H. (1954) 'Dual allegiance: a critique and a proposed research approach', *Personnel Psychology*, 7: 67–71.

Rosenthal, P., Hill, S. and Peccei, R. (1997) 'Checking out service: evaluating excellence, HRM and TQM in retailing', *Work, Employment and Society*, 11 (3): 481–503.

Rousseau, D. M. (1995) *Psychological Contracts in Organizations*, London: Sage.

Roy, D. (1952) 'Efficiency and "the fix": informal inter-group relations in a piecework machine shop', *American Journal of Sociology*, 57: 255–66.

Roy, D. (1953) 'Work satisfaction and social reward in quota achievement: an analysis of piecework incentive', *American Sociological Review*, 18: 507–14.

Roy, D. (1955) 'Quota restriction and goldbricking in a machine shop', *American Journal of Sociology*, 60: 427–42.

Roy, D. (1960) 'Banana time: job satisfaction and informal interaction', *Human Organization*, 18: 156–68.

Rubery, J. and Wilkinson, F. (1979) 'Notes on the nature of the labour process in the secondary sector', *Low Pay and Labour Market Segmentation Conference Papers*, Cambridge.

Rubery, J. Fagan, C. and Smith, M. (1995) *Changing Patterns of Work and Working Time in the European Union and the Impact on Gender Provisions*, Report for the Equal Opportunities Unit, Brussels: European Commission.

Rubinstein, M. (1984) *Equal Pay for Work of Equal Value*, London: Macmillan.

Russell, H. (1998) 'The rewards of work' in Jowell, R., Curtice, J., Park, A., Brook, L., Thomson, K. and Bryson, C. *British – and European – Social Attitudes: the 15th Report*, Aldershot: Ashgate, pp. 77–100.

Sabel, C. F. (1982) *Work and Politics: the Division of Labour in Industry*, Cambridge: Cambridge University Press.

Sadler, P. (1970) 'Sociological aspects of skill', *British Journal of Industrial Relations*, 8 (1): 22–31.

Saks, M. (1983) 'Removing the blinkers? A critique of recent contributions to the sociology of the professions', *Sociological Review*, 31 (1): 1–22.

Savery, L. K., Travaglione, A. and Firns, I. G. J. (1998) 'The links between absenteeism and commitment during downsizing', *Personnel Review*, 27 (4): 312–24.

Sayer, A. and Walker, R. (1992) *The New Social Economy: Reworking the Division of Labour*, Oxford: Blackwell.

Scarborough, H. (1999) 'Knowledge as work: conflicts in the management of knowledge workers', *Technology Analysis & Strategic Management*, 11 (1): 5–16.

Schaubroeck, J. and Jones, J. R. (2000) 'Antecedents of workplace emotional labor dimensions and moderators of their effects on physical symptoms', *Journal of Organizational Behavior*, 21: 163–83.

Schein, E. H. (1965) *Organizational Psychology*, Englewood Cliffs, NJ: Prentice-Hall.

Schor, J. (1991) *The Overworked American: The Unexpected Decline in Leisure*, New York: Basic Books.

Scott, A. (1994) *Willing Slaves: British Workers Under Human Resource Management*, Cambridge: Cambridge University Press.

Sennett, R. (1998) *The Corrosion of Character*, New York: Norton.

Sewell, G and Wilkinson, B. (1992a) 'Empowerment or emasculation? Shopfloor surveillance in a total quality organisation', in P. Blyton and P. Turnbull (eds) *Reassessing Human Resource Management*, London: Sage, pp. 97–115.

Sewell, G. and Wilkinson, B. (1992b) 'Someone to watch over me: surveillance, discipline and the just-in-time labour process', *Sociology*, 26 (2): 271–90.

Seymour, W. D. (1966) *Industrial Skills*, London: Pitman.

Shimonitsu, T. and Levi, L. (1992) 'Recent working life changes in Japan', *European Journal of Public Health*, 2: 76–96.

Shutt, J. and Whittington, R. (1987) 'Fragmentation strategies and the rise of small units: cases from the North West', *Regional Studies*, 21: 13–23.

Simpson, R. (2000) 'Presenteeism and the impact of long hours on managers', in D. Winstanley and J. Woodall (eds) *Ethical Issues in Contemporary Human Resource Management*, Basingstoke: Macmillan, pp. 156–71.

Smith, C. (1989) 'Flexible specialisation, automation and mass production', *Work, Employment and Society*, 3 (2): 203–22.

Smith, D. J. (1981) *Unemployment and Racial Minorities*, London: Policy Studies Institute.

Smith, S. and Wied-Nebbeling, S. (1986) *The Shadow Economy in Britain and Germany*, London: Anglo-German Foundation.

Snyder, M. (1987) *Public Appearances, Private Realities*, New York: Freeman.

Sorge, A., Hartman, G., Warner, M. and Nicholas, I. (1983) *Microelectronics and Manpower in Manufacturing Applications of Computer Numerical Control in Great Britain and West Germany*, Aldershot: Gower.

Sparks, K., Cooper, C., Fried, Y. and Shirom, A. (1997) 'The effects of hours of work on health: a meta-analytic review', *Journal of Occupational and Organizational Psychology*, 70: 391–408.

Sparrow, P. (1996) 'The changing nature of psychological contracts in the UK banking sector', *Human Resource Management Journal*, 6 (4): 75–92.

Spencer, D. (2000) 'Braverman and the contribution of labour process analysis to the critique of capitalist production – twenty-five years on', *Work, Employment and Society*, 14 (2): 223–43.

Spradley, J. P. and Mann, B. J. (1975) *The Cocktail Waitress: Women's Work in a Man's World*, New York: Wiley.

Steiger, T. L. (1993) 'Construction skill and skill construction', *Work, Employment and Society*, 7 (4): 535–60.

Steinberg, R. J. (1990) 'Social construction of skill', *Work and Occupations*, 17 (4): 449–82.

Stopford, J. and Turner, L. (1985) *Britain and the Multinationals*, Chichester: Wiley.

Sullivan, C. and Lewis, S. (2001) 'Home-based telework, gender and the synchronization of work and family: perspectives of teleworkers and their co-residents', *Gender, Work and Organization*, 8 (2): 123–45.

Tancred, P. (1995) 'Women's work: a challenge to the sociology of work', *Gender, Work and Organization*, 2 (1): 11–20.

Taylor, F. W. (1911) *The Principles of Scientific Management*, New York: Harper.

Taylor, L. and Walton, P. (1971) 'Industrial sabotage: motives and meanings', in S. Cohen (ed.) *Images of Deviance*, Harmondsworth: Penguin, pp. 219–45.

Taylor, P. and Bain, P. (1999) '"An assembly line in the head": work and employee relations in the call centre', *Industrial Relations Journal*, 30 (2): 101–17.

Taylor, S. (1998) 'Emotional labour and the new workplace', in P. Thompson and C. Warhurst (eds) *Workplaces of the Future*, Basingstoke: Macmillan, pp. 84–103.

Taylor, S. and Tyler, M. (2000) 'Emotional labour and sexual difference in the airline industry', *Work, Employment and Society*, 14 (1): 77–95.

The Guardian (2000) 'Hospital's macho culture goes on trial', 4 December.

The Guardian (2001) 'Suicide of black worker "caused by bullying"', 9 January.

The Independent (1999) 'Systematic racism at car plant "was ignored by Ford"', 24 September.

The Observer (1994) 'Baptism of fire for Brigades' ethnic recruits', 10 April.

Thomas, J. J. (1992) *Informal Economic Activities*, Hemel Hempstead: Harvester Wheatsheaf.

Thomas, K. (1999) 'Introduction' in K. Thomas (ed.) *The Oxford Book of Work*, Oxford: Oxford University Press, pp. xiii–xxiii.

Thomas, P. and Smith, K. (1995) 'Results of the 1993 Census of Employment', *Employment Gazette*, October: 369–77.

Thomason, G. F. (1980) *Job Evaluation: Objectives and Methods*, London: Institute of Personnel Management.

Thompson, E. P. (1967) 'Time, work-discipline and industrial capitalism', *Past and Present*, No. 38: 56–97.

Thompson, P. (1989) *The Nature of Work*, Second edition, London: Macmillan.

Tidd, K. L. and Lockard, J. S. (1978) 'Monetary significance of the affiliative smile', *Bulletin of the Psychonomic Society*, 11: 344–6.

Toninelli, P. A. (ed.) (2000) *The Rise and Fall of State-Owned Enterprise in the Western World*, Cambridge: Cambridge University Press.

Trades Union Congress (1998) *Working Time Regulations 1998*, London: Trades Union Congress.

Traxler, F., Blaschke, S. and Kittel, B. (2001) *National Labour Relations in International-ized Markets*, Oxford: Oxford University Press.

Turnbull, P. (1988) 'The limits to "Japanisation" – just-in-time, labour relations and the UK automotive industry', *New Technology, Work and Employment*, 3 (1): 7–20.

Turner, B. A. (1971) *Exploring the Industrial Subculture*, London: Macmillan.

Turner, H.A. (1962) *Trade Union Growth, Structure and Policy*, London: Allen & Urwin.

Turner, R., Bostyn, A.-M. and Wight, D. (1985) 'The work ethic in a Scottish town with declining employment', in B. Roberts, R. Finnegan and D. Gallie (eds) *New Approaches to Economic Life*, Manchester: Manchester University Press, pp. 476–89.

Ursell, G. and Blyton, P. (1988) *State, Capital and Labour: Changing Patterns of Power and Dependence*, London: Macmillan.

Van Maanen, J. and Kunda, G. (1989) '"Real feelings": emotional expression and organizational culture' in L. L. Cummings and B. M. Staw (eds) *Research in Organizational Behaviour*, Greenwich, CT: JAI Press, pp. 43–103.

Veal, A. J. (1989) 'Leisure and the future: considering the options', in F. Coalter (ed.) *Freedom and Constraint: The Paradoxes of Leisure*, London: Routledge. pp. 264–74.

Waddington, J. and Whitston, C. (1996) 'Empowerment versus intensification: union perspectives of change at the workplace' in P. Ackers, C. Smith and P. Smith (eds) *The New Workplace and Trade Unionism*, London: Routledge, pp 149–77.

Waddington, J. and Whitston, C. (1997) 'Why do people join unions in a period of membership decline?', *British Journal of Industrial Relations*, 35 (4): 515–46.

Wajcman, J. (1991) 'Patriarchy, technology and skill', *Work and Occupations*, 18 (1): 29–45.

Walby, S. (1986) *Patriarchy at Work*, Cambridge: Polity.

Walby, S. (1990) *Theorizing Patriarchy*, Oxford: Blackwell.

Walby, S. (1997) *Gender Transformations*, London: Routledge.

Wallace, C. and Pahl, R. (1986) 'Polarisation, unemployment and all forms of work', in S. Allen, A. Waton, K. Purcell and S. Wood (eds) *The Experience of Unemployment*, Basingstoke: Macmillan, pp. 116–33.

Wareing, A. (1992) 'Working arrangements and patterns of working hours in Britain', *Employment Gazette*, November: 88–100.

Warhurst, C. and Thompson, P. (1998) 'Hands, hearts and minds: changing work and workers at the end of the century', in P. Thompson and C. Warhurst (eds) *Workplaces of the Future*, Basingstoke: Macmillan, pp. 1–24.

Warr, P. (1987) *Work, Unemployment and Mental Health*, Oxford: Clarendon.

Waters, M. (1995) *Globalisation*, London: Routledge.

Watson, T. J. (1986) *Management, Organisation and Employment*, London: Routledge.

Watson, T. J. (1987) *Sociology, Work and Industry*, Second edition, London: Routledge & Kegan Paul.

Webb, J. and Liff, S. (1988) 'Play the white man: the social construction of fairness and competition in equal opportunity policies', *Sociological Review*, 36 (3): 532–51.

Webb, M. and Palmer, G. (1998) 'Evading surveillance and making time: an ethnographic view of the Japanese factory floor in Britain', *British Journal of Industrial Relations*, 36 (4): 611–27.

Weber, M. (1930) *The Protestant Ethic and the Spirit of Capitalism*, (translated by Talcott Parsons) London: Allen & Unwin.

Weber, M. (1949) *The Methodology of the Social Sciences*, Glencoe, Illinois: Free Press.

Webster, F. (1995) *Theories of the Information Society*, London: Routledge.

West, J. (2000) 'Prostitution: collectives and the politics of regulation', *Gender, Work and Organization*, 7 (2): 106–18.

Westwood, S. (1984) *All Day Every Day*, London: Pluto.

Wharton, A. (1993) 'The affective consequences of service work: managing emotions on the job', *Work and Occupations*, 20 (2): 205–32.

Wharton, A. and Erickson, R. (1993) 'Managing emotions on the job and at home: understanding the consequences of multiple emotional roles', *Academy of Management Review*, 18 (3): 457–86.

Wheeler, H. N. and McClendon, J. A. (1991) 'The individual decision to unionize', in G. Strauss, D. G. Gallagher and J. Fiorito (eds) *The State of the Unions*, Madison, WI: Industrial Relations Research Association, pp. 47–83.

Whipp, R. (1987) 'A time to every purpose: an essay on time and work', in P. Joyce (ed.) *The Historical Meanings of Work*, Cambridge: Cambridge University Press, pp. 210–36.

White, M. (1987) *Working Hours: Assessing the Potential for Reduction*, Geneva: International Labour Organization.

Williams, C. (1988) *Blue, White and Pink Collar Workers in Australia*, Sydney: Allen and Unwin.

Williams, K., Cutler, T., Williams, J. and Haslam, C. (1987) 'The end of mass production?', *Economy and Society*, 16 (3): 405–39.

Williams, K., Haslam, C. and Williams, J. (1992) 'Ford versus "Fordism": the beginning of mass production?', *Work, Employment and Society*, 6 (4): 517–55.

Willis, P. (1977) *Learning to Labour*, Farnborough: Saxon House.

Wilson C. P. (1979) *Jokes: Form, Content, Use and Function*, London: Academic Press.

Wilson, D. F. (1972) *Dockers: The Impact of Industrial Change*, London: Fontana Collins.

Winslow, C. D. and Bramer, W. L. (1994) *Future Work: Putting Knowledge to Work in the Knowledge Economy*, New York: Free Press.

Witz, A. (1992) *Professions and Patriarchy*, London: Routledge.

Womack, J. P., Jones, D. T. and Roos, D. (1990) *The Machine that Changed the World*, New York: Rawson Macmillan.

Wood, E. A. (2000) 'Working in the fantasy factory: the attention hypothesis and the enacting of masculine power in strip clubs', *Journal of Contemporary Ethnography*, 29 (1): 5–31.

Wood, S. (ed.) (1982) *The Degradation of Work? Skill, Deskilling and the Labour Process*, London: Hutchinson.

Wood, S. (ed.) (1989) *The Transformation of Work?*, London: Unwin Hyman.

Woollacott, J. (1980) 'Dirty and deviant work', in G. Esland and G. Salaman (eds) *The Politics of Work and Occupations*, Milton Keynes: Open University Press, pp. 192–212.

Wouters, C. (1989) 'The sociology of emotions and flight attendants: Hochschild's Managed Heart', *Theory, Culture and Society*, 6: 95–123.

Wrench, J. (1987) 'Unequal comrades: trade unions, equal opportunities and racism' in R. Jenkins and J. Solomos (eds) *Racism and Equal Opportunity Policies in the 1980s*, Cambridge: Cambridge University Press.

Yankelovich, D. (1973) 'The meaning of work', in R. Rosnow (ed.) *The Worker and the Job*, New York: Columbia University Press/Prentice Hall, pp. 19–47.

Yinger, M. (1986) 'Intersecting strands in the theorisation of race and ethnic relations', in J. Rex and D. Mason (eds) *Theories of Race and Ethnic Relations*, Cambridge: Cambridge University Press, pp. 20–41.

Yousef, D. A. (2001) 'Islamic work ethic', *Personnel Review*, 30 (2): 152–69.

Zimbalist, A. (ed.) (1979) *Case Studies on the Labour Process*, New York: Monthly Review Press.

Zuboff, S. (1988) *In the Age of the Smart Machine*, Oxford: Heinemann.

Author index

Subject index